Critical Essays
on Walt Whitman

Critical Essays
on Walt Whitman

James Woodress

G.K. Hall & Co. ● Boston, Massachusetts

Library of Congress Cataloging in Publication Data
Main entry under title:

   Critical essays on Walt Whitman.

   (Critical essays on American literature)
   Includes index.
   1. Whitman, Walt, 1819–1892—Criticism and interpretation—
Addresses, essays, lectures.   I. Woodress, James Leslie.   II. Series.
PS3238.C74   1983   811'.3   82–12078
ISBN 0–8161–8632–4

This publication is printed on permanent/durable acid-free paper
MANUFACTURED IN THE UNITED STATES OF AMERICA

CRITICAL ESSAYS ON AMERICAN LITERATURE

This series seeks to publish the most important reprinted criticism on writers and topics in American literature along with, in various volumes, original essays, interviews, bibliographies, letters, manuscript sections, and other materials brought to public attention for the first time. This volume on Walt Whitman, edited by James Woodress, Professor of English at the University of California, Davis, is in many ways a remarkable collection of criticism. It contains not only reprinted essays and comments by such notable figures as Ralph Waldo Emerson, Henry James, Ezra Pound, and D. H. Lawrence, but original articles by Jerome Loving and Roger Asselineau and an important introduction by Professor Woodress. We are confident that this collection will make a permanent and significant contribution to American literary study.

JAMES NAGEL, GENERAL EDITOR

Northeastern University

For Roberta

CONTENTS

ESSAYS AND OTHER FORMS OF CRITICISM

INTRODUCTION

Walt Whitman's critical reputation begins on 21 July 1855, seventeen days after the slim, green-bound, quarto-sized first edition of *Leaves of Grass* was issued anonymously from the Rome brothers' printing shop in Brooklyn. This is the date that Ralph Waldo Emerson wrote Whitman acknowledging his complimentary copy of *Leaves* as "the most extraordinary piece of wit and wisdom that America has yet contributed." From that moment the battle was joined: American and European literati either lined up behind Emerson or joined a noisy, often abusive opposition. No one concerned with literary matters remained indifferent, although some fence-straddlers damned with faint praise or couldn't make up their minds which way to jump. Thus was Whitman a figure of considerable controversy during his lifetime. The opposition became less and less significant as time went on, and by the time Whitman died in 1892, he had achieved the status of a national landmark; but it must be said that *Leaves of Grass* was not for many more years a book that respectable middle-class families kept on their living room tables or recommended to their teen-age daughters.

The early selections in this anthology give a representative sampling of the controversy that swirled about Whitman during the period when *Leaves of Grass* was a new book. Some of the wrong-headed judgments are amusing to read nearly a century and a third later, such as the anonymous British reviewer who thought Whitman "as unacquainted with art, as a hog is with mathematics."[1] And one can still be impressed with the clarity of Emerson's vision when he wrote Whitman: "I greet you at the beginning of a great career."[2] Emerson's fellow transcendentalists immediately embraced Whitman, and three of them, Bronson Alcott, Moncure Daniel Conway, and Henry Thoreau went to Brooklyn to look up this astonishing new poet. They were properly impressed, as their reports printed here indicate. Whitman, meantime, was busy promoting his book by writing anonymous reviews and preparing a new edition that he brought out the following year. He emblazoned across its spine, without any permission, Emerson's famous greeting. Emerson was taken aback by

1

this, but one had to accept Whitman as he was, or as he projected himself to be:

> Walt Whitman, An American, one of the roughs, a kosmos,
> Disorderly, fleshy and sensual . . . eating, drinking and breeding,
> No sentimentalist. . . . no stander above men and
> women or apart from them . . . no more modest
> than immodest,

as he announced in the long untitled initial poem that he later called "Song of Myself."[3]

From the first edition of 95 pages and 11 untitled poems to the "death-bed edition" of 1891–92, which contained 438 pages, Whitman constantly revised, expanded, and rearranged his life work. The organic growth of this central document in American cultural history is too complex to be recounted here, but the story is ably treated in Gay Wilson Allen's *The New Walt Whitman Handbook* (New York, 1975). Although some critics, notably Malcolm Cowley think the first edition is the best, most students of Whitman believe that he grew in skill and power in the decade following 1855. Roy Harvey Pearce nominated the 1860 third edition for first place when he edited a reprinting of it, and there is much to be said for this view. The *Leaves of Grass* that most readers know begins to take shape in this edition, and it includes "Enfans D'Adam" (later called "Children of Adam"), "Calamus," and "Out of the Cradle Endlessly Rocking," a poem that is generally considered one of Whitman's masterpieces. One can only marvel today at the vitriolic attack on this poem by the anonymous reviewer in the Cincinnati *Commercial* reprinted in this collection. That Whitman was beginning to establish himself by 1860 is evident from the fact that he was able to get the reputable Boston firm of Thayer and Eldridge to bring out his book. He would not, however, take Emerson's advice and delete some of the sexual passages. These helped keep him a controversial figure and perpetuated his reputation as the writer of a dirty book.

But whether or not Whitman was fired from his job in the Department of the Interior because *Leaves of Grass* was obscene has now become an open question. For 110 years Secretary James Harlan has been charged with this deed and motivation as the result of William Douglas O'Connor's impassioned pamphlet, *The Good Gray Poet: A Vindication* (partly included in this collection). Recently, Jerome Loving found a document from Harlan directing his bureau chiefs to prune the payroll, and he thinks that the obscenity issue became Harlan's defense only after O'Connor publicly excoriated him for dismissing Whitman.[4] Be that as it may, O'Connor's epithet of "Good Gray Poet" stuck to Whitman for the rest of his life and after, and the fervor of O'Connor's defense makes it clear in retrospect that Whitman was already becoming a cult figure, a subject that William James found significant when he wrote his *Varieties of Religious Experience*, a part of which also is reprinted here.

About the time that O'Connor was defending Whitman, the poet was bringing out *Drum-Taps*, which contained his Civil War poems, and its sequel, which held his Lincoln elegy, "When Lilacs Last in the Dooryard Bloom'd," one of the great elegies in the English language. These poems found many admirers, one of whom was the early French critic Thérèse Bentzon (reprinted here) who did not like Whitman's barbaric yawp but praised highly the war poems. It is one of the ironies of American literary history that the youthful William Dean Howells and Henry James, both of whom grew up to be excellent critics, disparaged *Drum-Taps* when they reviewed the book in 1865, as the documents collected here show; but the two novelists lived to change their minds.

Whitman's American reputation was enhanced considerably after he began to build a following in England. The Pre-Raphaelites discovered him, and William Michael Rossetti edited a selected edition of *Leaves of Grass* (1868). He also gave a copy of the complete *Leaves* to his friend Anne Gilchrist, who fell madly in love with Whitman and later traveled to America to meet and, she hoped, to marry him. Although this passion caused Whitman a good deal of embarrassment, her essay, reprinted here, "A Woman's Estimate of Walt Whitman," is a remarkable testament to the impact of the poems on a gifted woman, and it made a strong impression on its readers. In addition, the enthusiastic essays by Robert Buchanan and later Robert Louis Stevenson, plus the support of the scholar Edward Dowden, gave Whitman a solid footing among the British intelligentsia. It came as a surprise to Americans to learn that many European critics regarded Whitman as a towering figure among world writers. This judgment was not universal, of course, and the jaundiced essay (reproduced here) by Swinburne, "Whitmania," is representative of what was by that time in Europe (1883) a minority view. But even Swinburne as a young man had written a grateful poetic tribute "To Walt Whitman in America" (also printed here) before turning conservative in his later years.

By the 1880s, when Whitman was living quietly in Camden, New Jersey, much diminished by the stroke he had suffered during the previous decade, he was gradually assuming the stature he has enjoyed in the present century. Even establishment critics such as Edmund Clarence Stedman gave him a prominent chapter (partly reprinted here) in his *Poets of America* (1886), and his future literary executors, Richard M. Bucke, Thomas Harned, and Horace Traubel were hard at work promoting the man and the myth. The last of this triumvirate, Traubel, spent his days talking with Whitman and recording the old poet's conversation, six volumes of which eventually were published.

This is the period of Whitman's reputation that Allen calls "The American Apotheosis," and it extends through the decade following Whitman's death.[5] The executors published a memorial volume *In Re Walt Whitman*, which contained tributes from friends and admirers and a good bit of translated foreign criticism. Another friend of Whitman's old age, William Sloane Kennedy, brought out *Reminiscences of Walt Whitman* (1896) and eventually *The Fight of a Book for the World* (1926), which traced the history of *Leaves of Grass* during its first three-quarters of a century. Still another friend and disciple, John Burroughs, the naturalist, who had met Whitman in 1863 and been strongly attracted to him, was part of the apotheosis. His first contribution to the hagiology was *Notes on Walt Whitman as Poet and Person*, which Whitman partly wrote and which is partly reprinted here; then in 1896 he brought out another adulatory study. Another volume that Whitman also had a hand in was Bucke's *Walt Whitman* (1884), an excerpt of which is included here. The decade following Whitman's death culminated in the publication of the ten-volume Camden Edition of Whitman's poetical and prose works. This elegant edition was not superseded until the definitive New York University Press edition came out (1961–80).

Scholars and critics since Whitman's death have produced a quantity of writing commensurately as broad and as wide as the North American continent that Whitman's poetry embraces. The second part of this anthology can only reprint a tiny segment of this vast output. In this ninety-year period Whitman has been approached from every angle: his Americanness, his internationalism, his sex life, his language, his prosody, his sources, his influence, and so on. It would be hard to find a topic that has not been plowed more than once. In Lewis Leary's several volumes of *Articles on American Literature*, covering the years from 1900 through 1975, there are listed 1,686 articles on Whitman: 10 per year during the first half of this century; 37 per year during the years 1950–67; and 67 per year from 1968 through 1975.[6] In addition, Allen's *Handbook* (1975) lists about 90 books dealing entirely with Whitman, and there are innumerable other studies that devote significant portions to his work. As Roger Asselineau reports in a fine bibliographical essay on Whitman scholarship: "The reasons why this great cairn has been piled up are not in the least obscure. Whitman has always attracted antagonists eager to show that he is a shallow thinker and a second-rate poet. But his defenders have been more numerous than his detractors. Year by year they have added stones to the cairn of criticism and commentary."[7]

Much of the early writing has been superseded, but a considerable amount continues to be useful. One of the first books to appear after Whitman's death was J. A. Symonds' *Walt Whitman: A Study* (1893), a selection of which is included here. Symonds was the first to deal with the vexing problem of Whitman's sexual orientation. He had studied Greek friendships and Renaissance history, and the idea of homosexuality did not shock him. When he wrote Whitman asking candidly if he were homosexual, Whitman fabricated his claim to have had six illegitimate children, a red herring no doubt to cover his tracks. Symonds praises Whitman's treatment of love, both hetero- and homosexual, in the "Children of Adam" and "Calamus" sections of *Leaves of Grass*. His discussion still has value, though more up-to-date observations may be found in Asselineau's *The Evolution of Walt Whitman* (1962) and most recently in Robert K. Martin's *The Homosexual Tradition in American Poetry* (1979).

It is always interesting to read the youthful opinions of writers who later become important artists, and the early views on Whitman of Willa Cather and Ezra Pound are instructive. They were less myopic than Howells and James, but the ambivalence they express illustrates the impact that Whitman had on younger writers even while they resisted. Cather didn't understand Whitman's style and form, but there was a good bit of Whitman in her when she discovered her real subject in her Nebraska novels, and the title of her first prairie novel, *O Pioneers!*, is borrowed from Whitman's poems. Pound, as James E. Miller shows convincingly in *The American Quest for a Supreme Fiction* (see a selection reprinted in this volume), owes much to Whitman: "If Ezra Pound is sometimes conceived of as the father of the modern movement . . . then Whitman must clearly be cast in the role of grandfather."[8]

George Santayana's disenchanted essay, "The Poetry of Barbarism," included here, lined up the young philosopher with the Whitman-baiters and provoked a great deal of response, probably more, says Asselineau, than any other essay by a Whitman detractor. To Santayana, who thought that poetry had been in a state of decline ever since Homer, Whitman and Browning were the poets of barbarism. Such art while it "is not without its charm," has various defects: "lack of distinction, absence of beauty, confusion of ideas, incapacity to permanently please."[9] Stuart Sherman in *Americans* (1922) refuted Santayana with spirit, though he had not yet come to appreciate another barbarian, Theodore Dreiser.

Basil de Selincourt's *Walt Whitman: A Study* (1914) was a milestone in Whitman scholarship in its concentration on the form and structure of *Leaves of Grass*. In the biographical parts of his book he naively accepted the myth of a romance in New Orleans and Whitman's claim to have had six illegitimate children. But de Selincourt was very astute when he compared Whitman's verse to music and insisted on the importance of the line as a unit. His chapter on "Constructive Principles" is included in this collection.

A brief study of Whitman that is both fascinating and irritating is D. H. Lawrence's chapter in his *Studies in Classic American Literature* (1923). As reprinted in this volume, it shows Lawrence making some shrewd *aperçus* while at the same time indulging himself in some outrageous nonsense. As might be expected of a coal miner's son who had struggled fearfully to escape the squalor of his background, Lawrence hated Whitman's democratic merging with everyone and everything, but he was exhilarated by Whitman's fusing of body and spirit: "Whitman was the first heroic seer to seize the soul by the scruff of her neck and plant her down among the potsherds."[10] In the end Whitman became one of Lawrence's heroes, and the essay, the last in his book, was written after he had come to the United States and was living in New Mexico.

Whitman also was a hero to Vernon Parrington, whose influential *Main Currents in American Thought* appeared in 1930. There Whitman is treated as "the afterglow of the Enlightenment" in a perceptive chapter that traces his intellectual connections back to the founding fathers, Thomas Paine, and William Godwin.[11] This tracing of Whitman's intellectual heritage somewhat anticipates the argument in Floyd Stovall's essay, "Walt Whitman and the American Tradition," written in the centennial year of *Leaves of Grass* and reprinted here.

Following Parrington in the decade of the thirties and down to the beginning of World War II, a new generation of scholars appeared. They carried Whitman studies into the post-war era and produced books that still have value. There was Charles Glicksberg's *Walt Whitman and the Civil War* (1933); Harold Blodgett's *Walt Whitman in England* (1934); Newton Arvin's *Whitman* (1938), which concentrated on the poet as social thinker; Esther Shephard's *Walt Whitman's Pose* (1938), a carping source study that dealt particularly with the influence of George Sand. Meantime, outside of the United States an important book from France preceded the decade in Jean Catel's *Walt Whitman: la naissance du poète* (1929), which enlisted the aid of Freud to explain Whitman; and a significant study was published in Denmark: Frederik Schyberg's *Walt Whitman* (1933), although the latter was virtually unknown in the United States until Evie Allison Allen translated it in 1951.

As might be expected, the war years of 1941–45 did not produce much Whitman scholarship, but just before Pearl Harbor, F. O. Matthiessen's influential *American Renaissance* appeared, and the year after the war Allen brought out his useful original *Walt Whitman Handbook*. The former volume, which is subtitled "Art and Expression in the Age of Emerson and Whitman," deals with Emerson, Thoreau, Hawthorne, Melville, and Whitman. The study began with Matthiessen's realization that the half decade between 1850 and 1855 had produced an extraordinary number of American classics beginning with the *The Scarlet Letter* and ending with the first edition of *Leaves of Grass*. He set out to discover what these masterpieces were as works of art and to evaluate their "fusion of form and content." The 110 pages that he devotes to Whitman are full of insights and penetrating analysis, and he is particularly effective in explaining Whitman's form by three analogies: public speaking, music, and the sea. These were not new ideas, but Matthiessen brings them together in a highly illuminating fashion. Allen, whose handbook was preceded by a valuable discussion of Whitman's technique in his *American Prosody* (1935), produced in this volume a tool of enormous use to a generation of scholars and teachers. By 1946, when it appeared, there was a real need for someone to codify and organize the mountain of good, bad, and indifferent scholarship that by then had been accumulated. Nearly thirty years later at the end of his career, Allen again performed this service to scholarship by updating his vademecum in *The New Walt Whitman Handbook* (1975), a chapter of which is included here.

Between Matthiessen and Allen there were two book-length studies: Hugh I'Anson Fausset's *Walt Whitman: Poet of Democracy* (1942) and Henry S. Canby's *Walt Whitman: An American* (1943). The former has little importance today and suffers from being thesis-ridden. Fausset finds Whitman a split personality never able to resolve the contradictions between art and life, and while he thinks Whitman a great poet (at least sometimes), the book has a nagging, disparaging tone. Canby's book on the other hand was a major contribution to Whitman biography and criticism. As one of the editors of that large cooperative venture, *The Literary History of the United States* (1948), to which he contributed the essay on Whitman, Canby was a knowledgeable scholar-journalist ideally equipped by experience and temperament to bring together in a sensible volume much of the previous scholarship, to lay to rest some of the old myths, and to suggest reasonable conclusions regarding the problems in interpreting Whitman's life and work. This book still is a good introduction to Whitman, though it is not the final word on the subject.

One hates to call any book the last word on its subject, but by the 1950s, it finally had become possible to undertake a definitive critical biography. Allen set himself the task of writing the most complete study yet of Whitman and brought out during the centennial year 1955, *The Solitary Singer: A Critical Biography of Walt Whitman*, an important publishing event. Allen's aim was to "trace consecutively the physical life of the man, the growth of his mind, and the development of his art out of his physical and mental experience."[12] There is a great deal of new material in the book and the life is projected against a full-scale background of Whitman's social, political, and intellectual milieu. (For readers with neither the time nor the patience to read Allen's 686 pages, he also has written a brief biography published in 1961.)

Allen's biography was the culmination of one hundred years of Whitman's studies, but his book had a long foreground. The first attempt to tell Whitman's story completely and impartially was Bliss Perry's *Walt Whitman* (1906), a pioneering effort that was undertaken before the private notebooks and unpublished manuscripts became available. Where there were gaps in Whitman's life, Perry made no effort to fill the blanks with conjecture. He found Whitman no modern Christ or superman (to the dismay of the Whitmaniacs) but a real, fallible human being and a great poet. The next biography was George Rice Carpenter's *Walt Whitman* (1909), a contribution to the "English Men of Letters" series. It is sober, straight forward but does not go beyond Perry. The year before

Carpenter's book appeared Léon Bazalgette had published in France a
romantic account of Whitman's Life: *Walt Whitman: l'homme et son
oeuvre.* This is an unrestrainedly enthusiastic biography that follows the
idealized interpretations of John Burroughs and Richard Bucke, and accepts the New Orleans romance invented by Henry Binns in *A Life of
Walt Whitman* (1905). (American readers should be warned against a
bowdlerized translation that appeared in 1920.)

A landmark in Whitman biography was erected by Emory Holloway
in *Whitman: An Interpretation in Narrative* (1926), the product of thirteen years of research by a dedicated Whitman scholar. It was the best
biography yet, though Holloway was reticent about Whitman's sex life
and convinced that he was heterosexual. He also perpetuated the New
Orleans romance, but his scholarship was sound, and he had laid the
groundwork for his book by publishing the *Uncollected Poetry and Prose*
(1921), containing notebooks, early journalistic writings, and juvenilia in
poetry and prose. Holloway knew more than anyone else about
Whitman's background and early career when he began to write.

For nearly three decades after Holloway there appeared no general
biographies, only books attempting to analyze Whitman's complex
character and its impact on his work or specialized studies. The works by
Catel and Schyberg, already mentioned, are of the former type, while the
latter are represented by two limited but useful books, both of which appeared in 1951: Joseph Beaver's *Walt Whitman: Poet of Science* and
Robert Faner's *Walt Whitman and Opera.* By the time these last two
came out, Allen was at work on *The Solitary Singer* and another French
scholar, who since has become the dean of French Americanists, Roger
Asselineau, also was writing a study that has not been superseded.
Following the French pattern of the thesis for the *doctorat d'etat,* which
treats *l'homme et l'oeuvre,* Asselineau's work appeared in France in 1954
as *L'Evolution de Walt Whitman après la première edition des "Feuilles
d'herbe,"* the first half being biography and the second half criticism. It
became two books when it was translated into English: *The Evolution of
Walt Whitman: The Creation of a Personality* (1960) and *The Creation of
a Book* (1962). Asselineau and Allen, who are friends and had corresponded during their separate labors, share many points of view. Both
were influenced in their interpretations by Catel and Shyberg, but Allen
is more reticent about Whitman's sexual orientation; calling him
homoerotic whereas Asselineau used the term homosexual. This seemed a
significant difference in the mid-fifties, but today it does not appear to
matter much. Asselineau's critical interpretations of Whitman are
convincing and his scholarship is meticulously documented. His thesis is
this: of Whitman's many inner struggles the most difficult was the fight
against his homosexual desires. His art saved him by allowing him to express the turbulent emotions that bothered him. His song was not the
joyful outpouring of the demigod that Burroughs and Bucke depicted but

the sorrowful notes of a sick soul trying to understand itself and maintain its equilibrium.

Another significant book came out during the centennial year, Richard Chase's *Walt Whitman Reconsidered*. The biographical parts are hastily and inaccurately written, but Chase is a good critic and his analyses of Whitman's poetry are provocative. (See his discussion of "When Lilacs Last in the Dooryard Bloom'd" reprinted here.) Chase, like Asselineau, sees Whitman as a troubled spirit, a man whose poetry was created out of his inner turmoil. Chase introduces a new note into Whitman criticism by calling Whitman's masterpiece "Song of Myself," "the profound and lovely comic drama of the self"—comic because Whitman tried to play the role of moral leader and failed. Chase also is the author of the University of Minnesota pamphlet on Whitman, which in its forty-eight page format gives a good brief overview.

The centennial year also produced *Walt Whitman Abroad*, edited by Allen, which collected critical essays from Germany, France, Scandinavia, Russia, Italy, Spain, Latin America, Israel, Japan, and India. This volume made clear Whitman's international standing and included translations of writing on Whitman by a host of important writers and scholars: Thomas Mann, Knut Hamsun, Cesare Pavese, Jose Marti, Miguel de Unamuno, to name some. A follow-up volume, *Walt Whitman in Europe Today*, edited by Asselineau and William White, editor of the *Walt Whitman Review* (a journal founded in 1955), came out in 1972 and surveyed Whitman scholarship in both Eastern and Western Europe. Whitman was the first American poet to gain world recognition and is today well known around the globe. *Leaves of Grass* has been completely translated into French, German, Spanish, Italian, Greek, and Japanese, and selections are available in many, many languages. Whitman is especially popular in Russia where his works sell better than they do in America. The Russians make much of him as a proletarian poet but ignore the democratic aspects of his life and work. For anyone wishing to read a Russian study of Whitman, the work of a leading Soviet Americanist, Maurice Mendelson's *Life and Work of Walt Whitman: A Soviet View*, was translated into English and published in Moscow in 1976. It might have been subtitled "The Good Gray Poet Revolutionary." Whitman's foreign reputation is well treated in a complete chapter in Allen's *New Handbook*, and Asselineau's previously unpublished essay that concludes this collection deals in part with Whitman's internationalism.

Despite the flurry of scholarly activity that took place at the time of the centennial, Whitman's critical reputation was then at a low ebb among many contemporary poets, such as John Crow Ransom, Allen Tate, and T. S. Eliot, and among the New Critics. He was often disparaged or simply ignored. One of the exceptions was Karl Shapiro, who stood up for him vigorously in his 1958 essay, "The First White Aboriginal." He noted: "Walt Whitman is almost completely shunned by his fellows. He has no audience, neither a general audience nor a literary clique." Yet he is "the most original religious thinker we have; the poet of the greatest achievement; the first profound innovator; the most accomplished artist as well."[13] Randall Jarrell also was an exception, and his essay reprinted in this collection is an extraordinary defense of Whitman's verbal skill. Shapiro was overstating his case, for in the academies Whitman was always a standard part of the curriculum, and during the 1950s 19 dissertations were written on Whitman and another 8 on Whitman and other writers.

Twenty-seven years have passed since the centennial year, and during that period the torrent of Whitman scholarship has poured out far more work than can be summarized in this brief essay. One can only hit the high spots. In 1957 James E. Miller, Jr. published the first of his several volumes on Whitman: A Critical Guide to "Leaves of Grass," a very useful book that avoids biography and concentrates on studying the structural design of Whitman's final edition. His chapter on "Song of Myself" is especially provocative, as he sees the poem as an example of "inverted mystical experience."[14] The experience is inverted because Whitman, contrary to the usual mystical experience, achieves the mystical state through the senses rather than through an escape from the senses. Miller also is the author of the brief but competent Whitman volume in the Twayne series.

While the 1950s were perhaps the richest in Whitman scholarship, the decade of the 1960s brought several important books and two standard histories of American poetry in which Whitman is given his proper importance. The histories were Roy Harvey Pearce's The Continuity of American Poetry (1961), a book that has influenced two decades of graduate students, in which Whitman is viewed as "the supremely realized Emersonian poet."[15] Hyatt Waggoner's American Poets from the Puritans to the Present (1968) also does justice to Whitman and again places great stress on the Emersonian connection. It was literally true, Waggoner writers, that Whitman had been "simmering" and "Emerson had brought him 'to a boil'."[16]

It is not surprising that both of these critics stress the influence of Emerson, for it is documented from the very start in Emerson's letter of 1855 and in Whitman's long response in which he addresses Emerson as "master" in the second edition of Leaves of Grass. Many scholars have surveyed this relationship, but none has done it with more insight than Jerome Loving, whose new book on the subject may well be the final word. His essay commissioned for this collection distills from his study a sophisticated assessment of the parallel development and interrelatedness of the two writers.

Three other books of the 1960s should be noted briefly. V. K. Chari's Whitman in the Light of Vedantic Mysticism (1964) is a fine study by a Sanscrit scholar who shows a surprising number of parallels between

Leaves of Grass and Vedantic mysticism. Chari does not argue influences but makes the connections "as a critical instrument . . . to define and illustrate Whitman's most basic ideas."[17] This is the opposite direction taken by Chase, who connects Whitman to native American humor. The second book of this decade is Howard Waskow's *Whitman: Exploration in Form* (1966), a study that examines the "bipolar unity" of Whitman's mind, the structure of his poems that divide themselves in categories of didacticism, imagism, narrative, and monodrama. There are in addition many good explications of individual poems. The third book of the 1960s is E. H. Miller's *Walt Whitman's Poetry: A Psychological Journey* (1968). Miller, who is the editor of Whitman's letters in the definitive New York University edition of his works, knows Whitman well and writes with authority. Though he is a literary scholar, he is well versed in psychology and approaches Whitman as a "lyrical, autobiographical poet" whose poetry "has its origins in unconscious and infantile sources; hence the results are regressive imagery, fantasy, and reactivation of infantile longings."[18] In addition, the tensions are psychic, and the external world is of little importance. His inner drama has its own psychic tensions that must find release, and his genius reveals itself by its ability to put into artistic form what remains inarticulate in lesser minds. This is an important book, and part of one chapter of it is included in this anthology.

A quartet of books worth noting came out in the 1970s. Floyd Stovall, who edited Whitman for the old "American Men of Letters" series in 1934, climaxed a lifetime of Whitman scholarship by bringing out *The Foreground of "Leaves of Grass"* (1974). This is a meticulous review of the context of Whitman's world before 1855, not only his family. and personal life but the influences that aided in the change from journalist to poet. Stovall discusses popular literature, the New York stage, science, philosophy, and the influence of other writers. The flowering of Whitman's genius, says Stovall, was less a sudden illumination than "the gradual opening of latent faculties under the stimulation of his reading combined with a growing confidence in himself."[19] This book complements Joseph Jay Rubin's *The Historic Whitman* (1973), a storehouse of detail gathered from contemporary newspapers in which the author reconstructs the world of Whitman's youth, the life of the young journalist, teacher, wanderer, and political activist. Rubin is exhaustive and somewhat exhausting, but future Whitman scholars cannot afford to ignore his book. The third book of the 1970s is Stephen A. Black's *Whitman's Journeys into Chaos: A Psychoanalytic Study of the Poetic Process* (1975), a book that puts Whitman on the analyst's couch but is less interesting, illuminating, and readable than Miller's study. The last of this quartet but the first published is Thomas E. Crawley's *The Structure of "Leaves of Grass"* (1970), a study that searches for unity in Whitman through recurring themes and symbols. Crawley revives the Christ-prophet persona and traces it through the poems; he also extracts a theme of the unfolding of poet and nation which he supports through finding recurring symbols and relationships within and between groups of poems.

The 1980s have started off with a trio of books, each one very different from the other. The most widely circulated and publicized is Justin Kaplan's *Walt Whitman: A Life* (1980), the first important biography since Allen's. Kaplan's life, however, does not add any new facts to Whitman's life, nor does its critical stance differ from those of Allen and Asselineau. Kaplan also does not do much with the evaluation or interpretation of the major poems so that the biography is weak in showing how Whitman's life and art are related. Nevertheless, the book is written by a first-rate professional biographer. It is enormously readable, the facts are correct, and one comes away from it with a good sense of Whitman the man. Also appearing in 1980 is Harold Aspiz' *Walt Whitman and the Body Beautiful*, which focuses on Whitman's physical self, "the authentic, vital center of *Leaves of Grass*." Since Whitman was the self-proclaimed poet of both the body and the soul, this enterprise has legitimacy, and there are good chapters dealing with Whitman's "constantly retouched self-portrait" showing him as the model of untainted masculinity, his relationship with medicine, health, and hospitals, his interest in pseudosciences like phrenology. Aspiz concludes: "By hallowing his bodily drives and processes, he sanctified the animal element in everyone's life."[20] The third book of this trio is Betsy Erkkila's *Walt Whitman Among the French* (1980), an exhaustive study that traces the French influence on Whitman and his influence on French literature. The latter is somewhat problematical, but there is no doubt that French writers have always considered Whitman important.

This bibliographical survey concludes with a listing of the chief editions of Whitman's work.

WHITMAN WORKS: 1855–1892

Leaves of Grass (Brooklyn, 1855). [About 1,000 copies were printed. Bound in green cloth with gold letters. 95 pages. Several facsimile copies have been published.]

Leaves of Grass (Brooklyn, 1856). [Bound in green cloth, stamped on spine with quotation from Emerson's letter. 384 pages.]

Leaves of Grass (Boston: Thayer and Eldridge, 1860). [A facsimile of this third edition with introduction by Roy Harvey Pearce was published in 1960.]

Walt Whitman's Drum-Taps (New York, 1865). [A second issue with *Sequel* came out later in the same year containing "When Lilacs Last in the Dooryard Bloom'd" and other poems.]

Leaves of Grass (New York, 1867). [*Drum-Taps* and *Sequel* were incorporated into this fourth edition.]

Democratic Vistas (Washington, D.C., 1871).

Leaves of Grass (Washington, D.C., 1871). [Fifth edition. A second issue in 1872 included "Passage to India," 120 added pages.]

Leaves of Grass (Camden, N.J., 1876). [Not a new edition but a reprinting from the 1871–72 plates.]

Two Rivulets, Including Democratic Vistas, Centennial Songs, and Passage to India (Camden, N.J., 1876). [Bound uniformly with the above to constitute the author's *Complete Works* in two volumes.]

Leaves of Grass (Boston: James R. Osgood and Co., 1881–82). [Sixth edition. Poems arranged in final order, later additions being added as annexes. Reprinted in Philadelphia in 1882 and later.]

Specimen Days and Collect (Philadelphia: Rees Welsh and Co., 1882–83). [Prose. *Specimen Days* is informal autobiography.]

November Boughs (Philadelphia: David McKay, 1888). [Prose and poetry.]

Complete Poems and Prose of Walt Whitman (Philadelphia, 1888). [Not a new edition but a reprinting of the 1882 *Leaves* and *Specimen Days.*]

Good-Bye My Fancy (Philadelphia: David McKay, 1891). [Prose and poetry.]

Leaves of Grass (Philadelphia: David McKay, 1891–92). [Not a new edition but a reprint of the sixth with poems from *November Bough* added as First Annex and poems from *Good-Bye My Fancy* as Second Annex. This is the "Death-bed Edition" and the text that Whitman authorized for future printings.]

Complete Prose Works (Philadelphia: David McKay, 1892). [Contains *Specimen Days and Collect*, the prose from *November Boughs*, and *Good-Bye My Fancy*. Sold as Vol 2. of *Complete Works.*]

POSTHUMOUS EDITIONS OF WHITMAN'S WORKS

The Complete Writings of Walt Whitman (New York: Putnam's Sons, 1902). 10 vols. [Issued under the supervision of Whitman's literary executors, Richard Bucke, Thomas Harned, and Horace Traubel. It also included bibliographical and critical material by Oscar Triggs.]

The Collected Writings of Walt Whitman, general eds. Gay Wilson Allen and Sculley Bradley (New York: New York University Press, 1961–80).

Prose Works 1892, ed., Floyd Stovall. Vol. 1, *Specimen Days* (1968); Vol. 2, *Collect and Other Prose* (1964).

The Early Poems and the Fiction, ed. Thomas L. Brasher (1963).

Leaves of Grass. Reader's Edition. Including the Annexes, the Prefaces, "A Backward Glance O'er Travel'd Roads," "Old Age Echoes," the Excluded Poems and Fragments, and the Uncollected Poems and Fragments, ed. Harold W. Blodgett and Sculley Bradley (1965).

The Correspondence, ed. Edwin H. Miller. Vol. 1, 1842–1867 (1961);

Vol. 2, 1868–1875 (1961); Vol. 3, 1876–1885 (1964); Vol. 4, 1886–1889 (1969); Vol. 5, 1890–1892 (1969); Vol. 6, A Supplement with a Composite Index (1977).

Day-Books and Other Diaries, ed. William White. 3 vols (1978).

Leaves of Grass: A Textual Variorum of the Printed Poems, eds. Sculley Bradley, Harold Blodgett, Arthur Golden, and William White. Vol. 1, Poems, 1855–1856; Vol. 2, Poems, 1860–1867; Vol. 3, Poems, 1897–1891 (1980).

Notes

1. London *Critic*, 15 (1 April 1856), 170.

2. 21 July 1855, in *Walt Whitman: The Correspondence*, ed. E. H. Miller (New York: New York Univ. Press, 1961), I, 41.

3. *Leaves of Grass*, Comprehensive Reader's Edition, ed. Harold W. Blodgett and Sculley Bradley (New York: W. W. Norton and Co., 1968), p. 52.

4. See *American Literature*, 48 (1976), 219–22.

5. Gay Wilson Allen, *The New Walt Whitman Handbook* (New York: New York Univ. Press, 1975), p. 13.

6. (Durham, N.C.: Duke Univ. Press, 1954, 1970, 1979).

7. *Eight American Authors*, ed. James Woodress (New York: W. W. Norton and Co., 1971), p. 246.

8. (Chicago: Chicago Univ. Press, 1979), p. 15.

9. *Interpretations of Poetry and Religion* (New York: Charles Scribner's Sons, 1900), pp. 174–75.

10. (Garden City, N.Y.: Doubleday and Co.), p. 184.

11. *The Beginnings of Critical Realism in America: 1860–1920* (New York: Harcourt, Brace and World [1958], III, 69–86.

12. (New York: The Grove Press, n.d.), pp. ix–x.

13. *The Poetry Wreck: Selected Essays, 1950–1970* (New York: Random House [1975]), p. 157.

14. (Chicago: Univ. of Chicago Press), pp. 6–35.

15. (Princeton, N.J.: Princeton Univ. Press), p. 164.

16. (New York: Dell Publishing Co.), p. 154.

17. (Lincoln: Univ. of Nebraska Press), p. xi.

18. (New York: New York Univ. Press), p. vii.

19. (Charlottesville: Univ. Press of Virginia), p. 14.

20. (Urbana: Univ. of Illinois Press), p. 239.

REVIEWS AND OTHER
EARLY REACTIONS

[Emerson Writes Whitman]

R.W. Emerson*

Concord 21 July
Masstts. 1855

Dear Sir,

I am not blind to the worth of the wonderful gift of "Leaves of Grass." I find it the most extraordinary piece of wit and wisdom that America has yet contributed. I am very happy in reading it, as great power makes us happy. It meets the demand I am always making of what seemed the sterile & stingy nature, as if too much handiwork or too much lymph in the temperament were making our western wits fat and mean. I give you joy of your free brave thought. I have great joy in it. I find incomparable things said incomparably well, as they must be. I find the courage of *treatment*, which so delights us, & which large perception only can inspire. I greet you at the beginning of a great career, which yet must have had a long foreground somewhere for such a start. I rubbed my eyes a little to see if this sunbeam were no illusion; but the solid sense of the book is a sober certainty. It has the best merits, namely of fortifying & encouraging.

I did not know until I, last night, saw the book advertised in a newspaper, that I could trust the name as real and available for a post-office. I wish to see my benefactor, & have felt much like striking my tasks, & visiting New York to pay you my respects.

R. W. Emerson

Mr. Walter Whitman.

---

*This letter, which is probably the most famous letter in American literary history, is in the Feinberg Collection at the Library of Congress. It is reproduced in facsimile in *Walt Whitman: A Selection of the Manuscripts, Books, and Association Items* (Detroit: Detroit Public Library, 1955), a catalog of an exhibition held at the Detroit Public Library. It also appears in an accurate text in *Walt Whitman: The Correspondence*, ed. E. H. Miller (New York: New York Univ. Press, 1961), I, 41.

[The Initial Review of
Leaves of Grass]

[Charles A. Dana]*

From the unique effigies of the anonymous author of this volume which graces the frontispiece, we may infer that he belongs to the exemplary class of society sometimes irreverently styled "loafers." He is therein represented in a garb, half sailor's, half workman's, with no superfluous appendage of coat or waistcoat, a "wide-awake" perched jauntily on his head, one hand in his pocket and the other on his hip, with a certain air of mild defiance, and an expression of pensive insolence in his face which seems to betoken a consciousness of his mission as the "coming man." This view of the author is confirmed in the preface. He vouchsafes, before introducing us to his poetry, to enlighten our benighted minds as to the true function of the American poet. Evidently the original, which is embodied in the most extraordinary prose since the "Sayings" of the modern Orpheus, was found in the "interior consciousness" of the writer. Of the materials afforded by this country for the operations of poetic art we have a lucid account.

[Omitted is paragraph 2 and part of paragraph 6 of the preface to the 1855 edition.]

Of the nature of poetry the writer discourses in a somewhat too oracular strain, especially as he has been anticipated in his "utterances" by Emerson and other modern "prophets of the soul":

[Omitted is another passage from paragraph 8.]

Such is the poetic theory of our nameless bard. He furnishes a severe standard for the estimate of his own productions. His *Leaves of Grass* are doubtless intended as an illustration of the natural poet. They are certainly original in their external form, have been shaped on no pre-existent model out of the author's own brain. Indeed, his independence often becomes coarse and defiant. His language is too frequently reckless and indecent though this appears to arise from a naive unconsciousness rather than from an impure mind. His words might have passed between Adam and Eve in Paradise, before the want of fig-leaves brought no shame; but they are quite out of place amid the decorum of modern society, and will justly prevent his volume from free circulation in scrupulous circles. With these glaring faults, the *Leaves of Grass* are not destitute of peculiar poetic merits, which will awaken an interest in the lovers of literary curiosities. They are full of bold, stirring thoughts—with occasional passages of effective description, betraying a genuine intimacy with Nature and a keen appreciation of beauty—often presenting a rare felicity of diction, but so disfigured with eccentric fancies as to prevent a consecutive perusal without offense, though no impartial reader can fail to be im-

*Reprinted from the *New York Tribune*, 23 July 1855, p. 3.

pressed with the vigor and quaint beauty of isolated portions. A few specimens will suffice to give an idea of this odd genius.

[Omitted are 37 lines of Section 21 beginning at line 433 of "Song of Myself" in the present "Comprehensive Reader's Edition" of *Leaves of Grass*, 15 lines of Section 36, 10 lines from "A Song for Occupation," 12 lines from "To Think of Time," and 30 lines from "Faces."]

The volume contains many more "Leaves of Grass" of similar quality, as well as others which cannot be especially commended either for fragrance or form. Whatever severity of criticism they may challenge for their rude ingenuousness, and their frequent divergence into the domain of the fantastic, the taste of not over dainty fastidiousness will discern much of the essential spirit of poetry beneath an uncouth and grotesque embodiment.

["a curious and lawless collection."]

[Charles Eliot Norton]*

Our account of the last month's literature would be incomplete without some notice of a curious and lawless collection of poems, called *Leaves of Grass*, and issued in a thin quarto without the name of publisher or author. The poems, twelve in number, are neither in rhyme nor blank verse, but in a sort of excited prose broken into lines without any attempt at measure or regularity, and, as many readers will perhaps think, without any idea of sense or reason. The writer's scorn for the wonted usages of good writing extends to the vocabulary he adopts; words usually banished from polite society are here employed without reserve and with perfect indifference to their effect on the reader's mind; and not only is the book one not to be read aloud to a mixed audience, but the introduction of terms never before heard or seen, and of slang expressions, often renders an otherwise striking passage altogether laughable. But, as the writer is a new light in poetry, it is only fair to let him state his theory for himself. We extract from the preface:—

> The art of art, the glory of expression, is simplicity. Nothing is better than simplicity, and the sunlight of letters is simplicity. Nothing is better than simplicity—nothing can make up for excess, or for the lack of definiteness. . . . To speak in literature, with the perfect rectitude and the insouciance of the movements of animals and the unimpeachableness of the sentiment of trees in the woods, is the flawless triumph of art. . . .

*Reprinted from *Putnam's Monthly*, 6 (Sept. 1855), 321–23; also reprinted in *A Leaf of Grass from Shady Hill*, ed. Kenneth B. Murdock (Cambridge, Mass.: Harvard Univ. Press, 1928), pp. 27–31. Ellipsis marks are Norton's.

The greatest poet has less a marked style, and is more the channel of thought and things, without increase or diminution, and is the free channel of himself. He swears to his art, I will not be meddlesome. I will not have in my writing any elegance, or effect, or originality to hang in the way between me and the rest, like curtains. What I feel, I feel for precisely what it is. Let who may exalt, or startle, or fascinate, or soothe, I will have purposes, as health, or heat, or snow has, and be as regardless of observation. What I experience or portray shall go from my composition without a shred of my composition. You shall stand by my side to look in the mirror with me.

The application of these principles, and of many others equally peculiar, which are expounded in a style equally oracular throughout the long preface—is made *passim*, and often with comical success, in the poems themselves, which may briefly be described as a compound of the New England transcendentalist and New York rowdy. A fireman or omnibus driver, who had intelligence enough to absorb the speculations of that school of thought which culminated at Boston some fifteen or eighteen years ago, and resources of expression to put them forth again in a form of his own, with sufficient self-conceit and contempt for public taste to affront all usual propriety of diction, might have written this gross yet elevated, this superficial yet profound, this preposterous yet somehow fascinating book. As we say, it is a mixture of Yankee transcendentalism and New York rowdyism, and, what must be surprising to both these elements, they here seem to fuse and combine with the most perfect harmony. The vast and vague conceptions of the one, lose nothing of their quality in passing through the coarse and odd intellectual medium of the other; while there is an original perception of nature, a manly brawn, and an epic directness in our new poet, which belong to no other adept of the transcendental school. But we have no intention of regularly criticising this very irregular production; our aim is rather to cull, from the tough and ragged thicket of its pages, a few passages equally remarkable in point of thought and expression. Of course we do not select those which are the most transcendental or the most bold:—

[Omitted are 88 lines from "Song of Myself," "Faces," and "Great are the Myths." All poems were untitled in the 1855 edition. "Great are the Myths" was later dropped from *Leaves of Grass*.]

As seems very proper in a book of transcendental poetry, the author withholds his name from the title page, and presents his portrait, neatly engraved on steel, instead. This, no doubt, is upon the principle that the name is merely accidental; while the portrait affords an idea of the essential being from whom these utterances proceed. We must add, however, that this significant reticence does not prevail throughout the volume, for we learn on p. 29, that our poet is "Walt Whitman, an American, one of the roughs, a kosmos." That he was an American, we knew before, for, aside from America, there is no quarter of the universe where such a production could have had a genesis. That he was one of the roughs was also tolerably plain; but that he was a kosmos, is a piece of news we were hardly prepared for. Precisely what a kosmos is, we trust Mr. Whitman will take an early occasion to inform the impatient public.

["well worth going . . . to buy it"]

[Edward Everett Hale]*

Everything about the external arrangement of this book was odd and out of the way. The author printed it himself, and it seems to have been left to the winds of heaven to publish it. So it happened that we had not discovered it before our last number, although we believe the sheets had then passed the press. It bears no publisher's name, and, if the reader goes to a bookstore for it, he may expect to be told at first, as we were, that there is no such book, and has not been. Nevertheless, there is such a book, and it is well worth going twice to the bookstore to buy it. Walter Whitman, An American—one of the roughs—no sentimentalist—no stander above men and women, or apart from them—no more modest than immodest—has tried to write down here, in a sort of prose poetry, a good deal of what he has seen, felt, and guessed at in a pilgrimage of some thirty-five years. He has a horror of conventional language of any kind. His theory of expression is, that, "to speak in literature with the perfect rectitude and *insouciance* of the movement of animals, is the flawless triumph of art." Now a great many men have said this before. But generally, it is the introduction to something more artistic than ever—more conventional and strained. Antony began by saying he was no orator, but none the less did an oration follow. In this book, however, the prophecy is fairly fulfilled in the accomplishment. "What I experience or portray shall go from my composition without a shred of my composition. You shall stand by my side and look in the mirror with me."

So truly accomplished is this promise—which anywhere else would be a flourish of trumpets—that this thin quarto deserves its name. That is to say, one reads and enjoys the freshness, simplicity, and reality of what he reads, just as the tired man, lying on the hill-side in summer, enjoys the leaves of grass around him—enjoys the shadow—enjoys the flecks of sunshine—not for what they "suggest to him," but for what they are.

So completely does the author's remarkable power rest in his simplicity, that the preface to the book—which does not even have large letters at the beginning of the lines, as the rest has—is perhaps the very best thing in it. We find more to the point in the following analysis of the "genius of the United States," than we have found in many more pretentious studies of it.

*Reprinted from *North American Review*, 82 (Jan. 1856), 275–77.

Other states indicate themselves in their deputies, but the genius of the United States is not best or most in its executive or legislatures, nor in its ambassadors or authors or colleges or churches or parlors, nor even in its newspapers or inventors—but always most in the common people. Their manners, speech, dress, friendships—the freshness and candor of their physiognomy, the picturesque looseness of their carriage, their deathless attachment to freedom, their aversion to everything indecorous or soft or mean, the practical acknowledgement of the citizens of one State by the citizens of all other States, the fierceness of their roused resentment, their curiosity and welcome of novelty, their self-esteem and wonderful sympathy; their susceptibility to a slight, the air they have of persons who never knew how it felt to stand in the presence of superiors, the fluency of their speech, their delight in music (the sure symptom of manly tenderness and native elegance of soul), their good temper and open-handedness, the terrible significance of their elections, the President's taking off his hat to them, not they to him—these too are unrhymed poetry. It awaits the gigantic and generous treatment worthy of it.

The book is divided into a dozen or more sections, and in each one of these some thread of connection may be traced, now with ease, now with difficulty—each being a string of verses, which claim to be written without effort and with entire *abandon*. So the book is a collection of observations, speculations, memories, and prophecies, clad in the simplest, truest, and often the most nervous English—in the midst of which the reader comes upon something as much out of place as a piece of rotten wood would be among leaves of grass in the meadow, if the meadow had no object but to furnish a child's couch. So slender is the connection, that we hardly injure the following scraps by extracting them.

[Omitted are two passages quoted from sections 33 and 46 of "Song of Myself."]

Claiming in this way a personal interest in every thing that has ever happened in the world, and, by the wonderful sharpness and distinctness of his imagination, making the claim effective and reasonable, Mr. "Walt. Whitman" leaves it a matter of doubt where he has been in this world, and where not. It is very clear, that with him, as with most other effective writers, a keen, absolute memory, which takes in and holds every detail of the past—as they say the exaggerated power of the memory does when a man is drowning—is a gift of his organization as remarkable as his vivid imagination. What he has seen once, he has seen for ever. And thus there are in this curious book little thumb-nail sketches of life in the prairie, life in California, life at school, life in the nursery—life, indeed we know not where not—which, as they are unfolded one after another, strike us as real—so real that we wonder how they came on paper.

For the purpose of showing that he is above every conventionalism Mr. Whitman puts into the book one or two lines which he would not address to a woman nor to a company of men. There is not anything, perhaps, which modern usage would stamp as more indelicate than are some passages in Homer. There is not a word in it meant to attract readers by its grossness, as there is in half the literature of the last century, which holds its place unchallenged on the tables of our drawing-room. For all that, it is a pity that a book where everything else is natural should go out of the way to avoid the suspicion of being prudish.

[Whitman Reviews Himself]

[Walt Whitman]*

To give judgment on real poems, one needs an account of the poet himself. Very devilish to some, and very divine to some, will appear the poet of these new poems, the *Leaves of Grass*; an attempt, as they are, of a naive, masculine, affectionate, contemplative, sensual, imperious person, to cast into literature not only his own grit and arrogance, but his own flesh and form, undraped, regardless of models, regardless of modesty or law, and ignorant or slightly scornful, as at first appears, of all except his own presence and experience, and all outside the fiercely loved land of his birth and the birth of his parents, and their parents for several generations before him. Politeness this man has none, and regulation he has none. A rude child of the people!—no imitation—no foreigner—but a growth and idiom of America. No discontented—a careless slouch, enjoying today. No dilettante democrat—a man who is part-and-part with the commonalty, and with immediate life—loves the streets—loves the docks—loves the free rasping talk of men—likes to be called by his given name, and nobody at all need Mr. him—can laugh with laughers—likes the ungenteel ways of laborers—is not prejudiced one mite against the Irish—talks readily with them—talks readily with niggers—does not make a stand on being a gentleman, nor on learning or manners—eats cheap fare, likes the strong flavored coffee of the coffee-stands in the market, at sunrise—likes a supper of oysters fresh from the oyster-smack—likes to make one at the crowded table among sailors and work-people—would leave a select soirée of elegant people any time to go with tumultuous men, roughs, receive their caresses and welcome, listen to their noise, oaths, smut, fluency, laughter, repartee—and can preserve his presence perfectly among these, and the like of these. The effects he produces in his poems are no effects of artists or the arts, but effects of the original eye or arm, or the actual atmosphere, or tree, or bird. You may feel the unconscious teaching of a fine brute, but will never feel the artificial teaching of a fine writer or speaker.

*Reprinted from R. M. Bucke, *Walt Whitman* (Glasgow: Wilson and McCormick, 1884), pp. 195–96; originally published in the *Brooklyn Daily Times*, 29 September 1855. Whitman, of course, did not sign this review or two others that he wrote.

Other poets celebrate great events, personages, romances, wars, loves, passions, the victories and power of their country, or some real or imagined incident—and polish their work, and come to the conclusions, and satisfy the reader. This poet celebrates natural propensities in himself; and that is the way he celebrates all. He comes to no conclusions, and does not satisfy the reader. He certainly leaves him what the serpent left the woman and the man, the taste of the Paradisaic tree of the knowledge of good and evil, never to be erased again.

What good is it to argue about egotism? There can be no two thoughts on Walt Whitman's egotism. That is avowedly what he steps out of the crowd and turns and faces them for. Mark, critics! Otherwise is not used for you the key that leads to the use of the other keys to this well-enveloped man. His whole work, his life, manners, friendships, writings, all have among their leading purposes an evident purpose to stamp a new type of character, namely his own, and indelibly fix it and publish it, not for a model but an illustration, for the present and future of American letters and American young men, for the South the same as the North, and for the Pacific and Mississippi country, and Wisconsin and Texas and Kansas and Canada and Havana and Nicaragua, just as much as New York and Boston. Whatever is needed toward this achievement he puts his hand to, and lets imputations take their time to die.

First be yourself what you would show in your poem—such seems to be this man's example and inferred rebuke to the schools of poets. He makes no allusions to books or writers; their spirits do not seem to have touched him; he has not a word to say for or against them, or their theories or ways. He never offers others; what he continually offers is the man whom our Brooklynites know so well. Of pure American breed, large and lusty—age thirty-six years (1855)—never once using medicine—never dressed in black, always dressed freely and clean in strong clothes—neck open, shirt-collar flat and broad, countenance tawny transparent red, beard well-mottled with white, hair like hay after it has been mowed in the field and lies tossed and streaked—his physiology corroborating a rugged phrenology—a person singularly beloved and looked toward, especially by young men and the illiterate—one who has firm attachments there, and associates there—one who does not associate with literary people—a man never called upon to make speeches at public dinners—never on platforms amid the crowds of clergymen, or professors, or aldermen, or congressmen—rather down in the bay with pilots in their pilot-boat—or off on a cruise with fishers in a fishing-smack—or riding on a Broadway omnibus, side by side with the driver—or with a band of loungers over the open grounds of the country—fond of New York and Brooklyn—fond of the life of the great ferries—one whom, if you should meet, you need not expect to meet an extraordinary person—one in whom you will see the singularity which consists in no singularity—whose contact is no dazzle or fascination, nor requires any deference, but has the easy fascination of what is homely and accustomed—as of something you knew before, and was waiting for—there you have Walt Whitman, the begetter of a new offspring out of literature, taking with easy nonchalance the chances of its present reception, and, through all misunderstandings and distrusts, the chances of its future reception.

[A New York Journalist Finds Whitman a Scurvy Fellow]

[Rufus Griswold]*

An unconsidered letter of introduction has oftentimes procured the admittance of a scurvy fellow into good society, and our apology for permitting any allusion to the above volume in our columns is, that it has been unworthily recommended by a gentleman of wide repute, and might, on that account, obtain access to respectable people, unless its real character were exposed.

Mr. Ralph Waldo Emerson either recognizes and accepts these "leaves," as the gratifying result of his own peculiar doctrines, or else he has hastily indorsed them, after a partial and superficial reading. If it is of any importance, he may extricate himself from the dilemma. We, however, believe that this book does express the bolder results of a certain transcendental kind of thinking, which some may have styled philosophy.

As to the volume itself, we have only to remark, that it strongly fortifies the doctrines of the Metempsychosists, for it is impossible to imagine how any man's fancy could have conceived such a mass of stupid filth, unless he were possessed of the soul of a sentimental donkey that had died of disappointed love. This *poet* (?) without wit, but with a certain vagrant wildness, just serves to show the energy which natural imbecility is occasionally capable of under strong excitement.

There are too many persons, who imagine they demonstrate their superiority to their fellows, by disregarding all the politenesses and decencies of life, and, therefore, justify themselves in indulging the vilest imaginings and shamefullest license. But Nature, abhorring the abuse of the capacities she has given to man, retaliates upon him, by rendering extravagant indulgence in any direction followed by an insatiable, ever-consuming, and never to be appeased passion.

Thus, to these pitiful beings, virtue and honor are but names. Bloated with self-conceit, they strut abroad unabashed in the daylight,

*Reprinted from *Leaves of Grass Imprints* (Boston, 1860), pp. 55–56, a volume of notices printed by Whitman's publisher, Thayer and Eldridge, to promote the 1860 edition of *Leaves of Grass*. The review was published anonymously in the *Criterion*, but Griswold is identified as the author by Bliss Perry in a footnote to his *Walt Whitman: His Life and Work* (Boston: Houghton Mifflin, 1906), p. 100.

and expose to the world the festering sores that overlay them, like a garment. Unless we admit this exhibition to be beautiful, we are at once set down for non-progressive conservatives, destitute of the "inner light," the far-seeingness which, of course, characterizes those gifted individuals. Now, any one who has noticed the tendency of thought in these later years, must be aware that a quantity of this kind of nonsense is being constantly displayed. The immodesty of presumption exhibited by those *seers*; their arrogant pretentiousness; the complacent smile with which they listen to the echo of their own braying, should be, and we believe is, enough to disgust the great majority of sensible folks; but, unfortunately, there is a class that, mistaking sound for sense, attach some importance to all this rant and cant. These candid, these ingenuous, these honest "progressionists"; these human diamonds without flaws; these men that have *come*—detest furiously all shams; "to the pure, all things are pure"; they are pure, and, consequently, must thrust their reeking presence under every man's nose.

They seem to think that man has no instinctive delicacy; is not imbued with a conservative and preservative modesty, that acts as a restraint upon the violence of passions, which for a wise purpose, have been made so strong. No! these fellows have no secrets, no disguises; no, indeed! But they do have, conceal it by whatever language they choose a degrading, beastly sensuality, that is fast rotting the healthy core of all the social virtues.

There was a time when licentiousness laughed at reproval; now it writes essays and delivers lectures. Once it shunned the light; now it courts attention, writes books showing how grand and pure it is, and prophesies from its lecherous lips to its own ultimate triumph.

Shall we argue with such men? Shall we admit them into our houses, that they may leave a foul odor, contaminating the pure, healthful air? Or shall they be placed in the same category with the comparatively innocent slave of poverty, ignorance, and passion that skulks along in the shadows of byways; even in her deep degradation possessing some sparks of the Divine light, the germ of good that reveals itself by a sense of shame?

Thus, then, we leave this gathering of much to the laws which, certainly, if they fulfil their intent, must have power to suppress such obscenity. As it is entirely destitute of wit, there is no probability that any would, after this exposure, read it in the hope of finding that; and we trust no one will require further evidence—for, indeed, we do not believe there is a newspaper so vile that would print confirmatory extracts.

In our allusion to this book, we have found it impossible to convey any, even the most faint idea of its style and contents, and of our disgust and detestation of them, without employing language that cannot be pleasing to ears polite; but it does seem that some one should, under circumstances like these, undertake a most disagreeable, yet stern duty. The records of crime show that many monsters have gone on in impunity, because the exposure of their vileness was attended with too great indelicacy. *Peccatum illud horribile, inter Christianos non nominandum* [that horrible sin not to be mentioned among Christians].

[The *Boston Intelligencer* Seconds Griswold]

Anonymous*

We were attracted by the very singular title of the work to seek the work itself, and what we thought ridiculous in the title is eclipsed in the pages of this heterogeneous mass of bombast, egotism, vulgarity, and nonsense. The beastliness of the author is set forth in his own description of himself, and we can conceive no better reward than the lash for such a violation of decency as we have before us. Speaking of "this mass of stupid filth," the *Criterion* says: "It is impossible to imagine how any man's fancy could have conceived it, unless he were possessed of the soul of a sentimental donkey that had died of disappointed love." This book should find no place where humanity urges any claim to respect, and the author should be kicked from all decent society as below the level of the brute. There is neither wit nor method in his disjointed babbling, and it seems to us he must be some escaped lunatic raving in pitiable delirium.

[Whitman Victim of "the depravity of public taste"]

Anonymous*

Nothing can more clearly demonstrate the innate vulgarity of our American people, their radical immodesty, their internal licentiousness, their unchastity of heart, their foulness of feelings, than the tabooing of Walt Whitman's *Leaves of Grass*. It is quite impossible to find a publisher for the new edition which has long since been ready for the press, so measureless is the depravity of public taste. There is not an indecent word, an immodest expression, in the entire volume; not a suggestion which is not purity itself; and yet it is rejected on account of its indecency! So much do I think of this work by the healthiest and most original poet

*Dated 3 May 1856. Reprinted from Bucke, p. 198.

*Extracted from a book identified only as *Fourteen Thousand Miles Afoot* (1859); reprinted from Bucke, p. 198.

America has ever produced, so valuable a means is it of rightly estimating character, that I have been accustomed to try with it of what quality was the virtue my friends possessed. How few stood the test I shall not say. Some did, and praised it beyond measure. These I set down without hesitation as radically pure, as "born again," and fitted for the society of heaven and the angels. And this test I would recommend to everyone. Would you, reader, male or female, ascertain if you be actually modest, innocent, pure-minded? read the *Leaves of Grass*. If you find nothing improper there, you are one of the virtuous and pure. If, on the contrary, you find your sense of decency shocked, then is that sense of decency an exceedingly foul one, and you, man or woman, a very vulgar, dirty person.

The atmosphere of the *Leaves of Grass* is as sweet as that of a hayfield. Its pages exhale the fragrance of Nature. It takes you back to man's pristine state of innocence in Paradise, and lifts you Godwards. It is the healthiest book, morally, this century has produced; and if it were reprinted in the form of a cheap tract, and scattered broadcast over the land, put into the hands of youth, and into the hands of men and women everywhere, it would do more towards elevating our nature, towards eradicating this foul, vulgar, licentious, sham modesty which so degrades our people now, than any other means within my knowledge. What we want is not outward, but inward modesty; not external, but internal virtue; not silk and broadcloth decency, but a decency infused into every organ of the body and faculty of the soul. Is modesty a virtue? Is it then worn in clothes? Does it hang over the shoulders, or does it live and breathe in the heart? Our modesty is a Jewish phylactery, sewed up in the padding of a coat, and stitched into a woman's stays.

[The New York *Daily Times* is Both Attracted and Repelled]

[William Swinton]*

What Centaur have we here, half man, half beast, neighing shrill defiance to all the world? What conglomerate of thought is this before us, with insolence, philosophy, tenderness, blasphemy, beauty and gross indecency tumbling in drunken confusion through the pages? Who is this arrogant young man who proclaims himself the Poet of the Time, and who roots like a pig among a rotten garbage of licentious thoughts? Who is this flushed and full-blooded lover of Nature who studies her so affec-

*Reprinted from the *New York Daily Times*, 13 November 1856. The identification of this unsigned review as having been written by William Swinton was made by C. Carroll Hollis (see "Whitman and William Swinton: A Cooperative Friendship," *American Literature*, 30 (Jan. 1959), 425–49.

tionately, and who sometimes utters her teachings with a lofty tongue?
This mass of extraordinary contradictions, this fool and this wise man,
this lover of beauty and this sunken sensualist, this original thinker and
blind egotist, is Mr. WALT WHITMAN, author of *Leaves of Grass*, and,
according to his own account, "a Kosmos."

Some time since there was left at the office of this paper a thin quarto
volume bound in green and gold. On opening the book we first beheld, as
a frontispiece, the picture of a man in his shirt sleeves, wearing an expression of settled arrogance upon his countenance. We next arrived at a title
page of magnificent proportions, with letter-press at least an inch and a
half in length. From this title page we learned that the book was entitled
Leaves of Grass and was printed at Brooklyn in the year 1855. This in-
spected, we passed on to what seemed to be a sort of preface, only that it
had no beginning, was remarkable for a singular sparseness in the punctuation, and was broken up in a confusing manner by frequent rows of dots
separating the paragraphs. To this succeeded eighty-two pages of what
appeared at the first glance to be a number of prose sentences printed
somewhat after a biblical fashion. Almost at the first page we opened we
lighted upon the confession that the author was

> WALT WHITMAN, an American, one of the roughs,
>   a Kosmos,
> Disorderly, fleshy and sensual. . . .

This was sufficient basis for a theory. We accordingly arrived at the
conclusion that the insolent-looking young man on the frontispiece was
this same WALT WHITMAN, and author of the *Leaves of Grass*.

Then returning to the fore-part of the book, we found proof slips of
certain review articles written about the *Leaves of Grass*. One of these
purported to be extracted from a periodical entitled the *United States
Review*, the other was headed "From the *American Phrenological Journal*." These were accompanied by a printed copy of an extravagant letter
of praise addressed by Mr. RALPH WALDO EMERSON to Mr. WALT WHIT-
MAN, complimenting him on the benefaction conferred on society in the
present volume. On subsequently comparing the critiques from the
United States Review and the *Phrenological Journal* with the preface of
the *Leaves of Grass* we discovered unmistakable internal evidence that
Mr. WALT WHITMAN, true to his character as a Kosmos, was not content
with writing a book, but was also determined to review it; so Mr. WALT
WHITMAN, had concocted both those criticisms of his own work, treating
it we need not say how favorably. This little discovery of our "disorderly"
acquaintances' mode of proceeding rather damped any enthusiasm with
which Mr. EMERSON's extravagant letter may have inspired us. We
reflected, here is a man who sets himself up as the poet and teacher of his
time; who professes a scorn of everything mean and dastardly and double-
faced, who hisses with scorn as he passes one in the street whom he

suspects of the taint, hypocrisy—yet this self-contained teacher, this rough-and-ready scorner of dishonesty, this rowdy knight-errant who tilts against all lies and shams, himself perpetrates a lie and a sham at the very outset of his career. It is a lie to write a review of one's own book, then extract it from the work in which it appeared and send it out to the world as an impartial editorial utterance. It is an act that the most degraded helot of literature might blush to commit. It is a dishonesty committed against one's own nature, and all the world. Mr. WALT WHITMAN in one of his candid rhapsodies announces that he is "no more modest than immodest." Perhaps in literary matters he carries the theory farther, and is no more honest than dishonest. He likewise says in his preface: "The great poets are so known by the absence in them of tricks, and by the justification of perfect personal candor." Where, then, can we place Mr. WALT WHITMAN's claims upon immortality?

We confess we turn from Mr. WHITMAN as Critic, to Mr. WHITMAN as Poet, with considerable pleasure. We prefer occupying that independent position which Mr. WHITMAN claims for man, and forming our own opinions, rather than swallowing those ready-made. This gentleman begins his poetic life with a coarse and bitter scorn of the past. We have been living stale and unprofitable lives; we have been surfeited with luxury and high living, and are grown lethargic and dull; the age is fast decaying, when, lo! the trump of the Angel Whitman brings the dead to life, and animates the slumbering world. If we obey the dictates of that trumpet, we will do many strange things. We will fling off all moral clothing and walk naked over the earth. We will disembarrass our language of all the proprieties of speech, and talk indecency broad cast. We will act in short as if the Millennium were arrived in this our present day, when the absence of all vice would no longer necessitate a virtuous discretion. We fear much, Mr. WALT WHITMAN, that the time is not yet come for the nakedness of purity. We are not yet virtuous enough to be able to read your poetry aloud to our children and our wives. What might be pastoral simplicity five hundred years hence, would perhaps be stigmatized as the coarsest indecency now, and—we regret to think that you have spoken too soon.

The adoration of the "Me," the "Ego," the "eternal and universal I," to use the jargon of the Boston Oracle, is the prevailing motive of *Leaves of Grass*. Man embraces and comprehends the whole. He is everything, and everything is him. All nature ebbs and flows through him in ceaseless tides. He is "his own God and his own Devil," and everything that he does is good. He rejoices with all who rejoice; suffers with all who suffer. This doctrine is exemplified in the book by a panorama as it were of pictures, each of which is shared in by the author, who belongs to the universe, as the universe belongs to him. In detailing these pictures he hangs here and there shreds and tassels of his wild philosophy, till his work, like a maniac's robe, is bedizened with fluttering tags of a thousand colors.

With all his follies, insolence, and indecency, no modern poet that we know of has presented finer descriptive passages than Mr. WALT WHITMAN. His phrasing, and the strength and completeness of his epithets, are truly wonderful. He paints in a single line with marvellous power and comprehensiveness. The following rhapsody will illustrate his fulness of epithet:

> I am he that walks with the tender and growing night
> I call the earth and sea, half held by the night.
>
> Press close bare-bosomed night! Press close magnetic, nourishing
>   night!
> Night of South winds! Night of the large few stars!
> Still nodding night! Mad, naked, Summer night!
>
> Smile, O voluptuous cool-breathed earth!
> Earth of the slumbering and liquid trees!
> Earth of departed sunset! Earth of the mountains misty-topt!
> *Earth of the vitreous pour of the full moon just tinged*
>   *with blue!*
> Earth of shine and dark, mottling the tide of the river!
> Earth of the limpid gray of clouds brighter and clearer for
>   my sake!
> *Far-swooping elbowed earth!* Rich apple-blossomed earth!
> Smile, for your lover comes!
>
> You sea! I resign myself to you also . . . I guess what you mean,
> I behold from the beach your crooked inviting fingers,
> I believe you refuse to go back without feeling of me;
> We must have a turn together . . . I undress . . . hurry me out
>   of sight of the land.
> Cushion me soft . . . *rock me in billowy drowse,*
> Dash me with amorous wet . . . I can repay you.
>
> Sea of stretched ground-swells!
> Sea, breathing broad and convulsive breaths!
> Sea of the brine of life! *Sea of unshovelled and always ready*
>   *graves!*
> *Howler and scooper of storms!* Capricious and dainty sea!
> I am integral with you . . . I too am of one phase and of all
>   phases.

Here are fine expressions well placed. Mr. WHITMAN's study of nature has been close and intense. He has expressed certain things better than any other man who has gone before him. He talks well, and largely, and tenderly of sea and sky, and men and trees, and women and children. His observation and his imagination are both large and well-developed. Take this picture; how pathetic, how tenderly touched!

Agonies are one of my changes of garments;
I do not ask the wounded person how he feels . . . I myself
   become the wounded person,
My hurt turns livid upon me as I lean on a cane and observe.

I am the mashed fireman with breast-bone broken . . . tumbling
   walls buried me in their debris.
Heat and smoke I inspired . . . I heard the yelling shouts
   of my comrades,
I heard the distant click of their picks and shovels;
They have cleared the beams away . . . they tenderly lift me
   forth.
I lie in the night air in my red shirt . . . the pervading
   hush is for my sake,
Painless after all I lie, exhausted but not so unhappy.

White and beautiful are the faces around me . . . the heads
   are bared of their fire-caps.
The kneeling crowd faces with the light of the torches.

If it were permitted to us to outrage all precedent and print that which should not be printed, we could cull some passages from the *Leaves of Grass*, and place them in strange contrast with the extracts we have already made. If being a Kosmos is to set no limits to one's imagination; to use coarse epithets when coarseness is not needful; to roam like a drunken satyr, with inflamed blood, through every field of lascivious thought; to return time after time with a seemingly exhaustless prurient pleasure to the same licentious phrases and ideas, and to jumble all this up with bits of marvellously beautiful description, exquisite touches of nature, fragments of savagely uttered truth, shreds of unleavened philosophy; if to do all this is to be a Kosmos, then indeed we cede to Mr. WALT WHITMAN his arrogated title. Yet it seems to us that one may be profound without being beastly; one may teach philosophy without clothing it in slang; one may be a great poet without using a language which shall outlaw the minstrel from every decent hearth. Mr. WALT WHITMAN does not think so. He tears the veil from all that society by a well-ordered law shrouds in a decent mystery. He is proud of his nakedness of speech; he glories in his savage scorn of decorum. Like the priests of Belus, he wreathes around his brow the emblems of the Phallic worship.

With all this muck of abomination soiling the pages, there is a wondrous, unaccountable fascination about the *Leaves of Grass*. As we read it again and again, and we will confess that we have returned to it often, a singular order seems to arise out of its chaotic verses. Out of the mire and slough, edged thoughts and keen philosophy start suddenly, as the men of Cadmus sprang from the muddy loan. A lofty purpose still dominates the uncleanness and the ridiculous self-conceit in which the author, led astray by ignorance, indulges. He gives token everywhere that he is a huge uncultivated thinker. No country save this could have given birth to the man. His mind is Western—brawny, rough, and original. Wholly uncultivated, and beyond his associates, he has begotten within him the egotism of intellectual solitude. Had he mingled with scholars and men of intellect, those effete beings whom he so despises, he would have learned much that would have been beneficial. When we have none of our own size to measure ourselves with, we are apt to fancy ourselves broader and taller and stronger than we are. The poet of the little country town, who has reigned for years the Virgil or Anacreon of fifty square miles, finds, when he comes into the great metropolis, that he has not had all the thinking to himself. There he finds hundreds of men who have thought the same things as himself, and uttered them more fully. He is astonished to discover that his intellectual language is limited, when he thought that he had fathomed expression. He finds his verse unpolished, his structure defective, his best thoughts said before. He enters into the strife, clashes with his fellows, measures swords with this one, gives thrust for thrust with the other, until his muscles harden and his frame swells. He looks back upon his provincial intellectual existence with a smile; he laughs at his country arrogance and ignorant faith in himself. Now we gather from Mr. WHITMAN's own admissions—admissions that assume the form of boasts—that he has mingled but little with intellectual men. The love of the physical—which is the key-note of his entire book—has as yet altogether satisfied him. To mix with large-limbed, clean-skinned men, to look on ruddy, fair-proportioned women, is his highest social gratification. This love of the beautiful is by him largely and superbly expressed in many places, and it does one good to read those passages pulsating with the pure blood of animal life. But those associates, though manly and handsome, help but little to a man's inner appreciation of himself. Perhaps our author among his comrades had no equal in intellectual force. He reigned triumphantly in an unquestioning circle of admirers. How easy, then, to fancy one's self a wonderful being! How easy to look around and say, "There are none like me here. I am the coming man!" It may be said that books will teach such a man the existence of other powerful minds, but this will not do. Such communion is abstract, and has but little force. It is only in the actual combat of mind striving with mind that a man comes properly to estimate himself. Mr. WHITMAN has grown up in an intellectual isolation which has fully developed all the eccentricities of his nature. He has made some foolish theory that to be rough is to be original. Now, external softness of manner is in no degree incompatible with muscularity of intellect; and one thinks no more of a man's brains for his treading on one's toes without an apology, or his swearing in the presence of women. When Mr. WHITMAN shall have learned that a proper worship of the individual man need not be expressed so as to seem insolence, and that men are not to be bullied into receiving as a Messiah every man who sneers at them in his portrait, and disgusts them in his writings, we have no doubt that in some chastened mood of mind he will produce moving and powerful books. We select some passages exhibiting the different phases of Mr. WHITMAN's character. We do so more readily as, from the many indecencies contained in *Leaves of Grass*, we do not believe it will find its way into many families.

[Omitted are 42 lines from "Song of Myself," "To Think of Time," and "Europe."]

Since the foregoing was written—and it has been awaiting its turn at the printing press some months—Mr. WALT WHITMAN has published an enlarged edition of his works, from which it is fair to infer that his first has had a ready sale. From twelve poems, of which the original book was composed, he has brought the number up to thirty, all characterized by the same wonderful amalgamation of beauty and indecency. He has, however, been in his new edition guilty of a fresh immodesty. He has not alone printed Mr. EMERSON's private letter in an appendix, but he has absolutely printed a passage of that gentleman's note, "I greet you at the beginning of a great career," in gold letters on the back, and affixed the name of the writer. Now, Mr. EMERSON wrote a not very wise letter to Mr. WHITMAN on the publication of the first twelve poems—indorsing them, and so there might be some excuse for the poet's anxiety to let the public know that his first edition was commended from such a quarter. But with the additional poems, Mr. EMERSON has certainly nothing whatever to do; nevertheless, the same note that indorsed the twelve is used by Mr. WHITMAN in the coolest manner to indorse the thirty-two. This is making a private letter go very far indeed. It is as if after a man signed a deed, the person interested should introduce a number of additional clauses, making the original signature still cover them. It is a literary fraud, and Mr. WHITMAN ought to be ashamed of himself.

Still, this man has brave stuff in him. He is truly astonishing. The originality of his philosophy is of little account, for if it is truth, it must be ever the same, whether uttered by his lips or PLATO's. In manner only can we be novel, and truly Mr. WHITMAN is novelty itself. Since the greater portion of this review was written, we confess to having been attracted again and again to *Leaves of Grass*. It has a singular electric attraction. Its manly vigor, its brawny health, seem to incite and satisfy. We look forward with curious anticipation to Mr. WALT WHITMAN's future works. We are much mistaken if, after all, he does not yet contribute something to American Literature which shall awaken wonder.

[A Selection from
His Autobiography]

Moncure D. Conway*

An important event in 1855 was the appearance of Walt Whitman's "Leaves of Grass." Emerson spoke of the book at his house, and suggested that I should call on the new poet. I read the poem with joy. Democracy had at length its epic. It was prophetic of the good time coming when the vulgar herd should be transformed into noblemen. The portrait in the book was that of a working man, and if one labourer could so flower, genius was potential in all. That Walt was posing as one of a class to which he did not belong was not realized by me even after his own intimation of it, as related in my subjoined letter to Emerson (sent me by his son):

WASHINGTON, *September* 17, 1855.

MY DEAR MR. EMERSON—I immediately procured the *Leaves of Grass* after hearing you speak of it. I read it on board the steamer *Metropolis* on my way to New York the evening after seeing you, and resolved to see its author if I could while I was in the city. As you seemed much interested in him and his work, I have taken the earliest moment which I could command since my return to give you some account of my visit.

I found by the directory that one Walter Whitman lived fearfully far (out of Brooklyn, nearly), on Ryerton Street, a short way from Myrtle Avenue. The way to reach the house is to go down to Fulton Street Ferry, after crossing take the Fulton and Myrtle Avenue car, and get out at Ryerton Street. It is one of a row of small wooden houses with porches which all seem occupied by mechanics. I didn't find him there, however. His mother directed me to Rome's Printing Office (corner of Fulton and Cranberry Streets), which is much nearer, and where he often is.

I found him reviewing some proof. A man you would not have marked in a thousand; blue striped shirt, opening from a red throat; and sitting on a chair without a back, which, being the only one, he offered me and sat down on a round of the printer's desk himself. His manner was blunt enough also, without being disagreeably so.

I told him that I had just spent an evening with you, and that what you had said of him and the perusal of his book had resulted in my call. He seemed very eager to hear from you and about you, and what you thought of his book. He had once seen you and heard you in the lecture-room, and was anxious to know all he could of your life, yet not with any vulgar curiosity, but entire frankness. I told him of the occasions in which Mr. Bartol and others had attempted to read it in company and failed, at which he seemed much amused.

The likeness in the book is fair. His beard and hair are greyer than is usual with a man of thirty-six. His face and eyes are interesting, and his

*Reprinted from *Autobiography, Memories, and Experiences of Moncure Daniel Conway* (London: Cassell and Co., 1904), I, 189–92.

head rather narrow behind the eyes; he walked with me and crossed the Ferry; he seemed "hail fellow" with every man he met, all apparently in the labouring class. He says he is one of that class by choice; that he is personally dear to some thousands of such in New York, who "love him but cannot make head or tail of his book." He rides on the stage with the driver, stops to talk with the old man or woman selling fruit at the street corner; and his dress, etc., is consistent with that.

I am quite sure after talking with him that there is much in all this of what you might call "playing Providence a little with the baser sort" (so much to the distress of the Rev. Vaughan's nerves). . . . I could see that he had some books, if only a bottle-stick like Alton Locke to read them by; though he told me I thought too much of books. But I came off delighted with him. His eye can kindle strangely, and his words are ruddy with health. He is clearly his Book, and I went off impressed with the sense of a new city on my map, viz., Brooklyn, just as if it had suddenly risen through the boiling sea.

After reading the *Leaves of Grass*, Emerson wrote to the author an enthusiastic letter, greeting him "at the beginning of a great career." Whitman at once printed an edition prefaced with Emerson's letter. Emerson said that if he had known his letter would be published he might have qualified his praise. "There are parts of the book," he said, "where I hold my nose as I read. One must not be too squeamish when a chemist brings him to a mass of filth and says, 'See, the great laws are at work here also'; but it is a fine art if he can deodorise his illustration. However, I do not fear that any man who has eyes in his head will fail to see the genius in these poems. Those are terrible eyes to walk along Broadway. It is all there, as if in an auctioneer's catalogue."

Emerson did not complain seriously of the publication of his letter; it was not marked private, and appeared so carefully written that Walt considered it, as he said to me, "a serious thing that might be fairly printed." He did not, however, print any more of the edition containing it, and that second edition is rare. The incident made no difference in Emerson's friendliness towards the author, whom he welcomed cordially in Concord.

Walt Whitman did not wonder that Emerson and his Boston circle should sniff at his plain-spoken inclusion in his poetry, to use his words, "of every process, every concrete object, every human or other existence, not only considered from the point of view of all, but of each." He told me with a smile that he had heard of his poems being offered for sale by a vendor of obscene books. My own feeling after twice-reading *Leaves of Grass* was that his pantheistic inspiration had come from Emerson, and his style as well as his broadness mainly from the Bible. He had been reared among Quakers, had heard Elias Hicks preach, and the Quaker way of spiritualising everything in the Bible explained to me the refrains of psalms and Solomonic songs in *Leaves of Grass*.

My sister had been with me on this summer excursion, and I left her at the Metropolitan Hotel with a lady friend while I went to visit Walt. But I had read these young ladies select passages from the poem, and they had curiosity to see him. So I invited him to early dinner at our hotel next day, and he came in baize coat and chequered shirt, in fact, just like the portrait in his book. The ladies were pleased with him; his manners were good and his talk entertaining.

Walt Whitman told me that I was the first who had visited him because of his book. On my second visit, during the summer of 1857, he was not at home, but I found him at the top of a hill nearby lying on his back and gazing on the sky. It was Sunday morning, and he promptly agreed to a ramble. We first went to his house, where I talked a few moments with his mother, a plain pleasant old lady, not so grey as her son, and whose dark eyes had an apprehensive look. It was a small frame house. He took me to his little room, with its cot and poor furniture, the only decoration being two engravings, one of Silenus and the other of Bacchus. What he brought me up there to see was the barren solitude stretching from beneath his window towards the sea. There were no books in the room, and he told me he had very few, but had the use of good libraries. He possessed, however, a complete Shakespeare and a translation of Homer. He had received a common school education, and had been brought up in the Democratic party. He used to attend the gatherings of leading men in Tammany Hall in the days when its chief was the excellent John Fellowes. But he left the party when the Fugitive Slave Law was enacted, and then wrote his first poem, "Bloodmoney" never published.

We passed the day "loafing" on Staten Island, where we found groves and solitary beaches now built over. We had a good long bath in the sea, and I perceived that the reddish tanned face and neck of the poet crowned a body of lily-like whiteness and a shapely form.

Walt Whitman said to me as we parted, "I have not met anyone so charged with my ideas as you." The ideas had attracted me less than the style, because of its marvellous resemblance not only to biblical but to ancient Persian poetry which I was reading in the *Desatir* and other books which I found he had never heard of. It seemed like the colours of dawn reappearing in the sunset.

[A Selection from His Journals]

Bronson Alcott*

October 4 [1856]   *New York City*
    P.M. To Brooklyn, and see Walt Whitman. I pass a couple of hours, and find him to be an extraordinary person, full of brute power, certainly

*Reprinted from *The Journals of Bronson Alcott*, ed. Odell Shepard (Boston: Little Brown and Co., 1938), pp. 286-87, 289-91, 293-94.

of genius and audacity, and likely to make his mark on Young America—he affirming himself to be its representative man and poet. I must meet him again, and more than once, to mete his merits and place in this Pantheon of the West. He gives me his book of poems, the *Leaves of Grass*, 2nd. Edition, with new verses, and asks me to write to him if I have any more to say about him or his master, Emerson.

A nondescript, he is not so easily described, nor seen to be described. Broad-shouldered, rouge-fleshed, Bacchus-browed, bearded like a satyr, and rank, he wears his man-Bloomer in defiance of everybody, having these as everything else after his own fashion, and for example to all men hereafter. Red flannel undershirt, open-breasted, exposing his brawny neck; striped calico jacket over this, the collar Byroneal, with coarse cloth overalls buttoned to it; cowhide boots; a heavy round-about, with huge outside pockets and buttons to match; and a slouched hat, for house and street alike. Eyes gray, unimaginative, cautious yet sagacious; his voice deep, sharp, tender sometimes and almost melting. When talking will recline upon the couch at length, pillowing his head upon his bended arm, and informing you naively how lazy he is, and slow. Listens well; asks you to repeat what he has failed to catch at once, yet hesitates in speaking often, or gives over as if fearing to come short of the sharp, full, concrete meaning of his thought. Inquisitive, very; over-curious even; inviting criticism on himself, on his poems—pronouncing it "pomes."—In fine, an egotist, incapable of omitting, or suffering any one long to omit, noting Walt Whitman in discourse. Swaggy in his walk, burying both hands in his outside pockets. Has never been sick, he says, nor taken medicine, nor sinned; and so is quite innocent of repentance and man's fall. A bachelor, he professes great respect for women. Of Scotch descent by his father; by his mother, German. Age 38, and Long Island born.

November 10
This morning we call on Whitman, Mrs. Tyndall accompanying us to whet her curiosity on the demigod. He receives us kindly, yet awkwardly, and takes us up two narrow flights of stairs to sit or stand as we might in his attic study—also the bedchamber of himself and his feeble brother, the pressure of whose bodies was still apparent in the unmade bed standing in one corner, and the vessel scarcely hidden underneath. A few books were piled disorderly over the mantel-piece, and some characteristic pictures—a Hercules, a Bacchus, and a satyr—were pasted, unframed, upon the rude walls.

There was a rough table in the room, and but a single window, fronting Ellison Avenue, upon which he lives, his being the middle tenement of a single block of three private dwellings and far out on Myrtle Avenue, in the very suburbs of the city of Brooklyn.

He took occasion to inform us three, while surveying his premises aloft, of his bathing daily through the mid-winter; said he rode sometimes a-top of an omnibus up and down Broadway from morning till night beside the driver, and dined afterwards with the whipsters, frequented the opera during the season, and "lived to make pomes," and for nothing else particularly.

He had told me on my former visit of his being a housebuilder, but I learned from his mother that his brother was the house-builder, and not Walt, who, she said, had no business but going out and coming in to eat, drink, write, and sleep. And she told how all the common folks loved him. He had his faults, she knew, and was not a perfect man, but meant us to understand that she thought him an extraordinary son of a fond mother.

I said, while looking at the pictures in his study; "Which, now, of the three, particularly, is the new poet here—this Hercules, the Bacchus, or the satyr?" On which he begged me not to put my questions too close, meaning to take, as I inferred, the virtues of the three to himself unreservedly. And I think he might fairly, being himself the modern Pantheon—satyr, Silenus, and him of the twelve labours—combined.

He is very curious of criticism on himself or his book, inviting it from all quarters, nor suffering the conversation to stray very wide away from Walt's godhead without recalling it to that high mark. I hoped to put him in communication direct with Thoreau, and tried my hand a little after we came down stairs and sat in the parlour below; but each seemed planted fast in reserves, surveying the other curiously—like two beasts, each wondering what the other would do, whether to snap or run; and it came to no more than cold compliments between them. Whether Thoreau was mediating the possibility of Walt's stealing away his "out-of-doors" for some sinister ends, poetic or pecuniary, I could not well divine, nor was very curious to know; or whether Walt suspected or not that he had here, for once, and the first time, found his match and more at smelling out "all Nature," a sagacity potent, penetrating and peerless as his own, if indeed not more piercing and profound, finer and more formidable. I cannot say. At all events, our stay was not long, and we left the voluminous Mrs. Tyndall . . . with the savage sovereign of the flesh, he making an appointment to meet me at the International tomorrow and deliver himself further, if the mood favored and the place.

December 12
Today fair and sunny, and I walk for two hours in the Park. Walt Whitman comes, and we dine at Taylor's Saloon, discussing America, its men and institutions. Walt thinks the best thing it has done is the growing of Emerson, the only man there is in it—unless it be himself. Alcott, he fancies, may be somebody, perhaps, to be named by way of courtesy in a country so crude and so pregnant with coming great men and women. He tells me he is going presently to Washington City to see and smell of, or at, the pigmies assembled there at the Capitol, whom he will show up in his letters from there in some of the newspapers, and will send me samples of

his work by mail to me at Walpole. It will be curious to see what he will make of Congress and the Society at the Capitol. Walt has been editor of a paper once, at Brooklyn, and a contributor to the magazines sometimes. If a broader and finer intercourse with men serves to cure something of his arrogance and take out his egotism, good may come, and great things, of him.

[A Letter about Whitman]

Henry David Thoreau*

December 7
      That Walt Whitman, of whom I wrote to you, is the most interesting fact to me at present. I have just read his second edition (which he gave me), and it has done me more good than any reading for a long time. Perhaps I remember best the poem of Walt Whitman, an American, and the Sun-Down Poem. There are two or three pieces in the book which are disagreeable to say the least; simply sensual. He does not celebrate love at all. It is as if the beasts spoke. I think that men have not been ashamed of themselves without reason. No doubt there have always been dens where such deeds were unblushingly recited, and it is no merit to compete with their inhabitants.
      But even on this side he has spoken more truth than any American or modern that I know. I have found his poem exhilarating, encouraging. As for its sensuality—and it may turn out to be less sensual than it appears—I do not so much wish that those parts were not written, as that men and women were so pure, that they could read them without harm, that is, without understanding them. One woman told me that no woman could read it—as if a man could read what a woman could not. Of course Walt Whitman can communicate to us no experience, and if we are shocked, whose experience is it that we are reminded of?
      On the whole, it sounds to me very brave and American, after whatever deductions. I do not believe that all the sermons, so called, that have been preached in this land put together are equal to it for preaching.
      We ought to rejoice greatly in him. He occasionally suggests something a little more than human. You can't confound him with the other inhabitants of Brooklyn or New York. How they must shudder when they read him! He is awfully good.
      To be sure I sometimes feel a little imposed on. By his heartiness and broad generalities he puts me into a liberal frame of mind prepared to see wonders—as it were, sets me upon a hill or in the midst of a plain—stirs

*Letter to Harrison Blake; reprinted in *Letters to Various Persons* (Boston: Ticknor and Fields, 1865), pp. 146–48.

me up well, and then—throws in a thousand of brick. Though rude and sometimes ineffectual, it is a great primitive poem—an alarm or trumpet-note ringing through the American camp. Wonderfully like the Orientals, too, considering that when I asked him if he had read them, he answered, "No: tell me about them."

I did not get far in conversation with him—two more being present—and among the few things which I chanced to say, I remember that one was, in answer to him as representing America, that I did not think much of America or of politics, and so on, which may have been somewhat of a damper to him.

Since I have seen him, I find that I am not disturbed by any brag or egoism in his book. He may turn out the least of a braggart of all, having a better right to be confident.

He is a great fellow.

["as unacquainted with art as a hog is with mathematics"]

Anonymous*

We had ceased, we imagined, to be surprised at anything that America could produce. We had become stoically indifferent to her Woolly Horses, her Mermaids, her Sea Serpents, her Barnums, and her Fanny Ferns; but the last monstrous importation from Brooklyn, New York, has scattered our indifference to the winds. Here is a thin quarto volume without an author's name on the title-page; but to atone for which we have a portrait engraved on steel of the notorious individual who is the poet presumptive. This portrait expresses all the features of the hard democrat, and none of the flexile delicacy of the civilised poet. The damaged hat, the rough beard, the naked throat, the shirt exposed to the waist, are each and all presented to show that the man to whom those articles belong scorns the delicate arts of civilisation. The man is the true impersonation of his book—rough, uncouth, vulgar. It was by the merest accident that we discovered the name of this erratic and newest wonder; at page 29 we find that he is—

> Walt Whitman, an American, one of the roughs,
> a Kosmos,
> Disorderly, fleshly, and sensual.

The words, "an American" are a surplusage, "one of the roughs" too painfully apparent; but what is intended to be conveyed by "a Kosmos" we cannot tell, unless it means a man who thinks that the fine essence of

*Reprinted from the London *Critic*, 15 (1 April 1856), 170–71.

poetry consists in writing a book which an American reviewer is compelled to declare is "not to be read aloud to a mixed audience." We should have passed over this book, *Leaves of Grass*, with indignant contempt, had not some few Transatlantic critics attempted to "fix" this Walt Whitman as the poet who shall give a new and independent literature to America—who shall form a race of poets as Banquo's issue formed a line of kings. Is it possible that the most prudish nation in the world will adopt a poet whose indecencies stink in the nostrils? We hope not; and yet there is a probability, and we will show why, that this Walt Whitman will not meet with the stern rebuke which he so richly deserves. America has felt, oftener perhaps that we have declared, that she has no national poet—that each one of her children of song has relied too much on European inspiration, and clung too fervently to the old conventionalities. It is therefore not unlikely that she may believe in the dawn of a thoroughly original literature, now there has arisen a man who scorns the hellenic deities, who has no belief in, perhaps because he has no knowledge of, Homer and Shakespeare; who relies on his own rugged nature, and trusts to his own rugged language, being himself what he shows in his poems.

Once transfix him as the genesis of a new era, and the manner of the man may be forgiven or forgotten. But what claims has this Walt Whitman to be thus considered, or to be considered a poet at all? We grant freely enough that he has a strong relish for nature and freedom, just as an animal has; nay, further, that his crude mind is capable of appreciating some of nature's beauties; but it by no means follows that, because nature is excellent, therefore art is contemptible. Walt Whitman is as unacquainted with art, as a hog is with mathematics. His poems—we must call them so for convenience—twelve in number, are innocent of rhythm, and resemble nothing so much as the war-cry of the Red Indians. Indeed, Walt Whitman has had near and ample opportunities of studying the vociferation of a few amiable savages. Or rather perhaps, this Walt Whitman reminds us of Caliban flinging down his logs, and setting himself to write a poem. In fact Caliban, and not Walt Whitman, might have written this:

> I too am not a bit tamed—I too am untranslatable.
> I sound my barbaric yawp over the roofs of the world.

Is this man with the "barbaric yawp" to push Longfellow into the shade, and he meanwhile to stand and "make mouths" at the sun? The chance of this might be formidable were it not ridiculous. That object or that act which most develops the ridiculous element carries in its bosom the seeds of decay, and is wholly powerless to trample out of God's universe one spark of the beautiful. We do not, then, fear this Walt Whitman, who gives us slang in the place of melody, and rowdyism in the place of regularity. The depth of his indecencies will be the grave of his fame, or ought to be if all proper feeling is not extinct. The very nature of this man's compositions excludes us from proving by extracts the truth of our remarks; but we, who are not prudish, emphatically declare that the man who wrote page 79 of the *Leaves of Grass* deserves nothing so richly as the public executioner's whip. Walt Whitman libels the highest type of humanity, and calls his free speech the true utterance of a *man*: we, who may have been misdirected by civilisation, call it the expression of *a beast.* . . .[1]

Note

    1. This review continues for another column and one half, mostly containing exhibits from *Leaves of Grass* and ends with line 637 of "Song of Myself" ("I talk wildly, I have lost my wits . . .") altered to read "I talk wildly, I am mad."

["a pregnant text-book . . . minted gold"]

[William J. Fox]*

    We have before us one of the most extraordinary specimens of Yankee intelligence and American eccentricity in authorship it is possible to conceive. It is of a *genus* so peculiar as to embarrass us, and has an air at once so novel, so audacious, and so strange, as to verge upon absurdity, and yet it would be an injustice to pronounce it so, as the work is saved from this extreme by a certain mastery over diction not very easy of definition. What Emerson has pronounced to be good must not be lightly treated, and before we pronounced upon the merits of this performance it is but right to examine them. We have, then, a series of pithy prose sentences strung together—forming twelve grand divisions in all, but which, having a rude rhythmical cadence about them, admit of the designation poetical being applied. They are destitute of rhyme, measure of feet, and the like, every condition under which poetry is generally understood to exist being absent; but in their strength of expression, their fervor, hearty wholesomeness, their originality, mannerism, and freshness, one finds in them a singular harmony and flow, as if by reading they gradually formed themselves into melody, and adopted characteristics peculiar and appropriate to themselves alone. If, however, some

*Reprinted from *Leaves of Grass Imprints*, pp. 29–30. Although attributed to William Howitt by Gay Wilson Allen in *A Solitary Singer* (New York, 1955), p. 176, both W. M. Rossetti and W. D. O'Connor (see Bucke, pp. 106 and 240) say without qualification that the review which appeared in the *Weekly Dispatch*, (London), is by Fox. Also Harold Blodgett (*Walt Whitman in England* [Ithaca, N.Y.: Cornell Univ. Press, 1934], p. 14) assigns this review to Fox.

sentences be fine, there are others altogether laughable; nevertheless, in the bare strength, the unhesitating frankness of a man who "believes in the flesh and the appetites," and who dares to call simplest things by their plainest names, conveying also a large sense of the beautiful, and with an emphasis which gives a clearer conception of what manly modesty really is than anything we have, in all conventional forms of word, deed, and act so far known of, that we rid ourselves, little by little, of the strangeness with which we greet this bluff new-comer, and beginning to understand him better, appreciate him in proportion as he becomes more known. He will soon make his way into the confidence of his readers, and his poems in time will become a pregnant text-book, out of which quotations as sterling as the minted gold will be taken and applied to every form and phrase of the "inner" or the "outer" life; and we express our pleasure in making the acquaintance of Walt Whitman, hoping to know more of him in time to come.

["unmixed and hopeless drivel"]

Anonymous*

The author of *Leaves of Grass* has perpetrated another "poem." The N.Y. *Saturday Press*, in whose columns, we regret to say, it appears, calls it "a curious warble." Curious it may be; but warble it is not, in any sense of that mellifluous word. It is a shade less heavy and vulgar than the *Leaves of Grass*, whose unmitigated badness seemed to cap the climax of poetic nuisances. But the present performance has all the emptiness, without half the grossness, of the author's former efforts.

How in the name of all the Muses this so-called "poem" ever got into the columns of the *Saturday Press*, passes our poor comprehension. We had come to look upon that journal as the prince of literary weeklies, the *arbiter elegantiarum* of dramatic and poetic taste, into whose well-filled columns nothing stupid or inferior could intrude. The numerous delicious poems; the sparkling *bon mots*; the puns, juicy and classical, which almost redeemed that vicious practice, and raised it to the rank of a fine art; the crisp criticisms, and delicate dramatic humors of "Personne," and the charming piquancies of the *spirituelle* Ada Clare—all united to make up a paper of rare excellence. And it is into this gentle garden of the Muses that that unclean cub of the wilderness, Walt Whitman, has been suffered to intrude, trampling with his vulgar and profane hoofs among the

*From the Cincinnati *Commercial*, Jan. 1, 1860; reprinted in *Leaves of Grass Imprints*, pp. 57–60. Although the 3rd edition did not appear until May, 1860, this attack on "A Child's Reminiscence," later called "Out of the Cradle Endlessly Rocking," published in the N.Y. *Saturday Press*, December 24, 1859, was launched against what is generally regarded to be the finest poem in the 1860 edition.

delicate flowers which bloom there, and soiling the spotless white of its fair columns with lines of stupid and meaningless twaddle.

Perhaps our readers are blissfully ignorant of the history and achievements of Mr. Walt Whitman. Be it known, then, that he is a native and resident of Brooklyn, Long Island, born and bred in an obscurity from which it were well he never had emerged. A person of coarse nature, and strong, rude passions, he has passed his life in cultivating, not the amenities, but the rudenesses of character; and instead of tempering his native ferocity with the delicate influences of art and refined literature, he has studied to exaggerate his deformities, and to thrust into his composition all the brute force he could muster from a capacity not naturally sterile in the elements of strength. He has undertaken to be an artist, without leaving the first principle of art, and has presumed to put forth "poems" without possessing a spark of the poetic faculty. He affects swagger and independence, and blurts out his vulgar impertinence under a full assurance of "originality."

In his very first performance, this truculent tone was manifested. He exaggerated every sentiment, and piled up with endless repetition every epithet, till the reader grew weary, even to nausea, of his unmeaning rant. He announces himself to the world as a new and striking thinker who had something to reveal. His *Leaves of Grass* were a revelation from the Kingdom of Nature. Thus he screams to a gaping universe:

> I, Walt Whitman, an American, one of the roughs,
> a Cosmos; I shout my voice high and clear over the waves;
> I send my barbaric yawp over the roofs of the world!

Such was the style of his performance, only it was disfigured by far worse sins of morality than of taste. Never, since the days of Rabelais, was there such literature of uncleanness as some portions of this volume exhibited. All that is beautiful and sacred in love was dragged down to the brutal plane of animal passion, and the writer appeared to revel in language fit only for the lips of the Priapus of the old mythology.

We had hoped that the small reception accorded to his first performance had deterred Mr. Whitman from fresh trespasses in the realms of literature. Several years had passed away; his worse than worthless book had been forgotten, and we hoped that this Apollo of the Brooklyn marshes had returned to his native mud. But we grieve to say he revived last week, and although somewhat changed, changed very little for the better. We do not find so much that is offensive, but we do find a vast amount of irreclaimable drivel and inexplicable nonsense.

We have searched this "poem" through with the serious and deliberate endeavour to find out the reason of its being written; to discover some clue to the mystery of so vast an expenditure of words. But we honestly confess our utter inability to solve the problem. It is destitute of all the elements which are commonly desiderated in poetical composition;

it has neither rhythm nor melody, rhyme nor reason, metre nor sense. We do solemnly assert, that there is not to be discovered, throughout the whole performance, so much as a glimmering ghost of an idea.

[Omitted are 29 lines quoted from the poem.]

Now, what earthly object can there be in writing and printing such unmixed and hopeless drivel as that? If there were any relief to the unmeaning monotony, some glimpse of fine fancy, some oasis of sense, some spark of "the vision and the faculty divine," we would not say a word. But we do protest, in the name of the sanity of the human intellect, against being invited to read such stuff as this, by its publication in the columns of a highly respectable literary journal. What is the comment of the *Saturday Press* itself on the "poem"? It says:

> Like the *Leaves of Grass*, the purport of this wild and plaintive song, well enveloped, and eluding definition, is positive and unquestionable, like the effect of music. The piece will bear reading many times—perhaps, indeed, only comes forth, as from recesses, by many repetitions.

Well, Heaven help us, then, for as we are a living man, we would not read that poem "many times" for all the poetry that was ever perpetrated since the morning stars sang together. "Well enveloped, and eluding definition." Indeed! We should think so. For our part, we hope it will remain "well enveloped" till doomsday; and as for "definition" all we can do in that direction is to declare that either that "poem" is nonsense, or we are a lunatic.

If any of the tuneful Nine have ever descended upon Mr. Walt Whitman, it must have been long before that gentleman reached the present sphere of existence. His amorphous productions clearly belong to that school which it is said that neither gods nor men can endure. There is no meaning discoverable in his writings, and if there were, it would most certainly not be worth the finding out. He is the laureate of the empty deep of the incomprehensible; over that immortal limbo described by Milton, he has stretched the dragnet of his genius; and as he has no precedent and no rival, so we venture to hope that he will never have an imitator.

["the genuine stuff in this man"]

Anonymous*

Thayer & Eldridge, of Boston, advertise as nearly ready the redoubtable poems of Walt Whitman—a new and enlarged edition of the *Leaves of Grass*—which made so much astonishment in literary and other circles,

*From the *New York Illustrated News*, 5 May 1860, reprinted in *Leaves of Grass Imprints*, p. 65.

when it was first flung pell-mell at the heads of the reading public some eight [five] years ago. We shall have something to say about it when it comes to us in the due time and season of publication. In the mean while we warn our readers who may know nothing about this poet and his works, that strange as his speech is—wild, rude, and barbaric as they will find it at first—that there is the genuine stuff in this man, and that his sentences resound with the primordial music of nature, and are in harmony with the mountains and seas, and with the songs of the morning stars. Captious, flippant, and foolish people, who are also smart and brilliant, affect already, and will continue to affect, to despise these poems, and adjudge them to the trunk maker. But they are not to be disposed of thus. The "Court as of Angels," who, according to Emerson, make up the final verdict about every book, will dispose of it in quite another and far different manner. We find in it all sorts of marvellous insights and truths; the broadest intellectual and moral recognitions and suggestions; and a culture which is up to the high-water mark to which the age has risen. In our judgment—without of course indorsing either the phraseology or the sentiments of particular passages—it is the first true word which has been spoken of America—its people, institutions, laws, customs, its physical and moral portraitures—by an American. The genius of this continent and of this wonderful civilization speaks through his pen; and his sentences will one day become the Mosaics of the literature, and be woven into the common speech of the people of America. We know all this is treason at present, in the estimation of poodles and the snobs of literature and of society; but Whitman can afford to wait for the judgment of the "Court as of Angels," and smile at poodledom.

["these foul and rank leaves"]

Anonymous*

We have alluded just now to our incapability of comprehending the writings of Swedenborg, but still more, in some parts, do we acknowledge ourselves nonplussed and puzzled by these *Leaves of Grass*. It would be more correct, however, to say how utterly at a loss we are to understand by what motive or impulse so eminent a lecturer and writer, and, as we have always understood, with all his crotchety ideas and pantheistic prattlings, so pure-minded a man as R. Waldo Emerson could have written that eulogy of the *Leaves*, which certainly acted as our chief inducement for inspecting their structure.

Grass is the gift of God and the healthy sustenance of his creatures, and its name ought not to be desecrated by being so improperly bestowed

*From the *Boston Post*, May[?] 1860; reprinted in Bucke, pp. 201–02.

upon these foul and rank leaves of the poison-plants of egotism, ir-reverence, and of lust run rampant and holding high level in its shame!

We see that the volume arrogantly assumes to itself the claim of founding an original and independent American Literature. Woe and shame for the Land of Liberty if its literature's stream is thus to flow from the filthy foundations of licentious corruption! Little fear, however, should we have of such an issue from the *Leaves* themselves. The pure and elevated moral sense of America would leave them to decay and perish amid their own putridity. But there is danger of their corrupting in-fluences being diffused and extended to the great injury of society, when leaders of our literature, like Emerson, are so infatuated in judgment, and so untrue to the most solemn responsibilities of their position, as to indorse such a prurient and polluted work—to address its author in such terms as these, "I give you joy of your free and brave thought—I have great joy in it—I wish to see my benefactor."

The most charitable conclusion at which we can arrive is, that both Whitman's *Leaves* and Emerson's laudation had a common origin in tem-porary insanity.

It in no degree shakes our judgment to find more than one eminent Review coinciding more or less in the praise of this work, to which we ourselves by no means deny the possession of much originality of thought and vigor of expression. No amount, however, of such merits can in the judgment of sound and honest criticism—whose bounden duty it is to en-deavor to guide the mind of the nation in a healthy, moral course—atone for the exalting audacity of Priapus worshipping obscenity, which marks a large portion of the volume. Its vaunted manliness and independence, tested by the standard of a truthful judgment, is nothing but the deifica-tion of Self, and defiance of the Diety—its liberty is the wildest license; its love the essence of the lowest lust!

["A herculean fellow . . . with an entire gold mine"]

Anonymous*

In no other modern poems do we find such a lavish outpouring of wealth. It is as if, in the midst of a crowd of literati bringing handfuls of jewels, a few of pure metal elaborately wrought, but the rest merely pretty specimens of pinchbeck, suddenly a herculean fellow should come along with an entire gold mine. Right and left he scatters the glittering dust—and it is but dust in the eyes of those who look only for pleasing trinkets. Out of his deep California sacks, mingled with native quartz and

*From the *Boston Cosmopolite*, 4 August 1860; reprinted in Bucke, pp. 200–01.

sand, he empties the yellow ore—sufficient to set up fifty small practical jewellers dealing in galvanized ware, if they were not too much alarmed at the miner's rough garb to approach and help themselves. Down from his capacious pockets tumble astonishing nuggets—but we, who are accustomed to see the stuff never in its rude state, but only in fashionable shapes of breastpins, or caneheads, start back with affright, and scream for our toes.

It is much to be regretted that treasures of such rare value are lost to the age through the strange form and manner in which they are presented. But it is time lost blaming the miner. Perhaps he could have done differently, perhaps not; at all events, we must take him as he is, and if we are wise, make the best of him.

The first and greatest objection brought against Walt Whitman and his *Leaves of Grass* is their indecency. Nature is treated here without fig-leaves; things are called by their names, without any apparent sense of modesty or shame. Of this peculiarity—so shocking in an artificial era—the dainty reader should be especially warned. But it is a mistake to infer that the book is on this account necessarily immoral. It is the poet's design, not to entice to the perversion of Nature, which is vice, but to lead us back to Nature, which in his theory is the only virtue. His theory may be wrong, and the manner in which he carried it out repulsive, but no one who reads and understands him will question the sincerity of his motives, however much may be doubted the wisdom of attempting in this way to restore mankind to the days of undraped innocence.

In respect of plain speaking, and in most respects, the *Leaves* more resemble the Hebrew Scriptures than do any other modern writings. The style is wonderfully idiomatic and graphic. The commonest daily objects and the most exalted truths of the soul, this bard of Nature touches with the ease and freedom of a great master. He wonders at all things, he sympathizes with all things and with all men. The nameless something which makes the power and spirit of music, of poetry, of all art, throbs and whirls under and through his verse, affecting us we know not how, agitating and ravishing the soul. And this springs so genuinely from the inmost nature of the man, that it always appears singularly in keeping even with that extravagant egotism, and with those surprisingly quaint or common expressions, at which readers are at first inclined only to laugh. In his frenzy, in the fire of his inspiration, are fused and poured out together elements hitherto considered antagonistic in poetry—passion, arrogance, animality, philosophy, brag, humility, rowdyism, spirituality, laughter, tears, together with the most ardent and tender love, the most comprehensive human sympathy which ever radiated its divine glow through the pages of poems.

The Good Gray Poet: A Vindication

William Douglas O'Connor*

WASHINGTON, D.C., September 2, 1865

Nine weeks have elapsed since the commission of an outrage, to which I have not till now been able to give my attention, but which, in the interest of the sacred cause of free letters, and in that alone, I never meant should pass without its proper and enduring brand.

For years past, thousands of people in New York, in Brooklyn, in Boston, in New Orleans, and latterly in Washington, have seen, even as I saw two hours ago, tallying, one might say, the streets of our American cities, and fit to have for his background and accessories their streaming populations and ample and rich facades, a man of striking masculine beauty—a poet—powerful and venerable in appearance; large, calm, superbly formed; oftenest clad in the careless, rough, and always picturesque costume of the common people; resembling, and generally taken by strangers for some great mechanic or stevedore, or seaman, or grand laborer of one kind or another; and passing slowly in this guise, with nonchalant and haughty step along the pavement, with the sunlight and shadows falling around him. The dark sombrero he usually wears was, when I saw him just now, the day being warm, held for the moment in his hand; rich light an artist would have chosen, lay upon his uncovered head, majestic, large, Homeric, and set upon his strong shoulders with the grandeur of ancient sculpture. I marked the countenance, serene, proud, cheerful, florid, grave; the brow seamed with noble wrinkles; the features, massive and handsome, with firm blue eyes; the eyebrows and eyelids especially showing the fulness of arch seldom seen save in the antique busts; the flowing hair and fleecy beard, both very gray, and tempering with a look of age the youthful aspect of one who is but forty-five; the simplicity and purity of his dress, cheap and plain, but spotless, from snowy falling collar to burnished boot, and exhaling faint fragrance; the whole form surrounded with manliness as with a nimbus, and breathing, in its perfect health and vigor, the august charm of the strong.

We who have looked upon this figure, or listened to that clear, cheerful, vibrating voice, might thrill to think, could we but transcend our age, that we had been thus near to one of the greatest of the sons of men. But Dante stirs no deep pulse, unless it be of hate, as he walks the streets of Florence; that shabby, one-armed soldier, just out of jail and hardly noticed, though he has amused Europe, is Michael Cervantes; that son of a vine-dresser, whom Athens laughs at as an eccentric genius, before it is

*Separately published in New York (1866) as a pamphlet; reprinted in Bucke, pp. 99–130, from which I have selected the first six pages. O'Connor made 17 minor revisions in Bucke's version; see Jerome Loving's *Walt Whitman's Champion: William Douglas O'Connor* (College Station, Tex.: Texas A&M Press, 1978), pp. 237–38. Loving reprints the original pamphlet.

thought worth while to roar him into exile, is the century-shaking Aeschylus; that phantom whom the wits of the seventeenth century think not worth extraordinary notice, and the wits of the eighteenth century, spluttering with laughter, call a barbarian, is Shakespeare; that earth-soiled, vice-stained ploughman, with the noble heart and sweet bright eyes, abominated by the good and patronized by the gentry, subject now of anniversary banquets by gentlemen who, could they wander backward from those annual hiccups into time, would never help his life or keep his company—is Robert Burns; and this man, whose grave, perhaps, the next century will cover with passionate and splendid honors, goes regarded with careless curiosity or phlegmatic composure by his own age. Yet, perhaps, in a few hearts he has waked that deep thrill due to the passage of the sublime. I heard lately, with sad pleasure, of the letter introducing a friend, filled with noble courtesy, and dictated by the reverence for genius, which a distinguished English nobleman, a stranger, sent to this American bard. Nothing deepens my respect for the beautiful intellect of the scholar Alcott, like the bold sentence, "Greater than Plato," which he once uttered upon him. I hold it the surest proof of Thoreau's insight, that after a conversation, seeing how he incarnated the immense and new spirit of the age, and was the compend of America, he came away to speak the electric sentence, "He is Democracy!" I treasure to my latest hour, with swelling heart and springing tears, the remembrance that Abraham Lincoln seeing him for the first time from the window of the east room of the White House as he passed slowly by, and gazing at him long with that deep eye which read men, said, in the quaint, sweet tone, which those who have spoken with him will remember, and with a significant emphasis which the type can hardly convey. "Well, *he* looks like a Man!" Sublime tributes, great words; but none too high for their object, the author of *Leaves of Grass*, Walt Whitman, of Brooklyn.

On the 30th of June last, this true American man and author was dismissed, under circumstances of peculiar wrong, from a clerkship he had held for six months in the Department of the Interior. His dismissal was the act of the Hon. James Harlan, the Secretary of the Department, formerly a Methodist clergyman, and president of a Western college.

Upon the interrogation of an eminent officer of the Government, at whose instance the appointment had, under a former Secretary been made, Mr. Harlan averred that Walt Whitman had been in no way remiss in the discharge of his duties, but that, on the contrary, so far as he could learn, his conduct had been most exemplary. Indeed, during the first few months of his tenure of office, he had been promoted. The sole and only cause of his dismissal, Mr. Harlan said, was that he had written the book of poetry entitled *Leaves of Grass*. This book Mr. Harlan characterized as "full of indecent passages." The author, he said, was "a very bad man," a "free lover." Argument being had upon these propositions, Mr. Harlan was, as regards the book, utterly unable to maintain his assertions and, as regards the author, was forced to own that his opinion of him had been changed. Nevertheless, after this substantial admission of his injustice, he absolutely refused to revoke his action. Of course, under no circumstances would Walt Whitman, the proudest man that lives, have consented to again enter into office under Mr. Harlan; but the demand for his reinstatement was as honorable to the gentleman who made it as the refusal to accede to it was discreditable to the Secretary.

The closing feature of this transaction, and one which was a direct consequence of Mr. Harlan's course, was its remission to the scurrilous, and in some instances libellous, comment of a portion of the press. To sum up, an author solely and only for the publication, ten years ago, of an honest book, which no intelligent and candid person can regard as hurtful to morality, was expelled from office by the Secretary, and held up to public contumely by the newspapers. It only remains to be added here, that the Hon. James Harlan is the gentleman who, upon assuming the control of the Department, published a manifesto, announcing that it was thenceforth to be governed "upon the principles of Christian civilization."

This act of expulsion, and all that it encloses, is the outrage to which I referred in my opening paragraph.

I have had the honor, which I esteem a very high one, to know Walt Whitman intimately for several years, and am conversant with the details of his life and history. Scores and scores of persons, who know him well, can confirm my own report of him, and I have therefore no hesitation in saying that the scandalous assertions of Mr. Harlan, derived from who I know not, as to his being a bad man, a free lover, etc., belong to the category of those calumnies at which, as Napoleon said, innocence itself is confounded. A better man in all respects, or one more irreproachable in his relations to the other sex, lives not upon this earth. His is the great goodness, the great chastity of spiritual strength and sanity. I do not believe that from the hour of his infancy, when Lafayette held him in his arms, to the present hour, in which he bends over the last wounded and dying of the war, any one can say aught of him, which does not consort with the largest and truest manliness. I am perfectly aware of the miserable lies which have been put into circulation respecting him, of which the story of his dishonoring an invitation to dine with Emerson, by appearing at the table of the Astor House in a red shirt, and with the manners of a rowdy, is a mild specimen. I know too the inferences drawn by wretched fools, who, because they have seen him riding upon the top of an omnibus; or at Pfaff's restaurant; or dressed in rough clothes suitable for his purposes, and only remarkable because the wearer was a man of genius; or mixing freely and lovingly, like Lucretius, like Rabelais, like Francis Bacon, like Rembrandt, like all great students of the world, with low and equivocal and dissolute persons, as well as with those of a different character, must needs set him down as a brute, a scallawag, and a criminal. Mr. Harlan's allegations are of a piece with these. If I could associate the title with a really great person, or if the name of man were not radically superior, I should say that for solid nobleness of character, for native elegance and delicacy of soul, for a courtesy which is the very passion of thoughtful kindness and forbearance, for his tender and paternal respect and manly honor for woman, for love and heroism carried into the pettiest details of life, and for a large and homely beauty of manners, which makes the civilities of parlors fantastic and puerile in comparison, Walt Whitman deserves to be considered the grandest gentleman that treads this continent. I know well the habits and tendencies of his life. They are all simple, sane, domestic, worthy of him as one of an estimable family and a member of society. He is a tender and faithful son, a good brother, a loyal friend, an ardent and devoted citizen. He has been a laborer, working successively as a farmer, a carpenter, a printer. He has been a stalwart editor of the Republican party, and often, in that powerful and nervous prose of which he is master, done yeoman's service for the great cause of human liberty and the imperial conception of the indivisible Union. He has been a visitor of prisons, a protector of fugitive slaves, a constant voluntary nurse, night and day, at the hospitals, from the beginning of the war to the present time; a brother and friend through life to the neglected and the forgotten, the poor, the degraded, the criminal, the outcast, turning away from no man for his guilt, nor woman for her vileness. His is the strongest and truest compassion I have ever known. I remember here the anecdote told me by a witness, of his meeting in a by-street in Boston a poor ruffian, one whom he had known well as an innocent child, now a fullgrown youth, vicious far beyond his years, flying to Canada from the pursuit of the police, his sin-trampled features bearing marks of the recent bloody brawl in New York, in which, as he supposed, he had killed someone; and having heard his hurried story, freely confided to him, Walt Whitman separated not from the bad even by his own goodness, with well I know what tender and tranquil feeling for the ruined being, and with a love which makes me think of that love of God which deserts not any creature, quietly at parting, after assisting him from his means, held him for a moment, with his arm around his neck, and, bending to the face, horrible and battered and prematurely old, kissed him on the cheek, and the poor hunted wretch, perhaps for the first time in his low life, receiving a token of love and compassion like a touch from beyond the sun, hastened away in deep dejection, sobbing and in tears. It reminds me of the anecdotes Victor Hugo, in his portraiture of Bishop Myriel, tells, under a thin veil of fiction, of Charles Miolles, the good Bishop of Digne. I know not what talisman Walt Whitman carries, unless it be an unexcluding friendliness and goodness which is felt upon his approach like magnetism; but I know that in the subterranean life of cities, among the worst roughs, he goes safely; and I could recite instances where hands that, in mere wantonness of ferocity, assault anybody, raised against him, have of their own accord been lowered almost as quickly, or, in some cases, have been dragged promptly down by others; this, too, I mean when he and the assaulting gang were mutual strangers. I have seen singular evidence of the mysterious quality which not only guards him, but draws to him with intuition, rapid as light, simple and rude people, as to their natural mate and friend. I remember, as I passed the White House with him one evening, the startled feeling with which I saw a soldier on guard there—a stranger to us both, and with something in his action that curiously proved that he was a stranger—suddenly bring his musket to the "present" in military salute to him, quickly mingling with his respect due to the colonel, a gesture of greeting with the right hand as to a comrade, grinning, meanwhile, good fellow, with shy, spontaneous affection and deference, his ruddy, broad face glowing in the flare of lampions. I remember, on another occasion, as I crossed the street with him, the driver of a street-car, a stranger, stopping the conveyance, and inviting him to get on and ride with him. Adventures of this kind are frequent, and "I took a fancy to you," or "You look like one of my style," is the common explanation he gets upon their occurrence. It would be impossible to exaggerate the personal adhesion and strong, simple affection given him, in numerous instances on sight, by multitudes of plain persons, sailors, mechanics, drivers, soldiers, farmers, sempstresses, old people of the past generation, mothers of families—those powerful unlettered persons, among whom, as he says in his book, he has gone freely, and who never in most cases even suspect as an author him whom they love as a man, and who loves them in return.

His intellectual influence upon many young men and women —spirits of the morning sort, not willing to belong to that intellectual colony of Great Britain which our literary classes compose, nor helplessly tied, like them to the old forms—I note as kindred to that of Socrates upon the youth of ancient Attica, or Raleigh upon the gallant young England of his day. It is a power at once liberating, instructing, and inspiring. His conversation is a university. Those who have heard him in some roused hour, when the full afflatus of his spirit moved him, will agree with me that the grandeur of talk was accomplished. He is known as a passionate lover and powerful critic of the great music and of art. He is deeply cultured by some of the best books, especially those of the Bible, which he prefers above all other great literature, but principally by contact and communion with things themselves, which literature can only mirror and celebrate. He has travelled through most of the United States, intent on comprehending and absorbing the genius and history of his country, that he might do his best to start a literature worthy of her, sprung from her own polity, and tallying her own unexampled magnificence among the nations. To the same end, as he has been a long, patient, and laborious student of life, mixing intimately with all varieties of experience and men, with curiosity and with love. He has given his thought, his life, to this beautiful ambition, and still young, he has grown gray in its service. He has never married; like Giordano Bruno, he has made Thought in the service of his fellow-creatures his *bella donna*, his best beloved, his bride. His patriotism is boundless. It is no intellectual sentiment; it is a personal passion. He performs with scrupulous fidelity and zeal the duties of a citizen. For eighteen years, not missing once, his ballot has dropped on every national and local election day, and his influence has been ardently given for the good cause. Of all men I know, his life is most in the life of the nation. I remember, when the first draft was ordered, at a time when he was already performing an arduous and perilous duty as a volunteer attendant upon the wounded in the field—a duty which cost him the only illness he ever had in his life, and a very severe and dangerous illness it was, the result of poison absorbed in his devotion to the worse cases of hospital gangrene, and when it would have been the easiest thing in the world to evade duty, for though then only forty-two or three years old, and subject to the draft, he looked a hale sixty, and no enrolling officer would have paused for an instant before his gray hair—I remember, I say, how anxious and careful he was to get his name put on the enrollment lists, that he might stand his chance for martial service. This, too, at a time when so many gentlemen were skulking, dodging, agonizing for substitutes, and practicing every conceivable device to escape military duty. What music of speech, though Cicero's own—what scarlet and gold superlatives could adorn or dignify this simple, antique trait of private heroism? I recall his love for little children, for the young, and for very old persons, as if the dawn and the evening twilight of life awakened his deepest tenderness. I recall the affection for him of numbers of young men, and invariably of all good women. Who, knowing him, does not regard him as a man of the highest spiritual culture? I have never known one of greater and deeper religious feeling. To call one like him good seems an impertinence. In our sweet country phrase, he is one of God's men. And as I write these hurried and broken memoranda—as his strength and sweetness of nature, his moral health, his rich humor, his gentleness, his serenity, his charity, his simple-heartedness, his courage, his deep and varied knowledge of life and men, his calm wisdom, his singular and beautiful boy-innocence, his personal majesty, his rough scorn of mean actions, his magnetic and exterminating anger on due occasions—all that I have seen and heard of him, the testimony of associates, the anecdotes of friends, the remembrance of hours with him that should be immortal, the traits, lineaments, incidents of his life and being—as they come crowding into memory, his seems to me a character which only the heroic pen of Plutarch could record, and which Socrates himself might emulate or envy.

This is the man whom Mr. Harlan charges with having written a bad book.

[A Young Novelist Fails to Appreciate *Drum-Taps*]

William Dean Howells*

Will Saltpeter Explode? Is Walt Whitman a true poet? Doubts to be solved by the wise futurity which shall pay off our national debt. Poet or not, however, there was that in Walt Whitman's first book which compels attention to his second. There are obvious differences between the two: this is much smaller than that; and whereas you had at times to hold your nose (as a great sage observed) in reading *Leaves of Grass*, there is not an indecent thing in *Drum-Taps*. The artistic method of the poet remains, however, the same, and we must think it mistaken. The trouble about it is that it does not give you sensation in a portable shape; the thought is as intangible as aroma; it is no more put up than the atmosphere.

We are to suppose that Mr. Whitman first adopted his method as something that came to him of its own motion. This is the best possible reason, and only possible excuse, for it. In its way, it is quite as artificial as that of any other poet, while it is unspeakably inartistic. On this account it is a failure. The method of talking to one's self in rhythmic and ecstatic prose is one that surprises at first, but, in the end, the talker can only have the devil for a listener, as happens in other cases when people address their own individualities; not, however, the devil of the proverb, but the devil of reasonless, hopeless, all-defying egotism. An ingenious French critic said very acutely of Mr. Whitman that he made you partner of the poetical enterprise, which is perfectly true; but no one wants to share the enterprise. We want its effect, its success; we do not want to plant corn, to hoe it, to drive the crows away, to gather it, husk it, grind it, sift it, bake it, and butter it, before eating it, and then take the risk of its being at last moldy in our mouths. And this is what you have to do in reading Mr. Whitman's rhythm.

At first, a favorable impression is made by the lawlessness of this poet, and one asks himself if this is not the form which the unconscious poetry of American life would take, if it could find a general utterance. But there is really no evidence that such is the case. It is certain that among the rudest peoples the lurking sublimity of nature has always sought expression in artistic form, and there is no good reason to believe that the sentiment of a people with our high average culture would seek expression more rude and formless than that of the savagest tribes. It is not more probable that, if the passional principle of American life could find utterance, it would choose the highest, least dubious, most articulate speech? Could the finest, most shapely expression be too good for it?

If we are to judge the worth of Mr. Whitman's poetic theory (or impulse, or possession) by its popular success, we must confess that he is

*Reprinted from *The Round Table*, N.S. no. 10 (11 Nov. 1865), 147–48.

wrong. It is already many years since he first appeared with his claim of poet, and in that time he has employed criticism as much as any literary man in our country, and he has enjoyed the fructifying extremes of blame and praise. Yet he is, perhaps, less known to the popular mind, to which he has attempted to give an utterance, than the newest growth of the magazines and the newspaper notices. The people fairly rejected his former revelation, letter and spirit, and those who enjoyed it were readers with a cultivated taste for the quaint and the outlandish. The time to denounce or to ridicule Mr. Whitman for his first book is past. The case of *Leaves of Grass* was long ago taken out the hands of counsel and referred to the great jury. They have pronounced no audible verdict; but what does their silence mean? There were reasons in the preponderant beastliness of that book why a decent public should reject it; but now the poet has cleansed the old channels of their filth, and pours through them a stream of blameless purity, and the public has again to decide, and this time more directly, on the question of his poethood. As we said, his method remains the same, and he himself declares that, so far as concerns it, he has not changed nor grown in any way since we saw him last:

> Beginning my studies, the first step pleased me so much,
> The mere fact, consciousness—these forms—the power of motion,
> The least insect or animal—the senses—eye-sight;
> The first step, I say, aw'd me and pleas'd me so much,
> I have never gone, and never wish'd to go, any further
> But stop and loiter all my life to sing it in ecstatic songs.

Mr. Whitman has summed up his own poetical theory so well in these lines, that no criticism could possibly have done it better. It makes us doubt, indeed, if all we have said in consideration of him has not been said idly, and certainly releases us from further explanation of his method.

In *Drum-Taps*, there is far more equality than in *Leaves of Grass*, and though the poet is not the least changed in purpose, he is certainly changed in fact. The pieces of the new book are nearly all very brief, but generally his expression is freer and fuller than ever before. The reader understands, doubtless, from the title, that nearly all these pieces relate to the war; and they celebrate many of the experiences of the author in the noble part he took in the war. One imagines the burly tenderness of the man who went to supply the

> —lack of woman's nursing

that there was in the hospitals of the field, and woman's tears creep unconsciously to the eyes as the pity of his heart communicates itself to his reader's. No doubt the pathos of many of the poems gains something from the quaintness of the poet's speech. One is touched in reading them by the same inarticulate feeling as that which dwells in music; and is sensible that the poet conveys to the heart certain emotions which the brain cannot analyze, and only remotely perceives. This is especially true of his inspirations from nature; memories and yearnings come to you folded, mute, and motionless in his verse, as they come in the breath of a familiar perfume. They give a strange, shadowy sort of pleasure, but they do not satisfy, and you rise from the perusal of this man's book as you issue from the presence of one whose personal magnetism is very subtle and strong, but who has not added to this tacit attraction the charm of spoken ideas. We must not mistake this fascination for a higher quality. In the tender eyes of an ox lurks a melancholy, soft and pleasing to the glance as the pensive sweetness of a woman's eyes; but in the orb of the brute there is no hope of expression, and in the woman's look there is the endless delight of history, the heavenly possibility of utterance.

Art cannot greatly employ itself with things in embryo. The instinct of the beast may interest science; but poetry, which is nobler than science, must concern itself with natural instincts only as they can be developed into the sentiments and ideas of the soul of man. The mind will absorb from nature all that is speechless in her influences; and it will demand from kindred mind those higher things which can be spoken. Let us say our say here against the nonsense, long current, that there is, or can be, poetry *between the lines*, as is often sillily asserted. *Expression* will always suggest; but mere *suggestion* in art is unworthy of existence, vexes the heart, and shall not live. Every man has tender, and beautiful, and lofty emotions; but the poet was sent into this world to give these a tangible utterance, and if he do not this, but only give us back dumb emotion for dumb emotion, he is a cumberer of the earth. There is a yearning, almost to agony at times, in the human heart, to throw off the burden of inarticulate feeling, and if the poet will not help it in this effort, if, on the contrary, he shall seek to weigh it and sink it down under heavier burdens, he has not any reason to be.

So long, then, as Mr. Whitman chooses to stop at mere consciousness, he cannot be called a true poet. We all have consciousness; but we ask of art an utterance. We do not so much care in what way we get this expression; we will take it in ecstatic prose, though we think it is better subjected to the laws of prosody, since every good thing is subject to some law; but the expression we must have. Often, in spite of himself, Mr. Whitman grants it in this volume, and there is some hope that he will hereafter grant it more and more. There are such rich possibilities in the man that it is lamentable to contemplate his error of theory. He has truly and thoroughly absorbed the idea of our American life, and we say to him as he says to himself, "You've got enough in you, Walt; why don't you get it out?" A man's greatness is good for nothing folded up in him, and if emitted in barbaric yawps, it is not more filling than Ossian or the east wind.

[Another Fledgling Novelist Disparages *Drum-Taps*]

Henry James*

It has been a melancholy task to read this book; and it is a still more melancholy one to write about it. Perhaps since the day of Mr. Tupper's *Philosophy* there has been no more difficult reading of the poetic sort. It exhibits the effort of an essentially prosaic mind to lift itself, by a prolonged muscular strain, into poetry. Like hundreds of other good patriots, during the last four years, Mr. Walt Whitman has imagined that a certain amount of violent sympathy with the great deeds and sufferings of our soldiers, and of admiration for our national energy, together with a ready command of picturesque language, are sufficient inspiration for a poet. If this were the case we had been a nation of poets. The constant developments of the war moved us continually to strong feelings and to strong expression of it. But in those cases in which these expressions were written out and printed with all due regard to prosody, they failed to make poetry, as anyone may see by consulting now in cold blood the back volumes of the "Rebellion Record." *Of course* the city of Manhattan, as Mr. Whitman delights to call it, when regiments poured through it in the first months of the war, and its own sole god, to borrow the words of a real poet, ceased for a while to be the millionaire, was a noble spectacle, and a poetical statement to this effect is possible. *Of course* the tumult of a battle is grand, the results of a battle tragic, and the untimely deaths of young men a theme for elegies. But he is not a poet who merely reiterates these plain facts *ore rotundo*. He only sings them worthily who views them from a height. Every tragic event collects about it a number of persons who delight to dwell upon its superficial points—of minds which are bullied by the *accidents* of the affair. The temper of such minds seems to us to be the reverse of the poetic temper; for the poet, although he incidentally masters, grasps, and uses the superficial traits of his theme, is really a poet only in so far as he extracts its latent meaning and holds it up to common eyes. And yet from such minds most of our war-verses have come, and Mr. Whitman's utterances, much as the assertion may surprise his friends, are in this respect no exception to general fashion. They are an exception, however, in that they openly pretend to be something better; and this it is that makes them melancholy reading. Mr. Whitman is very fond of blowing his own trumpet, and he has made very explicit claims for his book. 'Shut not your doors,' he explains at the outset—

> Shut not your doors to me, proud libraries,
> For that which was lacking among you all, yet needed
>   most, I bring;

*Reprinted from the *Nation*, 16 Nov. 1865, pp. 593–94.

A book I have made for your dear sake, O soldiers,
And for you, O soul of man, and you, love of comrades;
The words of my book nothing, the life of it everything;
A book separate, not link'd with the rest, nor felt by
the intellect;
But you will feel every word, O Libertad! arm'd Libertad!
It shall pass by the intellect to swim the sea, the air,
With joy with you, O soul of man.

These are great pretentions, but it seems to us that the following are even greater:

From Paumanok starting, I fly like a bird,
Around and around to soar, to sing the idea of all;
To the north betaking myself, to sing there arctic songs,
To Kanada, 'till I absorb Kanada in myself—to Michigan
then,
To Wisconsin, Iowa, Minnesota, to sing their songs
(they are inimitable);
Then to Ohio and Indiana, to sing theirs—to Missouri
and Kansas and Arkansas to sing theirs,
To Tennessee and Kentucky—to the Carolinas and
Georgia, to sing theirs,
To Texas, and so along up toward California, to roam
accepted everywhere;
To sing first (to the top of the war-drum, if need be)
The idea of all—of the western world, one and
inseparable,
And then the song of each member of these States.

Mr. Whitman's primary purpose is to celebrate the greatness of our armies; his secondary purpose is to celebrate the greatness of the city of New York. He pursues these objects through a hundred pages of matter which remind us irresistibly of the story of the college professor who, on a venturesome youth's bringing him a theme done in blank verse, reminded him that it was not customary in writing prose to begin each line with a capital. The frequent capitals are the only marks of verse in Mr. Whitman's writing. There is, fortunately, but one attempt at rhyme. We say fortunately, for if the inequality of Mr. Whitman's lines were self-registering, as it would be in the case of an anticipated syllable at their close, the effect would be painful in the extreme. As the case stands, each line starts off by itself, in resolute independence of its companions, without a visible goal. But if Mr. Whitman does not write verse, he does not write ordinary prose. The reader has seen that liberty is "libertad." In like manner, comrade is "comerado." Americans are "Americanos," a pavement is a "trottoir," and Mr. Whitman himself is a "chansonnier." If there is one thing that Mr. Whitman is not, it is this, for Béranger was a *chansonnier*. To appreciate the force of our conjunction, the reader should compare his military lyrics with Mr. Whitman's declamations. Our author's novelty, however, is not in his words, but in the form of his writing. As we have said, it begins for all the world like verse and turns out to be arrant prose. It is more like Mr. Tupper's proverbs than anything we have met. But what if, in form it *is* prose? it may be asked. Very good poetry has come out of prose before this. To this we would reply that it must first have gone into it. Prose, in order to be good poetry, must first be good prose. As a general principle, we know of no circumstances more likely to impugn a writer's earnestness than the adoption of an anomalous style. He must have something very original to say if none of the old vehicles will carry his thoughts. Of course he *may* be surprisingly original. Still, presumption is against him. If on an examination the matter of his discourse proves very valuable, it justifies, or at any rate excuses, his literary innovation.

But if, on the other hand, it is of a common quality, with nothing new about it but its manners, the public will judge the writer harshly. The most that can be said of Mr. Whitman's vaticinations is, that, cast in a fluent and familiar manner, the average substance of them might escape unchallenged. But we have seen that Mr. Whitman prides himself especially on the substance—the life—of his poetry. It may be rough, it may be grim, it may be clumsy—such we take to be the author's argument—but it is sincere, it is sublime, it appeals to the soul of man, it is the voice of a people. He tells us, in the lines quoted, that the words of his book are nothing. To our perception they are everything, and very little at that. A great deal of verse that is nothing but words has, during the war, been sympathetically signed over and cut out of newspaper corners, because it has possessed a certain simple melody. But Mr. Whitman's verse, we are confident, would have failed even of this triumph, for the simple reason that no triumph, however small, is won but through the exercise of art, and that this volume is an offense against art. It is not enough to be grim and rough and careless; common sense is also necessary, for it is by common sense that we are judged. There exists in even the commonest minds, in literary matters, a certain precise instinct of conservatism, which is very shrewd in detecting wanton eccentricities. To this instinct Mr. Whitman's attitude seems monstrous. It is monstrous because it pretends to persuade the soul while it slights the intellect; because it pretends to gratify the feelings while it outrages the taste. The point is that it does this *on theory*, wilfully, consciously, arrogantly. It is the little nursery game of "open your mouth and shut your eyes." Our hearts are often touched through a compromise with the artistic sense, but never in direct violation of it. Mr. Whitman sits down at the outset and counts on the intelligence. This were indeed a wise precaution on his part if the intelligence were only submissive! But when she is deliberately insulted, she takes her revenge by simply standing erect and open-eyed.

This is assuredly the best she can do. And if she could find a voice she would probably address Mr. Whitman as follows:

You came to woo my sister, the human soul. Instead of giving me a kick as you approach, you should either greet me courteously, or, at least, steal in unobserved. But now you have me on your hands. Your chances are poor. What the human heart desires above all is sincerity, and you do not appear to me sincere. For a lover you talk entirely too much about yourself. In one place you threaten to absorb Kanada. In another you call upon the city of New York to incarnate you, as you have incarnated it. In another you inform us that neither youth pertains to you nor "delicatesse," that you are awkward in the parlor, that you do not dance, and that you have neither bearing, beauty, knowledge, nor fortune. In another place, by an allusion to your "little songs," you seem to identify yourself with the third person of the Trinity. For a poet who claims to sing "the idea of all," this is tolerably egotistical. We look in vain, however, through your book for a single idea. We find nothing but flashy imitations of ideas. We find a medley of extravagances and commonplaces. We find art, measure, grace, sense sneered at on every page, and nothing positive given us in their stead. To be positive one must have something to say; to be positive requires reason, labor, and art; and art requires, above all things, a suppression of one's self, a subordination of one's self to an idea. This will never do for you, whose plan is to adapt the scheme of the universe to your own limitations. You cannot entertain and exhibit ideas; but, as we have seen, you are prepared to incarnate them. It is for this reason, doubtless, that when once you have planted yourself squarely before the public and in view of the great service you have done to the ideal, have become as you say, "accepted everywhere," you can afford to deal exclusively in words. What would be bald nonsense and dreary platitudes in anyone else becomes sublimity in you. But all this is a mistake. To become adopted as a national poet, it is not enough to discard everything in particular and to accept everything in general, to amass crudity upon crudity, to discharge the undigested contents of your blotting-book into the lap of the public. You must respect the public which you address; for it has taste, it you have not. It delights in the grand, the heroic, and the masculine; but it delights to see these conceptions cast into worthy form. It is indifferent to brute sublimity. It will never do for you to thrust your hands into your pockets and cry out that, as the research of form is an intolerable bore, the shortest and most economical way for the public to embrace its idols—for the nation to realize its genius—is in your own person. This democratic, liberty-loving, American populace, this stern and war-tried people, is a great civilizer. It is devoted to refinement. If it has sustained a monstrous war, and practiced human nature's best in so many ways for the last five years, it is not to put up with spurious poetry afterwards. To sing aright our battles and our glories it is not enough to have served in a hospital (however praise-worthy the task in itself), to be aggressively careless, inelegant, and igno-rant, and to be constantly preoccupied with yourself. It is not enough to be rude, lugubrious, and grim. You must also be serious. You must forget yourself in your ideas. Your personal qualities—the vigor of your temperament, the manly independence of your nature, the tenderness of your heart—these facts are impertinent. You must be *possessed*, and you must strive to possess your possession. If in your striving you break into divine eloquence, then you are a poet. If the idea which possesses you is the idea of your country's greatness, then you are a national poet, and not otherwise.

[An Enthusiastic Reaction from Germany]

Ferdinand Freiligrath*

Walt Whitman! Who is Walt Whitman!

The answer is: a poet! A new American poet! His admirers say: the first, the only poet that America has produced so far. The only specifically American poet. No trekker in the worn footsteps of the European muse, no, fresh from the prairie and the settlements, fresh from the coasts and the great rivers, fresh from the moiling crowds in the ports and cities, fresh from the battlefields of the South, with the earthy scene of the soil, which begat him, in hair and beard and clothing; a new phenomenon, someone standing firmly and consciously on his own American feet, a pro-claimer of great things greatly, if often oddly. And even further his ad-mirers go: Walt Whitman is for them the only poet anywhere in whom the age, the laboring, struggling, seeking age, has found its expression; the poet *par excellence*; "*the* poet."

Thus, on the one side, the admirers; in their ranks even an Emerson is to be found; on the other of course the detractors, the disparagers. Along with the immoderate praise, the enthusiastic recognition, the bit-ter, the biting scorn, the insulting abuse.

But that does not bother the poet. The praise he accepts as owing to him; the scorn he meets with scorn. He believes in himself, his self-confi-dence is unlimited. "He is," says his English publisher W. M. Rossetti, "above all the one man who cherishes and affirms the serious conviction that he himself, now and for the future, is the founder of a new poetic literature—a great literature—one that is proportionate to America's

*Reprinted from the Augsburg *Allegemeine Zeitung*, 10 May 1868, reproduced in German in Bucke, pp. 202–203. A translation appeared in the *New Eclectic Magazine*, 2 (July 1868), 325–29. This translation is by Louise Schleiner.

material greatness and incalculable destinies." He believes that Columbus for the new world or Washington for the United States were no more truly founders and builders of this America than he himself will be in the future. Certainly a noble conviction, and declared by the poet more than once in splendid words—none more splendid than the poem which begins with the line:

Come I will make the continent indissoluble

That sounds proud. Is the man within his rights to speak this way? Let us step closer to him! Let us hear about his life and his achievement! First let us open his book!

Are these verses? The lines are set up like verses, certainly, but they are not verses. There is no meter, no rhyme, no stanzas. Rhythmic prose, stretched verses. At first sight rough, misshapen, formless; but neverthe-less for a finer ear not lacking in pleasing sounds. The language plain, strong, exact, calling a spade a spade, not holding back from anything, sometimes dark. The tone rhapsodic, prophetic, often uneven, mixing the lofty with the ordinary, even to the point of tastelessness. At times he reminds us, in spite of the difference between them, of our Hamann, or of Carlyle's oracular wisdom, or of *Paroles d'un Croyant*. Out of everything sounds the Bible—its language, not its doctrine.

And what is the poet presenting to us in this form? For one thing himself, his 'I,' Walt Whitman. This 'I' however is a part of America, a part of the earth, a part of humanity, a part of the cosmos. Thus he per-ceives himself, and linking the great with the small, always starting from America and coming back to America (the future belongs only to a free people!), he rolls out a splendid world panorama before us. Through this individual Walt Whitman and his Americanism, we would like to say, goes a cosmic drift, such as might unite contemplative spirits, who have passed solitary days on the shore of the sea, solitary nights under the starred heaven of the prairie, faced with infinity. He finds himself in everything, and everything in himself. He, the one human being Walt Whitman, is humanity and the world. And the world and humanity are to him a great poem. What he sees and hears, what he touches, whatever steps up to him, even the lowest, the least, the most everyday—everything is for him a symbol of something higher, something spiritual. Or rather, matter and the spirit, reality and the ideal are to him one and the same. Thus, realized through himself, he stands; thus, singing he strides forth; thus, a proud free person and only a person he discloses worldwide social and political perspectives.

A wonderful phenomenon! We admit that it grips us, unsettles us, and does not let us loose. But at the same time we notice that we are not finished with our evaluation, that we are still caught up in the first impression. Probably the first in Germany, we wish for the time being at least to take note of the existence and effects of this fresh power. It deserves from our poets and thinkers that they look more closely at this strange new comrade, who threatens to toss out our whole *Ars poetica*, all our aesthetic theories and canons. Indeed, if we have listened in on these serious pages, if the deep full-toned roaring of these rhapsodic utterances which like ocean waves in unbroken succession storm over us, has become familiar to us, then our accustomed verse making, our pressing of thoughts into some outmoded form or other, our games with ding and dong, our syllable counting and syllable measuring, our sonneteering and building of strophes and stanzas will seem almost childish to us. Have we really reached the point at which life, also in poetry, preemptorily demands new forms of expression? Does the age have so much and such important things to say that the old receptacles are no longer adequate for the new content? Are we faced with a poetry of the future, just as a music of the future was proclaimed to us years ago already? And is Walt Whitman more than Richard Wagner?

[A Mixed Review from France]

Thérèse Bentzon*

The contempt that he felt for the elegant sentimentalism which the poets of Tennyson's school have honored, and which for him was a more-or-less musical wordiness . . . , the hatred of this type of literature whose origin, according to him, is feudal, and conventional . . . the ambition, finally, to create an American poetry properly speaking, in relationship with the territorial immensity and the grandeur of the destinies of the New World, inspired him in this work which has had tremendous success while at the same time arousing enormous storms. Emerson did not fear to call *Leaves of Grass* the most extraordinary piece of wisdom and wit which America has as yet produced! Undoubtedly, its form is often careless or even baroque. If you are steeped in old prejudice against poems in prose, if you bear in mind the laws of versification, take care not to read what has been compared with too much indulgence to the poetry of the Bible and to the rhythmical prose of Plato. Besides, the author proclaims his breaking away from all the precedents; *today* is the test which must try the poet! What's the use of repeating the error of remote generations? The natural man, such is his hero; the United States are in themselves the greatest of all poems. Walt Whitman buries the past: he sings of the future, of America and of freedom; nothing frivolous or feminine should be expected from him. He prides himself, first and foremost, on a Herculean vitality.

*Extracts reprinted from *Revue des Deux Mondes*, 1 July 1872, reproduced in Bucke, pp. 207–09. Translated by Agnès Cazemajou.

What seems to us at least as bizarre as Mr. Whitman's philosophy and religion are his ethics. He doesn't admit evil, or rather he believes that good and evil are equal, since both exist; he takes man as he is and affirms that nothing can be better than what exists; if the crude appetites play a big part, it must be the necessary condition of things, and we must accept it. Why shouldn't what is seen, what we know, what is necessary and therefore just, be proclaimed in his verse? Backed up by such fallacies, no indecency will make him flinch; the French language would object to the translation of some erotic passages. Mr. Walt Whitman, admitting no difference between man and woman, nor even between ugliness and beauty, cannot use the word love in its ordinary meaning; he pronounces this word incessantly, but applies it indiscriminately to all beings; love, outside of human brotherhood, is for him merely physical pleasure expressed with the appropriate crudity. Therefore it is painful to hear him speak of the woman considered other than as a mother and a citizen. The only tribute, almost respectful and very eloquent besides, which he pays her in his whole work, has as a setting—believe it or not—the morgue, and it is about a prostitute. In short: is a prostitute worth less than a virgin?

English, which he celebrates emphatically as the language of progress, of faith, of freedom, of justice, of equality, of self-esteem, of common sense, of prudence, of revolution, of courage, and which, according to him, expresses almost the inexpressible, becomes under his pen a barbaric, often incomprehensible jargon. If only form were the only failing of his "Democratic Songs," but the contents are even more detestable. One cannot deny the presence of a certain grandeur and a lot of passion. Walt Whitman looks to us like the ominous sea-bird to which he has compared himself, with his big dark wings open above the ocean which separates him from the Old World, and uttering in the midst of tempests the cries of hatred, hoarse and shrill, which have unfortunately re-echoed in our country.

Walt Whitman, in *Drum-Taps*, excels in describing the enthusiasm of the recruits, the shipping of the old troops arriving from everywhere, covered with dust, steaming with sweat, the white tents that are being set up in the camp, the salutes of artillery at the crack of dawn, the hurried marches on unknown roads, the rapid halts underneath the nocturnal sky, studded with eternal stars; he excels in contrasting the immutable calm of nature with the human furores, in making us breathe the "fragrance of war."

On another occasion, he leads us to the ambulance, an improvised ambulance in the old church, in the heart of the woods; the lamps are hovering, streaking the darkness with a fitful gleam; a big tarred stationary torch casts its wild flame and clouds of smoke on the indistinct groups, on the vague shapes lying on the ground or which overload the benches. The poet spares us neither the smell of blood mingled with that of ether nor the sweat of the last spasms, nor the flashes which shoot up from the steel instrument working on the shredded flesh; he puts aside the woolen blanket which covers the face of the dead, he receives the half smile addressed to him by the young volunteer, a child, exhaling his last breath; he thinks of Christ, who died for his brothers; the religious feeling and divine piety enhance the roughness of some details so as to make of it an extra beauty. To be fair, one should quote everything from these eloquent and fierce *Drum-Taps*: "As Toilsome I wandered Virginia's Wood," the poor tomb of the soldier, ignored, lost in the woods of Virginia and which the poet who encountered it once finds again and again under his feet, in the midst of noisy streets and of celebrations of life; "First O Songs for a Prelude," which transports us amidst the slaughter with too much imitative music: the whistling of bullets, the explosion of shells; "By the Bivouac's Fitful Flame," where we taste for an instant the uneasy rest which follows forced marches and precedes the battles: "The Artilleryman's Vision," which brings back in the midst of the shooting the veteran who is now back home, while at midnight, he leans his elbow on the pillow of his sleeping wife and the soft breathing of the baby rises and falls in silence.

We are not far from the materialistic declarations teeming in the radical writings which we mentioned a little earlier only with repugnance. Walt Whitman contradicts himself singularly, and one cannot complain about it; besides, he doesn't pride himself in being consistent with himself. The fanatics lay the blame on the multiplicity of aspects presented by things and on Whitman's prodigious capacity to feel and understand everything, in one word, on his *universality*. We believe rather that he succeeded in writing lofty and strong things the day he decided to gather from the field of observation, instead of going astray in fruitless utopias, senseless paradoxes, and an unhealthy philosophy of which he is far from being the inventor—the day he drew his inspiration from the inexhaustible spectacle of human life, with its noble emotions, its pure joys and sufferings, instead of aspiring as he had done at first, to share the sensations with things, to assimilate himself with lilacs, flint, clouds, lambs, poultry from the poultry yard and even to the old drunkard who drags himself out of the tavern, stumbling!

It is notable that when Whitman chooses well his topics (as in *Drum-Taps*) the form is always more correct, which proves that the nobility of expression is inseparable from that of thought. Walt Whitman's much praised poem ("Song of Myself") brings us back to the height of brutality, selfishness, and paradox. However, we reaped from it[1] a beautiful thought which makes us hope that spiritualism will perhaps purify, one day, if the pride of the poet of the future allows it, this revolutionary muse who inspired him for too long. After a comparison between night and death, he exclaims:

I was thinking the day most splended till I saw what
the not-day exhibited,
I was thinking this globe enough till there sprang
out so noiseless around me myriads of other
globes.

. . . .

O I see now that life cannot exhibit all to me, as
the day cannot,
I see that I am to wait for what will be exhibited
by death.

Let us remain on these verses of good omen. Without admitting that the so-called Christopher Columbus of American art has discovered regions hitherto unexplored, one cannot deny that he possesses at a high degree the passion, the patriotic verve and a salutary contempt for triteness; but let him and his imitators (since he must be, alas! the father of a long generation of poets) stop believing that rudeness is strength, singularity is originality and license a noble boldness. Let them not mistake the obscurity of language for depth, cynicism for frankness, up-roar for music; let them not appeal to hatred, envy, to the worse feelings of the soul on pretense of arousing it: let them disengage themselves from factitious inspirations which would induce you to believe, while reading them, that they were hashish eaters, or one of these drinkers of whisky mixed with powder, as there are supposed to be in some wild corners of their homeland; let them respect the modesty of women, since they place them, so they say, higher than they ever were; let them allow the world to judge them, instead of judging themselves with such an arrogant confidence in their merits and their future destinies, so comically intoxicated with their own personality. "Comrade!" shouts Walt Whitman as he ends, after prophecies which prove he believes he is writing a new gospel, "Comerado, this is no book/ Who touches this touches a man."

Note
    1. This quotation actually is from "Night on the Prairies"—ed.

[The Good Gray Poet Lionized]

Anonymous*

WALT WHITMAN—HE VISITS NEW YORK AFTER FIVE YEARS' ABSENCE—HIGH TONE SOCIETY NOW TAKES HIM TO ITS BOSOM—YET HE RIDES AGAIN ATOP OF THE BROADWAY

*Reprinted from the *Camden Post*, 29 March 1877, in Bucke, pp. 216–17.

OMNIBUS AND FRATERNIZES WITH DRIVERS AND BOAT-
MEN—After an absence and sickness of nearly five years, says a New York
paper of March 28, 1877, the "old gray poet" has returned temporarily to
his

> Mast-hemm'd Manhattan,

and, in moderation, has been all the past month visiting, riding, receiving, and jaunting in and about the city, and, in good natured response to
pressure, has even appeared two or three times in brief, off-hand public
speeches.

Mr. Whitman, at present near his fifty-ninth birthday, is better in
health and appearance than at any time since his paralytic attack at
Washington in 1873. Passing through many grave experiences since that
period, he still remains tall and stout, with the same florid face, with his
great masses of hair and beard whiter than ever. Costumed in his usual
entire suit of English gray, with loose sack-coat and trousers, broad shirt-
collar open at the neck and guiltless of tie, he has, through the month,
been the recipient and centre of social gatherings, parlors, club meetings,
lunches, dinners, and even dress receptions—all of which he has taken
with steady good nature, coolness, and moderation.

As he sat on the platform of the Liberal Club on Friday night last he
looked like an old Quaker, especially as, in response to the suggestion of
the President, and sitting near a window-draught, he unhesitatingly put
on his old white broadbrim, and wore it the whole evening. In answer to
pressing requests, however, toward the close, he rose to let the audience
see him more fully, and, doffing his hat, smilingly said, in response to
calls for a speech, that he "must decline to take any other part than
listener, as he knew nothing of the subject under debate (blue glass) and
would not add to the general stock of misinformation."

At the full-dress reception of the Portfolio and Palette Clubs on the
Fifth Avenue, a few nights previous, as he slowly crossed the room to
withdraw, he was saluted by a markedly peculiar murmur of applause,
from a crowded audience of the most cultured and elegant society of New
York, including most of the artists of the city. It was a singularly spontaneous and *caressing* testimonial, joined in heartily by the ladies, and the
old man's cheeks, as he hobbled along through the kindly applause and
smiles, showed a deep flush of gratified feeling. . . .

[An Ovation in Boston]

Anonymous*

Walt Whitman is now on his second visit to Boston. He came quietly, but he finds himself the subject of an ovation given with such hearty cordialness as to prove with what a real affection he has come to be regarded. At about this time when the St. Botolph Club was organized, a few of the young fellows happening to speak of Lincoln, it was suggested by one of them that they ought to have Walt Whitman here to read his commemoration essay on the great President, a service that he reverently performs every year on the anniversary of Lincoln's death. The idea took root at once, and the arrangements were made that have resulted in the present occasion. It was a pleasant sight at the Hawthorne Rooms on Friday evening; the fine audience representing the best side of Boston literary activity, and the poet, with venerable hair and beard, but sturdy presence, reading his fine essay with the native eloquence born of sincere feeling—just as if reading to a few personal friends—but with none of the tricks of the elocutionizing trade.

He has been welcomed to Boston with open arms. Old and young, old friends and new, have gathered around him. The young men have taken to him as one with themselves, as one of those fresh natures that are ever youthful; the older ones, many of whom might once have been disposed to regard him with disfavor, now have grown to see the real core of the man in its soundness and sweetness, and are equally hearty in their welcome. "He is a grand old fellow" is everybody's verdict. Walt Whitman has in times past been, perhaps, more ignorantly than wilfully misunderstood, but time brings about its revenges, and his present position goes to prove that, let a man be true to himself, however he defies the world, the world will come to respect him for his loyalty. Perhaps frankness may be said to be the keynote of Walt Whitman's nature. He glows with responsive cordiality. He is not afraid to be himself, and he asserts it with ideal American unconventionality—that is, he is thoroughly individual in his personal ways and expressions, and all without offence to the individualism of others. He looks it in his strong features, full of the repose of force in reserve; his clear, friendly blue eyes, the open windows of a healthy brain; the pleasant, sympathetic voice; the easy suit of pleasant gray, and the open shirt with rolling collar; the broad, black felt hat contrasting with his white hair. All express the large-hearted, large-minded man. His ruddy face and powerful frame indicate good health, and it is only when he rises that one sees in his slow walk the invalid that he now is—"a half-paralytic," he calls himself. He is hearty in speaking of his contemporaries, and he thinks America is to be esteemed fortunate in having felt the influence of four such clean, pure and healthful natures as

*Reprinted from the *Boston Herald*, 18 April 1881, in Bucke, pp. 224–25.

Emerson, Bryant, Whittier and Longfellow. As his frank comments on others are without reserve, so his free talk of himself is without egotism, as can well be the case with a man of such large personality. . . .

["we are presented with the slop-bucket of Walt Whitman"]

Anonymous*

After the dilettante indelicacies of William H. Mallock and Oscar Wilde, we are presented with the slop-bucket of Walt Whitman. The celebrity of this phenomenal poet bears a curious disproportion to the circulation of his writings. Until now, it cannot be said that his verses have ever been published at all. They have been printed irregularly and read behind the door. They have been vaunted extravagantly by a band of extravagant disciples; and the possessors of the books have kept them locked up from the family. Some have valued them for the barbaric "yawp," which seems to them the note of a new, vigorous, democratic, American school of literature; some for the fragments of real poetry floating in the turbid mass; some for the nastiness and animal insensibility to shame which entitle a great many of the poems to a dubious reputation as curiosities. Now that they are thrust into our faces at the bookstalls there must be a re-examination of the myth of the Good Gray Poet. It seems to us that there is no need at this late day to consider Mr. Whitman's claims to the immortality of genius. That he is a poet most of us frankly admit. His merits have been set forth many times, and at great length, and if the world has erred materially in its judgment of them the error has been a lazy and unquestioning acquiescence in some of the extreme demands of his vociferous partisans. The chief question raised by this publication is whether anybody—even a poet—ought to take off his trousers in the market-place. Of late years we believe that Mr. Whitman has not chosen to be so shocking as he was when he had his notoriety to make, and many of his admirers—the rational ones—hoped that the *Leaves of Grass* would be weeded before he set them out again. But this has not been done; and indeed Mr. Whitman could hardly do it without falsifying the first principle of his philosophy, which is a belief in his own perfection, and the second principle, which is a belief in the preciousness of filth. "Divine am I," he cries, "Divine am I inside and out, and I make holy whatever I touch or am touched from. The scent of these arm-pits aroma finer than prayer. This head more than churches, Bibles, and all the creeds." He knows that he is "august." He does not care for anybody's opinion. He is

---

*Reprinted from the *New York Tribune*, 19 November 1881, in Bucke, pp. 227–28. The 1881 edition of *Leaves of Grass* was banned in Boston.

> Walt Whitman, a kosmos, of Manhattan the son,
> Turbulent, fleshy, sensual, eating, drinking, and breeding,
> No sentimentalist, no stander above men and women or
>   apart from them,
> No more modest than immodest.
> There is nothing in the universe better than Walt Whitman.

That is the burden of the "Song of Myself," which fills fifty pages of the present volume:

> I dote on myself, there is that lot of me, and all
>   so luscious.

Nothing is obscene or indecent to him. It is his mission to shout the forbidden voices, to tear the veil off everything, to clarify and transfigure all that is dirty and vile, to proclaim that garbage is just as good as nectar if you are only lusty enough to think so. His immodesty is free from glamour of every sort. Neither amatory sentiment nor susceptibility to physical beauty appears to have anything to do with it. It is entirely bestial; and in this respect we know nothing in literature which can be compared with it. Walt Whitman, despising what he calls conventionalism, and vaunting the athletic democracy, asks to be accepted as the master of a new poetical school, fresh, free, stalwart, "immense in passion, pulse, and power," the embodiment of the spirit of vigorous America. But the gross materialism of his verses represents art in its last degradation rather than its rude infancy.

ESSAYS AND OTHER
FORMS OF CRITICISM

Walt Whitman

Robert Buchanan*

In about ten thousand lines of unrhymed verse, very Biblical in form, and showing, indeed, on every page, the traces of Biblical influence, Walt Whitman professes to sow the first seeds of an indigenous literature, by putting in music the spiritual and fleshly yearnings of the cosmical man, and, more particularly, indicating the great elements which distinguish American freedom from the fabrics erected by European politicians. Starting from Paumanok, where he was born, he takes mankind in review, and sees everywhere but one wondrous life—the movement of the great masses, seeking incessantly under the sun for guarantees of personal liberty. He respects no particular creed, admits no specific morality prescribed by the civil law, but affirms in round terms the universal equality of men, subject to the action of particular revolutions, and guided *en masse* by the identity of particular leaders. The whole introduction is a reverie on the destiny of nations, with an undertone of forethought on the American future, which is to contain the surest and final triumph of the democratical man. A new race is to arise, dominating previous ones, and grander far, with new contests, new politics, new literatures and religions, new inventions and arts. But how dominating? By the perfect recognition of individual equality, by the recognition of personal responsibility and spiritual significance of each being, by the abrogation of distinctions such as set barriers in the way of perfect private action—action responsible only to the being of whom it is a consequence, and inevitably controlled, if diabolic, by the combined action of masses.

Briefly, Walt Whitman sees in the American future the grandest realization of centuries of idealism—equable distribution of property, luminous, enlargement of the spiritual horizon, perfect exercise of all the functions, no apathy, no prudery, no shame, none of that worst absenteeism wherein the soul deserts its proper and ample physical sphere, and sallies out into the regions of the impossible and the unknown. Very finely, indeed, does the writer set forth the divine func-

---

*Reprinted from *David Gray and Other Essays, Chiefly on Poetry* (London: S. Low, Son, and Marston, 1868), pp. 203–20. I have omitted the first four and one-half pages, which summarize biographical data apparently taken from *The Good Gray Poet*.

75

tions of the body—the dignity and the righteousness of a habitation existing only on the condition of personal exertion; and faintly, but truly, does he suggest how from that personal exertion issues *spirituality*, fashioning literatures, dreaming religions, and perfecting arts. "I will make," he exclaims, "the poems of materials, for I think they are to be the most spiritual poems; and I will make the poems of my body and of mortality: for I think I shall then supply myself with the poems of my soul and of immortality."

This, I hear the reader exclaim, is rank materialism; and, using the word in its big sense, materialism it doubtless is. I shall observe, further on, in what consists the peculiar value of the present manifestation. In the meantime, let me continue my survey of the work.

Having broadly premised, describing the great movements of masses, Walt Whitman proceeds, in a separate "poem" or "book," to select a member of the great democracy, representing typically the privileges, the immunities, the conditions, and the functions of all the rest. He cannot, he believes choose a better example than himself; so he calls this poem "Walt Whitman." He is, for the time being, and for poetical purposes, the cosmical man, an entity, a representative of the great forces. He describes the delight of his own physical being, the pleasure of the senses, the countless sensations through which he communicates with the material universe. All, he says, is sweet—smell, taste, thought, the play of his limbs, the fantasies of his mind; every attribute is welcome, and he is ashamed of none. He is not afraid of death; he is content to change, if it be the nature of things that he should change, but it is certain that he cannot perish. He pictures the pageant of life in the country and in cities; all is a fine panorama, wherein mountains and valleys, nations and religions, *genre* pictures and gleams of sunlight, babes on the breast and dead men in shrouds, pyramids and brothels, deserts and populated streets, sweep wonderfully by him. To all those things he is bound: wherever they force him, he is not wholly a free agent; but on one point he is very clear—that, so far as he is concerned, he is the most important thing of all. He has work to do; life is not merely a "suck or a sell"; nay, the whole business of ages has gone on with one object only—that he, the democrat, Walt Whitman, might have work to do. In these very strange passages, he proclaims the magnitude of the preparations for his private action:

> Who goes there? hankering, gross, mystical, nude;
> How is it I extract strength from the beef I eat?
>
> What is man, anyhow? What am I? What are you?
>
> All I mark as my own, you shall offset it with your own,
> Else it were time lost listening to me.

I do not snivel that snivel the world over,
That months are vacuums, and the ground but wallow
    and filth;
For room to me stars kept aside in their own rings;
They sent influences to look after what was to hold me.
Before I was born out of my mother, generations guided
    me;
My embryo has never been torpid—nothing could overlay
    it.
For it the nebula cohered to an orb,
The long slow strata piled to rest it on,
Vast vegetables gave it sustenance,
Monstrous sauroids transported it in their mouths, and
    deposited it with care.
All forces have been steadily employ'd to complete
    and delight me;
Now on this spot I stand with my robust Soul.

It is impossible in an extract to convey an idea of the mystic and coarse, yet living, force which pervades the poem called "Walt Whitman." I have chosen an extract where the utterance is unusually clear and vivid. But more extraordinary, in their strong sympathy, are the portions describing the occupations of men. In a few vivid touches we have striking pictures; the writer shifts his identity like Proteus, but breathes the same deep undertone in every shape. He can transfer himself into any personality, however base. "I am the man—I suffered—I was there." He cares for no man's pride. He holds no man unclean.

And afterwards, in the poem called "Children of Adam," he proceeds to particularise the privileges of flesh, and to assert that in his own personal living body there is no uncleanness. He sees that the beasts are not ashamed; why, therefore, should he be ashamed? Then comes passage after passage of daring animalism; the functions of the body are unhesitatingly described, and the man asserts that the basest of them is glorious. All the stuff which offended American virtue is to be found here. It is very coarse and silly, but, as we shall see, very important. It is never, however, inhuman; indeed, it is strongly masculine—unsicklied by Lesbian bestialities and Petronial abominations. It simply chronicles acts and functions which, however unfit for art, are natural, sane, and perfectly pure. I shall attempt to show, further on, that Walt Whitman is not an artist at all, not a poet, properly so called; and that this grossness, offensive in itself, is highly significant—an essential part of very imperfect work. The general question of literary immorality need not be introduced at all. No one is likely to read the book who is not intelligently chaste, or who is not familiar with numberless authors offensive to prudes—Lucretius, Virgil, Dante, Goethe, Byron, among poets; Tacitus, Rabelais, Montaigne, Cervantes, Swedenborg, among prose thinkers.

The remainder of *Leaves of Grass* is occupied with poems of democracy, and general monotonous prophecies. There is nothing more which it would serve my present purpose to describe in detail, or to interpret. The typical man continues his cry, encouraging all men,—on the open road, in the light of day, in the region of dreams. All is right with the world, he thinks. For religion he advises, "Reverence all things"; for morality, "Be not ashamed"; for political wisdom among peoples, "Resist much—obey little." He has no word for art; it is not in her temple that he burns incense. His language as even a short extract has shown, is strong, vehement, instantaneously chosen; always forcible, and sometimes even rhythmical, like the prose of Plato. Thoughts crowd so thick upon him, that he has no time to seek their artistic equivalent; he utters his thought in any way, and his expressions gain accidental beauty from the glamour of his sympathy. As he speaks, we more than once see a man's face at white heat, and a man's hand beating down emphasis at the end of periods. He is inspired, not angry, yet as even inspiration is not infallible, he sometimes talks rank nonsense.

The second part of the volume, "Drum-Taps," is a series of poetic soliloquies on the war. It is more American and somewhat less mystical than the *Leaves of Grass*, but we have again the old cry of democracy. Here, in proportion to the absence of self-consciousness, and the presence of vivid emotion, we find absolute music, culminating once or twice in poetry. The monody on the death of Lincoln—"When lilacs last in the door-yard bloom'd"—contains the three essentials of poetic art—perfect sight, supreme emotion, and true music. This, however, is unusual in Walt Whitman. Intellectual self-consciousness generally coerces emotion, insincerities and follies ensue, and instead of rising into poetry, the lines wail monotonously, and the sound drops into the circle of crabbed prose.

For there is this distinction between Walt Whitman and the poet—that Whitman is content to reiterate his truth over and over again in the same tones, with the same result; while the poet, having found a truth to utter, is coerced by his *artistic* sympathies into seeking fresh literary forms for its expression. "Bawling out the rights of man," wrote Horne Tooke, "is not singing." Artistic sympathies Walt Whitman has none; he is that curiously crying bird—a prophet with no taste. He is careless about beautifying his truth: he is heedless of the new forms—personal, dramatic, lyrical—in which another man would clothe it, and in which his disciples will be certain to clothe it for him. He sees vividly, but he is not always so naturally moved as to sing exquisitely. He has the swagger of the prophet, not the sweetness of the musician. Hence all these crude metaphors and false notes which must shock artists, those needless bestialities which repel prudes, that general want of balance and that mental dizziness which astonish most Europeans.

But when this has been said, all blame has been said—if, after all, a man is to incur blame for not being quite another sort of being than nature made him. Walt Whitman has arisen on the States to point the way to new literatures. He is the plain pioneer, pickaxe on shoulder, working and "roughing." The daintier gentlemen will follow, and build where he is delving.

Whitman himself would be the first to denounce those loose young gentlemen who admire him vaguely because he is loud and massive, gross and colossal, not for the sake of the truth he is teaching, and the grandeur of the result that may ensue. There are some men who can admire nothing unless it is "strong"; intellectual dram-drinkers, quite as far from the truth as sentimental tea-drinkers. Let it at once and unhesitatingly be admitted that Whitman's want of art, his grossness, his tall talk, his metaphorical word-piling are *faults*—prodigious ones; and then let us turn reverently to contemplate these signs which denote his ministry, his command of rude forces, his nationality, his manly earnestness, and, last and greatest, his wondrous sympathy with men as men. He emerges from the mass of unwelded materials—in shape much like the earth-spirit in *Faust*. He is loud and coarse, like most prophets, "sounding," as he himself phrases it, "his barbaric yawp over the roofs of the world." He is the voice of which America stood most in need—a voice at which ladies scream and whippersnappers titter with delight, but which clearly pertains to a man who means to be heard. He is the clear forerunner of the great American poets long yearned for, now prophesied, but not perhaps to be beheld till the vast American democracy has subsided a little from its last and grandest struggle. Honour in his generation is, of course, his due; but he does not seem to solicit honour. He is too thoroughly alive to care about being tickled into activity, too excited already to be much moved by finding himself that most badgered of functionaries, the recognized Sir Oracle.

[Whitman's English Editor
Writes a Friend]

William Michael Rossetti*

56 Euston Sq. N.W.
23 June. [1869]

My dear Mrs. Gilchrist,

Your letter has given me keen pleasure this morning. That glorious man Whitman will one day be known as one of the greatest sons of Earth, a few steps below Shakespeare on the throne of immortality. What a tearing-away of the obscuring veil of use & wont from the visage of man & of life!

I am doing myself the pleasure of at once ordering a copy of the Selection to you, wh. you will be so kind as to accept. Genuine—i.e. *enthusiastic*—appreciators are not so common, & must be cultivated when they appear.

I am obstinate enough to think I was right in missing out the whole poem, wherever a necessity arose of missing out so much as a word; indeed in one sense I *know* I was right, for, after some semi-misapprehension on the point, it turned out that any other course wd. be revolting to Whitman himself. It is also to be remembered that mine is confessedly & intentionally (this is the publisher's affair) a mere *Selection*, & the volume even as it stands is rather beyond the size proposed; &, as everything in it is excellent, to substitute other excellent things involving any complication of whatever sort mt. hardly have been well-judged. The sort of thing that people object to in Whitman's writings is not so easily surmised until one sees them. It mt. be expressed thus—that he puts into print physical matters with the same bluntness & directness almost as that with wh. they present themselves to the eye & mind, or are half-worded in the thought. From one point of view that is even blameless: but from another, the modern reader's point of view, it is quite intolerable. On the abstract question also I think I was more right than wrong. If Shakespeare were a new author requiring to form his public, & if one or two of his plays (suppose Measure for Measure & Pericles) were practically

*Reprinted from *Letters of William Michael Rossetti Concerning Whitman, Blake and Shelley to Anne Gilchrist and Her Son Herbert Gilchrist*, ed. Clarence Gohdes and Paull F. Baum (Durham, N.C.: Duke Univ. Press, 1934), pp. 23–24.

unacceptable, I shd. consider it pardonable to print other plays, avowedly missing out these: the volume wd. then consist of a certain (tho' not the whole) number of complete dramas. But I shd. contemn & abhor the plan (Bowdler's) of cutting out every startling phrase that can be found throughout the whole number of plays—equally the two above-named & such severe works as Macbeth or King John.

Anybody who values Whitman as you do ought to read the whole of him. If I have have the pleasure of seeing you before you leave for Colne, I will proffer you his book. My own quite complete copy is already lent out; but I have the unbound copy wh. Whitman himself sent over for possible English republication, with his own last corrections—also the separate original editions. I shd. like also to show you a letter he wrote me when the question of excision rather than total omission was mooted: it is manly & kind in the highest degree.

An Englishwoman's Estimate of Walt Whitman

Anne Gilchrist*

[Preface by William Michael Rossetti]

London: November 20, 1869.

The great satisfaction which I felt in arranging, about two years ago, the first edition (or rather selection) of Walt Whitman's poems published in England has been, in due course of time, followed by another satisfaction—and one which, rightly laid to heart, is both less mixed and more intense. A lady, whose friendship honours me, read the selection last summer, and immediately afterwards accepted from me the loan of the complete edition, and read that also. Both volumes raised in her a boundless and splended enthusiasm, ennobling to witness. This found expression in some letters which she addressed to me at the time, and which contain (I affirm it without misgiving, and I hope not without some title to form an opinion) about the fullest, farthest-reaching, and most eloquent appreciation of Whitman yet put into writing, and certainly the most valuable, whether or not I or other readers find cause for critical dissent at an item here and there. The most valuable, I say, because this is the expression of what *a woman* sees in Whitman's poems—a woman who has read and thought much, and whom to know is to respect and esteem in every relation, whether of character, intellect, or culture.

I longed that what this lady had written should be published for the benefit of English, and more especially of American readers. She has generously acceded to my request. The ensuing reflections upon Whitman's poems contains several passages reproduced verbatim from the letters in question, supplemented by others which the same lady has added so as more fully to define and convey the impression which those unparalleled and deathless writings have made upon her.

W. M. Rossetti.

June 22, 1869—I was calling on [Mr. Madox Brown] a fortnight ago, and he put into my hands your edition of Walt Whitman's poems. I shall not cease to thank him for that. Since I have had it, I can read no other

*Reprinted from *Anne Gilchrist: Her Life and Writings*, ed. Herbert H. Gilchrist (London: T. F. Unwin, 1887), pp. 287–307. The essay, written as letters to Rossetti, was published in the *Radical* (Boston, May 1870), 345–59.

82

book: it holds me entirely spell-bound, and I go through it again and again with deepening delight and wonder.

June 23—I am very sure you are right in your estimate of Walt Whitman. There is nothing in him that I shall ever let go my hold of. For me the reading of his poems is truly a new birth of the soul.

I shall quite fearlessly accept your kind offer of a loan of a complete edition, certain that great and divinely beautiful nature has not, could not infuse any poison into the wine he has poured out for us. And as for what you specially allude to, who so well able to bear it—I will say, to judge wisely of it—as one who, having been a happy wife and mother, has learned to accept all things with tenderness, to feel a sacredness in all? Perhaps Walt Whitman has forgotten—or, through some theory in his head, has overridden—the truth that our instincts are beautiful facts of nature, as well as our bodies; and that we have a strong instinct of silence about some things.

July 11—I think it was very manly and kind of you to put the whole of Walt Whitman's poems into my hands; and that I have no other friend who would have judged them and me so wisely and generously.

I had not dreamed that words could cease to be words, and become electric streams like these. I do assure you that, strong as I am, I feel sometimes as if I had not bodily strength to read many of these poems. In the series headed "Calamus," for instance, in some of the "Songs of Parting," the "Voice out of the Sea," the poem beginning "Tears, tears," &c., there is such a weight of emotion, such a tension of the heart, that mine refuses to beat under it—stands quite still—and I am obliged to lay the book down for a while. Or again, in the piece called "Walt Whitman," and one or two others of that type, I am as one hurried through stormy seas, over high mountains, dazed with sunlight, stunned with a crowd and tumult of faces and voices, till I am breathless, bewildered, half-dead. Then come parts and whole poems in which there is such calm wisdom and strength of thought, such a cheerful breadth of sunshine, that the soul bathes in them renewed and strengthened. Living impulses flow out of these that make me exult in life, yet look longingly towards "the superb vistas of Death." Those who admire this poem, and do not care for that, and talk of formlessness, absence of metre, and so forth, are quite as far from any genuine recognition of Walt Whitman as his bitter detractors. Not, of course, that all the pieces are equal in power and beauty, but that all are vital; they grew—they were not made. We criticise a palace or a cathedral; but what is the good of criticising a forest? Are not the hitherto-accepted masterpieces of literature akin rather to noble architecture; built up of material rendered precious by elaboration; planned with subtile art that makes beauty go hand in hand with rule and measure, and knows where the last stone will come, before the first is laid; the result stately, fixed, yet such as might, in every particular, have been different from what it is (therefore inviting criticism), contrasting proudly with the careless freedom of nature, opposing its own rigid adherence to symmetry to her wilful dallying with it? But not such is this book. Seeds brought by the winds from north, south, east, and west, lying long in the earth, not resting on it like the stately building, but hid in and assimilating it, shooting upwards to be nourished by the air and the sunshine and the rain which beat idly against that—each bough and twig and leaf growing in strength and beauty it own way, a law to itself, yet, with all this freedom of spontaneous growth, the result inevitable, unalterable (therefore setting criticism at naught), above all things vital—that is, a source of ever-generating vitality: such are these poems:

> Roots and leaves themselves alone are these,
> Scents brought to men and women from the wild woods
>   and from the pond-side,
> Breastsorrel and pinks of love, fingers that wind around
>   tighter than vines,
> Gushes from the throats of birds hid in the foliage of
>   trees as the sun is risen,
> Breezes of land and love, breezes set from living shores
>   out to you on the living sea,—to you, O sailors!
> Frost-mellowed berries and Third-month twigs,
>   offered fresh to young persons wandering out in
>   the fields when the winter breaks up,
> Love-buds put before you and within you, whoever you
>   are,
> Buds to be unfolded on the old terms.
> If you bring the warmth of the sun to them, they will
>   open, and bring form, color, perfume, to you:
> If you become the aliment and the wet, they will become
>   flowers, fruits, tall branches and trees.

And the music takes good care of itself too. As if it *could* be otherwise! As if those "large, melodious thoughts," those emotions, now so stormy and wild, now of unfathomed tenderness and gentleness, could fail to vibrate through the words in strong, sweeping, long-sustained chords, with lovely melodies winding in and out fitfully amongst them! Listen, for instance, to the penetrating sweetness, set in the midst of rugged grandeur, of the passage beginning—

> I am he that walks with the tender and growing
>   night;
> I call to the earth and sea half held by the night.

I see that no counting of syllables will reveal the mechanism of the music; and that this rushing spontaneity could not stay to bind itself with the letters of metre. But I know that the music is there, and that I would not for something change ears with those who cannot hear it. And I know that poetry must be one of two things—either own this man as equal with her highest, completest manifestors, or stand aside, and admit that there is something come into the world nobler, diviner than herself, one that is free of the universe, and can tell its secrets as none before.

I do not think or believe this; but see it with the same unmistakable definiteness of perception and full consciousness that I see the sun at this moment in the noonday sky, and feel his rays glowing down upon me as I write in the open air. What more can you ask of the words of a man's mouth than that they should "absorb into you as food and air, to appear again in your strength, gait, face"—that they should be "fibre and filter to your blood," joy and gladness to your whole nature?

I am persuaded that one great source of this kindling, vitalizing power—I suppose *the* great source—is the grasp laid upon the present, the fearless and comprehensive dealing with reality. Hitherto the leaders of thought have (except in science) been men with their faces resolutely turned backwards; men who have made of the past a tyrant that beggars and scorns the present, hardly seeing any greatness but what is shrouded away in the twilight, underground past; naming the present only for disparaging comparisons, humiliating distrust that tends to create the very barrenness it complains of; bidding me warm myself at fires that went out to mortal eyes centuries ago; insisting, in religion above all, that I must either "look through dead men's eyes," or shut my own in helpless darkness. Poets fancying themselves so happy over the chill and faded beauty of the past, but not making me happy at all—rebellious always at being dragged down out of the free air and sunshine of to-day.

But this poet, this "athlete, full of rich words, full of joy," takes you by the hand, and turns you with your face straight forwards. The present is great enough for him, because he is great enough for it. It flows through him as a "vast oceanic tide," lifting up a mighty voice. Earth, "the eloquent, dumb, great mother," is not old, has lost none of her fresh charms, none of her divine meanings; still bears great sons and daughters, if only they would possess themselves and accept their birthright—a richer, not a poorer, heritage than was ever provided before—richer by all the toil and suffering of the generations that have preceded, and by the further unfolding of the eternal purposes. Here is one come at last who can show them how; whose songs are the breath of a glad, strong, beautiful life, nourished sufficingly, kindled to unsurpassed intensity and greatness by the gifts of the present.

> Each moment and whatever happens thrills me with
>   joy.
> O the joy of my soul leaning poised on itself—
>   receiving identity through materials, and loving
>   them—observing characters, and absorbing them!
> O my soul vibrated back to me from them!

O the gleesome saunter over fields and hillsides!
The leaves and flowers of the commonest weeds, the
    moist, fresh stillness of the woods,
The exquisite smell of the earth at daybreak, and all
    through the forenoon.

O to realize space!
The plenteousness of all—that there are no bounds;
To emerge, and be of the sky—of the sun and moon
    and the flying clouds, as one with them.

O the joy of suffering—
To struggle against great odds, to meet enemies
    undaunted,
To be entirely alone with them—to find how much
    one can stand!

I used to think it was great to disregard happiness, to press on to a
high goal, careless, disdainful of it. But now I see that there is nothing so
great as to be capable of happiness; to pluck it out of "each moment and
whatever happens"; to find that one can ride as gay and buoyant on the
angry, menacing, tumultuous waves of life as on those that glide and glitter under a clear sky; that it is not defeat and wretchedness which come
out of the storm of adversity, but strength and calmness.

See, again, in the pieces gathered together under the title
"Calamus," and elsewhere, what it means for a man to love his fellow-
man. Did you dream it before? These "evangel-poems of comrades and of
love" speak, with the abiding, penetrating power of prophecy, of a "new
and superb friendship"; speak not as beautiful dreams, unrealizable
aspirations to be laid aside in sober moods, because they breathe out what
now glows within the poet's own breast, and flows out in action toward the
men around him. Had ever any land before her poet, not only to concen-
trate within himself her life, and, when she kindled with anger against
her children who were treacherous to the cause her life is bound up with,
to announce and justify her terrible purpose in words of unsurpassable
grandeur (as in the poem beginning, "Rise, O days, from your fathomless
deeps"), but also to go and with his own hands dress the wounds, with his
powerful presence soothe and sustain and nourish her suffering
soldiers—hundreds of them, thousands, tens of thousands—by day and
by night, for weeks, months, years?

I sit by the restless all the dark night; some are so
    young,
Some suffer so much: I recall the experience sweet
    and sad.
Many a soldier's loving arms about this neck have
    crossed and rested,
Many a soldier's kiss dwells on these bearded lips—

Kisses, that touched with the fire of a strange, new, undying eloquence the lips that received them! The most transcendent genius could not, untaught by that "experience sweet and sad," have breathed out hymns for her dead soldiers of such ineffably tender, sorrowful, yet triumphant beauty.

But the present spreads before us other things besides those of which it is easy to see the greatness and beauty; and the poet would leave us to learn the hardest part of our lesson unhelped if he took no heed of these; and would be unfaithful to his calling, as interpreter of man to himself and of the scheme of things in relation to him, if he did not accept all—if he did not teach "the great lesson of reception, neither preference nor denial." If he feared to stretch out the hand, not of condescending pity, but of fellowship, to the degraded, criminal, foolish, despised, knowing that they are only laggards in "the great procession winding along the roads of the universe," "the far-behind to come on in their turn," knowing the "amplitude of Time," how could he roll the stone of contempt off the heart as he does, and cut the strangling knot of the problem of inherited viciousness and degradation? And, if he were not bold and true to the utmost, and did not own in himself the threads of darkness mixed in with the threads of light, and own it with the same strength and directness that he tells of the light, and not in those vague generalities that everybody uses, and nobody means, in speaking on this head—in the worst, germs of all that is in the best; in the best, germs of all that is in the worst,—the *brotherhood* of the human race would be a mere flourish of rhetoric. And brotherhood is naught if it does not bring brother's love along with it. If the poet's heart were not "a measureless ocean of love" that seeks the lips and would quench the thirst of all, he were not the one we have waited for so long. Who but he could put at last the right meaning into that word "democracy," which has been made to bear such a burthen of incongruous notions?

> By God! I will have nothing that all cannot have
> their counterpart of on the same terms!

flashing it forth like a banner, making it draw the instant allegiance of every man and woman who loves justice. All occupations, however homely, all developments of the activities of man, need the poet's recognition, because every man needs the assurance that for him also the materials out of which to build up a great and satisfying life lie to hand, the sole magic in the use of them, all of the right stuff in the right hands. Hence those patient enumerations of every conceivable kind of industry;

> In them far more than you estimated—in them far
> less also.

For more as a means, next to nothing as an end; whereas we are wont to take it the other way, and think the result something, but the means a weariness. Out of all come strength, and the cheerfulness of strength. I murmured not a little, to say the truth, under these enumerations, at first. But now I think that not only is their purpose a justification, but that the musical ear and vividness of perception of the poet have enabled him to perform this task also with strength and grace, and that they are harmonious as well as necessary parts of the great whole.

Nor do I sympathize with those who grumble at the unexpected words that turn up now and then. A quarrel with words is always, more or less, a quarrel with meanings; and here we are to be as genial and as wide as nature, and quarrel with nothing. If the thing a word stands for exists by divine appointment (and what does not so exist?), the word need never be ashamed of itself; the shorter and more direct, the better. It is a gain to make friends with it, and see it in good company. Here, at all events, "poetic diction" would not serve—not pretty, soft, colourless words, laid by in lavender for the special uses of poetry, that have had none of the wear and tear of daily life; but such as have stood most, as tell of human heart-beats, as fit closest to the sense, and have taken deep hues of association from the varied experiences of life—those are the words wanted here. We only ask to seize and be seized swiftly, overmasteringly, by the great meanings. We see with the eyes of the soul, listen with the ears of the soul; the poor old words that have served so many generations for purposes, good, bad, and indifferent, and become warped and blurred in the process, grow young again, regenerate, translucent. It is not mere delight they give us—*that* the "sweet singers," with their subtly wrought gifts, their mellifluous speech, can give too in their degree; it is such life and health as enable us to pluck delights for ourselves out of every hour of the day, and taste the sunshine that ripened the corn in the crust we eat—I often seem to myself to do that.

Out of the scorn of the present came scepticism; and out of the large, loving acceptance of it comes faith. If *now* is so great and beautiful, I need no arguments to make me believe that the *nows* of the past and of the future were, and will be, great and beautiful too.

> I know I am deathless.
> I know this orbit of mine cannot be swept by the
>   carpenter's compass.
> I know I shall not pass, like a child's carlacue cut with
>   a burnt stick at night.
> I know I am august.
> I do not trouble my spirit to vindicate itself or be
>   understood.
>
> My foothold is tenoned and mortised in granite:
> I laugh at what you call dissolution,
> And I know the amplitude of Time.

> No array of terms can say how much I am at peace
> about God and Death.

You argued rightly that my confidence would not be betrayed by any of the poems in this book. None of them troubled me even for a moment; because I saw at a glance that it was not, as men had supposed, the heights brought down to the depths, but the depths lifted up level with the sunlit heights, that they might become clear and sunlit too. Always, for a woman, a veil woven out of her own soul—never touched upon even, with a rough hand, by this poet. But, for a man, a daring, fearless pride in himself, not a mock-modesty woven out of delusions—a very poor imitation of a woman's. Do they not see that this fearless pride, this complete acceptance of themselves, is needful for her pride, her justification? What! is it all so ignoble, so base, that it will not bear the honest light of speech from lips so gifted with "the divine power to use words?" Then what hateful, bitter humiliation for her, to have to give herself up to the reality! Do you think there is ever a bride who does not taste more or less this bitterness in her cup? But who put it there? It must surely be man's fault, not God's, that she has to say to herself, "Soul, look another way—you have no part in this. Motherhood is beautiful, fatherhood is beautiful; but the dawn of fatherhood and motherhood is not beautiful." Do they really think that God is ashamed of what He has made and appointed? And, if not, surely it is somewhat superfluous that they should undertake to be so for Him.

> The full-spread pride of man is calming and excellent
> to the soul,

Of a woman above all. It is true that instinct of silence I spoke of is a beautiful, imperishable part of nature too. But it is not beautiful when it means an ignominious shame brooding darkly. Shame is like a very flexible veil, that follows faithfully the shape of what it covers—beautiful when it hides a beautiful thing, ugly when it hides an ugly one. It has not covered what was beautiful here; it has covered a mean distrust of a man's self and of his Creator. It was needed that this silence, this evil spell, should for once be broken, and the daylight let in, that the dark cloud lying under might be scattered to the winds. It was needed that one who could here indicate for us "the path between reality and the soul" should speak. That is what these beautiful, despised poems, the "Children of Adam," do, read by the light that glows out of the rest of the volume: light of a clear, strong faith in God, of an unfathomably deep and tender love for humanity—light shed out of a soul that is "possessed of itself."

> Natural life of me faithfully praising things,
> Corroborating for ever the triumph of things.

Now silence may brood again; but lovingly, happily, as protecting what is beautiful, not as hiding what is unbeautiful; consciously enfolding a sweet and sacred mystery—august even as the mystery of Death, the dawn as the setting: kindred grandeurs, which to eyes that are opened shed a hallowing beauty on all that surrounds and preludes them.

> O vast and well-veiled Death!
> O the beautiful touch of Death, soothing and benumbing
> a few moments, for reasons!

He who can thus look with fearlessness at the beauty of Death may well dare to teach us to look with fearless, untroubled eyes at the perfect beauty of Love in all its appointed realizations. Now none need turn away their thoughts with pain or shame; though only lovers and poets may say what they will—the lover to his own, the poet to all, because all are in a sense his own. None need fear that this will be harmful to the woman. How should there be such a flaw in the scheme of creation that, for the two with whom there is no complete life, save in closest sympathy, perfect union, what is natural and happy for the one should be baneful to the other? The utmost faithful freedom of speech, such as there is in these poems, creates in her no thought or feeling that shuns the light of heaven, none that are not as innocent and serenely fair as the flowers that grow; would lead, not to harm, but to such deep and tender affection as makes harm or the thought of harm simply impossible. Far more beautiful care than man is aware of has been taken in the making of her, to fit her to be his mate. God has taken such care that *he* need take none; none, that is, which consists in disguisement, insincerity, painful hushing-up of his true, grand, initiating nature. And, as regards the poet's utterances, which, it might be thought, however harmless in themselves, would prove harmful by falling into the hands of those for whom they are manifestly unsuitable, I believe that even here fear is needless. For her innocence is folded round with such thick folds of ignorance, till the right way and time for it to accept knowledge, that what is unsuitable is also unintelligible to her; and, if no dark shadow from without be cast on the white page by misconstruction or by foolish mystery and hiding away of it, no hurt will ensue from its passing freely through her hands.

This is so, though it is little understood or realized by men. Wives and mothers will learn through the poet that there is rejoicing grandeur and beauty there wherein their hearts have so longed to find it; where foolish men, traitors to themselves, poorly comprehending the grandeur of their own or the beauty of a woman's nature, have taken such pains to make her believe there was none—nothing but miserable discrepancy.

One of the hardest things to make a child understand is, that down underneath your feet, if you go far enough, you come to blue sky and stars again; that there really is no "down" for the world, but only in every direction an "up." And that this is an all-embracing truth, including within its scope every created thing, and, with deepest significance, every part, faculty, attribute, healthful impulse, mind, and body of a man (each and all facing towards and related to the Infinite on every side), is what we grown children find it hardest to realize too. Novalis said, "We touch heaven when we lay our hand on the human body"; which, if it mean anything, must mean an ample justification of the poet who has dared to be the poet of the body as well as of the soul—to treat it with the freedom and grandeur of an ancient sculptor.

> Not physiognomy alone nor brain alone is worthy of
> the muse:—I say the form complete is worthier far.

> These are not parts and poems of the body only, but
> of the soul.

> O, I say now these are soul.

But while Novalis—who gazed at the truth a long way off, up in the air, in a safe, comfortable, German fashion—has been admiringly quoted by high authorities, the great American who has dared to rise up and wrestle with it, and bring it alive and full of power in the midst of us, has been greeted with a very different kind of reception, as has happened a few times before in the world in similar cases. Yet I feel deeply persuaded that a perfectly fearless, candid, ennobling treatment of the life of the body (so inextricably intertwined with, so potent in its influence on the life of the soul) will prove of inestimable value to all earnest and aspiring natures, impatient of the folly of the long prevalent belief that it is because of the greatness of the spirit that it has learned to despise the body, and to ignore its influences; knowing well that it is, on the contrary, just because the spirit is not great enough, not healthy and vigorous enough, to transfuse itself into the life of the body, elevating that and making it holy by its own triumphant intensity; knowing, too, how the body avenges this by dragging the soul down to the level assigned itself. Whereas the spirit must lovingly embrace the body, as the roots of a tree embrace the ground, drawing thence rich nourishment, warmth, impulse. Or, rather, the body is itself the root of the soul—that whereby it grows and feeds. The great tide of healthful life that carries all before it must surge through the whole man, not beat to and fro in one corner of his brain.

> O the life of my senses and flesh, transcending my
> senses and flesh!

For the sake of all that is highest, a truthful recognition of this life, and especially of that of it which underlies the fundamental ties of humanity—the love of husband and wife, fatherhood, motherhood—is needed. Religion needs it, now at last alive to the fact that the basis of all true worship is comprised in "the great lesson of reception, neither preference nor denial," interpreting, loving, rejoicing in all that is created, fearing and despising nothing.

I accept reality, and dare not question it.

The dignity of a man, the pride and affection of a woman, need it too. And so does the intellect. For science has opened up such elevating views of the mystery of material existence that, if poetry had not bestirred herself to handle this theme in her own way, she would have been left behind by her plodding sister. Science knows that matter is not, as we fancied, certain stolid atoms which the forces of nature vibrate through and push and pull about; but that the forces and the atoms are one mysterious, imperishable identity, neither conceivable without the other. She knows, as well as the poet, that destructibility is not one of nature's words; that it is only the relationship of things—tangibility, visibility—that are transitory. She knows that body and soul are one, and proclaims it undauntedly, regardless, and rightly regardless, of inferences. Timid onlookers, aghast, think it means that soul is body—means death for the soul. But the poet knows it means body is soul—the great whole imperishable; in life and in death continually changing substance, always retaining identity. For, if the man of science is happy about the atoms, if he is not baulked or baffled by apparent decay or destruction, but can see far enough into the dimness to know that not only is each atom imperishable, but that its endowments, characteristics, affinities, electric and other attractions and repulsions—however suspended, hid, dormant, masked, when it enters into new combinations—remain unchanged, be it for thousands of years, and, when it is again set free, manifest themselves in the old way, shall not the poet be happy about the vital whole? shall the highest force, the vital, that controls and compels into complete subservience for its own purposes the rest, be the only one that is destructible? and the love and thought that endow the whole be less enduring than the gravitating, chemical, electric powers that endow its atoms? But identity is the essence of love and thought—I still I, you still you. Certainly no man need ever again be scared by the "dark hush" and the little handful of refuse.

You are not scattered to the winds—you gather
    certainly and safely around yourself.

Sure as Life holds all parts together, Death holds all
    parts together.

All goes onward and outward: nothing collapses.

What I am, I am of my body; and what I shall be,
    I shall be of my body.

The body parts away at last for the journeys of the
    soul.

Science knows that whenever a thing passes from a solid to a subtle air, power is set free to a wider scope of action. The poet knows it too, and is dazzled as he turns his eyes toward "the superb vistas of death." He knows that "the perpetual transfers and promotions" and "the amplitude of time" are for a man as well as for the earth. The man of science, with unwearied, self-denying toil, finds the letters and joins them into words. But the poet alone can make complete sentences. The man of science furnishes the premises; but it is the poet who draws the final conclusion. Both together are "swiftly and surely preparing a future greater than all the past." But, while the man of science bequeaths to it the fruits of his toil, the poet, this mighty poet, bequeaths himself—"Death making him really undying." He will "stand as nigh as the nighest" to these men and women. For he taught them, in words which breathe out his very heart and soul into theirs, that "love of comrades" which, like the "soft-born measureless light," makes wholesome and fertile every spot it penetrates to, lighting up dark social and political problems, and kindling into a genial glow that great heart of justice which is the life-source of Democracy. He, the beloved friend of all, initiated for them a "new and superb friendship"; whispered that secret of a god-like pride in a man's self, and a perfect trust in a woman, whereby their love for each other, no longer poisoned and stifled, but basking in the light of God's smile, and sending up to Him a perfume of gratitude, attains at last a divine and tender completeness. He gave a faith-compelling utterance to that "wisdom which is the certainty of the reality and immortality of things, and of the excellence of things." Happy America, that he should be her son! One sees, indeed, that only a young giant of a nation could produce this kind of greatness, so full of the ardour, the elasticity, the inexhaustible vigour and freshness, the joyousness, the audacity of youth. But I, for one, cannot grudge anything to America. For, after all, the young giant is the old English giant—the great English race renewing its youth in that magnificent land, "Mexican-breathed, Arctic-braced," and girding up its loins to start on a new career that shall match with the greatness of the new home.

Notes on Walt Whitman as Poet and Person

John Burroughs*

Then further as to the question of finish or definite aim. To me the book is much like pure arterial blood. No other poems afford a parallel in this respect. Out of its very nature arises the objection from certain quarters that it has no distinct purpose or aim, and therefore has no artistic completion. It certainly has not the finish of a tale, romance, or any plot, which begins, goes on, and closes; neither has it the special purpose of a partisan book, or of a religious, scientific or philosophical treatise; but it has purpose again just as Nature has; to nourish, to strengthen, to fortify, to tantalize, to provoke curiosity, to hint, to suggest, to lead on and on, and never stop and never satisfy. Its final end is power; it walls no man in, but opens up to him endless prospects into space and the verities of the soul. The author himself says that the poems are not so much a good lesson, as that they take down the bars to a good lesson:

> . . . they are not the finish, but rather the
> outset;
> They bring none to his or her terminus, or to be
> contented and full;
> Whom they take, they take into space, to behold the
> birth of stars, to behold one of the meanings,
> To launch off with absolute faith—to sweep through the
> ceaseless rings, and never be quiet again.

The brilliant epigrammatist will surely find the book an offence, and will battle against it; because the poetry of Walt Whitman is, in a certain sort, death to epigrams, and is either the large poetry of the Whole, of Science, and of God, or it is nothing.

The profit of the book is largely in what it infers and necessitates. Like the bibles of nations, it is not so much what it gives in itself, as what it certainly gives birth to—a long train of revelations, new opinions, beliefs and institutions.

The highest art is not to express art, but to express life and communi-

*First published in 1867, Burroughs revised and expanded his book for publication by J. S. Redfield (New York, 1871), from which I have extracted pp. 44–49, 54–56. Whitman wrote parts, revised, and edited this work by his young disciple.

cate power. Let those persons who have been so fast to cr.
Grass in this respect reflect if Nature be not open to the sa.
and if the living figure be not less than the marble statue, be
not simulate the art faculty. Both readers and writers need to
a poet may propose to himself higher ends than lace or ne
Modern verse does not express the great liberating power of Art,
its conventional limitations, and the elegant finish of details to .vnich
society runs. It never once ceases to appeal directly to that part of the
mind which is cognizant of mere form—form denoted by regular lines. It
is never so bold as music, which in the analysis is discord, but in the synthesis harmony; and falls far short of painting, which puts in masses of
subdued color to one brilliant point, and which is forever escaping out of
more form into vista.

To accuse Walt Whitman, therefore, of want of art, is to overlook his
generic quality, and shows ignorance of the ends for which Nature and
Time exist to the mind. He has the art which surrounds all art, as the
sphere holds all form. He works, it may be said, after the pure method of
Nature, and nothing less; and includes not only the artist of the beautiful,
but forestalls the preacher and the moralist by his synthesis and kosmical
integrity.

Dating mainly from Wordsworth and his school, there is in modern
literature, and especially in current poetry, a great deal of what is
technically called Nature. Indeed it might seem that this subject was worn
threadbare long ago, and that something else was needed. The word
Nature, now, to most readers, suggests only some flower bank, or summer
cloud, or pretty scene that appeals to the sentiments. None of this is in
Walt Whitman. And it is because he corrects this false, artificial Nature,
and shows me the real article, that I hail his appearance as the most
important literary event of our times.

Wordsworth was truly a devout and loving observer of Nature, and
perhaps has indicated more surely than any other poet the healthful moral
influence of the milder aspects of rural scenery. But to have spoken in the
full spirit of the least fact which he describes would have rent him to
atoms. To have accepted Nature in her entirety, as the absolutely good
and the absolutely beautiful, would have been to him tantamount to
moral and intellectual, destruction. He is simply a rural and metaphysical
poet whose subjects are drawn mostly from Nature, instead of from society, or the domain of romance; and he tells in so many words what he sees
and feels in the presence of natural objects. He has definite aim, like a
preacher or moralist as he was, and his effects are nearer akin to those of
pretty vases and parlor ornaments than to trees or hills.

In Nature everything is held in solution; there are no discriminations,
or failures, or ends; there is no poetry or philosophy—but there is that
which is better, and which feeds the soul, diffusing itself through the

mind in calm and equable showers, to give the analogy of this in the least degree was not the success of Wordsworth. Neither has it been the success of any of the so-called poets of Nature since his time. Admirable as many of these poets are in some respects, but they are visiting-card-callers upon Nature, going to her for tropes and figures only. In the products of the lesser fry of them I recognize merely a small toying with Nature—a kind of sentimental flirtation with birds and butterflies.

I am aware, also, that the Germanic literary "storm and stress periods," during the latter part of the last century, screamed vehemently for "Nature" too; but they knew not what they said. The applauded works of that period and place were far from the spirit of Nature, which is health, not disease.

If it appears that I am devoting my pages to the exclusive consideration of literature from the point of view of Nature and the spirit of Nature, it is not because I am unaware of other and very important standards and points of view. But these others, at the present day, need no urging, nor even a statement from me. Their claims are not only acknowledged—they tyrannize out of all proportion. The standards of Nature apply just as much to what is called artificial life, all that belongs to cities and to modern manufacturers and machinery, and the life arising out of them. Walt Whitman's poems, though entirely gathered, as it were, under the banner of the Natural Universal, include, for themes, as has been already stated, all modern and artificial combinations, and the facts of machinery, trades, etc. These are an essential part of his chants. It is, indeed, all the more indispensable to resume and apply to these, the genuine standards.

Our civilization is not an escape from Nature, but a mastery over, and following out of, Nature. We do not keep the air and sunlight out of our houses, but only the rain and the cold; and the untamed and unrefined elements of the earth are just as truly the sources of our health and strength as they are of the savages'. In speaking of Walt Whitman's poetry, I do not mean raw, unreclaimed Nature. I mean the human absorption of Nature like the earths in fruit and grain, or in the animal economy. The dominant facts of his poetry, carried out strictly and invariably from these principles, are Life, Love, and the Immortal Identity of the Soul. Here he culminates, and here are the regions where, in all his themes, after treating them, he finally ascends with them, soaring high and cleaving the heavens.

Do I say, then, that beauty is not the object or attribute of *Leaves of Grass*? Not directly the object, but indirectly. The love of eternal beauty and of truth move the author to his work, producing a poem without a single piece of embroidery or hung-on ornament, yet in its quality and proportion dominating, in this very attribute, all rivals.

It is on the clear eye, the firm and limber step, the sweet breath, the loving lip, the magnetism of sex, the lofty and religious soul, eloquent in figure as in face, that Walt Whitman has depended for beauty's attractiveness in his poems.

He is by no means insensible to what is called the poetic aspect of things; only he uses this element sparingly, and well seasoned with the salt of the earth. Where others bring a flower from the woods or a shell from the shore, he brings the woods and the shore also, so that his charm lies in the completed integrity of his statements.

Of a long account of a battle which I once read in some old Grecian history I remember only the fact, casually mentioned by the historian, that the whereabouts of one army was betrayed to the other by the glint of the moonlight upon the shield of a soldier as he stood on a high hill. The touches in *Leaves of Grass* are of like significance, and by their singleness and peculiarity not one is lost to the mind.

But this is not the final statement. That which in every instance has been counted the defect of Walt Whitman's writings, namely, that they are not markedly poetical, as that term is used, constitutes their transcendent merit. Unlike all others, this poet's words seem dressed for work, with hands and arms bare. At first sight they appear as careless of mere beauty, or mere art, as do the leaves of the forest about numbers, or the snow-flakes as to where they shall fall; yet his poems do more to the mind, for this very reason, than the most ostentatiously elaborated works. They indicate fresh and near at hand the exhaustless sources of beauty and art. Comparatively few minds are impressed with the organic beauty of the world. That there are gleams and touches here and there which not only have no reference "to the compact truth of the whole," but which are lucky exceptions to the general rule, and which it is the province of art to fix and perpetuate in color or form, is the notion of all our poets and poetlings. Outside of *Leaves of Grass* there is no theory or practice in modern letters that keeps in view the principle after which the highest artists, like Michael Angelo, have wrought, namely, that in the unimpeachable health and rectitude and latent power of the world are to be found the true sources of beauty for purposes of Art.

The perception of such high kosmical beauty comes by a vital original process of the mind. It is in some measure a creative act, and those works that rest upon it make demands—perhaps extraordinary demands—upon the reader or beholder. We regard mere surface glitter, or mere verbal sweetness, in a mood entirely passive, and with a pleasure entirely profitless. The beauty of excellent stage scenery seems much more obvious and easy of apprehension than the beauty of trees and hills themselves, inasmuch as the act of association in the mind is easier and inferior to the act of originial perception.

Only the greatest works in any department afford any explanation of this wonder we call Nature, or aid the mind in arriving at correct notions concerning it. To copy here and there a line or a tint is no explanation;

but to translate Nature into another language—to repeat, in some sort, the act of creation itself—as is done in *Leaves of Grass*, is the final and crowning triumph of poetic art.

The Poet of Democracy: Walt Whitman

Edward Dowden*

At last steps forward a man unlike any of his predecessors, and announces himself, and is announced with a flourish of critical trumpets, as Bard of America, and Bard of democracy. What cannot be questioned after an hour's acquaintance with Walt Whitman and his *Leaves of Grass*, is that in him we meet a man not shaped out of old-world clay, not cast in any old-world mould, and hard to name by any old-world name. In his self-assertion there is a manner of powerful nonchalantness which is not assumed; he does not peep timidly from behind his works to glean our suffrages, but seems to say, "Take me or leave me, here I am, a solid and not an inconsiderable fact of the universe." He disturbs our classifications. He attracts us; he repels us; he excites our curiosity, wonder, admiration, love; or, our extreme repugnance. He does anything except leave us indifferent. However we feel towards him we cannot despise him. He is "a summons and a challenge." He must be understood and so accepted, or must be got rid of. Passed by he cannot be. His critics have, for the most part, confined their attention to the personality of the man; they have studied him, for the most part, as a phenomenon isolated from the surrounding society, the environment, the *milieu*, which has made such a phenomenon possible. In a general way it has been said that Whitman is the representative in art of American democracy, but the meaning of this has not been investigated in detail. It is purposed here to consider some of the characteritistics of democratic art, and to inquire in what manner they manifest themselves in Whitman's work.

A word of explanation is necessary. The representative man of a nation is not always the nation's favourite. Hebrew spiritualism, the deepest instincts, the highest reaches of the moral attainment of the Jewish race, appear in the cryings and communings of its prophets; yet the prophets sometimes cried in the wilderness, and the people went after strange gods. American democracy is as yet but half-formed. The framework of its in-

*Reprinted from *Studies in Literature* (London: Kegan Paul, Trench, Trübner and Co., 1878), pp. 468–523. I have excerpted pp. 473–90. The first five pages note that American writers prior to Whitman, such as Irving, Longfellow, Lowell, are more European than American.

stitutions exists, but the will, the conscience, the mature desires of the democratic society are still in process of formation. If Whitman's writings are spoken of as the poetry of American democracy, it is not implied that his are the volumes most inquired after in the libraries of New York or Boston. What we mean is that these are the poems which naturally arise when a man of imaginative genius stands face to face with a great democratic world, as yet but half-fashioned, such as society is in the United States of the present day. Successive editions of his works prove that Whitman has many readers. But whether he had them now, or waited for them in years to come, it would remain true that he is the first representative democrat in art of the American continent. Not that he is to be regarded as a model or a guide; great principles and great passions which must play their part in the future, are to be found in his writings; but these have not yet cleared themselves from their amorphous surroundings. At the same time he is before all else a living man, and must not be compelled to appear as mere official representative of anything. He will not be comprehended in a formula. No *view* of him can image the substance, the life and movement of his manhood, which contracts and dilates, and is all over sensitive and vital. Such views are, however, valuable in the study of literature, as hypotheses are in the natural sciences, at least for the colligation of facts. They have a tendency to render criticism rigid and doctrinaire; the critic must therefore ever be ready to escape from his own theory of a man, and come in contact with the man himself. Every one doubtless moves in some regular orbit, and all aberrations are only apparent, but what the precise orbit is we must be slow to pronounce. Meanwhile we may legitimately conjecture, as Kepler conjectured, if only we remain ready, as Kepler was, to vary our conjectures as the exigencies of the observed phenomena require.

A glance at the art of an aristocratic period will inform us in the way of contrast of much that we may expect to find under a democracy. And before all else we are impressed by the great regard which the artists of an aristocratic period pay to form. The dignity of letters maintains itself, like the dignity of the court, by a regulated propriety of manners. Ideas and feelings cannot be received unless they wear the courtly costume. Precise canons applicable to the drama, the ode, the epic, to painting, sculpture, architecture, music, are agreed upon, and are strictly enforced. They acquire traditional authority, the precedents of a great period of art (such, for example, as that of Louis XIV), being final and absolute with succeeding generations. "Style is deemed of almost as much importance as thought. . . . The tone of mind is always dignified, seldom very animated, and writers care more to perfect what they produce than to multiply their productions."[1] The peril to which an aristocratic literature is hereby exposed is of a singular kind; matter or substance may cease to exist, while an empty and elaborately studied form, a variegated surface with nothing below it, may remain. This condition of things was actually realized at different times in the literatures of Italy, of Spain, of France, and of England, when such a variegated surface of literature served for disport and display of the wits of courtiers, of ingenious authors, of noble and gentle persons male and female, and when reflection and imagination had ceased to have any relation with letters.

Again, the literature of an aristocracy is distinguished by its striving after selectness, by its exclusive spirit, and the number of things it proscribes. This is especially the case with the courtly art which has a great monarchy for its centre of inspiration. There is an ever-present terror of vulgarity. Certain words are ineligible in poetry; they are mean or undignified, and the things denoted by them must be described in an elegant periphrasis. Directness and vividness are sacrificed to propriety. The acquired associations of words are felt to be as important, and claim as much attention as their immediate significance, their spiritual power and personal character. In language as in life there is, so to speak, an aristocracy and a commonalty; words with a heritage of dignity, words which have been ennobled, and a rabble of words which are excluded from positions of honour and of trust. But this striving after selectness in forms of speech is the least important manifestation of the exclusive spirit of aristocratic art. Far the greater number of men and women, classes of society, conditions of life, modes of thought and feeling, are not even conceived as in any way susceptible of representation in art which aspires to be grave and beautiful. The common people do not show themselves *en masse* except as they may follow in a patient herd, or oppose in impotent and insolent revolt the leadership of their lords. Individually they are never objects of equal interest with persons of elevated worldly station. Even Shakespeare could hardly find in humble life other virtues than a humorous honesty and an affectionate fidelity. Robin Hood, the popular hero, could not be quite heroic were he not of noble extraction, and reputed Earl of Huntingdon.

In the decline of an aristocratic period, dramatic studies of individual character and the life of the peasant or artisan may be made *from a superor point of view*. The literature of benevolence and piety stooping down to view the sad bodies and souls of men tends in this direction. And there are poems and novels, and paintings and sculptures, which flatter the feeling of mild benevolence. Pictures like those of Faed, in which some aged cottager, some strong delver of the earth, or searcher of the sea, some hard-worked father of children, says appealingly, "By virtue of this love I exhibit towards my offspring, by virtue of the correct sense I have of the condescension of my betters, by virtue of this bit of pathos—indubitably human—in my eye, confess now *am* I not a man and a brother?"—pictures like these are produced, and may be purchased by amiable persons of the upper classes who would honour the admirable qualities which exist in humble life. But when the aristocratic period is in its strength, and especially in courtly art and literature, these condescending studies, not without a certain affection and sincerity in them, are unknown. It is as if the world were made up of none but the gently born and bred. At most rustic life is glanced at for the sake of the suggestions of pretty waywardness it may supply to the fancy of great people tired of greatness. To play at pastoral may be for a while the fashion, if the shepherds and shepherdesses are permitted to choose graceful classical names, if the crooks are dainty, and the duties of the penfold not severe, if Phyllis may set off a neat ankle with the latest shoe, and Corydon may complain of the cruel fair in the bitterness of roundel or sonnet. The middle classes, however, the *bourgeoisie*, figure considerably in one department of poetry—in the comic drama. Molière indeed, living under a stricter rule of courtliness, suffered disgrace in consequence of the introduction of so low-bred a person as the excellent M. Jourdain. But to the noble mind of our own Restoration period how rich a material of humour, inexhaustibly diverting, if somewhat monotonous in theme, was afforded by the relations of the high-born and the moneyed classes. The *bourgeois* aping the courtier, the lord making a fool of the merchant, while he makes love to the merchant's wife and daughter—what unextinguishable laughter have variations upon these elementary themes compelled from the occupants of the boxes in our Restoration theatres! There is an innocence quite touching in their openness to impressions from the same comic effects repeated again and again. Harlequin still at the close of the pantomime belabouring Pantaloon is not more sure of his success with the wide-eyed on-lookers in the front row than was the gallant engaged in seducing the draper's or hosier's pretty wife with gold supplied by her husband, in the playhouses favoured by our mirthful monarch and his companions.

All that is noblest in an aristocratic age embodies itself not in its comedy, but its serious art, and in the persons of heroic men and women. Very high and admirable types of character are realized in the creations of epic and dramatic poetry. All the virtues which a position of hereditary greatness, dignity, and peril calls forth—energy of character, vigour of will, disregard of life, of limb, and of property in comparison with honour, the virtues of generosity, loyalty, courtesy, magnificence—these are glorified and illustrated in man; and in woman all the virtues of dependence, all the graces insensibly acquired upon the surface of an externally beautiful world, and at times the rarer qualities called forth by occasional exigencies of her position, which demand virtues of the masculine kind. It is characteristic and right that our chief chivalric epic, the *Faerie Queene*, should set before itself as the general end of all the book "to fashion a gentleman or noble person in virtuous and gentle discipline." The feudal world with Artegall and Calidore, with Britomart and Una, was not wanting in lofty conceptions of human character, male and female.

Other characteristics of the art of an aristocratic period may be briefly noted. It is not deeply interested in the future, it gazes forward with no eyes of desire. Why should it? when nothing seems better than that things should remain as they are, or at most that things should be ameliorated, not that a new world should be created. The aristocratic society exists by inheritance, and it hopes from to-morrow chiefly a conserving of the good gifts handed down by yesterday and to-day. Its feeling of the continuity of history is in danger of becoming formal and materialistc; it does not always perceive that the abandonment of old things and the acceptance of new may be a necessary piece of continuity in government, in social life, in art, in religion. At the Present the artist of the period of aristocracy looks not very often, and then askance upon certain approved parts of the Present. But he loves to celebrate the glories of the Past. He displays a preference accordingly for antique subjects, chosen out of the history of his own land, or the histories of deceased nations. Shelley with his eyes fixed upon the golden age to come may stand as representative of the democratic tendencies in art; Scott, celebrating the glories of feudalism, its heroism and its refinements, will remain our great aristocratic artist of the period subsequent to the first French Revolution. The relation of the art to the religion of an age of aristocracy is peculiarly simple. The religious dogma which constitutes the foundation and formative principle of the existing society must have been fully established, and of supreme power, before the aristocratic form of social and political life can have acquired vigour and stability; the intellectual and moral habits favoured by the aristocratic polity—loyalty, obedience, veneration for authority, pride in the past, a willingness to accept things as they come to us from our fathers, a distrust of new things, all favour a permanence of belief. The art, therefore, will upon the whole (peculiar circumstances may of course produce remarkable exceptions) be little disturbed by the critical or sceptical spirit, and, untroubled by doubts, that art will either concern itself not at all with religion, or, accepting the religious dogma without dispute, will render it into artistic form in sublime allegory and symbol, and as it is found embodied in the venerable history of the Church. We may finally note from De Tocqueville the shrinking in an aristocratic society from whatever, even in pleasure, is too startling, violent, or acute and the especial approval of choice gratifications, of refined and delicate enjoyments.

Now in all these particulars the art of a democratic age exhibits characteristics precisely opposite to those of the art of an aristocracy. Form and style modelled on traditional examples are little valued. No canons of composition are agreed upon or observed without formal agreement. No critical dictator enacts laws which are accepted without dispute, and acquire additional authority during many years. Each new generation, with its new heave of life, its multitudinous energies, ideas, passions, is a law to itself. Except public opinion, there is no authority on earth above the authority of a man's own soul, and public opinion being strongly in favour of individualism, a writer is tempted to depreciate unduly the worth of order, propriety, regularity of the academic kind; he is encouraged to make new literary experiments as others make new experiments in religion; he is permitted to be true to his own instincts, whether they are beautiful instincts or the reverse. The appeal which a work of art makes is to the nation, not to a class, and diversities of style are consequently admissible. Every style can be tolerated except the vapid, everything can be accepted but that which fails to stimulate the intellect or the passions.

Turning to Whitman, we perceive at once that his work corresponds with this state of things. If he had written in England in the period of Queen Anne, if he had written in France in the period of the *grand monarque*, he must have either acknowledged the supremacy of authority in literature and submitted to it, or on the other hand revolted against it. As it is, he is remote from authority, and neither submits nor revolts. Whether we call what he has written verse or prose, we have no hesitation in saying that it is no copy, that it is something uncontrolled by any model or canon, something which takes whatever shape it possesses directly from the soul of its maker. With the Bible, Homer, and Shakespeare familiar to him, Whitman writes in the presence of great models, and some influences from each have doubtless entered into his nature; but that they should possess authority over him any more than that he should possess authority over them, does not occur to him as possible. The relation of democracy to the Past comes out very notably here. Entirely assured of its own right to the Present, it is prepared to acknowledge fully the right of past generations to the Past. It is not hostile to that Past, rather claims kinship with it, but also claims equality, as a full-grown son with a father:

> I conn'd old times;
> I sat studying at the feet of the great masters:
> Now, if eligible, O that the great masters might return and
>   study me!
> In the name of These States, shall I scorn the antique?
> Why These are the children of the antique, to justify it.
>
> Dead poets, philosophs, priests,
> Martyrs, artists, inventors, governments long since,
> Language-shapers on other shores,
> Nations once powerful, now reduced, withdrawn or desolate,
> I dare not proceed til' I respectfully credit what you have left,
>   wafted hither:
> I have perused it, own it is admirable (moving awhile among
>   it);
> Think nothing can ever be greater,—nothing can ever deserve
>   more than it deserves;
> Regarding it all intently a long while,—then dismissing it,
> I stand in my place, with my own day, here.

[Omitted are 380 words quoted from *Democratic Vistas* expressing sentiments similar to those just quoted from "Starting from Paumanok."]

As in all else, so with regard to the form of what he writes, Walt Whitman can find no authority superior to himself, or rather to the rights of the subject which engages him. There is, as Mr. Rossetti has observed, "a very powerful and majestic rhythmical sense" throughout his writings, prose and verse (if we consent to apply the term *verse* to any of them), and this rhythmical sense, as with every great poet, is original and inborn. His works, it may be, exhibit no perfect crystal of artistic form, but each is a menstruum saturated with form in solution. He fears to lose the instinctive in any process of elaboration, the vital in anything which looks like mechanism. He does not write with a full consciousness of the processes of creation, not does any true poet. Certain combinations of sound are preconceived, and his imagination excited by them works towards them by a kind of reflex action, automatically. His *ars poetica* is embodied in the precept that the poet should hold himself passive in presence of the material universe, in presence of society, in presence of his own soul, and become the blind yet unerringly guided force through which these seek artistic expression. No afterthought, no intrusion of reasoning, no calculating of effects, no stepping back to view his work is tolerated. The artist must create his art with as little hesitation, as little questioning of processes, and as much sureness of result as the beaver builds his house. Very nobly Whitman has spoken on this subject, and let those who, because they do not know him, suppose him insensible to any attractions in art except those of the extravagant, the incoherent, and the lawless, read what follows from the preface to *Leaves of Grass*:

> The art of art, the glory of expression, and the sunshine of the light of letters is simplicity. Nothing is better than simplicity—nothing can make up for excess, or for the lack of definiteness. To carry on the heave of impulse, and pierce intellectual depths, and give all subjects their articulations, are powers neither common nor very uncommon. But to speak in literature with the perfect rectitude and insouciance of the movements of animals, and the unimpeachableness of the sentiment of trees in the woods, and grass by the roadside, is the flawless triumph of art. If you have looked on him who has achieved it, you have looked on one of the masters of the artists of all nations and times. You shall not contemplate the flight of the grey-gull over the bay, or the mettlesome action of the blood-horse, or the tall leaning of sunflowers on their stalk, or the appearance of the sun journeying through heaven, or the appearance of the moon afterward, with any more satisfaction than you shall contemplate him. The greatest poet has less a marked style, and is more the channel of thoughts and things without increase or diminution, and is the free channel of himself. He swears to his art. . . . What I tell I tell for precisely what it is. Let who may exalt, or startle, or fascinate, or soothe, I will

have purposes as health, or heat, or snow has, and be as regardless of observation.

Seeing much of deep truth in this, it must be added that, when the poet broods over his half-formed creation, and fashions it with divine ingenuity, and gives it shapeliness and completion of detail, and the lustre of finished workmanship, he does not forsake his instincts, but is obedient to them; he does not remove from nature into a laboratory of art, but is the close companion of nature. The vital spontaneous movement of the faculties, far from ceasing, still goes on like "the flight of the grey-gull over the bay," while the poet seeks after order, proportion, comeliness, melody—in a word, beauty; or rather, as Whitman himself is fond of saying, does not seek but is sought—the perfect form preconceived but unattained, drawing the artist towards itself with an invincible attraction. An artist who does not yield to the desire for perfect order and beauty of form, instead of coming closer to nature is really forsaking nature, and doing violence to a genuine artistic instinct. Walt Whitman, however, knows this in all probability well enough, and does not need to be taught the mysteries of his craft. We will not say that his poems, as regards their form, do not, after all, come right, or that for the matter which he handles his manner of treatment may not be the best possible. One feels, as it has been well said, that although no counting of syllables will reveal the mechanism of the music, the music is there, and that "one would not for something change ears with those who cannot hear it." Whitman himself anticipates a new theory of literary composition for imaginative works, and especially for highest poetry, and desires the recognition of new forces in language, and the creation of a new manner of speech which cares less for what it actually realizes in definite form than "for impetus and effects, and for what it plants and invigorates to grow." Nevertheless, when we read not the lyrical portions of Whitman's poetry, but what may be called his poetical statements of thoughts and things, a suspicion arises that if the form be suitable here to the matter, it must be because the matter belongs rather to the chaos than the kosmos of the new-created world of art.

The principle of equality upon which the democratic form of society is founded, obviously opposes itself to the exclusive spirit of the aristocratical polity. The essential thing which gives one the freedom of the world is not to be born a man of this or that rank, or class, caste, but simply to be born a man. The literature of an aristocratic period is distinguished by its aim at selectness, and the number of things it proscribes; we should expect the literature of a democracy to be remarkable for its comprehensiveness, its acceptance of the persons of all men, its multiform sympathies. The difference between the President and the Broadway mason or hodman is inconsiderable—an accident of office; what is common to both is the inexpressibly important thing, their inalienable humanity. Rich and poor, high and low, powerful and feeble, healthy and diseased, deformed and beautiful, old and young, man and woman, have this in common, and by possession of this are in one essential thing equal, and brethren one of another. Even between the virtuous man and the vicious the difference is less than the agreement; they differ by a quality, but agree by the substance of their manhood. The *man* in all men, however it may be obscured by cruel shocks and wrenches of life which distort, by long unnatural uses which deform, by ignorance, by the well-meaning stupidity of others, or by one's own stupidity, by foul living, or by clean, hard, worldly living, is surely somewhere discoverable. How can any human creature be rejected, any scorned, any mocked? Such satire and such comedy as appear in aristocratic society are discouraged by the genius of democracy. The spirit of exclusiveness will, it is true, never fail to find material for its support, and baser prides may replace the calm, conservative, but unaggressive pride of hereditary dignity. Nevertheless it remains no less true that the spectacle of a great democracy present to the imagination, and the temper of the democracy accepted by the understanding heart, favour only such prides as are founded on nature—that is, on the possession, acquired or inherited, of personal qualities, personal powers, and virtues, and attainments.

If this be a true account of some characteristics of the art which arises when a man of imaginative genius stands face to face with a great democracy, Walt Whitman in these particulars is what he claims to be, a representative democrat in art. No human being is rejected by him, no one slighted, nor would he judge any, except as "the light falling around a helpless thing" judges. No one in his poems comes appealing "Am I not interesting, am I not deserving, am I not a man and a brother?" We have had, he thinks, "ducking and deprecating about enough." The poet studies no one from a superior point of view. He delights in men, and neither approaches deferentially those who are above him, nor condescendingly gazes upon those who are beneath. He is the comrade of every man, high and low. His admiration of a strong, healthy, and beautiful body, or a strong, healthy, and beautiful soul, is great when he sees it in a statesman or a savant; it is precisely as great when he sees it in the ploughman or the smith. Every variety of race and nation, every condition in society, every degree of culture, every season of human life, is accepted by Whitman as admirable and best, each in its own place. Working men of every name—all who engage in field-work, all who toil upon the sea, the city artisan, the woodsman and the trapper, fill him with pleasure by their presence; and that they are interesting to him not in a general way of theory or doctrine (a piece of the abstract democratic creed), but in the way of close, vital human sympathy, appears from the power he possesses of bringing before us with strange precision, vividness, and nearness in a few decisive strokes the essential characteristics of their respective modes of living. If the strong, full-grown working man wants a lover and comrade, he will think Walt Whitman especially made for him. If the young man wants one, he will think him especially the poet of young men. Yet a rarer and finer spell than that of the lush vitality of youth, or the trained activity of manhood, is exercised over the poet by the beautiful repose of unsubdued energy of old age. He is "the caresser of life, wherever moving." He does not search antiquity for heroic men and beautiful women; his own abundant vitality makes all the life which surrounds him a source of completest joy; "what is commonest, cheapest, nearest, easiest, is Me. . . . not asking the sky to come down to my goodwill; scattering it freely for ever."

Note

1. Alexis de Tocqueville, *Democracy in America*, 2d Part, First Book, Chapter 13 ("Literary Characteristics of Democratic Ages").

The Gospel According to
Walt Whitman

Robert Louis Stevenson*

This is a case of a second difficulty which lies continually before the writer of critical studies: that he has to mediate between the author whom he loves and the public who are certainly indifferent and frequently averse. Many articles had been written on this notable man. One after another had leaned, in my eyes, either to praise or blame unduly. In the last case, they helped to blindfold our fastidious public to an inspiring writer; in the other, by an excess of unadulterated praise, they moved the more candid to revolt. I was here on the horns of a dilemma; and between these horns I squeezed myself with perhaps some loss to the substance of the paper. Seeing so much in Whitman that was merely ridiculous, as well as so much more that was unsurpassed in force and fitness—seeing the true prophet doubled, so I thought, in places with a Bull in a China Shop—it appeared best to steer a middle course, and to laugh with the scorners when I thought they had any excuse, while I made haste to rejoice with the rejoicers over what is imperishably good, lovely, human, or divine, in his extraordinary poems. That was perhaps the right road; yet I cannot help feeling that in this attempt to trim my sails between an author whom I love and honour and a public too averse to recognise his merit, I have been led into a tone unbecoming from one of my stature to one of Whitman's. But the good and the great man will go on his way, not vexed with my little shafts of merriment. He, first of any one, will understand how, in the attempt to explain him credibly to Mrs. Grundy, I have been led into certain airs of the man of the world, which are merely ridiculous in me, and were not intentionally discourteous to himself. But there is a worse side to the question; for in my eagerness to be all things to all men, I am afraid I may have sinned against proportion. It will be enough to say here that Whitman's faults are few and unimportant when they are set beside his surprising merits. I had written another paper full of gratitude for the help that had been given me in my life, full of en-

*Reprinted from *Familiar Studies of Men and Books* (London: Cassell and Co., 1882), pp. xvii–xix, 91–128. The extracts are from the preface and parts one and five dealing with Whitman's program and his style. The parts omitted deal with Whitman's optimism, love of life, and character. Originally published in *New Quarterly*, 10 (Oct. 1878), 461–81.

thusiasm for the intrinsic merit of the poems, and conceived in the noisiest extreme of youthful eloquence. The present study was a *rifacimento*. From it, with the design already mentioned, and in a fit of horror at my old excess, the big words and emphatic passages were ruthlessly excised. But this sort of prudence is frequently its own punishment; along with the exaggeration, some of the truth is sacrificed; and the result is cold, constrained, and grudging. In short, I might almost everywhere have spoken more strongly than I did.

Whitman, it cannot be too soon explained, writes up to a system. He was a theoriser about society before he was a poet. He first perceived something wanting, and then sat down squarely to supply the want. The reader, running over his works, will find that he takes nearly as much pleasure in critically expounding his theory of poetry as in making poems. This is as far as it can be from the case of the spontaneous village minstrel dear to elegy, who has no theory whatever, although sometimes he may have fully as much poetry as Whitman. The whole of Whitman's work is deliberate and preconceived. A man born into a society comparatively new, full of conflicting elements and interests, could not fail, if he had any thoughts at all, to reflect upon the tendencies around him. He saw much good and evil on all sides, not yet settled down into some more or less unjust compromise as in older nations, but still in the act of settlement. And he could not but wonder what it would turn out; whether the compromise would be very just or very much the reverse, and give great or little scope for healthy human energies. From idle wonder to active speculation is but a step; and he seems to have been early struck with the inefficacy of literature and its extreme unsuitability to the conditions. What he calls "Feudal Literature" could have little living action on the tumult of American democracy; what he calls the "Literature of Woe," meaning the whole tribe of *Werther* and Byron, could have no action for good in any time or place. Both propositions, if art had none but a direct moral influence, would be true enough; and as this seems to be Whitman's view, they were true enough for him. He conceived the idea of a Literature which was to inhere in the life of the present; which was to be, first human, and next American; which was to be brave and cheerful as per contract; to give culture in a popular and poetical presentment; and, in so doing, catch and stereotype some democratic ideal of humanity which should be equally natural to all grades of wealth and education, and suited, in one of his favourite phrases, to "the average man." To the formation of some such literature as this his poems are to be regarded as so many contributions, one sometimes explaining, sometimes superseding, the other: and the whole together not so much a finished work as a body of suggestive hints. He does not profess to have built the castle, but he pretends he has traced the lines of the foundation. He has not made the poetry, but he flatters himself he has done something toward making the poets.

His notion of the poetic function is ambitious, and coincides roughly with what Schopenhauer has laid down as the province of the metaphysician. The poet is to gather together for men, and set in order, the materials of their existence. He is "The Answerer"; he is to find some way of speaking about life that shall satisfy, if only for the moment, man's enduring astonishment at his own position. And besides having an answer ready, it is he who shall provoke the question. He must shake people out of their indifference, and force them to make some election in this world, instead of sliding dully forward in a dream. Life is a business we are all apt to mismanage; either living recklessly from day to day, or suffering ourselves to be gulled out of our moments by the inanities of custom. We should despise a man who gave as little activity and forethought to the conduct of any other business. But in this, which is the one thing of all others, since it contains them all, we cannot see the forest for the trees. One brief impression obliterates another. There is something stupefying in the recurrence of unimportant things. And it is only on rare provocations that we can rise to take an outlook beyond daily concerns, and comprehend the narrow limits and great possibilities of our existence. It is the duty of the poet to induce such moments of clear sight. He is the declared enemy of all living by reflex action, of all that is done betwixt sleep and waking, of all the pleasureless pleasurings and imaginary duties in which we coin away our hearts and fritter invaluable years. He has to electrify his readers into an instant unflagging activity, founded on a wide and eager observation of the world, and make them direct their ways by a superior prudence, which has little or nothing in common with the maxims of the copy-book. That many of us lead such lives as they would heartily disown after two hours' serious reflection on the subject is, I am afraid, a true, and, I am sure, a very galling thought. The Enchanted Ground of dead-alive respectability is next, upon the map, to the Beulah of considerate virtue. But there they all slumber and take their rest in the middle of God's beautiful and wonderful universe; the drowsy heads have nodded together in the same position since first their fathers fell asleep; and not even the sound of the last trumpet can wake them to a single active thought. The poet has a hard task before him to stir up such fellows to a sense of their own and other people's principles in life.

And it happens that literature is, in some ways, but an indifferent means to such an end. Language is but a poor bull's-eye lantern wherewith to show off the vast cathedral of the world; and yet a particular thing once said in words is so definite and memorable, that it makes us forget the absence of the many which remain unexpressed; like a bright window in a distant view, which dazzles and confuses our sight of its surroundings. There are not words enough in all Shakespeare to express the merest fraction of a man's experience in an hour. The speed of the eyesight and the hearing, and the continual industry of the mind, produce, in ten minutes, what it would require a laborious volume to shadow forth by comparisons and roundabout approaches. If verbal logic were sufficient, life would be as plain sailing as a piece of Euclid. But, as a matter of fact, we make a travesty of the simplest process of thought when we put it into words; for the words are all coloured and forsworn, apply inaccurately, and bring with them, from former uses, ideas of praise and blame that have nothing to do with the question in hand. So we must always see to it nearly, that we judge by the realities of life and not by the partial terms that represent them in man's speech; and at times of choice, we must leave words upon one side, and act upon those brute convictions, unexpressed and perhaps inexpressible, which cannot be flourished in an argument, but which are truly the sum and fruit of our experience. Words are for communication, not for judgment. This is what every thoughtful man knows for himself, for only fools and silly schoolmasters push definitions over far into the domain of conduct; and the majority of women, not learned in these scholastic refinements, live all-of-a-piece and unconsciously, as a tree grows, without caring to put a name upon their acts or motives. Hence, a new difficulty for Whitman's scrupulous and argumentative poet; he must do more than waken up the sleepers to his words; he must persuade them to look over the book and at life with their own eye.

This side of truth is very present to Whitman; it is this that he means when he tells us that "To glance with an eye confounds the learning of all times." But he is not unready. He is never weary of descanting on the undebatable conviction that is forced upon our minds by the presence of other men, of animals, or of inanimate things. To glance with an eye, were it only at a chair or a park railing, is by far a more persuasive process, and brings us to a far more exact conclusion, than to read the works of all the logicians extant. If both, by a large allowance, may be said to end in certainty, the certainty in the one case transcends the other to an incalculable degree. If people see a lion, they run away; if they only apprehend a deduction, they keep wandering around in an experimental humour. Now, how is the poet to convince like nature, and not like books? Is there no actual piece of nature that he can show the man to his face, as he might show him a tree if they were walking together? Yes, there is one: the man's own thoughts. In fact, if the poet is to speak efficaciously, he must say what is already in his hearer's mind. That, alone, the hearer will believe; that, alone, he will be able to apply intelligently to the facts of life. Any conviction, even if it be a whole system or a whole religion, must pass into the condition of commonplace, or postulate, before it becomes fully operative. Strange excursions and high-flying theories may interest, but they cannot rule behaviour. Our faith is not the highest truth that we perceive, but the highest that we have been able to assimilate into the very texture and method of our thinking. It is not, therefore, by flashing before a man's eyes the weapons of dialectic; it is not by induction, deduction, or construction; it is not by forcing him on from one stage of reasoning to another, that the man will be effectually renewed. He cannot be made to believe anything; but he can be made to see that he has always believed it. And this is the practical canon. It is when the reader cries, "Oh, I know!" and is, perhaps, half irritated to see how nearly the author has forestalled his own thoughts, that he is on the way to what is called in theology a Saving Faith.

Here we have the key to Whitman's attitude. To give a certain unity of ideal to the average population of America—to gather their activities about some conception of humanity that shall be central and normal, if only for the moment—the poet must portray that population as it is. Like human law, human poetry is simply declaratory. If any ideal is possible, it must be already in the thoughts of the people; and, by the same reason, in the thoughts of the poet, who is one of them. And hence Whitman's own formula: "The poet is individual—he is complete in himself: the others are as good as he; only he sees it, and they do not." To show them how good they are, the poet must study his fellow-countrymen and himself somewhat like a traveller on the hunt for his book of travels. There is a sense, of course, in which all true books are books of travel; and all genuine poets must run their risk of being charged with the traveller's exaggeration; for to whom are such books more surprising than to those whose own life is faithfully and smartly pictured? But this danger is all upon one side; and you may judiciously flatter the portrait without any likelihood of the sitter's disowning it for a faithful likeness. And so Whitman has reasoned: that by drawing at first hand from himself and his neighbours, accepting without shame the inconsistencies and brutalities that go to make up man, and yet treating the whole in a high, magnanimous spirit, he would make sure of belief, and at the same time encourage people forward by the means of praise.

Something should be said of Whitman's style, for style is of the essence of thinking. And where a man is so critically deliberate as our author, and goes solemnly about his poetry for an ulterior end, every indication is worth notice. He has chosen a rough, unrhymed, lyrical verse; sometimes instinct with a fine processional movement; often so rugged and careless that it can only be described by saying that he has not taken the trouble to write prose. I believe myself that it was selected principally because it was easy to write, although not without recollections of the marching measures of some of the prose in our English Old Testament. According to Whitman, on the other hand, "the time has arrived to essentially break down the barriers of form between Prose and Poetry . . . for the most cogent purposes of those great inland states, and for Texas, and California, and Oregon"—a statement which is among the happiest achievements of American humour. He calls his verses "recitatives," in easily followed allusion to a musical form. "Easily-written, loose-fingered chords," he cries, "I feel the thrum of your climax and close." Too often, I fear, he is the only one who can perceive the rhythm; and in spite of Mr.

Swinburne, a great part of his work considered as verse is poor bald stuff. Considered, not as verse, but as speech, a great part of it is full of strange and admirable merits. The right detail is seized; the right word, bold and trenchant, is thrust into its place. Whitman has small regard to literary decencies, and is totally free from literary timidities. He is neither afraid of being slangy nor of being dull; nor, let me add, of being ridiculous. The result is a most surprising compound of plain grandeur, sentimental affection, and downright nonsense. It would be useless to follow his detractors and give instances of how bad he can be at his worst; and perhaps it would be not much wiser to give extracted specimens of how happily he can write when he is at his best. These come in to most advantage in their own place; owing something, it may be, to the offset of their curious surroundings. And one thing is certain, that no one can appreciate Whitman's excellences until he has grown accustomed to his faults. Until you are content to pick poetry out of his pages almost as you must pick it out of a Greek play in Bohn's translation, your gravity will be continually upset, your ears perpetually disappointed, and the whole book will be no more to you than a particularly flagrant production by the Poet Close.

A writer of this uncertain quality was, perhaps, unfortunate in taking for thesis the beauty of the world as it now is, not only on the hilltops, but in the factory; not only by the harbour full of stately ships, but in the magazine of the hopelessly prosaic hatter. To show beauty in common things is the work of the rarest tact. It is not to be done by the wishing. It is easy to posit as a theory, but to bring it home to men's minds is the problem of literature, and is only accomplished by rare talent and in comparatively rare instances. To bid the whole world stand and deliver, with a dogma in one's right hand by way of pistol; to cover reams of paper in a galloping, headstrong vein; to cry louder and louder over everything as it comes up and make no distinction in one's enthusiasm over the most incomparable matters; to prove one's entire want of sympathy for the jaded, literary palate, by calling, not a spade a spade, but a hatter a hatter, in a lyrical apostrophe—this, in spite of all the airs of inspiration, is not the way to do it. It may be very wrong, and very wounding to a respectable branch of industry, but the word "hatter" cannot be used seriously in emotional verse; not to understand this, is to have no literary tact; and I would, for his own sake, that this were the only inadmissible expression with which Whitman had bedecked his pages. The book teems with similar comicalities; and, to a reader who is determined to take it from that side only, presents a perfect carnival of fun.

A good deal of this is the result of theory playing its usual vile trick upon the artist. It is because he is a Democrat that Whitman must have in the hatter. If you may say Admiral, he reasons, why may you not say Hatter? One man is as good as another, and it is the business of the "great poet" to show poetry in the life of the one as well as the other. A most incontrovertible sentiment surely, and one which nobody would think of controverting, where—and here is the point—where any beauty has been shown. But how, where that is not the case? where the hatter is simply introduced, as God made him and as his fellow-men have miscalled him, at the crisis of a high-flown rhapsody? And what are we to say, where a man of Whitman's notable capacity for putting things in a bright, picturesque, and novel way, simply gives up the attempt, and indulges, with apparent exultation, in an inventory of trades or implements, with no more colour of coherence than so many index-words out of a dictionary? I do not know that we can say anything, but that it is a prodigiously amusing exhibition for a line or so. The worst of it is, that Whitman must have known better. The man is a great critic, and, so far as I can make out, a good one; and how much criticism does it require to know that capitulation is not description, or that fingering on a dumb keyboard, with whatever show of sentiment and execution, is not at all the same thing as discoursing music? I wish I could believe he was quite honest with us; but indeed, who was ever quite honest who wrote a book for a purpose? It is a flight beyond the reach of human magnanimity.

One other point, where his means failed him, must be touched upon, however shortly. In his desire to accept all facts loyally and simply, it fell within his programme to speak at some length and with some plainness on what is, for I really do not know what reason, the most delicate of subjects. Seeing in that one of the most serious and interesting parts of life, he was aggrieved that it should be looked upon as ridiculous or shameful. No one speaks of maternity with his tongue in his cheek; and Whitman made a bold push to set the sanctity of fatherhood beside the sanctity of motherhood, and introduce this also among the things that can be spoken of without either a blush or a wink. But the Philistines have been too strong; and, to say truth, Whitman has rather played the fool. We may be thoroughly conscious that his end is improving; that it would be a good thing if a window were opened on these close privacies of life; that on this subject, as on all others, he now and then lets fall a pregnant saying. But we are not satisfied. We feel that he was not the man for so difficult an enterprise. He loses our sympathy in the character of a poet by attracting too much of our attention in that of a Bull in a China Shop. And where, by a little more art, we might have been solemnised ourselves, it is too often Whitman alone who is solemn in the face of an audience somewhat indecorously amused.

[An Important American Critic Views Whitman]

Edmund Clarence Stedman*

The entire body of his work has a sign-metrical by which it is recognized—a peculiar and uncompromising style, conveyed in a still more peculiar unrhymed verse, irregular, yet capable of impressive rhythmical and lyrical effects.

The faults of his method, glaring enough in ruder passages, are quite his own; its merits often are original, but in his chosen form there is little original and new. It is an old fashion, always selected for dithyrambic oracular outpourings—that of the Hebrew lyrists and prophets, and their inspired English translators—of the Gaelic minstrels—of various Oriental and Shemitic peoples—of many barbarous dark-skinned tribes—and in recent times put to use by Blake, in the "Prophetic Visions," and by other and weaker men. There are symptoms in Whitman's earlier poems, and definite proof in the later, that his studies have included Blake—between whose traits and his own there is a superficial, not a genuine, likeness. Not as an invention, then, but as a striking and persistent renaissance, the form that has become its trademark, and his extreme claims for it should have fair consideration. An honest effort to enlarge the poet's equipment too long unaided, by something rich and strange, deserves praise, even though a failure; for there are failures worthier than triumphs. Our chanter can bear with dignity the provincial laughter of those to whom all is distasteful that is uncommon, and regard it as no unfavorable omen. From us the very strangeness of his chant shall gain for it a welcome, and the chance to benefit us as it may. Thereby we may escape the error pointed out by Mr. Benjamin, who says that people in approaching a work, instead of learning from it, try to estimate it from their preconceived notions. Hence, original artists at first endure neglect, because they express their own discoveries in nature of what others have not yet seen—a truth well to bear in mind whenever a singer arrives with a new method.

Probably the method under review has had a candid hearing in more

*Reprinted from *Scribner's*, 21 (Nov. 1880), 47–64. Republished in *Poets of America* (Boston: Houghton Mifflin, 1886), with some revisions. Omitted are Parts I–III, which are introductory, deal with the Whitman controversy, and sketch in biographical detail.

116

quarters than the author himself is aware of. If some men of independent thought and feeling have failed to accept his claims and his estimate of the claims of others, it possibly has not been through exclusiveness or malice, but upon their own impression of what has value in song.

Mr. Whitman never has swerved from his primal indictment of the wonted forms, rhymed and unrhymed, dependent upon accentual, balanced and stanzaic effects of sound and shape—and until recently has expressed his disdain not only of our poets who care for them, but of form itself. So far as this cry was raised against the technique of poetry, I not merely think it absurd, but that when he first made it he had not clearly thought out his own problem. Technique, *of some kind*, is an essential, though it is equally true that it cannot atone for poverty of thought and imagination. I hope to show that he never was more mistaken than when he supposed he was throwing off form and technique. But first it may be said that no "form" ever has sprung to life, and been handed from poet to poet, that was not engendered by instinct and natural law, and each will be accepted in a sound generalization. Whitman avers that the time has come to break down the barriers between prose and verse, and that only thus can the American bard utter anything commensurate with the liberty and splendor of his themes. Now, the mark of a poet is that he is at ease everywhere—that nothing can hamper his gifts, his exultant freedom. He is a master of expression. There are certain points—note this—where expression takes on rhythm, and certain other points where it ceases to be rhythmical—places where prose becomes poetical, and where verse grows prosaic; and throughout Whitman's productions these points are more frequent and unmistakable than in the work of any other writer of our time. However bald or formal a poet's own method, it is useless for him to decry forms that recognize the pulses of time and accent, and the linked sweetness of harmonic sound. Some may be tinkling, others majestic, but each is suited to its purpose, and has a spell to charm alike the philosopher and the child that knows not why. The human sense acknowledges them; they are the earliest utterance of divers peoples, and in their later excellence still hold their sway. Goethe discussed all this with Eckermann, and rightly said there were "great and mysterious agencies" in the various poetic forms. He even added that if a sort of poetic prose should be introduced, it would only show that the distinction between prose and poetry had been lost sight of completely. Rhyme, the most conventional feature of ballad verse, has its due place, and will keep it; it is an artifice, but a natural artifice, and pleases accordingly. Milton gave reasons for discarding it when he perfected an unrhymed measure for the stateliest English poem; but what an instrument rhyme was in his hands that made the sonnets and minor poems! How it has sustained the whole carnival of our heroic and lyric song, from the sweet pipings of Lodge and Chapman and Shakespeare, to the undertones of Swinburne and Poe. There are endless combinations yet in the gamut. The report is that Mr. Whitman's prejudice is specially strong against our noblest unrhymed form, "blank-verse." Its variety and freedom, within a range of accents, breaks, caesural effects—its rolling organ-harmonies—he appreciates not at all. Rhythmical as his own verse often can be, our future poets scarcely will discard blank-verse in its behalf—not if they shall recall *The Tempest*, "Hail, Holy Light," "Tintern Abbey," "Hyperion," the "Hellenics," "Ulysses," and "Thanatopsis." Mr. Parke Godwin, in a recent private letter, terms it "the grandest and most flexible of English measures," and adds, with quick enthusiasm; "Oh, what a glory there is in it, when we think of what Shakespeare, Milton, Wordsworth and Landor made of it, to say nothing of Tennyson and Bryant!" I doubt not that new handlings of this measure will produce new results, unsurpassed in any tongue. It is quite as fit as Mr. Whitman's own, if he knows the use of it, for "the expression of American democracy and manhood." Seeing how dull and prolix he often becomes, it may be that even for him his measure has been too facile, and that the curb of a more regular unrhymed form would have spared us many tedious curvetings and grewsome downfalls.

Strenuous as he may be in his belief that the old methods will be useless to poets of the future, I am sure that he has learned the value of technique through his long practice. He well knows that whatever claims to be the poetry of the future speedily will be forgotten in the past, unless consonant with the laws of expression in the language to which it belongs; that verse composed upon a theory, if too artificial in its contempt of art, may be taken up for a while, but, as a false fashion, anon will pass away. Not that his verse is of this class; but it justly has been declared that, in writing with a purpose to introduce a new mode or revolutionize thought, and not because an irresistible impulse seizes him, a poet is so much the less a poet. Our question, then, involves the spontaneity of his work, and the results attained by him.

His present theory, like most theories which have reason, seems to be derived from experience: he has learned to discern the good and bad in his work, and has arrived at a rationale of it. He sees that he has been feeling after the irregular, various harmonies of nature, the anthem of the winds, the roll of the surges, the countless laughter of the ocean waves. He tries to catch this "under-melody and rhythm." Here is an artistic motive, distinguishing his chainless dithyrambs from ordinary verse, somewhat as the new German music is distinguished from folk-melody, and from the products of an early, especially the Italian, school. Here is not only reason, but a theoretical advance to a grade of art demanding extreme resources, because it affords the widest range of combination and effect.

But this comprehension of his own aim is an after-thought, the result of long groping. The genesis of the early "Leaves" was in motives less artistic and penetrating. Finding that he could not think and work to advantage in the current mode, he concluded that the mode itself was at fault; especially, that the poet of a young, gigantic nation, the prophet of a new era, should have a new vehicle of song. Without looking farther, he spewed out the old forms, and avowed his contempt for American poets who use them. His off-hand course does not bring us to the conclusion of the whole matter. So far as the crudeness of the *juventus mundi* is assumed by him, it must be temporal and passing, like the work of some painters, who, for the sake of startling effects, use ephemeral pigments. A poet does not, perforce, restore the lost foundations of his art by copying the manner natural to an aboriginal time and people. He is merely exchanging masters, and certainly is not founding a new school. Only as he discovers the inherent tendencies of song does he belong to the future. Still, it is plain that Whitman found a style suited to his purposes, and was fortunate both as a poet and a diplomatist. He was sure to attract notice, and to seem original, by so pronounced a method. Quoth the monk to Gargantua, "A mass, a matin, or vesper, well rung, is half said." It was suited to him as a poet, because he has that somewhat wandering sense of form, and of melody, which often makes one's conceptions seem the more glorious to himself, as if invested with a halo or blended with concurrent sound, and prevents him from lessening or enlarging them by the decisive master-hand, or at once perfecting them by sure control.

A man who finds that his gloves cripple him does right in drawing them off. At first, Whitman certainly meant to escape all technique. But genius, in spite of itself, makes works that stand the test of scientific laws. And thus he now sees that he was groping toward a broader technique. Unrhymed verse, the easiest to write, is the hardest to excel in, and no measure for a bardling. And Mr. Whitman never more nearly displayed the feeling of a true artist than when he expressed a doubt as to his present handling of his own verse, but hoped that, in breaking loose from ultra-marine forms, he had sounded, at least, the key for a new paean. I have referred to his gradual advances in the finish of his song. Whether he has revived a form which others will carry to a still higher excellence, is doubtful. Blank-verse, limitless in its capacities, forces a poet to stand without disguise, and reveals all his defects. Whitman's verse, it is true, does not subject him to so severe a test. He can so twist and turn himself, and run and jump, that we are puzzled to inspect him at all, or make out his contour. Yet the few who have ventured to follow him have produced little that has not seemed like parody, or unpleasantly grotesque. It may be that his mode is suited to himself alone, and not to the future poets of These States—that the next original genius will have to sing "as Martin Luther sang," and the glorious army of poetic worthies. I suspect that the old forms, in endless combinations, will return as long as new poets arise with the old abiding sense of time and sound.

The greatest poet is many-sided, and will hold himself slavishly to no one thing for the sake of difference. He is a poet, too, in spite of measure and material, while, as to manner, the style is the man. Genius does not need a special language; it newly uses whatever tongue it finds. Thought, fire, passion, will overtop everything—will show, like the limbs of Teverino, through the clothes of a prince or a beggar. A cheap and common instrument, odious in foolish hands, becomes the slave of music under the touch of a master. I attach less importance, therefore, to Mr. Whitman's experiment in verse than he and his critics have, and inquire of his mannerism simply how far it represents the man. To show how little there is in itself, we only have to think of Tupper; to see how rich it may be, when the utterance of genius, listen to Whitman's teacher, William Blake. It does not prove much, but still is interesting, to note that the pieces whose quality never fails with any class of hearers—of which "My Captain" is an example—are those in which our poet has approached most nearly, and in a lyrical, melodious manner, to the ordinary forms.

He is far more original in his style proper than in his metrical inventions. His diction, on its good behavior, is copious and strong, full of surprises, utilizing the brave, homely words of the people, and assigning new duties to common verbs and nouns. He has a use of his own for Spanish and French catch-words, picked up, it may be, on his trip to Louisiana or in Mexican war times. Among all this is much slang that now has lived its life, and is not understood by a new generation with a slang of its own. This does not offend so much as the mouthing verbiage, the "ostent evanescent" phrases, wherein he seems profoundest to himself, and really is at his worst. The titles of his books and poems are varied and sonorous. Those of the latter often are taken from the opening lines, and are keynotes. What can be fresher than "Leaves of Grass" and "Calamus"? What richer than "The Mystic Trumpeter," "O Star of France!" "Proud Music of the Storm," or simpler than "Drum-Taps," "The Wound-Dresser," "The Ox-Tamer"? or more characteristic than "Give me the Splendid Silent Sun," "Mannahatta," "As a Strong Bird on Pinions Free," "Joy, Shipmate, Joy"? Some are obscure and grandiose—"Eidolons," "Chanting the Square Deific," but usually his titles arrest the eye and haunt the ear; it is an artist that invents them, and the best pieces have the finest names. He has the art of "saying things"; his epithets, also, are racier than those of other poets; there is something of the Greek in Whitman, and his lovers call him Homeric, but to me he shall be our old American Hesiod, teaching us works and days.

His surest hold, then, is as an American poet, gifted with language, feeling, imagination, and inspired by a determined purpose. Some estimate, as I have said, may be made of his excellence and short-comings, without waiting for that national absorption which he himself declares to be the test.

As an assimilating poet of nature he has positive genius, and seems to me to present his strongest claims. Who else, in fact, has so true a hand or eye for the details, the sweep and color, of American landscape? Like others, he confronts those superb physical aspects of the New World which have controlled our poetry and painting, and deferred the growth of a figure-school, but in this conflict with nature he is not overcome; if not the master, he is the joyous brother-in-arms. He has heard the message of the pushing, wind-swept sea, along Paumanok's shore; he knows the yellow, waning moon and the rising stars—the sunset, with its cloud-bar of gold above the horizon—the birds that sing by night or day, bush and brier, and every shining or swooning flower, the peaks, the prairie, the mighty, conscious river, the dear common grass that children fetch with full hands. Little escapes him, not even "the mossy scabs of the worm fence, and heap'd stones, mullen and poke-weed"; but his details are massed, blended—the wind saturates and the light of the American skies transfigures them. Not that to me, recalling the penetrative glance of Emerson, the wood and way-side craft that Lowell carried lightly as a sprig of fir, and recalling other things of others, does Whitman seem our "only" poet of nature; but that here he is on his own ground, and with no man his leader.

Furthermore, his intimacy with nature is always subjective—she furnishes the background for his self-portraiture and his images of men. None so apt as he to observe the panorama of life, to see the human figure—the hay-maker, wagoner, boatman, soldier, woman and babe and maiden, and brown, lusty boy—to hear not only "the bravuras of birds, bustle of growing wheat, gossip of flames, clack of sticks cooking my meals," but also "the sound I love, the sound of the human voice." His town and country scenes, in peace or in war, are idyllic. Above the *genre*, for utter want of sympathy, he can only name and designate—he does not depict. A single sketch, done in some original way, often makes a poem; such is that reminiscence (in rhyme) of the old Southern negress, "Ethiopia Saluting the Colors," and such the touching conceit of Old Ireland—no fair and green-robed Hibernia of the harp, but an ancient, sorrowful mother, white-haired, lean and tattered, seated on the ground, mourning for her children. He tells her that they are not dead, but risen again, with rosy and new blood, in another country. This is admirable, I say, and the true way to escape tradition; this is imaginative,—and there is imagination, too, in his apostrophe to "The Man-of-War-Bird" (carried beyond discretion by this highest mood, he finds it hard to avoid blank-verse:

> Thou who hast slept all night upon the storm,
> Waking renewed on thy prodigious pinions!
>
> *   *   *   *   *   *
>
> Thou, born to match the gale (thou art all wings)!
> To cope with heaven and earth and sea and hurricane;
> Thou ship of air that never furl'st thy sails,

Days, even weeks, untried and onward, through
  spaces—realms gyrating.
At dark that look'st on Senegal, at morn, America;
That sport'st amid the lightning-flash and thunder-
  cloud!
In these—in thy experiences—hadst thou my soul,
What joys! What joys were thine!

Imagination is the essential thing; without it poetry is as sounding
brass or a tinkling cymbal. Whitman shows it in his sudden and novel imagery, and in the subjective rapture of verse like this, but quite as often his
vision is crowded and inconsistent. The editor of a New York magazine
writes to me: "In so far as imagination is thinking through types
(*eidullia*), Whitman has no equal," adding that he does not use the term
as if applied to Coleridge, but as limited to the use of types, and that "in
this sense it is really more applicable to a master of science than to a poet.
In the poet the type is lodged in his own heart, and when the occasion
comes . . . he is mastered by it, and he must sing. In Whitman the type is
not so much in his heart as in his thought. . . . While he is moved by
thought, often grand and elementary, he does not give the intellectual
satisfaction warranted by the thought, but a moving panorama of objects.
He not only puts aside his 'singing robes,' but his 'thinking-cap,' and
resorts to the stereopticon." How acute, how true! There is, however, a
peculiar quality in these long catalogues of types—such as those in the
"Song of the Broad-Axe" and "Salut au Monde," or, more poetically
treated, in "Longings for Home." The poet appeals to our synthetic vision. Look through a window; you see not only the framed landscape, but
each tree and stone and living thing. His page must be seized with the eye,
as a journalist reads a column at a glance, until successive "types" and
pages blend in the mind like the diverse colors of a swift-turning wheel.
Whitman's most inartistic fault is that he overdoes this method, as if
usually unable to compose in any other way.

The tenderness of a strong and robust nature is a winning feature of
his song. There is no love-making, no yearning for some idol of the heart.
In the lack of so refining a contrast to his realism, we have gentle thoughts
of children, images of grand old men, and of women clothed with sanctity
and years. This tenderness, a kind of natural piety, marks also his poems
relating to the oppressed, the suffering, the wounded and dying soldiers.
It is the soul of the pathetic, melodious threne for Lincoln, and of the
epilogue—"My Captain!" These pieces remind us that he has gained some
command of his own music, and in the matter of tone has displayed
strength from the first. In revising his early poems he has improved their
effect as a whole. It must be owned that his wheat often is more welcome
for the chaff in which it is scattered; there is none of the persistent luxury
which compels much of Swinburne's unstinted wealth to go unreckoned.
Finally, let us note that Whitman, long ago, was not unread in the few

The *Leaves of Grass*, in thought and method, avowedly are a protest against a hackney breed of singers, singing the same old song. More poets than one are born in each generation, yet Whitman has derided his compeers, scouted the sincerity of their passion, and has borne on his mouth Heine's sneer at the eunuchs singing of love. In two things he fairly did take the initiative, and might, like a wise advocate, rest his case upon them. He essayed, without reserve or sophistry, the full presentment of the natural man. He devoted his song to the future of his own country, accepting and outvying the loudest peak-and-prairie brag, and pledging These States to work out a perfect democracy and the salvation of the world. Striking words and venturesome deeds, for which he must have full credit. But in our studies of the ideal and its votaries, the failings of the latter cannnot be lightly passed over. There is an inconsistency, despite the gloss, between his fearful arraignment, going beyond Carlyle's, of the outgrowth of our democracy, thus far, and his promise for the future. In his prose, he sees neither physical nor moral health among us: all is disease, impotency, fraud, decline. In his verse, the average American is lauded as no type ever was before. These matters renew questions which, to say the least, are still open. Are the lines of caste less sharply divided every year, or are the high growing higher, and the low lower, under our democracy? Is not the social law of more import than the form of government, and has not the quality of race much to do with both? Does Americanism in speech and literature depend upon the form and letter, or upon the spirit? Can the spirit of literature do much more than express the national spirit as far as it has gone, and has it not, in fact, varied with the atmosphere? Is a nation changed by literature, or the latter by the former, in times when journalism so swiftly represents the thought and fashion of each day? As to distinctions in form and spirit between the Old-World literature and our own, I have always looked for this to enlarge with time. But with the recent increase of travel and communication, each side of the Atlantic now more than ever seems to affect the other. Our "native flavor" still is distinct in proportion to the youth of a section, and inversely to the development. It is an intellectual narrowness that fails to meditate upon these things.

Thus we come to a defect in Mr. Whitman's theories, reasoning and general attitude. He professes universality, absolute sympathy, breadth in morals, thought, workmanship—exemption from prejudice and formalism. Under all the high poetic excellences which I carefully have pointed out, I half suspect that his faults lie in the region where, to use his own word, he is most complacent: in brief, that a certain *narrowness* holds him within well-defined bounds. In many ways he does not conform to his creed. Others have faith in the future of America, with her arts and letters, yet hesitate to lay down rules for her adoption. These must come of themselves, or not at all. Again, in this poet's specification of the objects of his sympathy, the members of every class, the lofty and the lowly, are duly named; yet there always is an implication that the employer is inferior to the employed—that the man of training, the civilizee, is less manly than the rough, the pioneer. He suspects those who, by chance or ability, rise above the crowd. What attention he does pay them is felt to be in the nature of patronage, and insufferable. Other things being equal, a scholar is as good as an ignoramus, a rich man as a poor man, a civilizee as a boor. Great champions of democracy—poets like Byron, Shelley, Landor, Swinburne, Hugo—often have come from the ranks of long descent. It would be easy to cite verses from Whitman that apparently refute this statement of his feeling, but the spirit of his whole work confirms it. Meanwhile, though various editions of his poems have found a sale, he is little read by our common people, who know him so well, and of whose democracy he is the self-avowed herald. In numberless homes of working-men—and all Americans are workers—the books of other poets are treasured. Some mental grip and culture are required, of course, to get hold of the poetry of the future. But Whittier, in this land, is a truer type of the people's poet—the word "people" here meaning a vast body of freemen, having a common-school education, homes, an honest living, and a general comprehension far above that of the masses in Europe. These folk have an instinct that Whittier, for example, has seized his day with as much alertness and self-devotion as this other bard of Quaker lineage, and has sung songs "fit for the New World" as he found it. Whitman is more truly the voice and product of the culture of which he bids us beware. At least, he utters the cry of culture for escape from over-culture, from the weariness, the finical precision, of its own satiety. His warmest admirers are of several classes: those who have carried the art of verse to super-refined limits, and seeing nothing farther in that direction, break up the mold for a change; those radical enthusiasts who, like myself, are interested in whatever hopes to bring us more speedily to the golden year; lastly, those who, radically inclined, do not think closely, and make no distinction between his strength and weakness. Thus he is, in a sense, the poet of the over-refined and the doctrinaires. Such men, too, as Thoreau and Burroughs have a welcome that scarcely would have been given them in an earlier time. From the discord and artifice of our social life we go with them to the woods, learn to name the birds, note the beauty of form and flower, and love these healthy comrades who know each spring that bubbles beneath the lichened crag and trailing hemlock. Theocritus learns his notes upon the mountain, but sings in courts of Alexandria and Syracuse. Whitman, through propagandists who care for his teachings from metaphysical and personal causes, and compose their own ideals of the man, may yet reach the people, in spite of the fact that lasting works usually have pleased all classes in their own time.

Reflecting upon his metrical theory, we also find narrowness instead of breadth. I have shown that the bent of a liberal artist may lead him to adopt a special form, but not to reject all others; he will see the uses of each, demanding only that it shall be good in its kind. Swinburne, with his cordial liking for Whitman, is too acute to overlook his formalism. Some of his eulogists, those whom I greatly respect, fail in their special analysis. One of them rightly says that Shakespeare's sonnets are artificial, and that three lines which he selects from "Measure for Measure" are of a higher grade of verse. But these are the reverse of "unmeasured" lines—they are in Shakespeare's free and artistic, yet most measured, vein. Here comes in the distinction between art and artifice; the blank-verse is conceived in the broad spirit of the former, the finish and pedantry of the sonnet make it an artificial form. A master enjoys the task of making its artifice artistic, but does not employ it exclusively. Whitman's irregular, manneristic chant is *at the other extreme of artificiality*, and equally monotonous. A poet can use it with feeling and majesty; but to use it invariably, to laud it as the one mode of future expression, to decry all others, is formalism of a pronounced kind. I have intimated that Whitman has carefully studied and improved it. Even Mr. Burroughs does him injustice in admitting that he is not a poet and artist in the current acceptation of those terms, and another writer simply is just in declaring that when he undertakes to give us poetry he can do it. True, the long prose sentences thrown within his ruder pieces resemble nothing so much as the comic recitativos in the buffo-songs of the concert-cellars. This is not art, nor wisdom, but sensationalism. There is narrowness in his failure to recast and modify these and other depressing portions of various poems, and it is sheer Philistinism for one to coddle all the weaknesses of his experimental period, because they have been a product of himself.

One effect of the constant reading of his poetry is that, like the use of certain refections, it mars our taste for the proper enjoyment of other kinds. Not, of course, because it is wholly superior, since the subtlest landscape by Corot or Rousseau might be utterly put to nought by a melodramatic neighbor, full of positive color and extravagance. Nor is it always, either, to our bard's advantage that he should be read with other poets. Consider Wordsworth's exquisite lyric upon the education which Nature gives the child whom to herself she takes, and of whom she declares:

> The stars of midnight shall be dear
> To her; and she shall lean her ear
> In many a secret place,
> Where rivulets dance their wayward round,
> And beauty born of murmuring sound
> Shall pass into her face.

It happens that Whitman has a poem on the same theme, describing the process of growth by sympathy and absorption, which thus begins and ends:

There was a child went forth every day;
And the first object he look'd upon, that object he
became;
And that object became part of him for the day,
or a certain part of the day, or for many years,
or stretching cycles of years.

*   *   *   *   *   *   *

The horizon's edge, the flying sea-crow, the
fragrance of salt-mash and shore-mud;
These became part of that child who went forth
every day, and who now goes, and will always go
forth every day.

Plainly there are some comparative advantages in Wordsworth's treatment of this idea. It would be just as easy to reverse this showing by quoting other passages from each poet: the purpose of my digression is to declare that by means of comparative criticism any poet may be judged unfairly, and without regard to his general claims.

So far as Mr. Whitman's formalism is natural to him, no matter how eccentric, we must bear with it; whenever it partakes of affectation, it is not to be desired. The charge of attitudinizing, so often brought against his writings and personal career, may be the result of a popular impression that the border-line is indistinct between his self-assertion as a type of Man, and the ordinary self-esteem and self-advancement displayed by men of common mold. Pretensions have this advantage, that they challenge analysis, and make a vast noise even as we are forced to examine them. In the early preface to the *Leaves* there is a passage modeled, in my opinion, upon the style of Emerson, concerning simplicity—with which I heartily agree, having constantly insisted upon the test of simplicity in my discussion of the English poets. Yet this quality is the last to be discerned in many portions of the *Leaves of Grass*. In its stead we often find boldness, and the "pride that apes humility"—until the reader is tempted to quote from the "Poet of Feudalism" those words of Cornwall upon the roughness which brought good Kent to the stocks. Our bard's self-assertion, when the expression of his real manhood, is bracing, is an element of poetic strength. When it even seems to be "posing," it is a weakness, or a shrewdness, and 'tis a weakness in a poet to be unduly shrewd. Or course a distinction must be carefully made between the fine extravagance of genius, the joy in its own conceptions, and self-conscious vanity or affectation—between, also, occasional weaknesses of the great, of men like Browning, and like the greatest of living masters, Hugo, and the afflatus of small men, who only thus far succeed in copying them. And it would be unjust to reckon Whitman among the latter class.

Doubtless his intolerant strictures upon the poets of his own land and time have made them hesitate to venture upon the first advances in brotherhood, or to intrude on him with their recognition of his birthright. As late as his latest edition, his opinion of their uselessness has been expressed in withering terms. It may be that this is merely consistent, an absolute corollary of his new propositions. There is no consistency, however, in a complaint of the silence in which they have submitted to his judgments. They listen to epithets which Heine spared Platen and his clique, and surely Heine would have disdained to permit a cry to go up in his behalf concerning a want of recognition and encouragement from the luckless victims of his irony. There is ground enough for his scorn of the time-serving, unsubstantial quality of much of our literature. But I should not be writing this series of papers, did I not well know that there are other poets than himself who hear the roll of the ages, who look before and after, above and below. The culture which he deprecates may have done them an ill turn in lessening their worldly tact. I am aware that Mr. Whitman's poems are the drama of his own life and passions. His subjectivity is so great that he not only absorbs all others into himself, but insists upon being absorbed by whomsoever he addresses. In his conception of the world's equality, the singer himself appears as the one Messianic personage, the answerer and sustainer, the universal solvent—in all these respects holding even "Him that was crucified" to be not one whit his superior. It is his kiss, his consolation, that all must receive—whoever you are, these are given especially to you. But men are egotists, and not all tolerant of one man's selfhood; they do not always deem the affinities elective. Whitman's personality is too strong and individual to be universal, and even to him it is not given to be all things to all men.

["I differ from him utterly"]

Sidney Lanier*

Here let me first carefully disclaim and condemn all that flippant and sneering tone which dominates so many discussions of Whitman. While I differ from him utterly as to every principle of artistic procedure; while he seems to me the most stupendously mistaken man in all history as to what constitutes true democracy, and the true advance of art and man; while I am immeasurably shocked at the sweeping invasions of those reserves which depend on the very personality I have so much insisted upon, and which the whole consensus of the ages has considered more and more sacred with every year of growth in delicacy; yet, after all these prodigious allowances, I owe some keen delights to a certain combination of bigness and naivety which make some of Whitman's passages so strong and taking, and indeed, on the one occasion when Whitman has abandoned his theory of formlessness and written in form he has made "My Captain, O my Captain," ["O Captain, My Captain"] surely one of the most tender and beautiful poems in any language.

I need quote but a few scraps from characteristic sentences here and there in a recent paper of Whitman's in order to present a perfectly fair view of his whole doctrine. When, for instance, he declares that Tennyson's poetry is not the poetry of the future because, although it is "the highest order of verbal melody, exquisitely clean and pure and almost always perfumed like the tube-rose to an extreme of sweetness," yet it has "never one democratic page," and is "never free, naive poetry, but involved, labored, quite sophisticated"; when we find him bragging of "the measureless viciousness of the great radical republic" (the United States, of course) "with its ruffianly nominations and elections; its loud, ill-pitched voice, utterly regardless whether the verb agrees with the nominative; its fights, errors, eructations, repulsions, dishonesties, audacities; those fearful and varied, long and continued storm-and-stress stages (so offensive to the well-regulated, college-bred mind) wherewith nature, history and time block out nationalities more powerful than the

*Reprinted from *The English Novel: A Study in the Development of Personality* (New York: Charles Scribner's Sons, 1897), pp. 45–47, 50–54, 62–65. These extracts originally were part of two lectures given at Johns Hopkins in 1881.

128

past"; and when finally we hear him tenderly declaring that "meanwhile democracy waits the coming of its bards in silence and in twilight—but 'tis the twilight of dawn"—we are in sufficient possession of the distinctive catch-words which summarize his doctrine.

In examining it, a circumstance occurs to me at the outset which throws a strange but effective light upon the whole argument. It seems curious to reflect that the two poets who have most avowedly written for the people, who have claimed most distinctively to represent and embody the thought of the people, and to be bone of people's bone and flesh of the people's flesh, are precisely the two who have most signally failed of all popular acceptance and who have most exclusively found audience at the other extreme of culture. These are Wordsworth and Whitman. We all know how strenuously and faithfully Wordsworth believed that in using the simplest words and treating the lowliest themes, he was bringing poetry back near to the popular heart; yet Wordsworth's greatest admirer is Mr. Matthew Arnold, the apostle of culture, the farthest remove from anything that could be called popular: and in point of fact it is probable that many a peasant who would feel his blood stir in hearing, *A man's a man for a' that*, would grin and guffaw if you read him Wordsworth's *Lambs* and *Peter Grays*.

And a precisely similar fate has met Whitman. Professing to be a mudsill and glorying in it, chanting democracy and shirt-sleeves and equal rights, declaring that he is nothing if not one of the people, nevertheless the people, the democracy, will yet have nothing to do with him, and it is safe to say that his sole audience has lain among such representatives of the highest culture as Emerson and the English *illuminated*.

The truth is, that if closely examined, Whitman, instead of being a true democrat, is simply the most incorrigible of aristocrats masquing in a peasant's costume, and his poetry, instead of being the natural outcome of a fresh young democracy, is a product which would be impossible except in a highly civilized society.

Returning to our outline of the last lecture: After we had discussed this matter, we advanced to the second of the great misconceptions of the function of form in art—that which holds that the imaginative effort of the future will be better than that of the present, and that this improvement will come through a progress towards formlessness. After quoting several sentences from Whitman which seemed to contain the substantial argument—to-wit, that the poetry of the future is to be signalized by the independence of form, and is, by virtue of this independence, to gain strength, and become a democratic poetry, as contrasted with the supposed weak and aristocratic poetry of the present—I called your attention to a notable circumstance which seems to throw a curious light along this inquiry: that circumstance being that the two English poets who have most exclusively laid claim to represent the people in poetry, to express nothing but the people's heart in the people's words, namely, Wordsworth and Whitman, are precisely the two whose audience has been most exclusively confined to the other extreme of culture. Wordsworth, instead of appealing to Hodge, Nokes, and Stiles, instead of being found in penny editions on the collier's shelves, is most cherished by Mr. Matthew Arnold, the high-priest of culture. And so with Whitman. We may say with safety that no preacher was ever so decisively rejected by his own: continually crying democracy in the market-place, and crying it in forms or no-forms professing to be nothing but products of the democratic spirit, nevertheless the democracy everywhere have turned a deaf ear, and it is only a few of the most sober and retired thinkers of our time that Whitman has found even a partial acceptance.

And finally by way of showing a reason for this state of things in Whitman's case, the last lecture closed with the assertion that Whitman's poetry, in spite of his belief (which I feel sure is most earnest) that it is democratic, is really aristocratic to the last degree; and instead of belonging, as he claims, to an early and fresh-thoughted stage of a republic, is really poetry which would be impossible except in a highly civilized state of society.

Here, then, let us take up the thread of that argument. In the quotations which were given from Whitman's paper, we have really the ideal democracy and democrat of this school. It is curious to reflect in the first place that in point of fact no such democracy, no such democrat, has ever existed in this country. For example: when Whitman tells us of "the measureless viciousness of the great radical republic, with its ruffianly nominations and elections; its loud, ill-pitched voice; its fights, errors, eructations, dishonesties, audacities, those fearful and varied storm-and-stress stages (so offensive to the well-regulated, college-bred mind) wherewith nature, history and time block out nationalities more powerful than the past"; when he tells us this, with a sort of caressing touch upon all the bad adjectives, rolling the "errors" and the "audacities" and the "visciousness" under his tongue and faithfully believing that the strength which recommends his future poetry is to come out of viciousness and ruffianly elections and the like: let us inquire, to what representative facts in our history does this picture correspond, what great democrat who has helped to block out this present republic sat for this portrait? Is it George Washington, that beautiful, broad, tranquil spirit whom, I sometimes think, even we Americans have never yet held quite at his true value—is it Washington who was vicious, dishonest, audacious, combative? But Washington had some hand in blocking out this republic. Or what would our courtly and philosophic Thomas Jefferson look like if you should put this slouch hat on him, and open his shirt-front at the bosom, and set him to presiding over a ruffianly nomination? Yet he had some hand in blocking out this republic. In one of Whitman's poems I find him crying out to Americans, in this same strain: "O lands! would you be freer than all that has ever been before? If you would be freer than all that has been before, come listen to me." And this is the deliverance:

> Fear grace—fear elegance, civilization, delicatesse,
> Fear the mellow sweet, the sucking of honey-juice;
> Beware the advancing mortal ripening of nature,
> Beware what precedes the decay of the ruggedness
>   of States and men.

And in another line, he rejoices in American because—"Here are the roughs, beards, . . . combativeness," and the like.

But where are these roughs, these beards, and this combativeness? Were the Adamses and Benjamin Franklin roughs? was it these who taught us to make ruffianly nominations? But they had some hand in blocking out this republic. In short, leaving each one to extend this list of names for himself, it may be fairly said that nowhere in history can one find less of that ruggedness which Whitman regards as the essential of democracy, nowhere more of that grace which he considers fatal to it, than among the very representative democrats who blocked out this republic. In truth, when Whitman cries, "fear the mellow sweet," and "beware the moral ripening of nature," we have an instructive instance of the extreme folly into which a man may be led by mistaking a metaphor for an argument. The argument here is, you observe, that because an apple in the course of nature rots soon after it mellows, *argal* a man cannot mellow his spirit with culture without decaying soon afterwards. Of course it is sufficient only to reflect *non sequitur*: for it is precisely the difference between the man and the apple that whereas every apple must rot after ripeness no man is bound to.

If therefore after an inquiry ranging from Washington and Jefferson down to William Cullen Bryant (that surely unrugged and graceful figure who was so often called the finest American gentleman) and Lowell and Longfellow and the rest who are really the men that are blocking out our republic—if we find not a single representative American democrat to whom any of these pet adjectives apply—not one who is measurelessly vicious, or ruffianly, or audacious, or purposely rugged, or contemptuous towards the graces of life—then we are obliged to affirm that the whole ideal drawn by Whitman, is a fancy picture with no counterpart in nature. It is perfectly true that we have ruffianly nominations; but we have them because the real democrats who govern our republic, who represent our democracy, stay away from nominating conventions and leave them to the ruffians. Surely no one can look with the most cursory eye upon our everyday American life without seeing that the real advance of our society goes on not only without, but largely in spite of that ostensible apparatus, legislative, executive, judicial which we call the Government—that really the most effective legislation in our country is that which is enacted in the breasts of the individual democrats who compose it. And this is true democratic growth: every day, more and more, each man perceives that the shortest and most effectual method of securing his own rights is to respect the rights of others, and so every day do we less and less need outside interference in our individual relations; so that every day we approach nearer and nearer towards that ideal government in which each man is mainly his own legislator, his own governor or president, and his own judge, and in which the public government is mainly a concert of measures for the common sanitation and police.

But again: it is true as Whitman says that we have dishonesties; but we punish them, they are not representative, they have no more relation to democracy than the English thief has to English aristocracy.

I find some deliverances in Epictetus which speak so closely to more than one of the points just discussed that I must quote a sentence or two. "What then," he says in the chapter "About Freedom," "is that which makes a man free from hindrance and makes him his own master? For wealth does not do it, nor consulship, nor provincial government, nor royal power; but something else must be discovered. What then is that which when we write makes us free from hindrance and unimpeded? The knowledge of the art of writing. What then is it (which gives freedom) in playing the lute? The science of playing the lute." If Whitman's doctrine is true, the proper method of acquiring freedom on the lute is to bring lute-music to that point where the loud jangling chord produced by a big hand sweeping at random across the strings is to take the place of the finical tunes and harmonies now held in esteem. "Therefore," continues Epictetus, "in life, also, it is the science of life. . . . When you wish the body to be sound, is it in your power or not?—It is not. When you wish it to be healthy? Neither is this in my power?" (I complain of Whitman's democracy that it has no provision for sick, or small, or puny, or plain-featured, or hump-backed, or any deformed people, and that his democracy is really the worst kind of aristocracy, being an aristocracy of nature's favorites in the matter of muscle.) And so of estate, house, horses, life and death—Epictetus continues; these are not in our power, they cannot make us free. So that, in another chapter, he cries: "This is the true athlete, the man who exercises himself against such appearances. Stay, wretch, do not be carried away. Great is the combat, divine is the work: it is for kingship, for freedom, for happiness."

And lastly, the Poetry of the Future holds that all modern poetry, Tennyson particularly, is dainty and over-perfumed, and Whitman speaks of it with the contempt which he everywhere affects for the dandy. But surely—I do not mean this disrespectfully—what age of time ever yielded such a dandy as the founder of this school, Whitman himself? The simpering beau who is the product of the tailor's art is certainly absurd enough; but what difference is there between that and the other dandy-upside-down who from equal motives of affection throws away coat and vest, dons a slouch hat, opens his shirt so as to expose his breast, and industriously circulates his portrait, thus taken, in his own books. And this dandyism—the dandyism of the roustabout—I find in Whitman's poetry from beginning to end. Everywhere it is conscious of itself, everywhere it is analyzing itself, everywhere it is posing to see if it cannot assume a naive and striking attitude, everywhere it is screwing up its eyes, not into an eyeglass like the conventional dandy, but into an expression supposed to be fearsomely rough and barbaric and frightful to the terror-stricken reader, and it is almost safe to say that one half of Whitman's poetic work has consisted of a detailed description of the song he is going to sing. It is the extreme of sophistication in writing.

But if we must have dandyism in our art, surely the softer sort, which at least leans towards decorum and gentility, is preferable; for that at worst becomes only laughable, while the rude dandyism, when it does acquire a factitious interest by being a blasphemy against real manhood, is simply tiresome.

I have thus dwelt upon these claims of the Whitman school, not so much because of any intrinsic weight they possess, as because they are advanced in such taking and sacred names—of democracy, of manhood, of freedom, of progress. Upon the most earnest examination, I can find it nothing but wholly undemocratic; not manful, but dandy; not free, because the slave of nature; not progressive, because its whole momentum is derived from the physical-large which ceased to astonish the world ages ago, in comparison with spiritual greatness.

Indeed, this matter has been pushed so far, with the apparent, but wholly unreal sanction of so many influential names, that in speaking to those who may be poets of the future, I cannot close these hasty words upon the Whitman school without a fervent protest, in the name of all art and all artists, against a poetry which has painted a great scrawling picture of the human body and has written under it, "This is the soul"; which shouts a profession of religion in every line, but of a religion that, when examined, reveals no tenet, no rubric, save that a man must be natural, must abandon himself to every passion; and which constantly roars its belief in God, but with a comerado air as if it were patting the Diety on the back and bidding Him *Cheer up* and hope for further encouragement.

It seems like a curious sarcasm of time that even the form of Whitman's poetry is not poetry of the future but tends constantly into the rhythm of

Brimmanna boda abeod eft ongean.

which is the earliest rhythm of our poetry. The only difference which Whitman makes is in rejecting the alliteration, in changing the line-division, so as to admit longer lines, and the allowance of much liberty in interrupting this general rhythm for a moment. It is remarkable indeed that this old rhythm is still distinctly the prevalent rhythm of English prose.

Some years ago Walter Savage Landor remarked that the dactyl was "the bindweed of English prose," and by the dactyl he means simply a word of three syllables with the accent on the first, like Brimmanna. For example

> I loaf and invite my soul;
> I lean and loaf at my ease, observing a spear of
>   summer grass.
> I exist as I am—that is enough;
> If no other in the world be aware, I sit content;
> And if each and all be aware I sit content
> Washes and razors for foofoos, and for me freckles
>   and a bristling beard.
>
> "Walt Whitman am I, a cosmos of mighty Manhattan
>   the sun."[1]

Note

1. ". . . of mighty Manhattan the son" is the reading in the 1867 edition of *Leaves of Grass*. Whether this is a typographical error or Lanier's attempt at a pun or a put-down is hard to say.

[A Letter to Robert Bridges]

Gerard Manly Hopkins*

Stonyhurst College, Blackburn.
Oct. 18, 1882.

Dearest Bridges—I have read of Whitman's (1) 'Pete' ["Come Up from the Fields Father"] in the library at Bedford Square (and perhaps something else; if so I forget), which you pointed out; (2) two pieces in the *Athenaeum* or *Academy*, one on the Man-of-War Bird, the other beginning "Spirit that formed this scene"; (3) short extracts in a review by Saintsbury in the *Academy*: this is all I remember. I cannot have read more than half a dozen pieces at most.

This, though very little, is quite enough to give a strong impression of his marked and original manner and way of thought and in particular of his rhythm. It might be even enough, I shall not deny, to originate or, much more, influence another's style: they say the French trace their whole modern school of landscape to a single piece of Constable's exhibited at the Salon early this century.

The question then is only about the fact. But first I may as well say what I should not otherwise have said, that I always knew in my heart Walt Whitman's mind to be more like my own than any other man's living. As he is a very great scoundrel this is not a pleasant confession. And this also makes me the more desirous to read him and the more determined that I will not.

Nevertheless I believe that you are quite mistaken about this piece and that on second thoughts you will find the fancied resemblance diminish and the imitation disappear.

And first of the rhythm. Of course I saw that there was to the eye something in my long lines like his, that the one would remind people of the other. And both are in irregular rhythms. There the likeness ends. The pieces of his I read were mostly in an irregular rhythmic prose: that is what they are thought to be meant for and what they seemed to me to be. Here is a fragment of a line I remember: "or a handkerchief designedly dropped." This is in a dactylic rhythm—or let us say anapaestic; for it is a

*Reprinted from *The Letters of Gerard Manly Hopkins to Robert Bridges*, ed. Claude Colleer Abbott (London: Oxford Univ. Press, 1935), pp. 154–58.

great convenience in English to assume that the stress is always at the end of the foot; the consequence of which assumption is that in ordinary verse there are only two English feet possible, the iamb and the anapaest, and even in my regular sprung rhythm only one additional, the fourth paeon: for convenience' sake assuming this, then the above fragment is anapaestic—"or a hánd | kerchíef . . . | . desígn | edly drópped"—and there is a break down, a designed break of rhythm, after "handkerchief," done no doubt that the line may not become downright verse, as it would be if he had said "or a handkerchief purposely dropped." Now you can of course say that he meant pure verse and that the foot is a paeon—"or a hánd | kerchíef desígn | edly drópped," or that he means, without fuss, what I should achieve by looping the syllable *de* and calling that foot an out-riding foot—for the result might be attained either way. Here then I must make the answer which will apply here and to all like cases and to the examples which may be found up and down the poets of the use of sprung rhythm—*if they could have done it they would*: sprung rhythm, once you hear it, is so eminently natural a thing and so effective a thing that if they had known of it they would have used it. Many a people, as we say, have been "burning," but they all missed it; they took it up and mislaid it again. So far as I know—I am enquiring and presently I shall be able to speak more decidedly—it existed in full force in Anglo saxon verse and in great beauty; in a degraded and doggrel shape in *Piers Ploughman* (I am reading that famous poem and am coming to the conclusion that it is not worth reading); Greene was the last who employed it at all consciously and he never continuously; then it disappeared—for one cadence in it here and there is not sprung rhythm and one swallow does not make a spring. (I put aside Milton's case, for it is altogether singular.) In a matter like this a thing does not exist, is not *done* unless it is wittingly and willingly done; to recognise the form you are employing and to mean it is everything. To apply this: there is (I suppose, but you will know) no sign that Whitman means to use paeons or outriding feet where these breaks in rhythm occur; it seems to me a mere extravagance to think he means people to understand of themselves what they are slow to understand even when marked or pointed out. If he does not mean it then he does not do it; or in short what he means to write—and writes—is rhythmic prose and that only. And after all, you probably grant this.

     Good. Now prose rhythm in English is always one of two things (allowing my convention about scanning upwards or from slack to stress and not from stress to slack)—either iambic or anapaestic. You may make a third measure (let us call it) by intermixing them. One of these three simple measures then, all iambic or all anapaestic or mingled iambic and anapaestic, is what he in every case means to write. He dreams of no other and he *means* a rugged or, as he calls it in that very piece "Spirit that formed this scene" (which is very instructive and should be read on this very subject), a "savage" art and rhythm.

Extremes meet, and (I must for truth's sake say what sounds pride) this savagery of his art, this rhythm in its last ruggedness and decomposition into common prose, comes near the last elaboration of mine. For that piece of mine is very highly wrought. The long lines are not rhythm run to seed: everything is weighed and timed in them. Wait till they have taken hold of your ear and you will find it so. No, but what it *is* like is the rhythm of Greek tragic choruses or of Pindar: which is pure sprung rhythm. And that has the same changes of cadence from point to point as this piece. If you want to try it, read one till you have settled the true places of the stress, mark these, then read it aloud, and you will see. Without this these choruses are prose bewitched; with it they are sprung rhythm like that piece of mine.

Besides, why did you not say *Binsey Poplars* was like Whitman? The present piece is in the same kind and vein, but developed, an advance. The lines and the stanzas (of which there are two in each poem and having much the same relation to one another) are both longer, but the two pieces are greatly alike: just look. If so how is this a being untrue to myself? I am sure it is no such thing.

The above remarks are not meant to run down Whitman. His "savage" style has advantages, and he has chosen it; he says so. But you cannot eat your cake and keep it: he eats his offhand, I keep mine. It makes a very great difference. Neither do I deny all resemblance. In particular I noticed in "Spirit that formed this scene" a preference for the alexandrine. I have the same preference: I came to it by degrees, I did not take it from him.

About diction the matter does not allow me so clearly to point out my independence as about rhythm. I cannot think that the present piece owes anything to him. I hope not, here especially, for it is not even spoken in my own person but in that of St. Winefred's maidens. It ought to sound like the thoughts of a good but lively girl and not at all like — not at all like Walt Whitman. But perhaps your mind may have changed by this.

I wish I had not spent so much time in defending the piece.

Believe me your affectionate friend

GERARD

Walt Whitman, Chapter III:
Analysis of Poems, Continued

Richard Maurice Bucke*

I have now reviewed briefly from my point of view the book in which Walt Whitman has, as far as such a thing is possible, embodied himself. It remains to state as well as I can the inner and more specific significance of the poems. After their unquestionable birthmarks, so different from European models or from any copied or foreign type whatever, the first thing to be noticed about *Leaves of Grass* (this is what strikes nearly every one immediately upon trying to read it) is the difficulty to the ordinary, even intelligent reader, of understanding it. On this point my own experience has been as follows. About eighteen years ago, I began to read it. For many months I could see absolutely nothing in the book, and at times I was strongly inclined to believe that there was nothing in it to see. But I could not let it alone; although one day I would throw it down in a sort of rage at its want of meaning, the next day or the day after I would take it up again with just as lively an interest as ever, persuaded that there was something there, and determined to find out what that might be. At first as I read, it seemed to me the writer was always on the point of saying something which he never actually said. Page after page seemed equally barren of any definite statement. Then after a time, I found that a few lines here and there were full of suggestion and beauty. Gradually these bright spots, as I may call them, grew larger, more numerous and more brilliant, until at last the whole surface was lit up with an almost unearthly splendor.

And still I am well aware that I do not yet fully understand this book. Neither do I expect ever to understand it entirely, though I learn something more about it almost everyday, and shall probably go on reading it as long as I live. I doubt whether I fully understand any part of it. For the more it is studied the more profound it is seen to be, stretching out vista beyond vista apparently interminably. Now it may seem strange that any person should go on reading a book he could not understand, and consequently, could in the ordinary way take no interest. The explanation is that there is the same peculiar magnetism about *Leaves of Grass* as about Walt Whitman himself, so that people who once really begin to read it

*Reprinted from Bucke, pp. 175–83.

138

and get into the range of its attraction, must go on reading it whether they comprehend it or not, or until they do comprehend it. As Walt Whitman says:

> I teach straying from me, yet who can stray from me?
> I follow you whoever you are from the present hour,
> My words itch at your ears till you understand them.

But after all, granting that this is true, is it worth while to read any book for years on the mere chance of understanding it at last? Certainly it would not be worth while with many books, but I will answer for it that no one who reads *Leaves of Grass* so as to understand it at all will ever repent the time and pains. For this is not a book that merely amuses or instructs. It does neither of these in the ordinary sense, but it does far more than amuse or instruct. It is capable of making whoever wishes to be so, wiser, happier, better; and it does these not by acting on the intellect, by telling us what is best for us, what we ought to do and avoid doing, and the like, but by acting directly on the moral nature itself, and elevating and purifying that. Why is this book so hard to understand? In the first place it is worth while to notice that the author of *Leaves of Grass* was himself well aware of this difficulty, as he says in the two following and in many other places:

> But these leaves conning you con at peril,
> For these leaves and me you will not understand,
> They will elude you at first, and still more afterward, I will certainly elude
>   you,
> Even while you should think you had unquestionably caught me, behold!
> Already you see I have escaped from you.

Then in the lines "To a Certain Civilian":

> Did you ask dulcet rhymes from me?
> Did you seek the civilian's peaceful and languishing rhymes?
> Did you find what I sang erewhile so hard to follow?
> Why I was not singing erewhile for you to follow, to understand—nor am I
>   now;
> (I have been born of the same as the war was born,
> The drum-corps' rattle is ever to me sweet music—I loved well the martial
>   dirge,
> With slow wail and convulsive throb leading the officer's funeral;)
> What to such as you anyhow such a poet as I? therefore leave my works,
> And go lull yourself with what you can understand, and with piano-tunes,
> For I lull nobody, and you will never understand me.

Are we to conclude that Walt Whitman wished and intended his writings to be difficult of comprehension? I do not think so at all. I think he would gladly have every one comprehend him at once if possible. Must we suppose then that he had not the ability to so write as to make himself easily intelligible? that in fact he is deficient in the faculty of clear expression? On the contrary I should say that Walt Whitman is a supreme master of the art of expression. In a case like this there is some one else besides the poet who may be to blame, and perhaps the fault may lie with—the reader. Must we say then that ordinary men, or even able men (for many of these have tried to read *Leaves of Grass* and failed), have not sufficient intelligence to comprehend the book? No, I neither say nor believe this.

The fact is, in the ordinary sense, there is nothing to understand about *Leaves of Grass* which any person of average intelligence could not comprehend with the greatest ease. The secret of the difficulty is, that the work, different from every popular book of poetry known, appeals almost entirely to the moral nature, and hardly at all to the intellect—that to understand it means putting oneself in emotional, and not simply mental relation with its author—means to thoroughly realize Walt Whitman—to be in sympathy with the heart and mind of perhaps the most advanced nature the world has yet produced. This, of course, is neither simple nor easy. *Leaves of Grass* is a picture of the world as seen from the standpoint of the highest moral elevation yet reached. It is at the same time an exposition of this highest moral nature itself. The real difficulty is for an ordinary person to rise to this spiritual altitude. Whoever can do so, even momentarily, or in imagination, will never cease to thank the man by whose aid this was accomplished. It is such assistance which Walt Whitman is destined to give to large sections of the human race, and doubtless it is this which he refers to in the following passages:

I am he bringing help for the sick as they pant on their backs,
And for strong upright men I bring yet more needed help.

Behold, I do not give lectures or a little charity,
When I give I give myself.

I bring what you much need yet always have,
Not money, amours, dress, eating, erudition, but as good,
I send no agent or medium, offer no representative of value, but offer the value
    itself.

For I myself am not one who bestows nothing upon man and woman.
For I bestow upon any man or woman the entrance to all the gifts of the universe.

Now, in the mouth of any man known to history, with very few exceptions, these claims would be ludicrous. They would not, however, have been ludicrous if we suppose them made by such men as Siddhartha Gautama, Confucius, Zoroaster, or Mohammed, for these men did as far as it was possible in their times and lands what Walt Whitman in these verses promises to do now—that is, they bestowed their own higher natures upon all who came under their influence, gave them the help they most needed, and opened to them (the best gift of all) the way to a higher spiritual life. They made such claims, and fulfilled them. Walt Whitman too makes them. Can he fulfil them? I say he has done so, and that he will do so throughout the future.

But let us examine this question and these claims a little more in detail, and see what they really mean. Whoever will consider them will see that they all amount essentially to the same thing, which is a promise on Walt Whitman's part to bestow upon any person who asks it, and who will put his or her mind in full relation with the poems, moral elevation. In other words, he will give to such person a greater amount of faith, a greater power of affection, and will consequently reduce in that person the liability to, and the capacity of, fear and hate. Now, love and faith are the elements of which happiness is composed, and hate and fear (their opposites) are the elements of which unhappiness is composed. If, therefore, Walt Whitman can produce in us moral elevation, he will increase our true happiness, and this, to my mind, is the most valuable of all the "gifts of the universe" so far, at all events, as we know at present. Again: modern science has made it capable of proof that this universe is so constructed as to justify on our part love and faith, and not hate and fear. For this reason, the man who has in his composition the most love and faith, and the least hate and fear, will stand (other things being equal) in the closest relation to universal truth—that is, he will be the wisest man. If, then, Walt Whitman gives us moral elevation, he will also give wisdom, which, it seems to me, is clearly another of the chief "gifts of the universe." Yet once more: conduct flows from moral nature. The man with a low moral nature who is full of hate and fear, and the compounds of these, such as envy and jealousy, cannot possibly live a beneficient and happy life. On the other hand, it is inconceivable that the man who is full of love and faith should, on the whole, live a bad life. So that moral elevation, besides giving us happiness and wisdom, gives us also the power and inclination to lead good lives; and this, I should say, is another "gift of the universe" really worth having, in contradistinction to mere wealth, education, social position, or fame, which the current standards make the main objects of existence.

Let us not forget that of all mental qualities, exceptional moral elevation is the hardest to see. So true is this, that in the whole history of our race, as far back as it is known, every man, without one exception, who has stood prominently in advance of and above his age by this quality, has not only not been considered exceptionally good, but has been in every instance looked upon by the majority of his contemporaries as a bad man, and has been consequently traduced, banished, burned, poisoned, or crucified.

In philosophy, science, art, religion, men's views, their ways of looking at things, are constantly altering. And it is equally plain that on the whole they are altering for the better—are constantly acquiring a more just and worthy mental attitude towards their surroundings, towards each other, and towards Nature. This progress necessitates the constant abandonment of old ideas, and the constant taking up of new intellectual and moral positions. These successive readjustments are always the cause of more or less social, political, and literary disturbance. The antagonism is naturally deeper and stronger in the case of religious and social changes than new departures in science, philosophy, or art, since in religious tenets the feelings are more deeply involved. The men who initiate such readjustments of the soul of man to its environment are the master minds of the race. These are the men Walt Whitman calls Poets. He says: "The true Poet is not the follower of beauty, but the august master of beauty." That is to say, he does not take merely the matter recognized as beautiful already and make it the theme of his verse, or amuse himself and his readers by dressing it up and admiring and praising it. This, in the language of *Leaves of Grass*, is the office of a "singer," not of a "Poet"; to do this is to be a follower of beauty. But the Poet is the master of beauty, and his mastery consists in commanding and causing things which were not before considered beautiful to become so. How does he do this? Before this question can be answered we must understand why one thing is beautiful to us and another not—why persons, combinations, etc., that are beautiful to one are often not so to another—and why one man sees so much beauty in the world, another so little. The explanation is, that beauty and love are correlatives; they are the objective and subjective aspects of the same thing. Beauty has no existence apart from love, and love has no existence apart from beauty. Beauty is the shadow of love thrown upon the outer world. We do not love a person or thing because the person or thing is beautiful, but whatever we love, that is beautiful to us, and whatever we do not love, is not beautiful. And the function of the true Poet is to love and appreciate all things, nationalities, laws, combinations, individuals. He alone illustrates the sublime reality and ideality of that verse of Genesis, how God after His entire creation looked forth, "and pronounced it *all* good." A parallel statement would be true of Faith. As that which is seen from without inwards is love, and seen from within outwards is beauty, so that which seen from without inwards is faith, is goodness when seen from within outwards.

The human race began by fearing or distrusting nearly everything, and trusting almost nothing; and this is yet the condition of savages. But from time to time, men arose who distrusted and feared less and less. These men have always been considered impious by those about them; but for all that, they have been the saviors and progressists of the race, and have been recognized as such when their views and feelings penetrated the generations succeeding them. Such evolution has always been going on, and will continue. So far, fear has been a part of every accepted religion, and it is still taught that to destroy fear is to destroy religion. But if faith is to increase, fear, its opposite, must continually decrease and at last disappear. Fear is the basis of superstition. Faith, its opposite, along with love, is the basis of religion. I know it is still said by some to-day in the name of religion, that men should hate this and that—sin for instance, and the devil, and that they should fear certain things, such as God and the Judgment. But this really is irreligion, not religion.

An important feature of *Leaves of Grass* is what I would call its continuity or endlessness. It does not teach something, and rest there. It does not make, in morals and religion, an important step in advance, and stop satisfied with that. It has unlimited vista. It clears the way ahead, with allowance and provision for new advances far, far beyond anything contained in itself. It brings no one to "a terminus," nor teaches any one to be "content and full." It is a ceaseless goad, a never-resting spur. To those to whom it speaks, it cries continually, forward ! forward ! and admits of no pause in the race. A second trait is its universality. There is nothing of which humanity has experience that it does not touch upon more or less directly. There must have been a deliberate intention on the part of the author to give the book this all-embracing character, and no doubt that was one reason for the catalogues of objects in a few of the poems which have so irritated the critics. I have often tried to think of something objective or subjective, material or immaterial, that was not taken cognizance of by *Leaves of Grass*, but always failed. A third feature is the manner in which the author avoids (either of set purpose, or more likely by a sure instinct) dealing specifically with any topics of mere class or ephemeral interest (though he really treats these too through the bases upon which they rest), and concerns himself solely with the elementary subjects of human life, which must necessarily have perennial interest.

Leaves of Grass is curiously a different book to each reader. To some, its merit consists in the keen thought which pierces to the kernel of things—or a perpetual and sunny cheeriness, in which respect it is the synonyme of pure air and health; to others it is chiefly valuble as being full of pictorial suggestions; to a third class of men it is a new Gospel containing fresh revelations of divine truth; to a fourth it is charged with ideas and suggestions in practical life and manners; to some its large, sweet, clear, animal physiology is its especial charm; to some, the strange abysses of its fervid emotions. Upon still others (on whom it produces its full effect), it exerts an irresistible and divine power, strengthening and elevating their lives unspeakably, driving them from all meanness and toward all good, giving them no rest, but compelling them to watch every act, word, thought, feeling—to guard their days and nights from weakness, baseness, littleness, or impurity—at the same time giving them extraordinary power to accomplish these ends.

There is still another class (altogether the most numerous so far), who see in the book nothing of all these fine things or good uses. To them it suggests contempt for laws and social forms, appears coarse, prosaic, senseless, full of impure ideas, and as seeking the destruction of religion, and all that is decent in human life. If men were really, as theologians tell us, inclined by Nature to evil, I could imagine *Leaves of Grass* might on the whole do some serious harm. But since, as I think is certainly the case, (for who would not rather be healthy than sick? loved than hated? happy than wretched?) humanity on the whole is far more disposed to good than evil, there is no question that whatever stimulates and encourages the native growth and independent vigor of the mind, as it does, must in the final result be beneficial.

[A Student Visits Whitman in 1886]

"I have read your books right through," I exclaimed beamingly as I entered.

"Oy! oy?—Did you make anything out of it?"

I then told him the various impressions his writings had made upon me, and finally asked: "Do you believe that mankind can be improved by books?"

WHITMAN: "I can hardly say that I had the idea to better mankind. I grew up like a tree—the poems are the fruit. Good literature ought to be the Roman cement; the older it grows—the better it serves its purpose."

An old peddler passed by. Whitman waved his hand, his famous Salut au Monde, as he did to nearly every passer-by.

The ragged old man stopped before the window and displayed his ware.

Whitman greeted him with a cordial "How do you do, sir?" and leaning a little out of the window pointed at a set of collar buttons: "How much are they?"

PEDDLER: (holding them up to him) "Five cents."

WHITMAN: "No thanks, I don't need any to-day."

Then followed an awkward pause.

I produced the copy of "After all Not to Create Only" with which he had presented me, handsomely bound.

"Why how nice it looks!" he exclaimed, scrutinizing it from all sides.

"Won't you inscribe something in it?" I asked.

"Thanks," he answered, and holding the book on his knee, his habitual way of writing, he penned down the words, "Given to C.S.H., by Walt Whitman" in his immense, uncouth, heavy-stroked handwriting, which offers marvelous opportunities to chirographists.

After this performance another pause, and a few vain attempts on my side to get him interested in some topic.

---

*Reprinted from *Conversations with Walt Whitman* (New York: E. P. Coby and Co., 1895), pp. 13–17. Hartmann, born of a Japanese mother and a German father in Japan, was a student of 19 in Philadelphia when he visited Whitman.

145

I mentioned at haphazard that my old Quaker friend had been one of his very first admirers, having studied the 1856 edition.

"Why I must go to see him," he exclaimed enthusiastically, "yes, that's what I am going to do!" He never did, but we talked for a while quite seriously about how it could be accomplished without exerting him.

"I want you to do me a favor—" and Whitman suddenly rose, dragging himself slowly step by step, with the help of a stick in a sideward direction through the room and upstairs. I looked after him for an explanation, but as none came, glanced over some books on the table, and was attracted by an old voluminous edition of Walter Scott's poems with numerous margin notes in red ink. He returned with a clipping of a German newspaper, handed it to me, and asked me to translate it. It was an ordinary newspaper concoction on *Leaves of Grass*, comparing his style with that of the psalmists.

Whitman smiled: "I don't know why some men compare my book with the Bible."

Another pause ensued.

For at least half an hour I spoke of a dozen different subjects or more, without getting anything else but an occasional oy! oy? as answer; nevertheless, one could presume from the way Whitman poised his head, that he was listening quite attentively most of the time.

At last I broke this silence by mentioning that I had read Bryant's "Thanatopsis." "There is something large about it," I remarked.

WHITMAN: "He is our greatest poet. He had a smack of Americanism, American individuality, smack of outdoor life, the wash of the sea, the mountains, forests, and animals. But he is too melancholy for a great representative of American poetry."

SADAKICHI: "It seems that the New England States have produced nine-tenths of all our American literati (a word I had learnt from Whitman, which he used with preference instead of authors, poets, etc). I cannot understand the worship of Emerson. Many of his ideas one can find in the Alexandrian philosophers."

WHITMAN: "Emerson's deficiency is that he doubts everything. He is a deep thinker, though he had hardly any influence on me; but people say so; maybe, without my knowledge. He had much of the Persians and Oriental people. He is only the offspring of other suns tumbling through the universe."

For a moment I thought of Whitman and Emerson, arguing under the old elms of Boston Common about certain passages in the "Children of Adam" and Whitman, after listening for two hours to the well nigh indisputable logic of Emerson, being "more settled than ever to adhere to his own theory." (American genre painters should tackle that subject!)

WHITMAN: "Did you read Holmes?"

SADAKICHI: "Very little. He serves his humor in a dainty fashion; yet I cannot digest it; it is too dry for me."

WHITMAN: "He is very witty, very smart, not first rank and not second rank; man of fine culture, who knows how to move in society; he takes the same place in modern society as the court singers and troubadours in the Middle Ages, who had a taste for castles, ladies, festivals, etc., who knew exactly how to move among kings and princes; but something was failing, that very thing which would have made him a poet."

His opinion about Mark Twain was similar.

SADAKICHI: "It seems to me, as if all these men produced nothing new. They are like imitators; for instance, was Washington Irving anything but a clever English essayist?"

WHITMAN: "Some people think they are poets if they have a feeling for jewels, paste gems, feathers, birds, flowers, perfume, etc. In a barbaric country among uncivilized people they would deserve some praise, but not in our time, when everybody can imagine these things."

SADAKICHI: "Like Gilder and Stoddard?"

WHITMAN: "Who?"

SADAKICHI: "Stoddard, for instance?"

WHITMAN: "Stoddard is fair, but many are like him."

SADAKICHI: "Whittier seems to reflect more of the milieu of his creed and country?"

WHITMAN: "Whittier was a strong poet, the favorite of Horace Greeley—as good and powerful in his old days as in his young. Much earnestness and fierceness bends all his Quaker peace."

SADAKICHI: "And the critical element, is it entirely lacking? Whipple? (I shrugged my shoulders) Lowell, of course."

WHITMAN: (nodded) "Cute, elegant, well dressed, somewhat of a Yankee—student—college."

SADAKICHI: "I think Stedman is after all the best we have."

WHITMAN: "Oy? (pause—smiling) Stedman is, after all, nothing but a sophisticated dancing master. If Hercules or Apollo himself would make their appearance he would look at them only from the standpoint of a dancing master. Now I have to be excused. I feel tired."

So I shook hands with him, and left satisfied with that afternoon's conversation at any rate.[1]

Note

1. Hartmann goes on to add that these estimates of contemporary authors "aroused quite a storm of indignation" when he published them in the *New York Herald* in 1889. When he published them again in 1893, one of Whitman's literary executors, Thomas Harned, wrote an admonishing letter saying that Whitman had repudiated the original article and claimed that Hartmann had made up the remarks. Hartmann goes on to protest that his transcripts of Whitman's remarks were accurate and that Whitman never had repudiated them to him and that he had seen Whitman often after the publication of the first article.

To Walt Whitman in America

Algernon Charles Swinburne*

Send but a song oversea for us
   Heart of their hearts who are free,
Heart of their singer, to be for us
   More than our singing can be;
Ours, in the tempest at error,
With no light but the twilight of terror;
   Send us a song oversea!

Sweet-smelling of pine-leaves and grasses,
   And blown as a tree through and through
With the winds of the keen mountain-passes,
   And tender as sun-smitten dew;
Sharp-tongued as the winter that shakes
The wastes of your limitless lakes,
   Wide-eyed as the sea-line's blue.

O strong-winged soul with prophetic
   Lips hot with the bloodbeats of song,
With tremor of heartstrings magnetic,
   With thoughts as thunders in throng,
With consonant ardours of chords
That pierce men's souls as with swords
   And hale them hearing along.

Make us too music, to be with us
   As a word from a world's heart warm,
To sail the dark as a sea with us,
   Full-sailed, outsinging the storm,
A song to put fire in our ears
Whose burning shall burn up tears,
   Whose sign bid battle reform;

*Reprinted from *Songs Before Sunrise* (London: Chatto and Windus, 1883), pp. 143–44.
Originally published in 1871 when Swinburne was most enthusiastic about Whitman. I have
quoted only five of the 22 stanzas.

A note in the ranks of a clarion,
  A word in the wind of cheer,
To consume as with lightning the carrion
  That makes time foul for us here;
In the air that our dead things infest
A blast of the breath of the west,
  Till east way as west way is clear.

Whitmania

Algernon Charles Swinburne*

The remarkable American rhapsodist who has inoculated a certain number of English readers and writers with the singular form of ethical and aesthetic rabies for which his name supplies the proper medical term of definition is usually regarded by others than Whitmaniacs as simply a blatant quack—a vehement and emphatic dunce, of incomparable vanity and volubility, inconceivable pretention and incompetence. That such is by no means altogether my own view I need scarcely take the trouble to protest. Walt Whitman has written some pages to which I have before now given praise enough to exonerate me, I should presume, from any charge of prejudice or prepossession against a writer whose claims to occasional notice and occasional respect no man can be less desirous to dispute than I am. Nor should I have thought it necessary to comment on the symptoms of a disorder which happily is not likely to become epidemic in an island or on a continent not utterly barren of poetry, had the sufferers not given such painfully singular signs of inability to realize a condition only too obvious to the compassionate bystander. While the preachers or the proselytes of the gospel according to Whitman were content to admit that he was either no poet at all, or the only poet who had ever been born into this world—that those who accepted him were bound to reject all others as nullities—they had at least the merit of irrefragable logic; they could claim at least the credit of indisputable consistency. But when other gods or godlings are accepted as participants in the divine nature; when his temple is transformed into a pantheon, and a place assigned his godhead a little beneath Shakespeare, a little above Dante, or cheek by jowl with Homer; when Isaiah and Aeschylus, for anything we know, may be admitted to a greater or lesser share in his incommunicable and indivisible supremacy—then, indeed, it is high time to enter a strenuous and (if it be possible) a serious protest. The first apostles alone were the depositaries of the pure and perfect evangel: these later and comparatively heterodox disciples have adulterated and debased the genuine metal of absolute, coherent, unalloyed and unqualified nonsense.

*Reprinted from *Studies in Prose and Poetry* (London: Chatto and Windus, 1894), pp. 129–40; originally published in *The Fortnightly Review*, 48 (August 1887), 170–76.

To the better qualities discernible in the voluminous and incoherent effusions of Walt Whitman it should not be difficult for any reader not unduly exasperated by the rabid idiocy of the Whitmaniacs to do full and ample justice: for these qualities are no less simple and obvious than laudable and valuable. A just enthusiasm, a genuine passion of patriotic and imaginative sympathy, a sincere though limited and distorted love of nature, an eager and earnest faith in freedom and in loyalty—in the loyalty that can only be born of liberty; a really manful and nobly rational tone of mind with regard to the crowning questions of duty and of death; these excellent qualities of emotion and reflection find here and there a not inadequate expression in a style of rhetoric not always flatulent or inharmonious. Originality of matter or of manner, of structure or of thought, it would be equally difficult for any reader not endowed with a quite exceptional gift of ignorance or of hebetude to discover in any part of Mr. Whitman's political or ethical or physical or proverbial philosophy. But he has said wise and noble things upon such simple and eternal subjects as life and death, pity and enmity, friendship and fighting; and even the intensely conventional nature of its elaborate and artificial simplicity should not be allowed, by a magnanimous and candid reader, too absolutely to eclipse the genuine energy and the occasional beauty of his feverish and convulsive style of writing.

All this may be cordially concealed by the lovers of good work in any kind, however imperfect, incomposite, and infirm; and more than this the present writer at any rate most decidedly never intended to convey by any tribute of sympathy or admiration which may have earned for him the wholly unmerited honour of an imaginary enlistment in the noble army of Whitmaniacs. He has therefore no palinode to chant, no recantation to intone; for if it seems and is unreasonable to attribute a capacity of thought to one who has never given any sign of thinking, a faculty of song to one who has never shown ability to sing, it must be remembered, on the other hand, that such qualities of energetic emotion and sonorous expression as distinguish the happier moments and the more sincere inspirations of such writers as Whitman or as Byron have always, in common parlance, been allowed to pass muster and do duty for the faculty of thinking or the capacity of singing. Such an use of common terms is doubtless inaccurate and inexact, if judged by the "just but severe law" of logical definition or of mathematical precision: but such abuse or misuse of plain words is generally understood as conveying no more than a conventional import such as may be expressed by the terms with which we subscribe an ordinary letter, or by the formula through which we decline an untimely visit. Assuredly, I never have meant to imply what most assuredly I never have said—that I regarded Mr. Whitman as a poet or a thinker in the proper sense; the sense in which the one term is applicable to Coleridge or to Shelley, the other to Bacon or to Mill. Whoever may have abdicated his natural right, as a being not born without a sense of music or a sense of reason, to protest against the judgment which discerns in *Childe Harold* or in *Drum-Taps* a masterpiece of imagination and expression, of intelligence or of song, I never have abdicated mine. The highest literary quality discoverable in either book is rhetoric: and very excellent rhetoric in either case it sometimes is; what it is at other times I see no present necessity to say. But Whitmaniacs and Byronites have yet to learn that if rhetoric were poetry John Bright would be a poet at least equal to John Milton, Demosthenes to Sophocles, and Cicero to Catullus. Poetry may be something more—I certainly am not concerned to deny it—than an art or a science; but not because it is not, strictly speaking, a science or an art. There is a science of verse as surely as there is a science of mathematics: there is an art of expression by metre as certainly as there is an art of representation by painting. To some poets the understanding of this science, the mastery of this art, would seem to come by a natural instinct which needs nothing but practice for its development, its application, and its perfection: others by patient and conscientious study of their own abilities attain a no less unmistakable and a scarcely less admirable success. But the man of genius and the dullard who cannot write good verse are equally out of the running. "Did you ask dulcet rhymes from me?" inquires Mr. Whitman of some extraordinary if not imaginary interlocutor; and proceeds, with some not ineffective energy of expression, to explain that "I lull nobody—and you will never understand me." No, my dear good sir—or camerado, if that be the more courteous and conventional address (a modest reader might deferentially reply): not in the wildest visions of a distempered slumber could I ever have dreamed of doing anything of the kind. Nor do we ask them even from such other and inferior scribes or bards as the humble Homer, the modest Milton, or the obsolete and narrow-minded Shakespeare—poets of sickly feudality, or hidebound classicism, of effete and barbarous incompetence. But metre, rhythm, cadence not merely appreciable but definable and reducible to rule and measurement, though we do not expect from you, we demand from all who claim, we discern in the works of all who have achieved, any place among poets of any class whatsoever. The question whether your work is in any sense poetry has no more to do with dulcet rhymes than with the differential calculus. The question is whether you have any more right to call yourself a poet, or to be called a poet by any man who knows verse from prose, or black from white, or speech from silence, or his right hand from his left, than to call yourself or to be called, on the strength of your published writings, a mathematician, a logician, a painter, a political economist, a sculptor, a dynamiter, an old parliamentary hand, a civil engineer, a dealer in marine stores, an amphimacer, a triptych, a rhomboid, or a rectangular parallelogram. "*Vois-tu bien, tu es baron comme ma pantoufle!*" said old Gillenormand—the creature of one who was indeed a creator or a poet: and the humblest of critics who knows any one thing from any one other thing has a right to say to the man who offers as poetry what the exuberant incontinence of a Whitman presents for our acceptance, *"Tu es poète comme mon—soulier."*

But the student has other and better evidence than any merely negative indication of impotence in the case of the American as in the case of the British despiser and disclaimer of so pitiful a profession or ambition as that of a versifier. Mr. Carlyle and Mr. Whitman have both been good enough to try their hands at lyric verse: and the ear which has once absorbed their dulcet rhymes will never need to be reminded of the reason for their contemptuous abhorrence of a diversion so contemptible as the art of Coleridge and Shelly.

> Out of eternity
>   This new day is born:
> Into eternity
>   This day shall return.

Such were the flute-notes of Diogenes Devilsdung: comparable by those who would verify the value of his estimate with any stanza of Shelley's "To a Skylark." And here is a sample of the dulcet rhymes which a most tragic occasion succeeded in evoking from the orotund oratist of Manhattan:

> The port is near, the bells I hear, the people all exulting,
> *While follow eyes the steady keel*, the vessel grim and daring;

> For you bouquets and ribbon'd wreaths—for you the shores
>   a-crowding; (*sic*)
> For you they call, the surging mass, their eager faces
>   turning.

'Ioù ioù, ẅ ẅ kakà. Upon the whole, I prefer Burns—or Hogg—to Carlyle, and Dibdin—or Catnach—to Whitman.

A pedantic writer of poems distilled from other poems (which, as the immortal author of the imperishable *Leaves of Grass* is well aware, must "pass away")—a Wordsworth, for example, or a Tennyson—would hardly have made "eyes" follow the verb they must be supposed to govern. Nor would a poor creature whose ear was yet unattuned to the cadence of "chants democratic" have permitted his Pegasus so remarkable a capriole as to result in the rhythmic reverberation of such rhymes as these. When a boy who remains unable after many efforts to cross the Asses' Bridge expresses his opinion that Euclid was a beastly old fool, his obviously impartial verdict is generally received by his elders with exactly the same amount of respectful attention as is accorded by any competent reader to the equally valuable and judicial deliverances of Messrs. Whitman, Emerson, and Carlyle on the subject of poetry—that is, of lyrical or creative literature. The first critic of our time—perhaps the largest-minded and surest-sighted of any age—has pointed out, in an essay on poetry which should not be too long left buried in the columns of the *Encyclopaedia Britannica*, the exhaustive accuracy of the Greek terms which define every claimant to the laurel as either a singer or a maker. There is no third term, as there is no third class. If then it appears that Mr. Walt Whitman has about as much gift of song as his precursors and apparent models in rhythmic structure and style, Mr. James Macpherson and Mr. Martin Tupper, his capacity for creation is the only thing that remains for us to consider. And on that score we find him, beyond all question, rather like the later than like the earlier of his masters. Macpherson could at least evoke shadows: Mr. Tupper and Mr. Whitman can only accumulate words. As to his originality in the matter of free speaking, it need only be observed that no remarkable mental gift is requisite to qualify man or woman for membership of a sect mentioned by Dr. Johnson—the Adamites, who believed in the virtue of public nudity. If those worthies claimed the right to bid their children run about the streets stark naked, the magistrate, observed Johnson, "would have a right to flog them into their doublets"; a right no plainer than the right of common sense and sound criticism to flog the Whitmaniacs into their strait-waistcoats; or, were there any female members of such a sect, into their strait-petticoats. If nothing that concerns the physical organism of men or of women is common or unclean or improper for literary manipulation, it may be maintained, by others than the disciples of a contemporary French novelist who has amply proved the sincerity of his own opinion to that effect, that it is not beyond the province of literature to describe with realistic exuberance of detail the functions of digestion or indigestion in all its processes—the objects and the results of an aperient or an emetic medicine. Into "the troughs of Zolaism," as Lord Tennyson calls them (a phrase which bears rather unduly hard on the quadrupedal pig), I am happy to believe that Mr. Whitman has never dipped a passing nose: he is a writer of something occasionally like English, and a man of something occasionally like genius. But in his treatment of topics usually regarded as no less unfit for public exposition and literary illustration than those which have obtained notoriety for the would-be bastard of Balzac—the Davenant of the (French) prose Shakespeare, he has contrived to make "the way of a man with a maid" (Proverbs xxx, 19) almost as loathsomely ludicrous and almost as ludicrously loathsome—I speak merely of the aesthetic or literary aspect of his effusions—as the Swiftian or Zolaesque enthusiasm of bestiality which insists on handling what "goeth into the belly, and is cast out into the draught" (St. Matthew xv, 17). The Zolas and the Whitmen, to whom nothing, absolutely and literally nothing, is unclean or common, have an obvious and incalculable advantage over the unconverted who have never enjoyed the privilege of a vision like St. Peter's, and received the benefit of a supernatural prohibition to call anything common or unclean. They cannot possibly be exposed, and they cannot possibly be put to shame: for that best of all imaginable reasons which makes it proverbially difficult to "take the breeks off a Highlander."

It would really seem as though, in literary and other matters, the very plainness and certitude of a principle made it doubly necessary for those who maintain it to enforce and reinforce it over and over again; as though, the more obvious it were, the more it needed indication and demonstration, assertion and reassertion. There is no more important, no more radical and fundamental truth of criticism than this: that, in poetry perhaps above all other arts, the method or treatment, the manner of touch, the tone of expression, is the first and last thing to be considered. There is no subject which may not be treated with success (I do not say there are no subjects which on other than artistic grounds it may not be as well to avoid, it may not be better to pass by) if the poet, by instinct or by training, knows exactly how to handle it aright, to present it without danger of just or rational offence. For evidence of this truth we need look no further than the pastorals of Virgil and Theocritus. But under the dirty clumsy paws of a harper whose plectrum is a muck-rake any tune will become a chaos of discords, though the motive of the tune should be the first principle of nature—the passion of man for woman or the passion of woman for man. And the unhealthily demonstrative and obtrusive animalism of the Whitmaniad is as unnatural, as incompatible with the wholesome instincts of human passion, as even the filthy and inhuman asceticism of SS. Macarius and Simeon Stylites. If anything can justify the serious and deliberate display of merely physical emotion in literature or in art, it must be one of two things: intense depth of feeling expressed with inspired perfection of simplicity, with divine sublimity of fascination, as by Sappho; or transcendent supremacy of actual and irresistible beauty in such revelation of naked nature as was possible to Titian. But Mr. Whitman's Eve is a drunken apple-woman, indecently sprawling in the slush and garbage of the gutter amid the rotten refuse of her overturned fruit-stall: but Mr. Whitman's Venus is a Hottentot wench under the influence of cantharides and adulterated rum. Cotytto herself would repudiate the ministration of such priestesses as these.

But what then, if anything, is it that a rational creature who has studied and understood the work of any poet, great or small, from Homer down to Moschus, from Lucretius down to Martial, from Dante down to Metastasio, from Villon down to Voltaire, from Shakespeare down to Byron, can find to applaud, to approve, or to condone to the work of Mr. Whitman? To this very reasonable and inevitable question the answer is not far to seek. I have myself repeatedly pointed out—it may be (I have often been told so) with too unqualified sympathy and too uncritical enthusiasm—the qualities which give a certain touch of greatness to his work, the sources of inspiration which infuse into its chaotic jargon some passing or seeming notes of cosmic beauty, and diversify with something of occasional harmony the strident and barren discord of its jarring and erring atoms. His sympathies, I repeat, are usually generous, his views of life are occasionally just, and his views of death are invariably noble. In other words, he generally means well, having a good stock on hand of honest emotion; he sometimes sees well, having a natural sensibility to such aspects of nature as appeal to an eye rather quick than penetrating; he seldom writes well, being cabined, cribbed, confined, bound in, to the limits of a thoroughly unnatural imitative, histrionic and affected style. But there is a thrilling and fiery force in his finest bursts of gusty rhetoric which makes us wonder whether with a little more sense and a good deal more cultivation he might not have made a noticeable orator. As a poet, no amount of improvement that self-knowledge and self-culture might have brought to bear upon such exceptionally raw material could ever have raised him higher than a station to which his homely and manly patriotism would be the best claim that could be preferred for him; a seat beside such writers as Ebenezer Elliot—or possibly a little higher, on such an elevation as might be occupied by poet whom careful training had reared and matured into a rather inferior kind of Southey. But to fit himself for such promotion he would have in the first place to resign all claim to the laurels of Gotham, with which the critical sages of that famous borough have bedecked his unbashful brows; he would have to recognize that he is no more, in the proper sense of the word, a poet, than Communalists or Dissolutionists are, in any sense of the word, Republicans; that he has exactly as much claim to a place beside Dante as any Vermersch or Vermorel or other verminous and murderous muckworm of the Parisian Commune to a place beside Mazzini; in other words, that the informing principle of his work is not so much the negation as the contradiction of the creative principle of poetry. And this is not to be expected that such a man should bring himself to believe, as long as he hears himself proclaimed the inheritor of a seat assigned a hundred years ago by the fantastic adulation of more or less distinguished literary eccentrics to a person of the name of Jephson—whose triumphs as a tragic poet made his admirers tremble for Shakespeare.

[The Years Work a Change]

William Dean Howells*

Mr. Walt Whitman calls his latest book *November Boughs*, and in more ways than one it testifies and it appeals beyond the letter to the reader's interest. For the poet the long fight is over; he rests his cause with what he has done; and we think no one now would like to consider the result without respect, without deference, even if one cannot approach it with entire submission. It is time, certainly, while such a poet is still with us, to own that his literary intention was as generous as his spirit was bold, and that if he has not accomplished all he intended, he has been a force that is by no means spent. Apart from the social import of his first book ("without yielding an inch, the working-man and working-woman were to be in my pages from first to last"), he aimed in it at the emancipation of poetry from what he felt to be the trammels of rhyme and metre. He did not achieve this; but he produced a new kind of literature, which we may or may not allow to be poetry, but which we cannot deny is something eloquent, suggestive, moving, with a lawless, formless beauty of its own. He dealt literary conventionality one of those blows which eventually show as internal injuries, whatever the immediate effect seems to be. He made it possible for poetry hereafter to be more direct and natural than hitherto; the hearing which he has braved nearly half a century of contumely and mockery to win would now be granted on very different terms to a man of his greatness, this is always the way; and it is always the way that the reformer (perhaps in helpless confession of the weakness he shares with all humankind) champions some error which seems as dear to him as the truth he was born to proclaim. Walt Whitman was not the first to observe that we are all naked under our clothes, but he was one of the greatest, if not the first, to preach a gospel of nudity; not as one of his Quaker ancestry might have done for a witness against the spiritual nakedness of his hearers, but in celebration of the five senses of their equal origin with the three virtues of which the greatest is charity. His offence, if rank, is quantitatively small; a few lines at most; and it is one which the judicious pencil of the editor will some day remove for him, though for the present he "takes occasion to confirm those lines with the

*Reprinted from the "Editor's Study," *Harper's*, 78 (Feb. 1889), 448.

157

settled convictions and deliberate renewals of thirty years." We hope for that day, not only because it will give to all a kind in poetry which none can afford to ignore, and which his cherished lines bar to most of those who read most in our time and country, but because we think the five senses do not need any celebration. In that duality which every thoughtful person must have noticed composes him, we believe the universal experience is that the beast half from first to last is fully able to take care of itself. But it is a vast subject, and, as the poet says, "it does not stand by itself; the vitality of it is altogether in its relations, bearings, significance." In the mean while we can assure the reader that these *November Boughs* are as innocent as so many sprays of apple blossom, and that he may take the book home without misgiving.

We think he will find in reading it that the prose passages are, some of them, more poetic than the most poetic of the rhythmical passages. "Some War Memoranda" and "The Last of the War Cases"—notes made twenty-five years ago—are alive with a simple pathos and instinct with a love of truth which recall the best new Russian work, and which make the poet's psalms seem vague and thin as wandering smoke in comparison. Yet these have the beauty of undulant, sinuous desultory smoke forms, and they sometimes take the light with a response of such color as dwells in autumn sunsets. The book is well named *November Boughs*: it is meditative and reminiscent, with a sober fragrance in it like the scent of fallen leaves in woods where the leaves that still linger overhead,

> Or few, or none, do shake against the cold—
> Bare ruined choirs where late the sweet birds sang.

It is the hymn of the runner resting after the race, and much the same as he chants always, whether the race has been lost or won.

[Spoken at Whitman's Funeral]

Robert G. Ingersoll*

My Friends: Again we, in the mystery of Life, are brought face to face with the mystery of Death. A great man, a great American, the most eminent citizen of this Republic, lies dead before us, and we have met to pay a tribute to his greatness and his worth.

I know he needs no words of mine. His fame is secure. He laid the foundations of it deep in the human heart and brain. He was, above all I have known, the poet of humanity, or sympathy. He was so great that he rose above the greatest that he stooped to the lowest without conscious condescension. He never claimed to be lower or greater than any of the sons of men.

He came into our generation a free, untrammeled spirit, with sympathy for all. His arm was beneath the form of the sick. He sympathized with the imprisoned and despised, and even on the brow of crime he was great enough to place the kiss of human sympathy.

One of the greatest lines in our literature is his, and the line is great enough to do honor to the greatest genius that has ever lived. He said, speaking of an outcast: "Not till the sun excludes you do I exclude you."

His charity was as wide as the sky, and wherever there was human suffering, human misfortune, the sympathy of Whitman bent above it as the firmament bends above the earth.

He was built on a broad and splendid plan—ample, without appearing to have limitations—passing easily for a brother of mountains and seas and constellations; caring nothing for the little maps and charts with which timid pilots hug the shore, but giving himself freely with recklessness of genius to winds and waves and tides; caring for nothing as long as the stars were above him. He walked among men, among writers, among verbal varnishers and veneerers, among literary milliners and tailors, with the unconscious majesty of an antique god.

He was the poet of that divine democracy which gives equal rights to all the sons and daughters of men. He uttered the great American voice; uttered a song worthy of the great Republic. No man ever said more for

*Reprinted from *The Works of Robert G. Ingersoll* (New York: Dresden Publishing Co., C. P. Farrell, 1902), XII, 473–77. Delivered at Camden, N.J., 30 March 1892.

the rights of humanity, more in favor of real democracy, of real justice. He neither scorned nor cringed, was neither tyrant nor slave. He asked only to stand the equal of his fellows beneath the great flag of nature, the blue and stars.

He was the poet of Life. It was a joy simply to breathe. He loved the clouds; he enjoyed the breath of morning, the twilight, the wind, the winding streams. He loved to look at the sea when the waves burst into the whitecaps of joy. He loved the fields, the hills; he was acquainted with the trees, with birds, with all the beautiful objects of the earth. He not only saw these objects, but understood their meaning, and he used them that he might exhibit his heart to his fellow-men.

He was the poet of Love. He was not ashamed of that divine passion that has built every home in the world; that divine passion that has painted every picture and given us every real work of art; that divine passion that has made the world worth living in and has given some value to human life.

He was the poet of the natural, and taught men not to be ashamed of that which is natural. He was not only the poet of democracy, not only the poet of the great Republic, but he was the poet of the human race. He was not confined to the limits of this country, but his sympathy went out over the seas to all the nations of the earth.

He stretched out his hand and felt himself the equal of all kings and of all princes, and the brother of all men, no matter how high, no matter how low.

He has uttered more supreme words than any writer of our century, possibly of almost any other. He was, above all things, a man, and above genius, above all the snow-capped peaks of intelligence, above all art, rises the true man. Greater than all is the true man, and he walked among his fellow-men as such.

He was the poet of Death. He accepted all life and all death, and he justified all. He had the courage to meet all, and was great enough and splendid enough to harmonize all and to accept all there is of life as a divine melody.

You know better than I what his life has been, but let me say one thing. Knowing, as he did, what others can know and what they cannot, he accepted and absorbed all theories, all creeds, all religions, and believed in none. His philosophy was a sky that embraced all clouds and accounted for all clouds. He had a philosophy and a religion of his own, broader, as he believed—and as I believe—than others. He accepted all, he understood all, and he was above all.

He was absolutely true to himself. He had frankness and courage, and he was as candid as light. He was willing that all the sons of men should be absolutely acquainted with his heart and brain. He had nothing to conceal. Frank, candid, pure, serene, noble, and yet for years he was maligned and slandered, simply because he had the candor of nature. He will be understood yet, and that for which he was condemned—his frankness, his candor—will add to the glory and greatness of his fame.

He wrote a liturgy for mankind; he wrote a great and splendid psalm of life, and he gave to us the gospel of humanity—the greatest gospel that can be preached.

He was not afraid to live, not afraid to die. For many years he and death were near neighbors. He was always willing and ready to meet and greet this king called death, and for many months he sat in the deepening twilight waiting for the night, waiting for the light.

He never lost his hope. When the mists filled the valleys, he looked upon the mountain tops, and when the mountains in darkness disappeared, he fixed his gaze upon the stars.

In his brain were the blessed memories of the day, and in his heart were mingled the dawn and dusk of life.

He was not afraid; he was cheerful every moment. The laughing nymphs of day did not desert him. They remained that they might clasp the hands and greet with smiles the veiled and silent sisters of the night. And when they did come, Walt Whitman stretched his hand to them. On one side were the nymphs of the day, and on the other the silent sisters of the night, and so, hand in hand, between smiles and tears, he reached his journey's end.

From the frontier of life, from the western wave-kissed shore, he sent us messages of content and hope, and these messages seem now like strains of music blown by the "Mystic Trumpeter" from Death's pale realm.

To-day we give back to Mother Nature, to her clasp and kiss, one of the bravest, sweetest souls that ever lived in human clay.

Charitable as the air and generous as Nature, he was negligent of all except to do and say what he believed he should do and should say.

And I to-day thank him, not only for you but for myself, for all the brave words he has uttered. I thank him for all the great and splendid words he has said in favor of liberty, in favor of man and woman, in favor of motherhood, in favor of fathers, in favor of children, and I thank him for the brave words that he has said of death.

He has lived, he has died, and death is less terrible than it was before. Thousands and millions will walk down into the "dark valley of the shadow" holding Walt Whitman by the hand. Long after we are dead the brave words he has spoken will sound like trumpets to the dying.

And so I lay this little wreath upon this great man's tomb. I loved him living, and I love him still.

[A British Critic Probes Whitman's Treatment of Love]

John Addington Symonds*

The transition from Personality to Sex offers no difficulty. Sex, the passions, the affections, love, are clearly the main things in life.

In his treatment of Love, Whitman distinguishes two broad kinds of human affection; the one being the ordinary sexual relation, the other comradeship or an impassioned relation between man and man. the former he describes as "amativeness," the latter as "adhesiveness." There is no reason why both forms of emotion should not co-exist in the same person. Indeed Whitman makes it plain that a completely endowed individuality, one who, as Horace might have said, is "entirely rounded and without ragged edges," will be highly susceptible of both. The exact bearing of amativeness and adhesiveness upon one another, and upon the spiritual nature of the individual, has been fully expressed in the following poem:

> Fast-anchored eternal O love! O woman I love!
> O bride! O wife! more resistless than I can tell, the thought
>   of you!
> Then separate, as disembodied or another born,
> Ethereal, the last athletic reality, my consolation,
> I ascend, I float in the regions of your love, O man,
> O sharer of my roving life.

Since this is the most condensed and weighty of Whitman's utterances upon the subject of love, every word in it may be supposed to have been carefully considered. It is not therefore insignificant to notice that, in the edition of 1860–61, "primeval" stood for "fast-anchored" in the first line, and "the purest born" for "or another born" in the third line.

The section of his complete works which deals exclusively with sexual love, is entitled "Children of Adam." The frankness and the rankness of the pieces composing this chapter called down a storm of insults, calumnies, unpopularity, on Whitman. Yet the attitude which he assumed as poet and prophet demanded this frankness, while the spirit of his treatment deprived the subject-matter of its rankness.

*Reprinted from *Walt Whitman: A Study* (London: John C. Nimmo, 1893), pp. 54–85.

His originality consisted, I have said, in giving the idealism of poetry and powerful emotion to the blank results of modern science. Now it is in the very nature of science to consider nothing as "common or unclean," to accept all the facts presented to its vision with indifference, caring for nothing in the process of analysis except the proof of reality, the elucidation of truth. Science, in her wise impartiality, regards morbid phenomena, disease and decay, crime and aberration, as worthy of attention, upon the same lines as healthy and normal products. She knows that pathology is an indispensable adjunct to the study of organic structure.

Sharing the scientific spirit in his quality of poet, Whitman was not called to celebrate what is unhealthy and abnormal in humanity. That is a proper subject for the laboratory. The poet's function is to stimulate and to invigorate. It is his duty to insist upon what is wholesome, the things in life which conduce to organic growth, the natural instincts and normal appetites upon which the continuation of the species, the energy of the individual, the welfare of the family, the fabric of the commonwealth, eventually rest. Feeling thus, and being penetrated with the scientific spirit, Whitman was justified in claiming the whole of healthy manhood and womanhood for his province. To exclude sex from his account of human nature would have been absurd; for it is precisely sex by which men and women are differentiated; sex which brings them into mutual relations of amativeness; sex which determines the preservation and the future of the species. The inspiration which prompted him, first among modern poets, to penetrate the blank results of science with imagination and emotion, led him inevitably to a frank treatment of sexual relations. Each portion of the healthy human body had for a thinker of his type to be considered "sweet and clean." He could not shrink from the facts of paternity and maternity, these being the most important both for men and women, and through them for society at large. For him "the parts and poems of the body" are not "of the body only, but of the soul"—indeed "these are the soul." Following the impulse which forced him to insist upon a vigorous and healthy personality or self as the fundamental integer of human life, he proceeded to impress upon his nation the paramount duty of maintaining a robust and healthy breed. Scientific pathology may be left to deal with abnormalities and diseases. The social conscience is sufficiently, if dimly, acquainted with those evils. For the poet, who has accepted the scientific point of view, it is enough to indicate their wrongness. But he enjoys the privilege of proclaiming the beauty and the goodness of functions and organs which constitute the central reality of human life. To recognise the dignity of sex, to teach personalities, both male and female, that they have the right to take a pride in it, and that this pride is their duty, was for a poet of Whitman's stamp a prime consideration. Those mediaeval lies regarding sexual sinfulness, those foolish panegyrics of chaste abstinence, those base insinuations of foul-minded priests, had to be swept away—not by polemic or vituperation, but by a plain proclamation of the truth which had been veiled from sight so long. Delicacy in matters of sex had become indelicacy by a false habit of envisaging the fact. All falsehood is inconsistent of society.

Having entered upon this region with the objects I have hinted at—a recognition of fundamental truths, an acceptance of scientific as opposed to theological principles, a deep sense of personality, and a conviction that the maintenance of the breed at its highest level of efficiency is a prime condition of national well-being—Whitman naturally treated the ordinary sexual relations with a breadth and simplicity which appear to more sophisticated minds as brutal. He does not shrink from images and descriptions, from metaphors and phrases, as closely borrowed from the facts of sex as are his pictures of the outer world, or his transcripts from the occupations of mankind. Sex, being for him so serious and excellent a thing, has the right to equal freedom of speech with sunrise or sunsetting, the stars in their courses, the woods and fields, the industries of carpenter or typesetter, the courage of soldiers, the inevitable fact of death. Therefore he speaks plainly about many things which hitherto were tacitly ignored in poetry, or were touched upon by seekers after obscene literary effects. It is not inconsequent that he should have been accused of indecency, because the things he talked of had so long been held to be indecent. Wishing to remove the stigma of indecency and obscenity, which he rightly considered due to conventionally imported prejudices, he had to face the misconstruction of those who could not comprehend his real intention.

Whitman thought and wrote habitually, not with people of culture, refined tastes, literary and social traditions in view, but for the needs and aspirations of what he called "the divine average." He aimed at depicting robust and sane humanity in his verse. He wanted to brace character, and to create through his art-work a type applicable to all sorts and conditions of men, irrespective of their previous differentiation by specific temperament or class-association. For this reason, his treatment of the sexual relations will be felt by some persons not only to be crudely frank in detail, but also to lack delicacy in its general outlines. The overwhelming attractions of sex, swaying the physique of men and women, are broadly insisted upon. The intercourse established in matrimony is regarded not so much as an intellectual and moral union, but as an association for mutual assistance in the labours of life, and for the production of noble human specimens. It is an Adamic hygienic view of marriage, satisfying the instincts of the primeval man. Take this passage, in which he describes the qualities of the help-mate for his typical male.

> Without shame the man I like knows and avows the delicious-
>   ness of his sex,
> Without shame the woman I like knows and avows hers.

Now I will dismiss myself from impassive women,
I will go stay with her who waits for me, and with those
    women that are warm-blooded and sufficient for me;
I see that they understand me, and do not deny me;
I see that they are worthy of me—I will be the robust
    husband of these women.

They are not one jot less than I am,
They are tanned in the face by shining suns and blowing
    winds,
Their flesh has the old divine suppleness and strength,
They know how to swim, row, ride, wrestle, shoot, run, strike,
    retreat, advance, resist, defend themselves.
They are ultimate in their own right—they are calm, clear,
    well-possessed of themselves.

I draw you close to me, you women!
I cannot let you go, I would do you good,
I am for you, and you are for me, not only for our own sake,
    but for others' sake;
Envelop'd in you sleep greater heroes and bards,
They refuse to awake at the touch of any man but me.

It is obvious, from this slightly humorous, but pregnant, passage, that
Whitman abandoned those dregs of mediaeval sentimentalism and
platonism, which filtering through the middle-class minds of an un-
chivalrous modern age, have resulted in commonplace notions about "the
weaker and the fairer sex," "woman's mission to console and elevate," the
"protection rendered by the stronger to the frailer," "the feminine ornament of our homes"—notions and phrases which the active-minded and
able-bodied woman of the present day repudiates, and from the thraldom
of which she is rapidly working out her way toward freedom. Whitman,
to use a phrase of Clough, looked upon love as "fellow-service." He
recognised the woman's right to share alike with man in labour and in
privilege. And it was not for nothing, as appears from some sentences in
the quotation, that he spoke in another place about "the athletic
American matron."[1]

    A theory of sexual relations, so primitive, so archetypal, so based and
planted on the primal needs and instincts, must of necessity lack much of
delicacy and fine gradations. It is, however, bracing to return to this from
the psychological studies of the modern French school, from such silly and
nauseous lucubrations as Bourget's "Physiologie de l'Amour Moderne,"
from all that stifling literature of "L'Amour Coupable," which lands us at
last in nothing better than what Whitman calls "the sly settee, and the un-
wholesome adulterous couple."

    There is an Aeschylean largeness, a Lucretian energy, in Whitman's

"Children of Adam." Sex is once again recognised; not in its aspect of the boudoir, the alcove, the brothel; but as the bass-note of the world, the universal Pan, unseen, yet omnipresent, felt by all, responded to by all, without which the whole vast symphony of things would have for man no value. By subtle associations, he connects the life of nature, in dewy forests and night-winds, in scents of fruits and pungent plants, in crushed herbs, and the rustling of rain-drenched foliage against our faces, with impressions of the sexual imagination. He finds the choicest images to shadow forth the acts of sex.

> The hairy wild bee that murmurs and hankers up and down
> —that gripes the full-grown lady-flower, curves upon
> her with amorous firm legs, takes his will of her, and
> holds himself tremulous and tight till he is satisfied.

That is audacious, in spite of its consummate style, a critic will exclaim. But the same critic, being accustomed by habit to the exercise, reads with equanimity the long-drawn paragraphs and chapters which lay bare the latest secrets of the "sly settee." The boudoir, the alcove, the brothel, have come to be recognised as legitimate subjects for analytical art. Even Bourget, even Catulle Mendès, are accepted and acclaimed. From these taints of the city and civilisation Whitman calls us away. He says in passing:

> Have you seen the fool that corrupted his own live body? or
> the fool that corrupted her own live body?
> For they do not conceal themselves, and cannot conceal them-
> selves.

Here and there he returns to this point and repeats the warning. He insists upon the truth that sins against the body, self-contamination, uncleanly lusts and refinements of sensuality, carry their own punishment. But he knows that their analysis in literature, except for the professed pathologist and psychiatrist, is harmful to the manhood of a nation; whereas the rehabitation of healthy and legitimate functions restores the natural man to a sense of his own dignity and responsibility. Nor does Whitman neglect that superflux of sense, which also claims a part in human life, that phallic ecstasy of which the pagan poets sang. A much-criticised piece from "Children of Adam" puts the matter very plainly. It is called "Native Moments," and need not be enlarged upon. Were we not expressly told by him that it is useless to extract a coherent system from his utterances, we might be puzzled to explain the logical connection of that poem with the rest of the section. I take it that he recognised the right and the necessity of "native moments" in that free play of the normal senses which he is upholding. Only, the ground-thoughts which penetrate the whole of his work upon this topic, the pervading essence whereof will remain longest with those who have imbibed its spirit, are expressed in lines like these:

> If any thing is sacred, the human body is sacred,
> And the glory and sweet of a man is the token of manhood
>   untainted;
> And in man or woman, a clean, strong, firm-fibred body is
>   beautiful as the most beautiful face.

If Aeschylus could come again, he would recognise Whitman's treatment of Aphrodite as akin to these lines of his own:

> Love throbs in holy heaven to wound the earth;
> And love still prompts the hand to yearn for bridals;
> The rain that falls in rivers from the sky,
> Impregnates earth, and she brings forth the men
> The flocks and herds and life of teeming Ceres;
> The bloom of forests by dews hymeneal
> Is perfected: in all which things I rule.

If we are to have sex handled openly in literature—and I do not see why we should not have it, or how we are to avoid it—surely it is better to be in the company of poets like Aeschylus and Whitman, who place human love among the large and universal mysteries of nature, than to dwell with theologians who confound its simple truth with sinfulness, or with self-dubbed "psychologues" who dabble in its morbid pruriencies.

The section of Whitman's works which deals with adhesiveness, or the love of comrades, is fully as important, and in some ways more difficult to deal with, than his "Children of Adam." He gave it the title "Calamus," from the root of a water-rush, adopted by him as the symbol of this love.[2] Here the element of spirituality in passion, of romantic feeling, and of deep enduring sentiment, which was almost conspicuous by its absence from the section on sexual love, emerges into vivid prominence, and lends peculiar warmth of poetry to the artistic treatment. We had to expect so much from the poem quoted by me at the commencement of this disquisition. There Whitman described the love of man for woman as "fast-anchor'd, eternal"; the thought of the bride, the wife, as "more resistless than I can tell." But for the love of man for man he finds quite a different class of descriptive phrases: "separate, disembodied, another born, ethereal, the last athletic reality, my consolation." He hints that we have left the realm of sex and sense, and have ascended into a different and rarer atmosphere, where passion, though it has not lost its strength, is clarified. "Largior hic aether, et campos lumine vestit purpureo."

This emphatic treatment of an emotion which is usually talked about under the vague and formal term of friendship, gives peculiar importance to "Calamus." No man in the modern world has expressed so strong a conviction that "manly attachment," "athletic love," "the high towering love of comrades," is a main factor in human life, a virtue upon which society will have to lay its firm foundations, and a passion equal in permanence, superior in spirituality, to the sexual affection. Whitman regards this emotion not only as the "consolation" of the individual, but also as a new and hitherto unapprehended force for stimulating national vitality.

There is no softness or sweetness in his treatment of this theme. His tone is sustained throughout at a high pitch of virile enthusiasm, which, at the same time, vibrates with acutest feeling, thrills with an undercurrent of the tenderest sensibility. Not only the sublimest thoughts and aspirations, but also the shyest, most shame-faced, yearnings are reserved for this love. At one time he exclaims:

> O I think it is not for life that I am chanting here my chant
>   of lovers—I think it must be for Death,
> For how calm, how solemn it grows, to ascend to the atmo-
>   sphere of lovers,
> Death or life I am then indifferent—my soul declines to
>   prefer,
> I am not sure but the high soul of lovers welcomes death
>   most;
> Indeed, O Death, I think now these leaves mean precisely the
>   same as you mean;
> Grow up taller, sweet leaves, that I may see! Grow up out
>   of my breast!
> Spring away from the concealed heart there!
> Do not fold yourselves so, in your pink-tinged roots, timid
>   leaves!
> Do not remain down there so ashamed, herbage of my breast!

The leaves are Whitman's emotions and the poems they engender; the root from which they spring is "manly attachment," "athletic love," symbolised for him in the blushing root of the pond-calamus which he plucked one day and chose to be the emblem of the love of lovers:

> O here I last saw him that tenderly loves me—and returns
>   again, never to separate from me,
> And this, O this shall henceforth be the token of comrades—
>   this Calamus-root shall,
> Interchange it, youths, with each other! Let none render it
>   back!

At another time, in minor key, he writes as follows:

> O you when I often and silently come where you are, that I
>   may be with you;
> As I walk by your side, or sit near, or remain in the same
>   room with you,
> Little you know the subtle, electric fire that for your sake is
>   playing within me.

These extracts were necessary, because there is some misapprehension abroad regarding the precise nature of what Whitman meant by "Calamus." His method of treatment has, to a certain extent, exposed him to misconstruction. Still, as his friend and commentator, Mr. Burroughs, puts it: "The sentiment is primitive, athletic, taking form in all manner of large and homely out-of-door images, and springs, as any one may see, directly from the heart and experience of the poet." The language has a passionate glow, a warmth of devotion, beyond anything to which the world is used in the celebration of friendship. At the same time the false note of insincerity or sensuousness is never heard. The melody is in the Dorian mood—recalling to our minds that fellowship in arms which flourished among the Dorian tribes, and formed the chivalry of pre-historic Hellas.

In the preface to the 1880 edition of *Leaves of Grass* and *Two Rivulets*, Whitman gives his own explanation of "Calamus," and of the feelings which inspired that section of his work.

> Something more may be added—for, while I am about it, I would make a full confession. I also sent out *Leaves of Grass* to arouse and set flowing in men's and women's hearts, young and old, endless streams of living, pulsating love and friendship, directly from them to myself, now and ever. To this terrible, irrepressible yearning (surely more or less down underneath in most human souls), this never-satisfied appetite for sympathy, and this boundless offering of sympathy, this universal democratic comradeship, this old, eternal, yet ever-new interchange of adhesiveness, so fitly emblematic of America, I have given in that book, undisguisedly, declaredly, the openest expression. Besides, important as they are in my purpose as emotional expressions for humanity, the special meaning of the "Calamus," cluster of *Leaves of Grass* (and more or less running through the book and cropping out in "Drum Taps"), mainly resides in its political significance. In my opinion, it is by a fervent accepted development of comradeship, the beautiful and sane affection of man for man, latent in all the young fellows, north and south, east and west—it is by this, I say, and by what goes directly and indirectly along with it, that the United States of the future (I cannot too often repeat) are to be the most effectu-ally welded together, intercalated, annealed into a living union.

This being so, Whitman never suggests that comradeship may occa-sion the development of physical desire. On the other hand, he does not in set terms condemn desires, or warn his disciples against their perils. There is indeed a distinctly sensuous side to his conception of adhesiveness. To a Western Boy he says:

> If you be not silently selected by lovers, and do not silently
>   select lovers,
> Of what use is it that you seek to become elect of mine?

Like Plato, in the *Phædrus*, Whitman describes an enthusiastic type of masculine emotion, leaving its private details to the moral sense and special inclination of the individuals concerned.

The poet himself appears to be not wholly unconscious that there are dangers and difficulties involved in the highly-pitched emotions he is praising. The whole tenor of two carefully-toned compositions, entitled, "Whoever you are, Holding me now in hand," and "Trickle, Drops," suggest an underlying sense of spiritual conflict. The following poem, again, is sufficiently significant and typical to call for literal transcription:

> Earthy, my likeness!
> Though you look so impassive, ample and spheric there,
> I now suspect that is not all;
> I now suspect there is something fierce in you, eligible to burst
>   forth;
> For an athlete is enamoured of me—and I of him,
> But toward him there is something fierce and terrible in me,
>   eligible to burst forth,
> I dare not tell it in word—not even in these songs.

The reality of Whitman's feeling, the intense delight which he derives from the personal presence and physical contact of a beloved man, find luminous expression in "A Glimpse," "Recorders Ages Hence," "When I Heard at the Close of the Day," "I Saw in Lousiana a Live-Oak Growing," "I Thought that Knowledge Alone Would Suffice Me,"[3] "O Tan-faced Prairie-Boy," and "Vigil Strange I Kept on the Field One Night."[4]

It is clear then that, in his treatment of comradeship, or the impassioned love of man for man, Whitman has struck a keynote, to the emotional intensity of which the modern world is unaccustomed. It therefore becomes of much importance to discover the poet-prophet's *Stimmung*—his radical instinct with regard to the moral quality of the feeling he encourages. Studying his works by their own light, and by the light of their author's character, interpreting each part by reference to the whole and in the spirit of the whole, an impartial critic will, I think, be drawn to the conclusion that what he calls the "adhesiveness" of comradeship is meant to have no interblending with the "amativeness" of sexual love. Personally, it is undeniable that Whitman possessed a specially keen sense of the fine restraint and continence, the cleanliness and chastity, that are inseparable from the perfectly virile and physically complete nature of healthy manhood. Still we have the right to predicate the same ground-qualities in the early Dorians, those founders of the martial institution of Greek love; and yet it is notorious to students of Greek civilisation that the lofty sentiment of their masculine chivalry was intertwined with much that is repulsive to modern sentiment.

Whitman does not appear to have taken some of the phenomena of contemporary morals into due account, although he must have been aware of them. Else he would have foreseen that, human nature being what it is, we cannot expect to eliminate all sensual alloy from emotions raised to a high pitch of passionate intensity, and that permanent elements within the midst of our society will imperil the absolute purity of the ideal he attempts to establish. It is obvious that those unenviable mortals who are the inheritors of sexual anomalies, will recognise their own emotion in Whitman's "superb friendship, exalté, previously unknown," which "waits, and has been always waiting, latent in all men," the "something fierce in me, eligible to burst forth," "ethereal comradeship," "the last comradeship," "the last athletic reality." Had I not the strongest proof in Whitman's private correspondence with myself that he repudiated any such deductions from his "Calamus," I admit that I should have regarded them as justified; and I am not certain whether his own feelings upon this delicate topic may not have altered since the time when "Calamus" was first composed.

These considerations do not, however, affect the spiritual quality of his ideal. After acknowledging, what Whitman omitted to perceive, that there are inevitable points of contact between sexual anomaly and his doctrine of comradeship, the question now remains whether he has not suggested the way whereby abnormal instincts may be moralised and raised to higher value. In other words, are those exceptional instincts provided in "Calamus" with the means of their salvation from the filth and mire of brutal appetite? It is difficult to answer this question; for the issue involved is nothing less momentous than the possibility of evoking a new chivalrous enthusiasm, analogous to that of primitive Hellenic society, from emotions which are at present classified among the turpitudes of human nature.

Let us look a little closer at the expression which Whitman has given to his own feelings about friendship. The first thing that strikes us is the mystic emblem he has chosen for masculine love. That is the water-plant, or scented rush, called "Calamus," which springs in wild places, "in paths untrodden, in the growth by margins of pond-waters." He has chosen these "emblematic and capricious blades" because of their shyness, their aromatic perfume, their aloofness from the patent life of the world. He calls them "sweet leaves, pink-tinged roots, timid leaves," "scented herbage of my breast." Finally, he says:

> Here my last words, and the most baffling,
> Here the frailest leaves of me, and yet my strongest-lasting.
> Here I shade down, and hide my thoughts—I do not expose them.
> And yet they expose me more than all my other poems.[5]

The manliness of the emotion which is thus so shyly, allegorically indicated, appears in the magnificent address to soldiers at the close of the great war: "Over the Carnage Rose Prophetic a Voice."[6] Its tenderness emerges in the elegy on a slain comrade:

> Vigil for boy of responding kisses (never again on earth
>   responding):
> Vigil for comrade swiftly slain—vigil I never forget, how as
>   day brightened,
> I rose from the chill ground, and folded my soldier well in his
>   blanket,
> And buried him where he fell.[7]

Its pathos and clinging intensity transpire through the last lines of the following piece, which may have been suggested by the legends of David and Jonathan, Achilles and Patroclus, Orestes and Pylades:

> When I peruse the conquered fame of heroes, and the victories,
>   of mighty generals,
> I do not envy the generals.
> Nor the President in his Presidency, nor the rich in his great
>   house;
> But when I read of the brotherhood of lovers, how it was with
>   them,
> How through life, through dangers, odium, unchanging, long
>   and long,
> Through youth, and through middle and old age, how un-
>   faltering, how affectionate and faithful they were,
> Then I am pensive—I hastily put down the book, and walk
>   away, filled with the bitterest envy.[8]

But Whitman does not conceive of comradeship as a merely personal possession, delightful to the friends it links in bonds of amity. He regards it eventually as a social and political virtue. This human emotion is destined to cement society and to render commonwealths inviolable. Reading some of his poems, we are carried back to ancient Greece—to Plato's *Symposium*, to Philip gazing on the sacred band of Thebans after the fight at Chaeronea.

> I dream'd in a dream, I saw a city invincible to the attacks of
>   the whole of the rest of the earth;
> I dream'd that was the new City of Friends;
> Nothing was greater there than the quality of robust love—it
>   led the rest;
> It was seen every hour in the actions of the men of that city,
> And in all their looks and words.[9]

And again:

> I believe the main purport of These States is to found a superb
>   friendship, exalté, previously unknown,

> Because I perceive it waits, and has been always waiting,
>   latent in all men.[10]

And once again:

> Come, I will make the continent indissoluble;
> I will make the most splendid race the sun ever yet shone
>   upon;
> I will make divine magnetic lands,
>   With the love of comrades,
>   With the life-long love of comrades.[11]
> I will plant companionship thick as trees all along the rivers
>   of America, and along the shores of the great lakes, and
>   all over the prairies;
> I will make inseparable cities, with their arms about each
>   other's necks;
>   By the love of comrades,
>   By the manly love of comrades.

> For you these from me, O Democracy, to serve you *ma
>   femme*!
> For you, for you I am trilling these songs.

We may return from this analysis to the inquiry whether anything like a new chivalry is to be expected from the doctrines of "Calamus," which shall in the future utilise for noble purposes some of those unhappy instincts which at present run to waste in vice and shame. It may be asked what these passions have in common with the topic of Whitman's prophecy? They have this in common with it. Whitman recognises among the sacred emotions and social virtues, destined to regenerate political life and to cement nations, an intense, jealous, throbbing, sensitive, expectant love of man for man: a love which yearns in absence, droops under the sense of neglect, revives at the return of the beloved: a love that finds honest delight in hand-touch, meeting lips, hours of privacy, close personal contact. He proclaims this love to be not only a daily fact in the present, but also a saving and ennobling aspiration. While he expressly repudiates, disowns, and brands as "damnable" all "morbid inferences" which may be drawn by malevolence or vicious cunning from his doctrine, he is prepared to extend the gospel of comradeship to the whole human race. He expects democracy, the new social and political medium, the new religious ideal of mankind, to develop and extend "that fervid comradeship," and by its means to counterbalance and to spiritualise what is vulgar and materialistic in the modern world. "Democracy," he maintains, "infers such loving comradeship, as its most inevitable twin or counterpart, without which it will be incomplete, in vain, and incapable of perpetuating itself."[12]

If this be not a dream, if he is right in believing that "threads of manly friendship, fond and loving, pure and sweet, strong and life-long, carried to degrees hitherto unknown," will penetrate the organism of society, "not only giving tone to individual character, and making it unprecedentedly emotional, muscular, heroic, and refined, but having deepest relations to general politics"—then are we perhaps justified in foreseeing here the advent of an enthusiasm which shall rehabilitate those outcast instincts, by giving them a spiritual atmosphere, an environment of recognised and healthy emotions, wherein to expand at liberty and purge away the grossness and the madness of their pariahdom?

This prospect, like all ideals, until they are realised in experience, may seem fantastically visionary. Moreover, the substance of human nature is so mixed that it would perhaps be fanatical to expect from Whitman's chivalry of "adhesiveness," a more immaculate purity than was attained by the mediaeval chivalry of "amativeness." Nevertheless, that mediaeval chivalry, the great emotional product of feudalism, though it fell short of its own aspiration, bequeathed incalculable good to modern society by refining and clarifying the crudest of male appetites. In like manner, this democratic chivalry, announced by Whitman, may be destined to absorb, control, and elevate those darker, more mysterious, apparently abnormal appetites, which we know to be widely diffused and ineradicable in the ground-work of human nature.

Returning from the dream, the vision of a future possibility, it will, at any rate, be conceded that Whitman has founded comradeship, the enthusiasm which binds man to man in fervent love, upon a natural basis. Eliminating classical associations of corruption, ignoring the perplexed questions of a guilty passion doomed by law and popular antipathy to failure, he begins anew with sound and primitive humanity. There he discovers "a superb friendship, exalté, previously unknown." He perceives that "it waits, and has been always waiting, latent in all men." His method of treatment, fearless, and uncowed by any thought of evil, his touch upon the matter, chaste and wholesome and aspiring, reveal the possibility of restoring in all innocence to human life a portion of its alienated or unclaimed moral birthright.

It were well to close upon this note. The half, as the Greeks said, is more than the whole; and the time has not yet come to raise the question whether the love of man for man shall be elevated through a hitherto unapprehended chivalry to nobler powers, even as the barbarous love of man for woman once was. This question at the present moment is deficient in actuality. The world cannot be invited to entertain it.

Notes

1. In the preface to the 1872 edition of *Leaves of Grass*, Whitman asserts that this book "is, in its intentions, the song of a great composite *democratic individual*, male or female."

2. Its botanical name is Acorus Calamus. We call it "sweet-rush" or "sweet sedge."

3. Not included in the *Complete Poems and Prose*. It will be found in *Leaves of Grass* (Boston, 1860–61).

4. The two last are from "Drum-Taps."

5. This I cannot find in *Complete Poems and Prose*. It is included in the Boston edition, 1860–61, and the Camden edition, 1876.

6. "Drum-Taps," *Complete Poems*, p. 247.

7. *Ibid.*, p. 238.

8. "Leaves of Grass," *Complete Poems*, p. 107. Since writing the above, I have been privileged to read a series of letters addressed by Whitman to a young man, whom I will call P[eter Doyle]., and who was tenderly beloved by him. They throw a flood of light upon "Calamus," and are superior to any commentary. It is greatly to be hoped that they may be published. Whitman, it seems, met P. at Washington not long before the year 1869, when the lad was about eighteen years of age. They soon became attached, Whitman's friendship being returned with at least equal warmth by P. The letters breathe a purity and simplicity of affection, a *naïveté* and reasonableness, which are very remarkable considering the unmistakable intensity of the emotion. Throughout them, Whitman shows the tenderest and wisest care for his young friend's welfare, helps him in material ways, and bestows upon him the best advice, the heartiest encouragement, without betraying any sign of patronage or preaching. Illness soon attacked Walt. He retired to Camden, and P., who was employed as "baggage-master on the freight-trains" of a railway, was for long unable to visit him. There is something very wistful in the words addressed from a distance by the aging poet to this "son of responding kisses." I regret that we do not possess P.'s answers. Yet, probably, to most readers, they would not appear highly interesting; for it is clear he was only an artless and uncultured workman.

9. *Complete Poems*, p. 109. Compare, "I hear it was charged against me," *ibid.*, p. 107.

10. *Complete Poems*, p. 110.

11. Camden edition, 1876, p. 127; *Complete Poems*, p. 99. Compare "Democratic Vistas," *Complete Prose*, p. 247, note.

12. These prose passages are taken from "Democratic Vistas," cited above, p. 94, note.

[*"sometimes sublime, sometimes ridiculous"*]

Speaking of monuments reminds one that there is more talk about a monument to Walt Whitman, "the good, gray poet." Just why the adjective good is always applied to Whitman it is difficult to discover, probably because people who could not understand him at all took it for granted that he meant well. If ever there was a poet who had no literary ethics at all beyond those of nature, it was he. He was neither good nor bad, any more than are the animals he continually admired and envied. He was a poet without an exclusive sense of the poetic, a man without the finer discriminations, enjoying everything with the unreasoning enthusiasm of a boy. He was the poet of the dung hill as well as of the mountains, which is admirable in theory but excruciating in verse. In the same paragraph he informs you that, "The pure contralto sings in the organ loft," and that "The malformed limbs are tied to the table, what is removed drop horribly into a pail." No branch of surgery is poetic, and that hopelessly prosaic word "pail" would kill a whole volume of sonnets. Whitman's poems are reckless rhapsodies over creation in general, sometimes sublime, sometimes ridiculous. He declares that the ocean with its "imperious waves, commanding" is beautiful, and that the fly-specks on the walls are also beautiful. Such catholic taste may go in science, but in poetry their results are sad. The poet's task is usually to select the poetic. Whitman never bothers to do that, he takes everything in the universe from fly-specks to the fixed stars. His *Leaves of Grass* is a sort of dictionary of the English language, and in it is the name of everything in creation set down with great reverence but without any particular connection.

But however ridiculous Whitman may be there is a primitive elemental force about him. He is so full of hardiness and of the joy of life. He looks at all nature in the delighted, admiring way in which the old Greeks and the primitive poets did. He exults so in the red blood in his body and the strength in his arms. He has such a passion for the warmth and dignity

*Reprinted from *The Kingdom of Art: Willa Cather's First Principles and Critical Statements, 1893–1896*, ed. Bernice Slote (Lincoln: Univ. of Nebr. Press, 1966), pp. 351–53, with the permission of the Univ. of Nebr. Press. The essay originally appeared in the *Nebraska State Journal* for 19 Jan. 1896.

of all that is natural. He has no code but to be natural, a code that this complex world has so long outgrown. He is sensual, not after the manner of Swinburne and Gautier, who are always seeking for perverted and bizarre effects on the senses, but in the frank fashion of the old barbarians who ate and slept and married and smacked their lips over the mead horn. He is rigidly limited to the physical, things that quicken his pulses, please his eyes or delight his nostrils. There is an element of poetry in all this, but it is by no means the highest. If a joyous elephant should break forth into song, his lay would probably be very much like Whitman's famous "Song of Myself." It would have just about as much delicacy and deftness and discrimination. He says: "I think I could turn and live with the animals. They are so placid and self-contained, I stand and look at them long and long. They do not sweat and whine about their condition. They do not lie awake in the dark and weep for their sins. They do not make me sick discussing their duty to God. Not one is dissatisfied nor not one is demented with the mania of many things. Not one kneels to another nor to his kind that lived thousands of years ago. Not one is respectable or unhappy, over the whole earth." And that is not irony on nature, he means just that, life meant no more to him. He accepted the world just as it is and glorified it, the seemly and unseemly, the good and the bad. He had no conception of a difference in people or in things. All men had bodies and were alike to him, one about as good as another. To live was to fulfil all natural laws and impulses. To be comfortable was to be happy. To be happy was the ultimatum. He did not realize the existence of a conscience or a responsibility. He had no more thought of good or evil than the folks in Kipling's *Jungle Book*.

And yet there is an undeniable charm about this optimistic vagabond who is made so happy by the warm sunshine and the smell of spring fields. A sort of good fellowship and whole-heartedness in every line he wrote. His veneration for things physical and material, for all that is in water or air or land, is so real that as you read him you think for the moment that you would rather like to live so if you could. For the time you half believe that a sound body and a strong arm are the greatest things in the world. Perhaps no book shows so much as *Leaves of Grass* that keen senses do not make a poet. When you read it you realize how spirited a thing poetry really is and how great a part spiritual perceptions play in apparently sensuous verse, if only to select the beautiful from the gross.

The Poetry of Barbarism

George Santayana*

It is an observation at first sight melancholy but in the end, perhaps, enlightening, that the earliest poets are the most ideal, and that primitive ages furnish the most heroic characters and have the clearest vision of a perfect life. The Homeric times must have been full of ignorance and suffering. In those little barbaric towns, in those camps and farms, in those shipyards, there must have been much insecurity and superstition. That age was singularly poor in all that concerns the convenience of life and the entertainment of the mind with arts and sciences. Yet it had a sense for civilization. That machinery of life which men were beginning to devise appealed to them as poetical; they knew its ultimate justification and studied its incipient processes with delight. The poetry of that simple and ignorant age was, accordingly, the sweetest and sanest that the world has known; the most faultless in taste, and the most even and lofty in inspiration. Without lacking variety and homeliness, it bathed all things human in the golden light of morning; it clothed sorrow in a kind of majesty, instinct with both self-control and heroic frankness. Nowhere else can we find so noble a rendering of human nature, so spontaneous a delight in life, so uncompromising a dedication to beauty, and such a gift of seeing beauty in everything. Homer, the first of poets, was also the best and the most poetical.

From this beginning, if we look down the history of Occidental literature, we see the power of idealization steadily decline. For while it finds here and there, as in Dante, a more spiritual theme and a subtler and riper intellect, it pays for that advantage by a more than equivalent loss in breadth, sanity, and happy vigour. And if ever imagination bursts out with a greater potency, as in Shakespeare (who excels the patriarch of poetry in depth of passion and vividness of characterization, and in those exquisite bubblings of poetry and humour in which English genius is at its best), yet Shakespeare also pays the price by a notable loss in taste, in sustained inspiration, in consecration, and in rationality. There is more or less rubbish in his greatest works. When we come down to our own day

*Reprinted from *Interpretations of Poetry and Religion* (New York: Charles Scribner's Sons, 1900), pp. 166–87.

we find poets of hardly less natural endowment (for in endowment all ages are perhaps alike) and with vastly richer sources of inspiration; for they have many arts and literatures behind them, with the spectacle of a varied and agitated society, a world which is the living microcosm of its own history and presents in one picture many races, arts, and religions. Our poets have more wonderful tragedies of the imagination to depict than had Homer, whose world was innocent of any essential defeat, or Dante, who believed in the world's definitive redemption. Or, if perhaps their inspiration is comic, they have the pageant of mediaeval manners, with its picturesque artifices and passionate fancies, and the long comedy of modern social revolutions, so illusory in their aims and so productive in their aimlessness. They have, moreover, the new and marvellous conception which natural science has given us of the world and of the conditions of human progress.

With all these lessons of experience behind them, however, we find our contemporary poets incapable of any high wisdom, incapable of any imaginative rendering of human life and its meaning. Our poets are things of shreds and patches; they give us episodes and studies, a sketch of this curiosity, a glimpse of that romance; they have no total vision, no grasp of the whole reality, and consequently no capacity for a sane and steady idealization. The comparatively barbarous ages had a poetry of the ideal; they had visions of beauty, order, and perfection. This age of material elaboration has no sense for those things. Its fancy is retrospective, whimsical, and flickering; its ideals, when it has any, are negative and partial; its moral strength is a blind and miscellaneous vehemence. Its poetry, in a word, is the poetry of barbarism.

This poetry should be viewed in relation to the general moral crisis and imaginative disintegration of which it gives a verbal echo; then we shall avoid the injustice of passing it over as insignificant, no less than the imbecility of hailing it as essentially glorious and successful. We must remember that the imagination of our race has been subject to a double discipline. It has been formed partly in the school of classic literature and polity, and partly in the school of Christian piety. This duality of inspiration, this contradiction between the two accepted methods of rationalizing the world, has been a chief source of that incoherence, that romantic indistinctness and imperfection, which largely characterize the products of the modern arts. A man cannot serve two masters; yet the conditions have not been such as to allow him wholly to despise the one or wholly to obey the other. To be wholly Pagan is impossible after the dissolution of that civilization which had seemed universal, and that empire which had believed itself eternal. To be wholly Christian is impossible for a similar reason, now that the illusion and cohesion of Christian ages is lost, and for the further reason that Christianity was itself fundamentally eclectic. Before it could succeed and dominate men even for a time, it was obliged to adjust itself to reality, to incorporate many elements of Pagan wisdom, and to accommodate itself to many habits and passions at variance with its own ideal.

In these latter times, with the prodigious growth of material life in elaboration and of mental life in diffusion, there has supervened upon this old dualism a new faith in man's absolute power, a kind of return to the inexperience and self-assurance of youth. This new inspiration has made many minds indifferent to the two traditional disciplines; neither is seriously accepted by them, for the reason, excellent from their own point of view, that no discipline whatever is needed. The memory of ancient disillusions has faded with time. Ignorance of the past has bred contempt for the lessons which the past might teach. Men prefer to repeat the old experiment without knowing that they repeat it.

I say advisedly ignorance of the past, in spite of the unprecedented historical erudition of our time; for life is an art not to be learned by observation, and the most minute and comprehensive studies do not teach us what the spirit of man should have learned by its long living. We study the past as a dead object, as a ruin, not as an authority and as an experiment. One reason why history was less interesting to former ages was that they were less conscious of separation from the past. The perspective of time was less clear because the synthesis of experience was more complete. The mind does not easily discriminate the successive phases of an action in which it is still engaged; it does not arrange in a temporal series the elements of a single perception, but posits them all together as constituting a permanent and real object. Human nature and the life of the world were real and stable objects to the apprehension of our forefathers; the actors changed, but not the characters or the play. Men were then less studious derivations because they were more conscious of identities. They thought of all reality as in a sense contemporary, and in considering the maxims of a philosopher or the style of a poet, they were not primarily concerned with settling his date and describing his environment. The standard by which they judged was eternal; the environment in which man found himself did not seem to them subject of any essential change.

To us the picturesque element in history is more striking because we feel ourselves the children of our own age only, an age which being itself singular and revolutionary, tends to read its own character into the past, and to regard all other periods as no less fragmentary and effervescent than itself. The changing and the permanent elements are, indeed, everywhere present, and the bias of the observer may emphasize the one or the other as it will: the only question is whether we find the significance of things in their variations or in their similarities.

Now the habit of regarding the past as effete and as merely a stepping-stone to something present or future, is unfavourable to any true apprehension of that element in the past which was vital and which remains eternal. It is a habit of thought that destroys the sense of the moral identity of all ages, by virtue of its very insistence on the mechanical derivation of one age from another. Existences that cause one another exclude one another; each is alien to the rest inasmuch as it is the product of new and different conditions. Ideas that cause nothing unite all things by giving them a common point of reference and a single standard of value.

The classic and the Christian systems were both systems of ideas, attempts to seize the eternal morphology of reality and describe its unchanging constitution. The imagination was summoned thereby to contemplate the highest objects, and the essence of things being thus described, their insignificant variations could retain little importance and the study of these variations might well seem superficial. Mechanical science, the science of causes, was accordingly neglected, while the science of values, with the arts that express these values, was exclusively pursued. The reverse has now occurred and the spirit of life, innocent of any rationalizing discipline and deprived of an authoritative and adequate method of expression, has relapsed into miscellaneous and shallow exuberance. Religion and art have become short-winded. They have forgotten the old maxim that we should copy in order to be copied and remember in order to be remembered. It is true that the multiplicity of these incompetent efforts seems to many a compensation for their ill success, or even a ground for asserting their absolute superiority. Incompetence, when it flatters the passions, can always find a greater incompetence to approve of it. Indeed, some people would have regarded the Tower of Babel as the best academy of eloquence on account of the variety of oratorical methods prevailing there.

It is thus that the imagination of our time has relapsed into barbarism. But discipline of the heart and fancy is always so rare a thing that the neglect of it need not be supposed to involve any very terrible or obvious loss. The triumphs of reason have been few and partial at any time, and perfect works of art are almost unknown. The failure of art and reason, because their principle is ignored, is therefore hardly more conspicuous than it was when their principle, although perhaps acknowledged, was misunderstood or disobeyed. Indeed, to one who fixes his eye on the ideal goal, the greatest art often seems the greatest failure, because it alone reminds him of what it should have been. Trivial stimulations coming from vulgar objects, on the contrary, by making us forget altogether the possibility of a deep satisfaction, often succeed in interesting and in winning applause. The pleasure they give us is so brief and superficial that the wave of essential disappointment which would ultimately drown it has not time to rise from the heart.

The poetry of barbarism is not without its charm. It can play with sense and passion the more readily and freely in that it does not aspire to subordinate them to a clear thought or a tenable attitude of the will. 't can impart the transitive emotions which it expresses; it can find many partial harmonies of mood and fancy; it can, by virtue of its red-hot irrationality, utter wilder cries, surrender itself and us to more absolute passion, and heap up a more indiscriminate wealth of images than belong to poets of seasoned experience or of heavenly inspiration. Irrational stimulation may tire us in the end, but it excites us in the beginning; and how many conventional poets, tender and prolix, have there not been, who tire us now without ever having excited anybody? The power to stimulate is the beginning of greatness, and when the barbarous poet has genius, as he well may have, he stimulates all the more powerfully on account of the crudity of his methods and the recklessness of his emotions. The defects of such art—lack of distinction, absence of beauty, confusion of ideas, incapacity permanently to please—will hardly be felt by the contemporary public, if once its attention is arrested; for no poet is so undisciplined that he will not find many readers, if he finds readers at all, less disciplined than himself.

These considerations may perhaps be best enforced by applying them to two writers of great influence over the present generation who seem to illustrate them on different planes—Robert Browning and Walt Whitman. They are both analytic poets—poets who seek to reveal and express the elemental as opposed to the conventional; but the dissolution has progressed much farther in Whitman than in Browning, doubtless because Whitman began at a much lower stage of moral and intellectual organization; for the good will to be radical was present in both. The elements to which Browning reduces experience are still passions, characters, persons; Whitman carries the disintegration further and knows nothing but moods and particular images. The world of Browning is a world of history with civilization for its setting and with the conventional passions for its motive forces. The world of Whitman is innocent of these things and contains only far simpler and more chaotic elements. In him the barbarism is much more pronounced; it is, indeed, avowed, and the "barbaric yawp" is sent "over the roofs of the world" in full consciousness of its inarticulate character; but in Browning the barbarism is no less real though disguised by a literary and scientific language, since the passions of civilized life with which he deals are treated as so many "barbaric yawps," complex indeed in their conditions, puffings of an intricate engine, but aimless in their vehemence and mere ebullitions of lustiness in adventurous and profoundly ungoverned souls.

Irrationality on this level is viewed by Browning with the same satisfaction with which, on a lower level, it is viewed by Whitman; and the admirers of each hail it as the secret of a new poetry which pierces to the quick and awakens the imagination to a new and genuine vitality. It is in the rebellion against discipline, in the abandonment of the ideals of classic and Christian tradition, that this rejuvenation is found. Both poets represent, therefore, and are admired for representing, what may be called the poetry of barbarism in the most accurate and descriptive sense of this word. For the barbarian is the man who regards his passions as their own excuse for being; who does not domesticate them either by understanding their cause or by conceiving their ideal goal. He is the man who does not know his derivations nor perceive his tendencies, but who merely feels and acts, valuing in his life its force and its filling, but being careless of its purpose and its form. His delight is in abundance and vehemence; his art, like his life, shows an exclusive respect for quantity and splendour of materials. His scorn for what is poorer and weaker than himself is only surpassed by his ignorance of what is higher.

Walt Whitman

The works of Walt Whitman offer an extreme illustration of this phase of genius, both by their form and by their substance. It was the singularity of his literary form—the challenge it threw to the conventions of verse and of language—that first gave Whitman notoriety: but this notoriety has become fame, because those incapacities and solecisms which glare at us from his pages are only the obverse of a profound inspiration and of a genuine courage. Even the idiosyncrasies of his style have a side which is not mere peversity or affectation; the order of his words, the procession of his images, reproduce the method of a rich, spontaneous, absolutely lazy fancy. In most poets such a natural order is modified by various governing motives—the thought, the metrical form, the echo of other poems in the memory. By Walt Whitman these conventional influences are resolutely banished. We find the swarms of men and objects rendered as they might strike the retina in a sort of waking dream. It is the most sincere possible confession of the lowest—I mean the most primitive—type of perception. All ancient poets are sophisticated in comparison and give proof of longer intellectual and moral training. Walt Whitman has gone back to the innocent style of Adam, when the animals filed before him one by one and he called each of them by its name.

In fact, the influences to which Walt Whitman was subject were as favourable as possible to the imaginary experiment of beginning the world over again. Liberalism, and transcendentalism both harboured some illusions on that score; and they were in the air which our poet breathed. Moreover he breathed this air in America, where the newness of the material environment made it easier to ignore the fatal antiquity of human nature. When he afterward became aware that there was or had been a world with a history, he studied that world with curiosity and spoke of it not without a certain shrewdness. But he still regarded it as a foreign world and imagined, as not a few Americans have done, that his own world was a fresh creation, not amenable to the same laws as the old. The difference in the conditions blinded him, in his merely sensuous apprehension, to the identity of the principles.

His parents were farmers in central Long Island and his early years were spent in that district. The family seems to have been not too prosperous and somewhat nomadic; Whitman himself drifted through

boyhood without much guidance. We find him now at school, now help-
ing the labourers at the farms, now wandering along the beaches of Long
Island, finally at Brooklyn working in an apparently desultory way as a
printer and sometimes as a writer for a local newspaper. He must have
read or heard something, at this early period, of the English classics; his
style often betrays the deep effect made upon him by the grandiloquence
of the Bible, of Shakespeare, and of Milton. But his chief interest, if we
may trust his account, was already in his own sensations. The aspects of
Nature, the forms and habits of animals, the sights of cities, the movement and talk of common people, were his constant delight. His mind was
flooded with these images, keenly felt and afterward to be vividly
rendered with bold strokes of realism and imagination.

Many poets have had this faculty to seize the elementary aspects of
things, but none has had it so exclusively; with Whitman the surface is absolutely all and the underlying structure is without interest and almost
without existence. He had had no education and his natural delight in im-
bibing sensations had not been trained to the uses of practical or
theoretical intelligence. He basked in the sunshine of perception and
wallowed in the stream of his own sensibility, as later at Camden in the
shallows of his favourite brook. Even during the civil war, when he heard
the drum-taps so clearly, he could only gaze at the picturesque and terrible aspects of the struggle, and linger among the wounded day after day
with a canine devotion; he could not be aroused either to clear thought or
to positive action. So also in his poems; a multiplicity of images pass
before him and he yields himself to each in turn with absolute passivity.
The world has no inside; it is a phantasmagoria of continuous visions,
vivid, impressive, but monotonous and hard to distinguish in memory,
like the waves of the sea or the decorations of some barbarous temple,
sublime only by the infinite aggregation of parts.

This abundance of detail without organization, this wealth of
perception without intelligence and of imagination without taste, makes
the singularity of Whitman's genius. Full of sympathy and receptivity,
with a wonderful gift of graphic characterization and an occasional rare
grandeur of diction, he fills us with a sense of the individuality and the
universality of what he describes—it is a drop in itself yet a drop in the
ocean. The absence of any principle of selection or of a sustained style
enables him to render aspects of things and of emotion which would have
eluded a trained writer. He is, therefore, interesting even where he is grotesque or perverse. He has accomplished, by the sacrifice of almost every
other good quality, something never so well done before. He has approached common life without bringing in his mind any higher standard
by which to criticise it; he has seen it, not in contrast with an ideal, but as
the expression of forces more indeterminate and elementary than itself;
and the vulgar, in this cosmic setting, has appeared to him sublime.

There is clearly some analogy between a mass of images without structure and the notion of an absolute democracy. Whitman, inclined by his genius and habits to see life without relief or organization, believed that his inclination in this respect corresponded with the spirit of his age and country, and that Nature and society, at least in the United States, were constituted after the fashion of his own mind. Being the poet of the average man, he wished all men to be specimens of that average, and being the poet of a fluid Nature, he believed that Nature was or should be a formless flux. This personal bias of Whitman's was further encouraged by the actual absence of distinction in his immediate environment. Surrounded by ugly things and common people, he felt himself happy, ecstatic, overflowing with a kind of patriarchal love. He accordingly came to think that there was a spirit of the New World which he embodied, and which was in complete opposition to that of the Old, and that a literature upon novel principles was needed to express and strengthen this American spirit.

Democracy was not to be merely a constitutional device for the better government of given nations, not merely a movement for the material improvement of the lot of the poorer classes. It was to be a social and a moral democracy and to involve an actual equality among all men. Whatever kept them apart and made it impossible for them to be messmates together was to be discarded. The literature of democracy was to ignore all extraordinary gifts of genius or virtue, all distinction drawn even from great passions or romantic adventures. In Whitman's works, in which this new literature is foreshadowed, there is accordingly not a single character nor a single story. His only hero is Myself, the "single separate person," endowed with the primary impulses, with health, and with sensitiveness to the elementary aspects of Nature. The perfect man of the future, the prolific begetter of other perfect men, is to work with his hands, chanting the poems of some future Walt, some ideally democratic bard. Women are to have as nearly as possible the same character as men: the emphasis is to pass from family life and local ties to the friendship of comrades and the general brotherhood of man. Men are to be vigorous, comfortable, sentimental, and irresponsible.

This dream is, of course, unrealized and unrealizable, in America as elsewhere. Undeniably there are in America many suggestions of such a society and such a national character. But the growing complexity and fixity of institutions necessarily tends to obscure these traits of a primitive and crude democracy. What Whitman seized upon as the promise of the future was in reality the survival of the past. He sings the songs of pioneers, but it is in the nature of the pioneer that the greater his success the quicker must be his transformation into something different. When Whitman made the initial and amorphous phase of society his ideal, he became the prophet of a lost cause. That cause was lost, not merely when wealth and intelligence began to take shape in the American Commonwealth, but it was lost at the very foundation of the world, when those laws of evolution were established which Whitman, like Rousseau, failed to understand. If we may trust Mr. Herbert Spencer, these laws involve a passage from the homogeneous to the heterogeneous, and a constant progress at once in differentiation and in organization—all, in a word, that Whitman systematically deprecated or ignored. He is surely not the spokesman of the tendencies of his country, although he describes some aspects of its past and present condition: nor does he appeal to those whom he describes, but rather to the *dilettanti* he despises. He is regarded as representative chiefly by foreigners, who look for some grotesque expression of the genius of so young and prodigious a people.

Whitman, it is true, loved and comprehended men; but his love and comprehension had the same limits as his love and comprehension of Nature. He observed truly and responded to his observation with genuine and pervasive emotion. A great gregariousness, an innocent tolerance of moral weakness, a genuine admiration for bodily health and strength, made him bubble over with affection for the generic human creature. Incapable of an ideal passion, he was full of the milk of human kindness. Yet, for all his acquaintance with the ways and thoughts of the common man of his choice, he did not truly understand him. For to understand people is to go much deeper than they go themselves; to penetrate to their characters and disentangle their inmost ideals. Whitman's insight into man did not go beyond a sensuous sympathy; it consisted in a vicarious satisfaction in their pleasures, and an instinctive love of their persons. It never approached a scientific or imaginative knowledge of their hearts.

Therefore Whitman failed radically in his dearest ambition: he can never be a poet of the people. For the people, like the early races whose poetry was ideal, are natural believers in perfection. They have no doubts about the absolute desirability of wealth and learning and power, none about the worth of pure goodness and pure love. Their chosen poets, if they have any, will be always those who have known how to paint these ideals in lively even if in gaudy colours. Nothing is farther from the common people than the corrupt desire to be primitive. They instinctively look toward a more exalted life, which they imagine to be full of distinction and pleasure, and the idea of that brighter existence fills them with hope or with envy or with humble admiration.

If the people are ever won over to hostility to such ideals, it is only because they are cheated by demagogues who tell them that if all the flowers of civilization were destroyed its fruits would become more abundant. A greater share of happiness, people think, would fall to their lot could they destroy everything beyond their own possible possessions. But they are made thus envious and ignoble only by a deception: what they really desire is an ideal good for themselves which they are told they may secure by depriving others of their preëminence. Their hope is always to enjoy perfect satisfaction themselves, and therefore a poet who loves the picturesque aspects of labour and vagrancy will hardly be the poet of the poor. He may have described their figure and occupation, in neither of which they are much interested; he will not have read their souls. They will prefer to him any sentimental story-teller, any sensational dramatist, any moralizing poet; for they are hero-worshippers by temperament, and are too wise or too unfortunate to be much enamoured of themselves or of the conditions of their existence.

Fortunately, the political theory that makes Whitman's principle of literary prophecy and criticism does not always inspire his chants, nor is it presented, even in his prose works, quite bare and unadorned. In *Democratic Vistas* we find it clothed with something of the same poetic passion and lighted up with the same flashes of intuition which we admire in the poems. Even there the temperament is finer than the ideas and the poet wiser than the thinker. His ultimate appeal is really to something more primitive and general than any social aspirations, to something more elementary than an ideal of any kind. He speaks to those minds and to those moods in which sensuality is touched with mysticism. When the intellect is in abeyance, when we would "turn and live with the animals, they are so placid and self-contained," when we are weary of conscience and of ambition, and would yield ourselves for a while to the dream of sense, Walt Whitman is a welcome companion. The images he arouses in us, fresh, full of light and health and of a kind of frankness and beauty, are prized all the more at such a time because they are not choice, but drawn perhaps from a hideous and sordid environment. For this circumstance makes them a better means of escape from convention and from that fatigue and despair which lurk not far beneath the surface of conventional life. In casting off with self-assurance and a sense of fresh vitality the distinctions of tradition and reason a man may feel, as he sinks back comfortably to a lower level of sense and instinct, that he is returning to Nature or escaping into the infinite. Mysticism makes us proud and happy to renounce the work of intelligence, both in thought and in life, and persuades us that we become divine by remaining imperfectly human. Walt Whitman gives a new expression to this ancient and multiform tendency. He feels his own cosmic justification and he would lend the sanction of his inspiration to all loafers and holiday-makers. He would be the congenial patron of farmers and factory hands in their crude pleasures and pieties, as Pan was the patron of the shepherds of Arcadia: for he is sure that in spite of his hairiness and animality, the gods will acknowledge him as one of themselves and smile upon him from the serenity of Olympus.

The Religion of Healthy-Mindedness

William James*

The supreme contemporary example of such an inability to feel evil is of course Walt Whitman.

"His favorite occupation," writes his disciple, Dr. Bucke, "seemed to be strolling or sauntering about outdoors by himself, looking at the grass, the trees, the flowers, the vistas of light, the varying aspects of the sky, and listening to the birds, the crickets, the tree frogs, and all the hundreds of natural sounds. It was evident that these things gave him a pleasure far beyond what they give to ordinary people. Until I knew the man," continues Dr. Bucke, "it had not occurred to me that any one could derive so much absolute happiness from these things as he did. He was very fond of flowers, either wild or cultivated; liked all sorts. I think he admired lilacs and sunflowers just as much as roses. Perhaps, indeed, no man who ever lived liked so many things and disliked so few as Walt Whitman. All natural objects seemed to have a charm for him. All sights and sounds seemed to please him. He appeared to like (and I believe he did like) all the men, women, and children he saw (though I never knew him to say that he liked any one), but each who knew him felt that he liked him or her, and that he liked others also. I never knew him to argue or dispute, and he never spoke about money. He always justified, sometimes playfully, sometimes quite seriously, those who spoke harshly of himself or his writings, and I often thought he even took pleasures in the opposition of enemies. When I first knew [him], I used to think that he watched himself, and would not allow his tongue to give expression to fretfulness, antipathy, complaint, and remonstrance. It did not occur to me as possible that these mental states could be absent to him. After long observation, however, I satisfied myself that such absence or unconsciousness was entirely real. He never spoke deprecatingly of any nationality or class of men, or time in the world's history, or against any trades or occupations—not even against any animals, insects, or inanimate things, nor any of the laws of nature, nor any of the results of those laws, such as illness, deformity, and death. He never complained or grumbled either at the

*Reprinted from *The Varieties of Religious Experience* (New York: Longmans, Green and Co., 1902), pp. 84–87.

188

weather, pain, illness, or anything else. He never swore. He could not very well, since he never spoke in anger and apparently never was angry. He never exhibited fear, and I do not believe he ever felt it."[1]

Walt Whitman owes his importance in literature to the systematic expulsion from his writings of all contractile elements. The only sentiments he allowed himself to express were of the expansive order; and he expressed these in the first person, not as your mere monstrously conceited individual might so express them, but vicariously for all men, so that a passionate and mystic ontological emotion suffuses his words, and ends by persuading the reader that men and women, life and death, and all things are divinely good.

Thus it has come about that many persons to-day regard Walt Whitman as the restorer of the eternal natural religion. He has infected them with his own love of comrades, with his own gladness that he and they exist. Societies are actually formed for his cult; a periodical organ exists for its propagation, in which the lines of orthodoxy and heterodoxy are already beginning to be drawn[2]; hymns are written by others in his peculiar prosody; and he is even explicitly compared with the founder of the Christian religion, not altogether to the advantage of the latter.

Whitman is often spoken of as a "pagan." The word nowadays means sometimes the mere natural animal man without a sense of sin; sometimes it means a Greek or Roman with his own peculiar religious consciousness. In neither of these senses does it fitly define this poet. He is more than your mere animal man who has not tasted of the tree of good and evil. He is aware enough of sin for a swagger to be present in his indifference towards it, a conscious pride in his freedom from flexions and contractions, which your genuine pagan in the first sense of the word would never show.

> I could turn and live with animals, they are so placid and self-contained,
> I stand and look at them and long;
> They do not sweat and whine about their condition.
> They do not lie awake in the dark and weep for their sins.
> Not one is dissatisfied, not one is demented with the mania of owning
>   things,
> Not one kneels to another, nor to his kind that lived thousands of years
>   ago,
> Not one is respectable or unhappy over the whole earth.[3]

No natural pagan could have written these well-known lines. But on the other hand Whitman is less than a Greek or Roman; for their consciousness, even in Homeric times, was full to the brim of the sad mortality of this sunlit world, and such a consciousness Walt Whitman resolutely refuses to adopt. When, for example, Achilles, about to slay Lycaon, Priam's young son, hears him sue for mercy, he stops to say:—

"Ah friend, thou too must die: why thus lamentest thou? Patroclos too is dead, who was better far than thou. . . . Over me too hang death and forceful fate. There cometh morn or eve or some noonday when my life too some man shall take in battle, whether with spear he smite, or arrow from the string."[4]

Then Achilles savagely severs the poor boy's neck with his sword, heaves him by the foot into the Scamander, and calls to the fishes of the river to eat the white fat of Lycaon. Just as here the cruelty and the sympathy each ring true, and do not mix or interfere with one another, so did the Greeks and Romans keep all their sadnesses and gladnesses unmingled and entire. Instinctive good they did not reckon sin; nor had they any such desire to save the credit of the universe as to make them insist, as so many of *us* insist, that what immediately appears as evil must be "good in the making," or something equally ingenious. Good was good, and bad just bad, for the earlier Greeks. They neither denied the ills of nature—Walt Whitman's verse, "What is called good is perfect and what is called bad is just as perfect," would have been mere silliness to them—nor did they, in order to escape from those ills, invent "another and a better world" of the imagination, in which, along with the ills, the innocent goods of sense would also find no place. This integrity of the instinctive reactions, this freedom from all moral sophistry and strain, gives a pathetic dignity to ancient pagan feeling. And this quality Whitman's outpourings have not got. His optimism is too voluntary and defiant; his gospel has a touch of bravado and an affected twist[5] and this diminishes its effect on many readers who yet are well disposed towards optimism, and on the whole quite willing to admit that in important respects Whitman is of the genuine lineage of the prophets.

Notes

1. R. M. Bucke, *Cosmic Consciousness*, pp. 182–86, abridged.

2. I refer to *The Conservator*, edited by Horace Traubel, and published monthly at Philadelphia.

3. "Song of Myself," 32.

4. *Iliad*, xxi, E. Myers's translation.

5. "God is afraid of me!" remarked such a titantic-optimistic friend in my presence one morning when he was feeling particularly hearty and cannibalistic. The defiance of the phrase showed that a Christian education in humility still rankled in his breast.

What I Feel About Walt Whitman

Ezra Pound*

From this side of the Atlantic I am for the first time able to read Whitman, and from the vantage of my education—if it be permitted a man of my scant years—my world citizenship: I see him America's poet. The only Poet before the artists of the Carman-Hovey period, or better, the only one of the conventionally recognized "American Poets" who is worth reading.

He *is* America. His crudity is an exceeding great stench, but it *is* America. He is the hollow place in the rock that echos with his time. He *does* "chant the crucial stage" and he is the "voice triumphant." He is disgusting. He is an exceedingly nauseating pill, but he accomplishes his mission.

Entirely free from the renaissance humanist ideal of the complete man or from the Greek idealism, he is content to be what he is, and he is his time and his people. He is a genius because he has vision of what he is and of his function. He knows that he is a beginning and not a classically finished work.

I honor him for he prophesied me while I can only recognize him as a forebearer of whom I ought to be proud.

In America there is much for the healing of the nations, but woe unto him of the cultured palate who attempts the dose.

As for Whitman, I read him (in many parts) with acute pain, but when I write of certain things I find myself using his rhythms. The expression of uncertain things related to cosmic consciousness seems tainted with this maramis.

I am (in common with every educated man) an heir of the ages and I demand my birth-right. Yet if Whitman represented his time in language acceptable to one accustomed to my standard of intellectual artistic living he would belie his time and nation. And yet I am but one of his "ages and ages' encrustations" or to be exact an encrustation of the next age. The

*Reprinted from *American Literature* 27 (1955), 59–61, with the permission of the Duke University Press and New Directions Publishing Corp., agent for the Ezra Pound Literary Property Trust. The MS is in the Yale University Library. I have regularized Pound's idiosyncratic spelling and punctuation and corrected the spelling of Bliss Carman's name in line four.

vital part of my message, taken from the sap and fibre of America, is the same as his.

Mentally I am a Walt Whitman who has learned to wear a collar and a dress shirt (although at times inimical to both). Personally I might be very glad to conceal my relationship to my spiritual father and brag about my more congenial ancestry—Dante, Shakespeare, Theocritus, Villon, but the descent is a bit difficult to establish. And, to be frank, Whitman is to my fatherland (Patriam quam odi et amo for no uncertain reasons) what Dante is to Italy and I at my best can only be a strife for a renaissance in America of all the lost or temporarily mislaid beauty, truth, valor, glory of Greece, Italy, England and all the rest of it.

And yet if a man has written lines like Whitman's to the "Sunset breeze" one has to love him. I think we have not yet paid enough attention to the deliberate artistry of the man, not in details but in the large.

I am immortal even as he is, yet with a lesser vitality as I am the more in love with beauty (If I really do love it more than he did). Like Dante he wrote in the "vulgar tongue"; in a new metric. The first great man to write in the language of the people.

Et ego Petrarca in lingua vetera scribo, and in a tongue my people understand not.

It seems to me I should like to drive Whitman into the old world. I sledge, he drill—and to scourge America with all the old beauty. (For Beauty *is* an accusation) and with a thousand thongs from Homer to Yeats, from Theocritus to Marcel Schwob. This desire is because I am young and impatient; were I old and wise I should content myself in seeing and saying that these things will come. But now, since I am by no means sure it would be true prophecy, I am fain set my own hand to the labour.

It is a great thing, reading a man to know, not "His Tricks are not as yet my Tricks, but I can easily make them mine" but "His message is my message. We will see that men hear it."

The Form: Constructive Principles

Our understanding of Whitman's form is incomplete till we see what it excludes; for a thing has no positive if it has no negative qualities. Of course the idea of *Leaves of Grass* was to be all-inclusive; the poem was conceived in a spirit of universal hospitality, and such a spirit would be unfavourable to conscious method of any kind, would be likely to pride itself on having none. But this more or less inevitable pose must not bluff the critic. The form of a work which aims at impressing us with the spiritual coherence of all things may well share the elusiveness of its theme and be as inapprehensible as life itself. Yet unless some connecting thread, however fine, holds its divergences in a unity, the aim is unaccomplished.

Form in verse means, as a rule, metre. Whitman felt rightly that no metre or combination of metres could serve the peculiar purpose he had in view. At the same time he was not averse, as we have seen, to the introduction of metrical fragments here and there, and even shows a partiality for jingling effects. If we are right in thinking that he made a mistake in this, we have only to analyse the grounds on which our judgment rests, and we shall find the principle of exclusion which we are looking for.

But first let us note that the mistake itself was of secondary importance. The primary requisite for the form of *Leaves of Grass* was that its spaciousness should be recognised and that the composer should write to scale. No one afflicted with sensitiveness about the minor literary proprieties would have been likely to rise to the careless amplitude of manner necessary to the filling of so gigantic a mould. We recognise this easily enough if we compare the master with his followers, the originator with the mimics. The normal writer of Whitmanesque verse feels in every line the influence of the metre he has dispensed with and exhibits the affectations of a disdainful culture. But Whitman, like all who bring a revelation through art, is faithful to nature, and his method turns upon the discovery of nature in what had seemed unnatural. He aimed at being himself in his poetry, and this required him to stand out as poetry per-

*Reprinted from Basil de Selincourt, *Walt Whitman: A Critical Study* (London: Martin Secker, 1914), pp. 94–118.

sonified in solitary relief against the whole poetic achievement of the past. He seemed to ask less than others of the Muse. It devolved upon him to give more. Choosing informality, he chose in effect a form which permitted him no concealment, no breathing-space. We cannot wonder if he did not stay to consider what his ideals denied to him; his task was to be ready with what they exacted. Only the intrusion, the conspicuous and abiding presence of matter inconsistent with the common forms could justify his departure from them.

Yet if he rather transcends than refuses metre, it is not the less true that recognisably metrical lines are out of keeping with the spirit of his poetry. His lines are not metrical; what are they, then? We glanced earlier at an objection often taken to the form of *Leaves of Grass* to the effect that it has a spurious emotionality; that the line-system has the same relation to poetry as the habitual use of italics has to prose. The objection, we think, is inapplicable; but obviously the presentment of a composition in lines is meaningless and otiose, unless the lines have some common measure and are identities in nature as well as in name.

The identity of the lines in metrical poetry is an identity of pattern. The identity of the lines in *Leaves of Grass* is an identity of substance; and this is in effect by far the subtler and more exacting condition of the two. Tyrannous spontaneity allows the poet so little respite that every line must, as it were, contain his personality in the germ. Whitman himself never, I think, formulated this demand, and in the course of his work he frequently overrides it. But it is a natural deduction from his admitted principles. He looked upon each of his poems as the leaf or branch of a tree. The line is to the poem what the poet is to the work as a whole. To say this is to say that certain forms are excluded, that certain kinds of line will not do.

A quotation from early manuscript passages written before Whitman had quite found his bearings will show better than anything else what his form rejects and why. Among the variorum readings given in the third volume of the Camden Edition of the collected works (p. 128) we find the following:—

> There is no word in my tongue,
> No array, no form of symbol,
> To tell his infatuation
> Who would define the scope and purpose of God.

Readers familiar with *Leaves of Grass* will at once feel a want of equivalence in these four lines; and what does the sensation point to if not to the presence of equivalence in Whitman's lines generally? Each true line of Whitman's comes to us, as I have said, floated separately on an independent breath. Like the sea-waves to which he himself so often compared them, his lines are not less recognisably units because of their variable shapes and sizes. And in the third of those quoted above, some principle of equivalence is violated. It is violated, therefore it exists. The words "to tell his infatuation" are merely transitional; they explain what precedes, prepare for what follows, and offer the mind no substantial resting place. The passage as it continues becomes still more instructive:—

> Mostly this we have of God: we have man.
> Lo, the Sun:
> Its glory floods the moon,
> Which of a night shines in some turbid pool,
> Shaken by soughing winds;
> And there are sparkles mad and tossed and broken,
> And their archetype is the sun.
>
> Of God I know not;
> But this I know:
> I can comprehend no being more wonderful than man;
> Man, before the rage of whose passions the storms of
>   heaven are but a breath;
> Before whose caprices the lightning is slow and less fatal;
> Man, microcosm of all Creation's wildness, terror, beauty
>   and power,
> And whose folly and wickedness are in nothing else
>   existent.

The weakness here is quite as obvious, if not quite so transparent. In the first passage one of the lines was like a plank bridging a chasm over which the reader walked insecurely, feeling as if there was nothing under him. Here the effect is of a succession of steppingstones. The lines are independent, but they are discontinuous. And the reason soon appears. The observations of the first stanza are not really made for their own sake; they are made with a purpose: in fact, in order to prepare us for a simile. Even their independence, therefore, is apparent rather than real. It is not independence; it is insulation. The turbid pool, the soughing winds, do not appear before us substantively; they are counted out like symbols, and each has its stage in the process of ethical deduction in which the simile is applied. The lines that hold them are, in fact, dependencies; they are not full lines; they demand their unit of attention from us and do not satisfy it.

It is to the junction in them of these two seemingly incompatible qualities, continuity and independence, that Whitman's mature lines owe their integrity, and it is this that dictates their behaviour in company, so to speak, explaining the shape of the poems, their formal development, and the difficulties and resources of the craftsman. The line is a personality, the poem is a battalion, the book is an army. To illustrate the point, let us quote a paragraph in full:—

> Here is the efflux of the soul,
> The efflux of the soul comes from within through em-
>   bower'd gates, ever provoking questions.
> These yearnings why are they? these thoughts in the
>   darkness why are they?
> Why are there men and women that while they are nigh
>   me the sunlight expands my blood?
> Why when they leave me do my pennants of joy sink flat
>   and lank?
> Why are there trees I never walk under but large and
>   melodious thoughts descend upon me?
> (I think they hang there winter and summer on those
>   trees and always drop fruit as I pass;)
> What is it I interchange so suddenly with strangers?
> What with some driver as I ride on the seat by his side?
> What with some fisherman drawing his seine by the shore
>   as I walk by and pause?
> What gives me to be free to a woman's and man's good-
>   will? what gives them to be free to mine?

The importance of continuity to the form is displayed at once here in that *epanaphora*, that taking up of words or phrases, which is a pronounced characteristic of the style of *Leaves of Grass*. Each line hangs by a loop from the line before it. The motion is like the motion of walking; we continually catch up our foremost foot and take a half step beyond. It is of course the substantial self-sufficiency of the lines that necessitates this interlocking. And their equivalence turns upon their relation to a progressive, an accumulating idea. For example, the repetition of such a phrase as "the efflux of the soul," though it lengthens the line in which it occurs, does nothing to help that line to take us further; it has a different function; it joins the line more closely to its predecessor than the pronoun "it" would do and, by demanding less attention from the reader, decreases the weight of the line, thus actually preserving the equivalence it seems at first sight to impair.

In what sense, then, finally are the lines

> Here is the efflux of the soul

and

> The efflux of the soul comes from within through em-
>   bower'd gates, ever provoking questions,

equivalent lines? We have seen that their equivalence is in their content; to say this is to say that it is in their context also—that it depends upon their association together. They have not the equivalence that two lines of blank verse have and which they have equally whether they stand next to one another or not. The second is equivalent to the first only as consequent upon it. In the first, an image is, as it were, posited: the conception of the soul as a radiating centre. In the second, the same image is elaborated. Suppose then that for the second line, stumbled at first sight by its length and complexity, we substitute

> The efflux of the soul comes from within through em-
>   bower'd gates,

and stop there, we shall find, not only that the line has lost poetry, but that it has lost equilibrium also. Why is this? Surely because, in the line as Whitman wrote it, we take the phrase

> comes from within through embower'd gates

transitionally, and because it is when so taken that its true value appears. If we emphasise it, as would be necessary were it to stand alone, we lose its suggestiveness and go searching for some precise significance which we do not find. But if we pass by way of it to the words

> ever provoking questions

and look to them for the first purpose of the line, the phrase falls into its relative place with beautiful accuracy. Is it because the gates are embowered that the questions are provoked? This, or something like it, gives the line, no doubt, its coherence of idea. But the point is that a mystical and an everyday expression have been weighed together and that their effect is felt in their juxtaposition. We weigh them in this way together because they are placed before us as constituents of a single line; and, having so weighed them, we find that the momentum set by

> Here is the efflux of the soul

is preserved and carried one stage further. The equivalence of the two lines is thus an equivalence of movement and of weight.

The problem of each succeeding line will be the same; to preserve the movement, to advance it by a stage and to maintain equilibrium in the advance. Reading to the end of the paragraph with this idea in view, we shall find that each line solves the problem in its own way. One has an element of surprise, another brings us into closer contact with the object, a third has its expanding generalisation, a fourth its illuminating detail; and the line in parenthesis is especially noticeable, niched there like some light obstacle in flowing water and revealing the current which it checks. To put the matter in general terms: the constitution of a line in *Leaves of Grass* is such that, taken in its context, the poetic idea to be conveyed by the words is only perfectly derivable from them when they are related to the line as a unit; and the equivalence of the lines is their equivalent appeal to our attention as contributors to the developing expression of the poetic idea of the whole.

Thus the progress of Whitman's verse has much in common with that of a musical composition. For we are carrying the sense of past effects along with us more closely and depending more intimately upon them than is possible in normal verse. What we can achieve at any point of our structure depends upon the trains of association we have set up, the number of balls we have kept spinning, the speed and quality of movement we have attacked or attained. And just as the context limits, so it also lays its claim upon us. For if no line can do more than maintain and add its unit to the general flow, none may do less. And just as in music, so here; it is impossible to lay down any rule for the maintenance of equivalence of effect, for the retaining of attention and accumulation of interest to the close. The condition of the effect that we are to produce now is the effect we have produced up to now; it lies with the modifications we have produced in our hearer's receptivity, the anticipations we have formed there. Here a *fortissimo* seems necessary; but its place is taken perhaps by a *pianissimo*, perhaps by a silence, and the effect is sustained. There we have a *diminuendo*; its point lies in the *crescendo* that preceded it; and behold! while the sound lessens, the meaning grows. Throughout, the test is whether the emotional pitch propounded is maintained, whether the piece continues to expand in significance as it expands in volume.

Perhaps it is because the significance of words accumulates faster than that of notes of music that frequent division into paragraphs becomes necessary, and also the frequent interpolation of parenthetical reflections. We go back and begin again where we began before in order, not that we may travel the same route a second time, but that we may travel to the same goal by a neighbouring route:—

> Allons! whoever you are come travel with me!
> Traveling with me you find what never tires.
>
> The earth never tires,
> The earth is rude, silent, incomprehensible at first,
>   Nature is rude and incomprehensible at first.
> Be not discouraged, keep on, there are divine things well
>   envelop'd,
> I swear to you there are divine things more beautiful
>   than words can tell.
>
> Allons! we must not stop here,
> However sweet these laid-up stores, however convenient
>   this dwelling we cannot remain here,
> However shelter'd this port and however calm these
>   waters we must not anchor here,
> However welcome the hospitality that surrounds us we
>   are permitted to receive it but a little while.

These lines exhibit splendidly the alternating *crescendo* and *diminuendo* spoken of above. In "Traveling with me you find what never tires" we come immediately to a climax; there is no carrying the idea further; we must have a line of silence and start afresh. "The earth never tires" takes up the idea again, and in a sense is an addition to it; but it is a concessive, an explanatory addition; it is a concrete example and suggestion, and, as such, is taken as platform for a new "flight into the wordless." The poet soars, using a marked *crescendo*, which comes freely because the theme is simple. The line "I swear to you" is an easy and yet an enjoyable *fortissimo*. Again there is a pause; and then a new theme develops (the transitoriness of life on earth), needing tenderer handling; and so we have the deliberate and delicious *diminuendo* which brings the paragraph to a close.

The use of parenthesis is a recurring feature of Whitman's technique, and no explanation of his form can be adequate which does not relate this peculiarity to the constructive principles of the whole. He frequently begins a paragraph or ends one with a bracketed sentence, or begins or ends some section of a poem with a bracketed paragraph, sometimes even begins or ends a poem parenthetically. Thus the "Song of Exposition" opens with the beautiful aside: —

> (Ah little recks the laborer,
> How near his work is holding him to God.
> The loving Laborer through space and time.)

and the last piece of "Calamus" significantly closes: —

> Be it as if I were with you. (Be not so certain but I am
> now with you.)

This persistent bracketing falls well into the scheme we have laid down of independent units that serve an accumulating effect. The bracket, one need not remark, secures a peculiar detachment for its contents; it also, by placing them outside the current and main flow of the sense, relates them to it in a peculiar way. And although for the time being the flow is broken, it by no means follows, as we saw, that our sense of the flow is broken; on the contrary, it is probably enhanced. We look down upon the stream from a point of vantage and gauge its speed and direction. More precisely, the bracket opening a poem or paragraph gives us, of course, the idea which that whole poem or paragraph presupposes, while the closing bracket gives the idea by which what precedes is to be qualified and tempered. We have thus as it were a poem within a poem; or sometimes, when a series of brackets is used, we have a double stream of poetry, as in "By Blue Ontario's Shore" where the waters blend and yet remain discriminate, a deeper and more personal current of feeling persisting under the strength and buoyant onrush of the surface. All this carries out and amplifies the peculiar formal significance of *Leaves of Grass*, with its strange submission of words to unfamiliar musical associations. Continuity and independence being Whitman's opposing principles of composition, independence emerges in the bracket into relative prominence. The disjunctive spirit of language asserts itself; literature contemplates music.

But the analogy with music is still unexhausted. Not only is the method of progression similar, the means of progression have also much in common. The chief difference between musical and verbal expression, as a rule, is that words, carrying each their modicum of meaning, have done their part when they have delivered it, while notes, being meaningless except in combination, develop new meanings by presenting a single combination in varying contexts or with varying accompaniment. In fact, repetition, which the artist in language scrupulously avoids, is the foundation and substance of musical expression. Now Whitman, for reasons we have touched on, uses words and phrases more as if they were notes of music than any other writer. As we shall see elsewhere, it was to him part of the virtue and essence of life that its forms and processes were endlessly reduplicated; and poetry, which was delight in life, must somehow, he thought, mirror this elemental abundance. Language generally expects us, when an object has been mentioned, to hold that object in view until all that has to be said about it has been said. But the object, if it were actually before us, would continue to assert itself in a thousand ways, and its persistency—its refusal, as it were, to believe that it can be monotonous to us—is its reality, and if its reality, then surely its poetry also.

> You have waited, you always wait, you dumb, beautiful
>   ministers,
> We receive you with free sense at last, and are insatiate
>   henceforward.

Why should not words imitate things and keep up the same patient knocking at the mind's doors until we genuinely admit them?

The meaning of repetition lies of course in the fact that it is impossible to have the same experience twice. If there is to be value in the repeating over and over of some form of words, there must be something in them or in their varying contexts to enable the mind to pass from a first to a second impression of them, and from a second to a third and a fourth, feeling at each stage that more is added in discovery than is lost through the trouble of treading the old path. Words, we must recollect, are partly vehicles of truth, partly vehicles of emotion; they may exhibit a simple relation or suggest a complex one. Now the more complex the relation suggested, the more familiar we must be with the words that suggest it if we are to profit by every breath of suggestion they contain. We have only to grasp the sense of a geometrical proposition and we have done with the words of it; we have no disposition to say them over. But the words of a poem we often learn by heart and repeat them to ourselves as we might repeat a prayer. We are conscious that they proceed out of a certain state of feeling which we desire to enter into and to make our own; to enter into a state we must become familiar with it as an experience; and so we repeat the poem over and over to ourselves, at each repetition experiencing more intimately and more profoundly the spiritual state reflected in it. The poem thus becomes less and less a form of words to us and more and more a key to life. The reason is that the disposition of the words demands from the mind that is to understand them a corresponding disposition. They emanate from and represent a harmony into which we enter only by reproducing it in our own being.

What applies to our deliberate repetition of a poem to ourselves can be applied to the handling of a poem by its composer if he so chooses. His object is not to state truths but to convey feelings; and the feeling with which we hear a certain form of words may well depend precisely upon the fact that we are not hearing it for the first time, the feeling itself changing and developing as its occasion is repeated. Lyric poetry acknowledges the virtue of repetition in the refrain, which, though in the main a concession to the forms of the musical accompaniment, has its value in reviving and sustaining the implied emotional mood.

But there is a further point. A truth necessarily continues true. Of an emotion our chief test is the degree to which it admits constancy; feelings are habitually proved and established by a frequent reiteration of the expression of them. Now poetry gives us this assurance as a rule by the elevation of manner, the unified tone, the remoteness, which are in themselves evidences of sustained feeling, being unattainable without it. Repetition (with certain exceptions irrelevant here) is thus more otiose in poetry than in prose. For the web of expression is more tightly woven, every word has full force, and a higher concentration is demanded of the reader who is to assimilate the mood. The poem does not so much rise to a certain altitude, as exist there; and the danger is not that we may doubt the emotion, but that we may fail to recognise the objects to which it attaches—a failing which sometimes extends beyond a poet's readers to the poet himself.

Now the absence of recognised formalities which is characteristic of *Leaves of Grass* robs language of these high-pitched associations, and obliges us to interpret it in accordance with the dictates of mere common sense. When Whitman bids us

> Behold this compost, behold it well,

we know that if we take up a handful of garden soil and turn it over in our hands, we shall be quite in the spirit of his intention. It was one of his ideals in poetry not to lose sight of these everyday simplicities. Yet a form or style which begins from and reverts to such simplicities must forge instruments of some kind to carry it from the simplicities to the profundities. Poetic exaltation is not the less necessary because it is not presupposed. And of Whitman's instruments for obtaining it, repetition—repetition of forms, of phrases, of themes—is perhaps the chief. It is not only that it assists him, as we have seen, to carry out the principle of accumulating weight, his first law of construction. It is also that by it he brings home to us the increasing value for emotion of expressions the value of which, at first hearing, seemed to lie in their very divorce from it, in their cool substantiality. His most astonishing effects are thus often produced by means least compatible with ordinary poetry, the means, like the effects they serve, being peculiarly his own. "Crossing Brooklyn Ferry" is perhaps the greatest and boldest example of them:—

> Flood-tide below me! I see you face to face!
> Clouds of the west—sun there half an hour high—I see
>   you also face to face!

Beginning thus with the common attitude to common objects, we find ourselves gradually, as it were, intermingled with them and caught up through the medium of the poet's interpretation into the sentiment and atmosphere they create:—

> Ah! what can ever be more stately and admirable to me
>   than mast-hemm'd Manhattan?
> River and sunset and scallop-edg'd waves of flood-tide?

Without losing touch with our own experience, we make a passage from natural to impassioned vision. We do more than read poetry. We feel it in its process and formation; not lifted into another world, but acquainted with the deepening and extending vistas of the world we live in:—

> Flow on, river! flow with the flood-tide, and ebb with the
>   ebb-tide!
> Frolic on, crested and scallop-edg'd waves!
> Gorgeous clouds of the sunset! drench with your splendor
>   me, or the men and women generations after me!
> Cross from shore to shore, countless crowds of passengers!
> Stand up, tall masts of Mannahatta! stand up, beautiful
>   hills of Brooklyn! . . .
> You have waited, you always wait, you dumb, beautiful
>   ministers,
> We receive you with free sense at last, and are in-
>   satiate henceforward,
> Not you any more shall be able to foil us, or withhold
>   yourselves from us,
> We use you, and do not cast you aside—we plant you
>   permanently within us,
> We fathom you not—we love you—there is perfection
>   in you also,
> You furnish your parts toward eternity,
> Great or small, you furnish your parts toward the soul.

There is in this a living presentment of the condition out of which all poetry springs. It is sometimes made a criticism of Whitman that, instead of writing poetry, he writes about it and tries to explain what it is. Often he does so; but often when he seems to be doing so, he is in reality doing much more. He is communicating not merely a poem, an example of poetry, but the spiritual attitude, which if we can assimilate it, will make us according to our measure poets ourselves. No process of explanation serves here. It is work for the greatest of poets in their moments of greatest inspiration. "Crossing Brooklyn Ferry" is such a 'poem of poetry'; it summarises experience, offers a new key to that dark door, would endow us with a new experiencing faculty. A purpose so sublime may well have demanded this strange blend of the ecstasies of music, the exactitudes of speech.

It will be pertinent to observe, finally, that Whitman has discovered and elaborated in *Leaves of Grass* a form for which other poets seem to have searched in vain. What after all was Goethe seeking for in those splendid lyrics "Prometheus," "Ganymed" and their like, if not some principle of equivalence for his lines which would be independent of metrical ties or would at least enable him to override them? Such a lyric as "Prometheus" has of course a sustained exaltation of manner, a conciseness of symbolic allusion, which Whitman never aims at and which, even if he had aimed at it, he probably could not have compassed. But considering it on its formal side only, may we not attribute to the lack of Whitman's 'substantial equivalence' that element of trickery or experimentation which the lines seem so often to display? The poet halts, as it were, between two principles, only half conscious of their antagonism, with the result that justice is done to neither:—

> Ihr nähret kummerlich
> Von Opfersteuern
> Und Gebetshauch
> Eure Majestät,
> Und darbtet, wären
> Nicht Kinder und Bettler
> Hoffnungsvoller Thoren.

Irony towers here, and it is piled up on something like the substantial principle, until at the word 'wären' the spell is broken, and we revert to measurement by syllables. The next stanza:—

> Da ich ein Kind war,
> Nicht wusste wo aus noch ein,
> Kehrt' ich mein verirrtes Auge
> Zur Sonne, als wenn drüber wär'
> Ein Ohr, zu hören meine Klage,
> Ein Herz, wie mein's,
> Sich des Bedrängten zu erbarmen.—

exhibits precisely those faults of which Whitman was sensitive in his first drafts for *Leaves of Grass*. The actual line division is not the real one. There is an inherent discrepancy between the style and the form. Exactly the same defect appears in the English imitations of Goethe to which Matthew Arnold was so much addicted. Some of his best thought is to be found in work which he has thrown into this irregular recitative; but the poetic result is, by general admission, unsatisfactory. Sometimes his themes are Whitmanesque:—

> They see the Scythian
> On the wide steppe, unharnessing
> His wheel'd house at noon.
> He tethers his beast down, and makes his meal,
> Mare's milk, and bread
> Baked on the embers: all around . . .

Such a passage as this fails, again, precisely for lack of any determining principle in the lines, anything to assure us that, in the absence of metrical regularity, they do not simply begin and end at haphazard. Mere variableness is not only unpleasing but unintelligible. In order that changes should have a meaning, we must have with it an instrument for measuring it, a standard to which it may be applied. Whitman makes an original contribution to poetic craft in that he discovers and exhibits a new standard, a new basis for variation. The freedom of his lines is pleasurable to us and conveys an intelligible impression only in so far as we instinctively recognise the common principle they exemplify, and measure them by tacit reference to it.

Whitman

D. H. Lawrence*

Post mortem effects?
　But what of Walt Whitman?
　The "good grey poet."
　Was he a ghost, with all his physicality?
　The good grey poet.
　Post mortem effects. Ghosts.
　A certain ghoulish insistency. A certain horrible pottage
of human parts. A certain stridency and portentousness. A
luridness about his beatitudes.
　DEMOCRACY! THESE STATES! EIDOLONS! LOVERS, END-
LESS LOVERS!
　ONE IDENTITY!
　ONE IDENTITY!
　I AM HE THAT ACHES WITH AMOROUS LOVE.
　Do you believe me, when I say post mortem effects?

When the *Pequod* went down, she left many a rank and dirty steam-
boat still fussing in the seas. The *Pequod* sinks with all her souls, but their
bodies rise again to man innumerable tramp steamers, and ocean-crossing
liners. Corpses.

What we mean is that people may go on, keep on, and rush on,
without souls. They have their ego and their will, that is enough to keep
them going.

So that you see, the sinking of the *Pequod* was only a metaphysical
tragedy after all. The world goes on just the same. The ship of the *soul* is
sunk. But the machine manipulating body works just the same: digests,
chews gum, admires Botticelli and aches with amorous love.

　　I AM HE THAT ACHES WITH AMOROUS LOVE.

What do you make of that? I AM HE THAT ACHES. First generalization.
First uncomfortable universalization. WITH AMOROUS LOVE! Oh, God!

*Reprinted from *Studies in Classic American Literature* (Garden City, N.Y.: Doubleday &
Co., Inc., 1953), pp. 174–191; copyright 1923 by Thomas Seltzer, Inc., renewed 1950 by
Frieda Lawrence; reprinted by permission of Viking Penguin, Inc.

Better a bellyache. A bellyache is at least specific. But the ACHE OF AMOROUS LOVE!

Think of having that under your skin. All that!

I AM HE THAT ACHES WITH AMOROUS LOVE.

Walter, leave off. You are not HE. You are just a limited Walter. And your ache doesn't include all Amorous Love, by any means. If you ache you only ache with a small bit of amorous love, and there's so much more stays outside the cover of your ache, that you might be a bit milder about it.

> I AM HE THAT ACHES WITH AMOROUS LOVE.
> CHUFF! CHUFF! CHUFF!
> CHU-CHU-CHU-CHU-CHUFF!

Reminds one of a steam-engine. A locomotive. They're the only things that seem to me to ache with amorous love. All that steam inside them. Forty million foot-pounds pressure. The ache of AMOROUS LOVE. Steam-pressure. CHUFF!

An ordinary man aches with love for Belinda, or his Native Land, or the Ocean, or the Stars, or the Oversoul: if he feels that an ache is in the fashion.

It takes a steam-engine to ache with AMOROUS LOVE. All of it.

Walt was really too superhuman. The danger of the superman is that he is mechanical.

They talk of his "splendid animality." Well, he'd got it on the brain, if that's the place for animality.

> I am he that aches with amorous love:
> Does the earth gravitate, does not all matter, aching, attract
>   all matter?
> So the body of me to all I meet or know.

What can be more mechanical? The difference between life and matter is that life, living things, living creatures, have the instinct of turning right away from *some* matter, and of blissfully ignoring the bulk of most matter, and of turning towards only some certain bits of specially selected matter. As for living creatures all helplessly hurtling together into one great snowball, why, most very living creatures spend the greater part of their time getting out of the sight, smell or sound of the rest of living creatures. Even bees only cluster on their own queen. And that is sickening enough. Fancy all white humanity clustering on one another like a lump of bees.

No, Walt, you give yourself away. Matter *does* gravitate, helplessly. But men are tricky-tricksy, and they shy all sorts of ways.

Matter gravitates because it *is* helpless and mechanical.

And if you gravitate the same, if the body of you gravitates to all you meet or know, why, something must have gone seriously wrong with you. You must have broken your mainspring.

You must have fallen also into mechanization.

Your Moby Dick must be really dead. That lonely phallic monster of the individual you. Dead mentalized.

I only know that my body doesn't by any means gravitate to all I meet or know. I find I can shake hands with a few people. But most I wouldn't touch with a long prop.

Your mainspring is broken, Walt Whitman. The mainspring of your own individuality. And so you run down with a great whirr, merging with everything.

You have killed your isolate Moby Dick. You have mentalized your deep sensual body, and that's the death of it.

I am everything and everything is me and so we're all One in One Identity, like the Mundane Egg, which has been addled quite a while.

> Whoever you are, to endless announcements—
> And of these one and all I weave the song of myself.

Do you? Well, then, it just shows you haven't *got* any self. It's a mush, not a woven thing. A hotch-potch, not a tissue. Your self.

Oh, Walter, Walter, what have you done with it? What have you done with yourself? With your own individual self? For it sounds as if it had all leaked out of you, leaked into the universe.

Post mortem effects. The individuality had leaked out of him.

No, no, don't lay this down to poetry. These are post mortem effects. And Walt's great poems are really huge fat tomb-plants, great rank grave-yard growths.

All that false exuberance. All those lists of things boiled in one pudding-cloth! No, no!

I don't want all those things inside me, thank you.

"I reject nothing," says Walt.

If that is so, one must be a pipe open at both ends, so everything runs through.

Post mortem effects.

"I embrace ALL," says Whitman. "I weave all things into myself."

Do you really! There can't be much left of *you* when you've done. When you've cooked the awful pudding of One Identity.

And whoever walks a furlong without sympathy walks to his own funeral dressed in his own shroud."

Take off your hat then, my funeral procession of one is passing.

This awful Whitman. This post mortem poet. This poet with the private soul leaking out of him all the time. All his privacy leaking out in a sort of dribble, oozing into the universe.

Walt becomes in his own person the whole world, the whole

iverse, the whole eternity of time. As far as his rather sketchy knowledge of history will carry him, that is. Because to *be* a thing he had to
know it. In order to assume the identity of a thing, he had to know that
thing. He was not able to assume one identity with Charlie Chaplin, for
example, because Walt didn't know Charlie. What a pity! He'd have done
poems, paeans and what not, Chants, Songs of Cinematernity.

Oh, Charlie, my Charlie, another film is done—

As soon as Walt *knew* a thing, he assumed a One Identity with it. If
he knew that an Esquimo sat in a kyak, immediately there was Walt being
little and yellow and greasy, sitting in a kyak.

Now will you tell me exactly what a kyak is?

Who is he that demands petty definition? Let him behold me *sitting
in a kyak*.

I behold no such thing. I behold a rather fat old man full of a rather
senile, self-conscious sensuosity.

> DEMOCRACY. EN MASSE. ONE IDENTITY.
> The universe, in short, adds up to ONE.
> ONE.

1.

Which is Walt.

His poems, *Democracy, En Masse, One Identity*, they are long sums
in addition and multiplication, of which the answer is invariably MYSELF.

He reaches the state of ALLNESS.

And what then? It's all empty. Just an empty Allness. An addled egg.

Walt wasn't an esquimo. A little, yellow, sly, cunning, greasy little
Esquimo. And when Walt blandly assumed Allness, including Es-
quimoness, unto himself, he was just sucking the wind out of a blown egg-
shell, no more. Esquimos are not minor little Walts. They are something
that I am not, I know that. Outside the egg of my Allness chuckles the
greasy little Esquimo. Outside the egg of Whitman's Allness too.

But Walt wouldn't have it. He was everything and everything was in
him. He drove an automobile with a very fierce headlight, along the track
of a fixed idea, through the darkness of this world. And he saw Everything
that way. Just as a motorist does in the night.

I, who happen to be asleep under the bushes in the dark, hoping a
snake won't crawl into my neck; I, seeing Walt go by in his great fierce
poetic machine, think to myself: What a funny world that fellow sees!

ONE DIRECTION! toots Walt in the car, whizzing along it.

Whereas there are myriads of ways in the dark, not to mention
trackless wildernesses. As anyone will know who cares to come off the
road, even the Open Road.

ONE DIRECTION! whoops America, and sets off also in an automobile.

ALLNESS! shrieks Walt at a cross-road, going whizz over an unwary Red Indian.

ONE IDENTITY! chants democratic En Masse, pelting behind in motor-cars, oblivious of the corpses under the wheels.

God save me, I feel like creeping down a rabbit-hole, to get away from all these automobiles rushing down the ONE IDENTITY track to the goal of ALLNESS.

> A woman waits for—

He might as well have said: "The femaleness waits for my maleness." Oh, beautiful generalization and abstraction! Oh, biological function.

"Athletic mothers of these Sates—" Muscles and wombs. They needn't have had faces at all.

> As I see myself reflected in Nature,
> As I see through a mist, One with inexpressible com-
>   pleteness, sanity, beauty,
> See the bent head, and arms folded over the breast, the
>   Female I see.

Everything was female to him: even himself. Nature just one great function.

> This is the nucleus—after the child is born of woman,
>   man is born of woman,
> This is the bath of birth, the merge of small and large,
>   and the outlet again—

> The Female I see—

If I'd been one of his women, I'd have given him Female. With a flea in his ear.

Always wanting to merge himself into the womb of something or other.

> The Female I see—

Anything, so long as he could merge himself.

Just a horror. A sort of white flux.

Post mortem effects.

He found, like all men find, that you can't really merge in a woman, though you go a long way. You can't manage the last bit. So you have to give it up, and try elsewhere. If you *insist* on merging.

In "Calamus" he changes his tune. He doesn't shout and thump and exult any more. He begins to hesitate, reluctant, wistful.

The strange calamus has its pink-tinged root by the pond, and it sends up its leaves of comradeship, comrades from one root, without the intervention of woman, female.

So he sings of the mystery of manly love, the love of comrades. Over and over he says the same thing: the new world will be built on the love of comrades, the new great dynamic of life will be manly love. Out of this manly love will come the inspiration for the future.

Will it though? Will it?

Comradeship! Comrades! This is to be the new Democracy: of Comrades. This is the new cohering principle in the world: Comradeship.

Is it? Are you sure?

It is the cohering principle of true soldiery, we are told in *Drum Taps*. It is the cohering principle in the new unison for creative activity. And it is extreme and alone, touching the confines of death. Something terrible to bear, terrible to be responsible for. Even Walt Whitman felt it. The soul's last and most poignant responsibility, the responsibility of comradeship, of manly love.

> Yet you are beautiful to me, you faint-tinged roots, you
>   make me think of death.
> Death is beautiful from you (what indeed is finally beauti-
>   ful except death and love?)
> I think it is not for life I am chanting here my chant of
>   lovers, I think it must be for death,
> For how calm, how solemn it grows to ascend to the atmos-
>   phere of lovers,
> Death or life, I am then indifferent, my soul declines to
>   prefer
> (I am not sure but the high soul of lovers welcomes death
>   most)
> Indeed, O death, I think now these leaves mean precisely
>   the same as you mean—

This is strange, from the exultant Walt.

Death!

Death is now his chant! Death!

Merging! And Death! Which is the final merge.

The great merge into the womb. Woman.

And after that, the merge of comrades: man-for-man love.

And almost immediately with this, death, the final merge of death.

There you have the progression of merging. For the great mergers, woman at last becomes inadequate. For those who love to extremes. Woman is inadequate for the last mergings. So the next step is the merging of the man-for-man love. And this is on the brink of death. It slides over into death.

> David and Jonathan. And the death of Jonathan.
> It always slides into death.
> The love of comrades.
> Merging.

So that if the new Democracy is to be based on the love of comrades, it will be based on death too. It will slip so soon into death.

The last merging. The last Democracy. The last love. The love of comrades.

Fatality. And fatality.

Whitman would not have been the great poet he is if he had not taken the last steps and looked over into death. Death, the last merging, that was the goal of his manhood.

To the mergers, there remains the brief love of comrades, and then Death.

> Whereto answering, the sea
> Delaying not, hurrying not
> Whispered me through the night, very plainly before day-
>   break,
> Lisp'd to me the low and delicious word death,
> And again death, death, death, death.
> Hissing melodions, neither like the bird nor like my arous'd
>   child's heart,
> But edging near as privately for me rustling at my feet,
> Creeping thence steadily up to my ears and laving me
>   softly all over
> Death, death, death, death, death—

Whitman is a very great poet, of the end of life. A very great post mortem poet, of the transitions of the soul as it loses its integrity. The poet of the soul's last shout and shriek, on the confines of death. *Après moi le déluge.*

But we have all got to die, and disintegrate.

We have got to die in life, too, and disintegrate while we live.

But even then the goal is not death.

Something else will come.

> Out of the cradle endlessly rocking.

We've got to die first, anyhow. And disintegrate while we still live.

Only we know this much. Death is not the *goal*. And Love, and merging, are now only part of the death-process. Comradeship—part of the death-process. Democracy—part of the death-process. The new Democracy—the brink of death. One Identity—death itself.

We have died, and we are still disintegrating.

But IT IS FINISHED.

Consummatum est.

Whitman, the great poet, has meant so much to me. Whitman, the one man breaking a way ahead. Whitman, the one pioneer. And only Whitman. No English pioneers, no French. No European pioneer-poets. In Europe the would-be pioneers are mere innovators. The same in America. Ahead of Whitman, nothing. Ahead of all poets, pioneering into the wilderness of unopened life, Whitman. Beyond him, none. His wide, strange camp at the end of the great high-road. And lots of new little poets camping on Whitman's camping ground now. But none going really beyond. Because Whitman's camp is at the end of the road, and on the edge of a great precipice. Over the precipice, blue distances, and the blue hollow of the future. But there is no way down. It is a dead end.

Pisgah. Pisgah sights. And Death. Whitman like a strange, modern, American Moses. Fearfully mistaken. And yet the great leader.

The essential function of art is moral. Not aesthetic, not decorative, not pastime and recreation. But moral. The essential function of art is moral.

But a passionate, implicit morality, not didactic. A morality which changes the blood, rather than the mind. Changes the blood first. The mind follows later, in the wake.

Now Whitman was a great moralist. He was a great leader. He was a great changer of the blood in the veins of men.

Surely it is especially true of American art, that it is all essentially moral. Hawthorne, Poe, Longfellow, Emerson, Melville: it is the moral issue which engages them. They all feel uneasy about the old morality. Sensuously, passionally, they all attack the old morality. But they know nothing better, mentally. Therefore they give tight mental allegiance to a morality which all their passion goes to destroy. Hence the duplicity which is the fatal flaw in them: most fatal in the most perfect American work of art. *The Scarlet Letter*. Tight mental allegiance given to a morality which the passional self repudiates.

Whitman was the first to break the mental allegiance. He was the first to smash the old moral conception, that the soul of man is something "superior" and "above" the flesh. Even Emerson still maintained this tiresome "superiority" of the soul. Even Melville could not get over it. Whitman was the first heroic seer to seize the soul by the scruff of her neck and plant her down among the potsherds.

"There!" he said to the soul. "Stay there!"

Stay there. Stay in the flesh. Stay in the limbs and lips and in the belly. Stay in the breast and womb. Stay there, O Soul, where you belong.

Stay in the dark limbs of negroes. Stay in the body of the prostitute. Stay in the sick flesh of the syphilitic. Stay in the marsh where the calamus grows. Stay there, Soul, where you belong.

The Open Road. The great home of the Soul is the open road. Not heaven, not paradise. Not "above." Not even "within." The soul is neither "above" nor "within." It is a wayfarer down the open road.

Not by meditating. Not by fasting. Not by exploring heaven after heaven, inwardly, in the manner of the great mystics. Not by exaltation. Not by ecstasy. Not by any of these ways does the soul come into her own.

Only by taking the open road.

Not through charity. Not through sacrifice. Not even through love.

Not through good works. Not through these does the soul accomplish herself.

Only through the journey down the open road.

The journey itself, down the open road. Exposed to full contact. On two slow feet. Meeting whatever comes down the open road. In company with those that drift in the same measure along the way. Towards no goal. Always the open road.

Having no known direction, even. Only the soul remaining true to herself in her going.

Meeting all the other wayfarers along the road. And how? How meet them, and how pass? With sympathy, says Whitman. Sympathy. He does not say love. He says sympathy. Feeling with. Feel with them as they feel with themselves. Catching the vibration of their soul and flesh as we pass.

It is a new great doctrine. A doctrine of life. A new great morality. A morality of actual living, not of salvation. Europe has never got beyond the morality of salvation. America to this day is deathly sick with saviourism. But Whitman, the greatest and the first and the only American teacher, was no Saviour. His morality was no morality of salvation. His was a morality of the soul living her life, not saving herself. Accepting the contact with other souls along the open way, as they lived their lives. Never trying to save them. As leave try to arrest them and throw them in gaol. The soul living her life along the incarnate mystery of the open road.

This was Whitman. And the true rhythm of the American continent speaking out in him. He is the first white aboriginal.

> In my Father's house are many mansions.

"No," said Whitman. "Keep out of mansions. A mansion may be heaven on earth, but you might as well be dead. Strictly avoid mansions. The soul is herself when she is going on foot down the open road."

It is the American heroic message. The soul is not to pile up defenses round herself. She is not to withdraw and seek her heavens inwardly, in mystical ecstasies. She is not to cry to some God beyond, for salvation. She is to go down the open road, as the road opens, into the unknown, keeping company with those whose soul draws them near to her, accomplishing nothing save the journey, and the works incident to the journey, in the long life-travel into the unknown, the soul in her subtle sympathies accomplishing herself by the way.

This is Whitman's essential message. The heroic message of the American future. It is the inspiration of thousands of Americans today, the best souls of today, men and women. And it is a message that only in America can be fully understood, finally accepted.

Then Whitman's mistake. The mistake of his interpretation of his watchword: Sympathy. The mystery of SYMPATHY. He still confounded it with Jesus' LOVE, and with Paul's CHARITY. Whitman, like all the rest of us, was at the end of the great emotional highway of Love. And because he couldn't help himself, he carried on his Open Road as a prolongation of the emotional highway of Love, beyond Calvary. The highway of Love ends at the foot of the Cross. There is no beyond. It was a hopeless attempt, to prolong the highway of Love.

He didn't follow his Sympathy. Try as he might, he kept on automatically interpreting it as Love, as Charity. Merging.

This merging, en masse, One Identity, Myself monomania was a carry-over from the old Love idea. It was carrying the idea of Love to its logical physical conclusion. Like Flaubert and the leper. The decree of unqualified Charity, as the soul's one means of salvation, still in force.

Now Whitman wanted his soul to save itself, *he* didn't want to save it. Therefore he did not need the great Christian receipt for saving the soul. He needed to supersede the Christian Charity, the Christian Love, within himself, in order to give his Soul her last freedom. The highroad of Love is no Open Road. It is a narrow, tight way, where the soul walks hemmed in between compulsions.

Whitman wanted to take his Soul down the open road. And he failed in so far as he failed to get out of the old rut of Salvation. He forced his Soul to the edge of a cliff, and he looked down into death. And there he camped, powerless. He had carried out his Sympathy as an extension of Love and Charity. And it had brought him almost to madness and soul-death. It gave him his forced, unhealthy, post-mortem quality.

His message was really the opposite of Henley's rant:

> I am the master of my fate.
> I am the captain of my soul.

Whitman's essential message was the Open Road. The leaving of the soul free unto herself, the leaving of his fate to her and to the loom of the open road. Which is the bravest doctrine man has ever proposed to himself.

Alas, he didn't quite carry it out. He couldn't quite break the old maddening bond of the love-compulsion, he couldn't quite get out of the rut of the charity habit. For Love and Charity have degenerated now into habit: a bad habit.

Whitman said Sympathy. If only he had stuck to it! Because Sympathy means feeling with, not feeling for. He kept on having a passionate feeling *for* the negro slave, or the prostitute, or the syphilitic. Which is merging. A sinking of Walt Whitman's soul in the souls of these others.

He wasn't keeping to his open road. He was forcing his soul down an old rut. He wasn't leaving her free. He was forcing her into other peoples' circumstances.

Supposing he had felt true sympathy with the negro slave? He would have felt *with* the negro slave. Sympathy—compassion—which is partaking of the passion which was in the soul of the negro slave.

What was the feeling in the negro's soul?

"Ah, I am a slave! Ah, it is bad to be a slave! I must free myself. My soul will die unless she frees herself. My soul says I must free myself."

Whitman came along, and saw the slave, and said to himself: "That negro slave is a man like myself. We share the same identity. And he is bleeding with wounds. Oh, oh, is it not myself who am also bleeding with wounds?"

This was not *sympathy*. It was merging and self-sacrifice. "Bear ye one another's burdens."—"Love thy neighbour as thyself."—"Whatsoever ye do unto him, ye do unto me."

If Whitman had truly *sympathised*, he would have said: "That negro slave suffers from slavery. He wants to free himself. His soul wants to free him. He has wounds, but they are the price of freedom. The soul has a long journey from slavery to freedom. If I can help him I will: I will not take over his wounds and his slavery to myself. But I will help him fight the power that enslaves him when he wants to be free, if he wants my help. Since I see in his face that he needs to be free. But even when he is free, his soul has many journeys down the open road, before it is a free soul."

And of the prostitute Whitman would have said:

"Look at that prostitute! Her nature has turned evil under her mental lust for prostitution. She has lost her soul. She knows it herself. She likes to make men lose their souls. If she tried to make me lose my soul, I would kill her. I wish she may die."

But of another prostitute he would have said:

"Look! She is fascinated by the Priapic mysteries. Look, she will soon be worn to death by the Priapic usage. It is the way of her soul. She wishes it so."

Of the syphilitic he would say:

"Look! She wants to infect all men with syphilis. We ought to kill her."

And of another syphilitic:

"Look! She has a horror of her syphilis. If she looks my way I will help her to get cured."

This is sympathy. The soul judging for herself, and preserving her own integrity.

But when, in Flaubert, the man takes the leper to his naked body; when Bubi de Montparnasse takes the girl because he knows she's got syphilis; when Whitman embraces an evil prostitute: that is not sympathy. The evil prostitute has no desire to be embraced with love; so if you sympathise with her, you won't try to embrace her with love. The leper loathes his leprosy, so if you sympathise with him, you'll loathe it too. The evil woman who wishes to infect all men with her syphilis hates you if you haven't got syphilis. If you sympathise, you'll feel her hatred, and you'll hate too, you'll hate her. Her feeling is hate, and you'll share it. Only your soul will choose the direction of its own hatred.

The soul is a very perfect judge of her own motions, if your mind doesn't dictate to her. Because the mind says Charity! Charity! you don't have to force your soul into kissing lepers or embracing syphilitics. Your lips are the lips of your soul, your body is the body of your soul; your own single, individual soul. That is Whitman's message. And your soul hates syphilis and leprosy. Because it *is* a soul, it hates these things which are against the soul. And therefore to force the body of your soul into contact with uncleanness is a great violation of your soul. The soul wishes to keep clean and whole. The soul's deepest will is to preserve its own integrity, against the mind and the whole mass of disintegrating forces.

Soul sympathises with soul. And that which tries to kill my soul, my soul hates. My soul and my body are one. Soul and body wish to keep clean and whole. Only the mind is capable of great perversion. Only the mind tries to drive my soul and body into uncleanness and unwholesomeness.

What my soul loves, I love.

What my soul hates, I hate.

When my soul is stirred with compassion, I am compassionate.

What my soul turns away from I turn away from.

That is the *true* interpretation of Whitman's creed: the true revelation of his Sympathy.

And my soul takes the open road. She meets the souls that are passing, she goes along with the souls that are going her way. And for one and all, she has sympathy. The sympathy of love, the sympathy of hate, the sympathy of simple proximity: all the subtle sympathisings of the incalculable soul, from the bitterest hate to the passionate love.

It is not I who guide my soul to heaven. It is I who am guided by my own soul along the open road, where all men tread. Therefore, I must accept her deep motions of love, or hate, or compassion, or dislike, or indifference. And I must go where she takes me. For my feet and my lips and my body are my soul. It is I who must submit to her.

This is Whitman's message of American democracy.

The true democracy, where soul meets soul, in the open road. Democracy. American democracy where all journey down the open road. And where a soul is known at once in its going. Not by its clothes or appearance. Whitman did away with that. Not by its family name. Not even by its reputation. Whitman and Melville both discounted that. Not by a progression of piety, or by works of Charity. Not by works at all. Not by anything but just itself. The soul passing unenhanced, passing on foot and being no more than itself. And recognized, and passed by or greeted according to the soul's dictate. If it be a great soul, it will be worshipped in the road.

The love of man and woman: a recognition of souls, and a communion of worship. The love of comrades: a recognition of souls, and a communion of worship. Democracy: a recognition of souls, all down the open road, and a great soul seen in its greatness, as it travels on foot among the rest, down the common way of the living. A glad recognition of souls, and a gladder worship of great and greater souls, because they are the only riches.

Love, and Merging, brought Whitman to the Edge of Death! Death! Death!

But the exultance of his message still remains. Purified of MERGING, purified of MYSELF, the exultant message of American Democracy, souls in the Open Road, full of glad recognition, full of fierce readiness, full of joy of worship, when one soul sees a greater soul.

The only riches, the great souls.

Explication de Texte Applied to Walt Whitman's "Out of the Cradle Endlessly Rocking"

Leo Spitzer*

After this rapid and over-simplified survey it should have become clear that in the poem "Out of the Cradle" Whitman has offered a powerful original synthesis of motifs which have been elaborated through a period of 1500 years of Occidental poetry. The poems I have mentioned are not necessarily his immediate material sources; but I am convinced that his "bird or demon" is a descendant of Shelley's "Sprite bird," that the brother mocking-bird is one of Saint Francis' brother creatures, that his "feathered guests from Alabama" is a derivate from Arnold's "wanderer from a Grecian shore," that the conception of "a thousand singers, a thousand songs . . . a thousand echoes" all present in the poet is a re-elaboration of Victor Hugo's "ame aux mille voix" and "écho sonore." Be this as it may, the basic motifs in which the idea of world harmony has taken shape in Europe must be in our mind when we read Whitman's poem, which becomes greater to the degree that it can be shown as ranking with, and sometimes excelling, the great parallel poems of world literature.

Our poem is organized in three parts: a *prooemium* (l. 1–22), the tale of the bird (l. 23–143), and the conclusion in which the influence of the bird on the "outsetting bard" is stated (l. 144–to the end). Parts one and three correspond to each other and occasionally offer parallel wording.

The proem, composed in the epic style of *arma virumque cano*, not only defines the theme of the whole poem clearly but translates this definition into poetry. The proem consists of one long, "oceanic" sentence which symbolizes by its structure the poetic victory achieved by the poet: "Out of the Cradle . . . down . . . up . . . out . . . from . . . I, chanter of pains and joys, uniter of here and hereafter . . . A reminiscence sing." Out of the maze of the world, symbolized by those numerous parallel phrases, introduced by contrasting prepositions, which invite the inner

*Reprinted by permission of the Johns Hopkins University Press from *English Literary History*, 16 (1949), 235–49. The first seven pages of the essay, which have been omitted, survey from classical literature to the 19th Century what Spitzer calls the "age-old theme of world harmony within which the bird is one voice, the sea another, and the poet the third." Spitzer's footnotes, which are not needed for the explication, also have been omitted.

eye of the reader to look in manifold directions, though *out of* and *from* predominate—out of the maze of the world emerges the powerful Ego, the "I" of the poet, who has extricated himself from the labyrinth (his victory being as it were sealed by the clipped last line "a reminiscence sing").

The longer the sentence, the longer the reader must wait for its subject, the more we sense the feeling of triumph once this subject is reached: the Ego of the poet that dominates the cosmos. It is well known that this is the basic attitude of Walt Whitman toward the world. "Walt Whitman, a kosmos, of Manhattan the son, turbulent, fleshy, sensual . . .", he says in the "Song of Myself." He felt himself to be a microcosm reflecting the macrocosm. He shares with Dante the conviction that the Here and the Hereafter collaborate toward his poetry, and as with Dante this attitude is not one of boastfulness. Dante felt impelled to include his own human self (with all his faults) because in his poem his Ego is necessary as a representative of Christendom on its voyage to the Beyond. Walt Whitman felt impelled to include in his poetry his own self (with all his faults) as the representative of American democracy undertaking this worldly voyage of exploration. "And I say to mankind, Be not curious about God . . . I see God each hour of the twenty-four, . . . In the faces of men and women I see God, and in my own face in the glass." "I am of old and young, of the foolish as much as the wise, one of the Nation of many nations . . . A Southerner soon as a Northerner . . . Of every hue and caste am I, of every rank and religion." But in contrast to Dante who knew of an eternal order in this world as in the Beyond, Whitman finds himself faced with an earthly reality whose increasing complexity made correspondingly more difficult his achievement of poetic mastery. Therefore Whitman must emphasize more his personal triumph. The complexity of the modern world finds its usual expression with Whitman in the endless catalogues, so rarely understood by commentators: in what I have called his "chaotic enumeration" ("La enumeración caótica en las literaturas modernas," Buenos Aires 1945), a device, much imitated after him by Rubén Darío, Claudel, and Werfel. This poetic device consists of lumping together things spiritual and physical, as the raw material of our rich, but unordered modern civilization which is made to resemble an oriental bazaar. In this poem it is only one specific situation whose material and spiritual ingredients Whitman enumerates: the natural scene (Paumanok beach at night), the birds, the sea, the thousand responses of the heart of the boy-poet, and his "myriad thence-arous'd words,"—they are all on one plane in this poem, no one subordinated to another, because this arrangement corresponds to Whitman's chaotic experience. Similarly the two temporal planes, the moment when the boy felt the "myriad words" aroused in him on Paumanok beach, and the other when the mature poet feels the rise of "the words such as now start the scene revisiting," are made to coincide because, at the time of the composition of the poem, they are felt as one chaotic but finally mastered experience: the boy who observed the birds now has become the poet. When defining his creative rôle here in the poem, Whitman does not indulge in chaotic enumeration of his qualities as he does in the passage from the "Song of Myself" in which he appears as a Protean demigod. Now he presents himself simply and succinctly as: "I, chanter of pains and joys, uniter of here and hereafter." Out of hydra-like anarchy he has created unity; and, as we see, he has gained not only an emotional, but an intellectual triumph; he represents himself as "taking all hints, but swiftly leaping beyond them" like a master philologian or medieval glossator (later he will insist on his rôle as cautious "translator of the birds' cry," 31 and 69). Whitman takes care to impress upon us the intellectual side of the synthesis he has achieved; a claim that is not unjustified and an aspect that should be stressed more in a poet in whose work generally only the sensuous and chaotic aspect is emphasized.

His "uniting" powers have been revealed to us in his first stanza; in fact in the first line of the poem which gives it its title. With its rocking rhythm, the line suggests the cradle of the infinite sea from which later, at the end of the poem, *death* will emerge. At this stage, however, death is already a part of the situation. It is present in the phrase "From a word stronger and more delicious than any," which the reader is not yet able to understand. Now we can visualize only the ocean, the main instrument in the concert of world harmony with which the song of the bird and the thousand responses of the poet fuse. Whitman restores the Ambrosian fullness and the unity of *Stimmung* of the world concert of love, music, and ocean (but obviously without Ambrose's theism). There will be no dainty *Vogelkonzert* in a German romantic nook, no dolorous dialogue between a soul estranged from nature and a bird-sprite in an English countryside; the American ocean, "the savage old mother" will provide the background and the undertone to the whole poem. In this Ambrosian concert of world harmony we may distinguish also the Hugoian voice of the poet consisting of a thousand voices; but the insistent repetitions "a thousand singers, a thousand echoes" give rather the effect of a struggle on the poet's part, a struggle with the infinite, than that of a complacent equation ("I am the universe!") such as we find in Hugo.

After the organ- and tuba-notes that resound in the proem, the tone changes entirely in the main part, which is devoted to the reminiscence proper, to the singing of the mocking-birds and the listening of the boy. Here we find a straightforward narrative interrupted by the lyrical songs or "arias" of the birds. Given the setting of nature within which the boy and the bird meet, the term *aria* (130, 138) with its operatic, theatrical connotation as well as the musicological term *trio* (140) that immediately follows (applied to the ears, the tears, and the soul of the boy), may seem too *précieux*. In "Song of Myself," we recall, Whitman speaks of the tree-toad as "a *chef-d'oeuvre* for the highest." But we must also remember that Whitman's world-embracing vision is able to contain in itself opposite aspects of the world at once together. In this vision the man-made or artificial has its genuine place near the product of nature and may even be only another aspect of the natural. The song of the mocking-bird, so naturally sweet, is an artefact of nature that teaches the human artist Whitman.

To return to our narrative, this offers us a development in time of the theme that had been compressed to one plane in the proem: the boy become poet. In such a development, we would expect, according to conventional syntax, to find the historical flow of events expressed by verbs. But to the contrary, this narrative section offers throughout an almost exclusively nominal style, that is, the coupling of nouns with adjectives or participles, without benefit of finite verbs or copulas. This is an impressionistic device known in French as *écriture artiste*, which was introduced by the Goncourts in their diary in the 1850's; for example, "Dans la rue. Tête de femme aux cheveux restroussés en arrière, dégageant le bossuage d'un front étroit, les sourcils remontés vers les tempes . . . ; un type physique curieux de l'énergie et de la volonté féminines" (*Journal des Goncourt*, [1856], I, 134). This we call impressionistic because with the suppression of the verb the concatenation and development of happenings gives way to the listing of unconnected ingredients, or, in pictorial terms, to touches of color irrespective of the units to which the colored objects belong. Accordingly, we find with Whitman: "Once Paumanok . . . two feathered guests . . . and their nest . . . and every day the he-bird to and fro . . . and every day . . . I cautiously peering . . .", a procedure that is brought to a high point of perfection in that masterpiece of the last stanza of the second part: "The aria sinking, all else continuing, the stars shining . . . The boy ecstatic . . . The love in the heart long pent . . ." I see in these participles nervous notations of the moment which serve not to reenact actions, but to perpetuate the momentary impressions which these have made on the boy when he was perceiving them. When the boy sensed that the melancholy song was subsiding, he jotted down in the book of memory the words: "Aria sinking," and we the readers may still perceive that first nervous reaction. The development of the boy is then given the style appropriate to a "reminiscence." The style here chosen is such as to impress upon us the fragmentary nature of the naked "reminiscence." Because of the non-finite form of the participles, single moments are forever arrested, but, owing to the verbal nature of these forms, the moment is one of movement, of movement crystallized. Of course, such vivid rendering of a reminiscence is possible only in languages, such as English or Spanish, that possess the progressive form, of which the simple participle may represent the elliptical variant.

Now, from line 138 on, while the initial rhythm of the stanza seems to continue, there appear strange inversions such as "The aria's meaning, the ears, the soul, swiftly depositing" (for "the ears, the soul swiftly depositing the aria's meaning" and similarly in 140 and 141), inversions quite unusual in English, even jarring upon the English *Sprachgefühl*. We must evidently suppose that the "extasis" (l. 136) of the boy is working in an effort comparable to travail toward an intellectual achievement. It is "the aria's *meaning*" that is now being found by him and the jarring construction is the "impressionistic" rendering of the difficulty with which this inner event is made to happen. It has already been noted that the activities here reflected by the sequence of participles and other modifiers are all of equal weight. We have not yet stressed the extent to which the "enumerative" procedure has been carried out in our stanza, which indeed consists only of detached phrases of the type "the . . . . -ing (-ed)." The chaotic enumeration offered us here is intended to show the collaboration of the whole world ("all else," "the stars," "the winds," "the fierce old mother," "the yellow half-moon," "the boy ecstatic," "the love," "the ears, the soul," "the strange tears," "the colloquy, the trio," and "the undertone of the sea") toward that unique event—the birth of a poet out of a child who has grasped the meaning of the world. The nervous, impressionistic enumeration is symbolic of the travail of this birth. On the other hand, the repetition in this whole stanza of the atonic rhyme *-ing*, an ending that appeared already in the first line with the suggestion of *rocking*, evokes the all-embracing rhythm and permanent undertone or counterpoint of the sea, whether fiercely howling or softly rocking, as it comes to drown out the chamber-music, the *trio* of ears, soul and tears in the boy. The rhyme in *-ing* is a *leitmotif* that orchestrates the arias of boy and bird and gives the poem a Wagnerian musical density of texture.

As for the songs of the birds, let us note first that Whitman has chosen to replace the hackneyed literary nightingale by a domestic bird of America, the mocking-bird, compared to which, Jefferson once declared, the European nightingale is a third-rate singer. The manner in which Whitman has "translated," to use his modest expression, the song of the mockingbird into words deserves boundless admiration. I know of no other poem in which we find such a heart-rending impersonation of a bird by a poet, such a welding of bird's voice and human word, such an empathy for the joy and pain expressed by nature's singers. The European poets we have listed above have accurately defined or admiringly praised the musical tone of the bird-notes issuing from tiny throats, but no one attempted to choose just those human articulate words which would correspond to birds' song if these creatures had possessed the faculty of speech (Eichendorff had the bird sing in the first person, but it sang conventional Romantic lines): the simple, over and over repeated exclamations of a helpless being haunted by pain, which, while monotonously repeating the same *oh*! or giving in to the automatism that is characteristic of overwhelming emotion ("my love, my love"), call upon all elements to bring back the mate. Thus in one common purpose the whole creation is united by the bird in the manner of Saint Francis, but this time in a dirge that associates the creation ("Oh night,"—"Low-hanging moon," "Land,

land, land," "Oh rising stars," "Oh darkness") with the mourner, with his
elemental body and his elemental desires "Oh throat," . . . "Oh throbbing heart," . . . "Oh past," "Oh happy life," "O songs of joy." The
mournful bird shakes out "reckless despairing carols," songs of *world
disharmony* in which love and death are felt as irreconcilable enemies
("carols of lonesome love,"—"death's carols"). The long outdrawn
refrains of despair ("soothe soothe soothe," "land land land," "loved loved
loved . . .") alternate with everyday speech whose minimum of ex-
pressivity becomes a maximum in a moment of tribulation that is beyond
words ("so faint, I must be still, be still to listen, but not altogether still,
for then she might not come immediately to me," or "O darkness, O in
vain! O I am very sick and sorrowful"). The most dynamic American poet
has here become the gentlest. We remember Musset's lines quoted above;
Whitman's bird's song is a *pur sanglot*.

We may surmise that this lyric section (within a lyric poem) has
been somewhat influenced by Mathew Arnold's "Forsaken Merman,"
("Come dear children, let us away, down and always below. / Come dear
children, come away down, call no more . . ."). But Arnold's merman is
one of the last offsprings on that futile masquerade of elementary spirits
revived by the Romantics, a pagan demon who is presented as *defeated* by
Christianity instead of a figure dangerously seductive to Christians. But
Whitman's mocking-bird, the spirit become human, who symbolizes all
earthly loveliness subject to grief and death, will live forever. It is one of
those historical miracles we can not explain that in the age of machines
and capitalism there should arise a poet who feels himself to be a brother
to nature as naturally as did Saint Francis, but who at the same time was
enough of an intellectual to know the uniqueness of his gift. To *him* the
bird poured forth the "meanings which I of all men know, Yes my brother
I know, the rest might not." This is again no boasting; this is the simple
truth, a perspicacious self-definition of one who has a primeval genius of
empathy for nature.

Now let us turn to the last part of the poem which begins with the
words "demon *or* bird" (14), an expression followed later (175) by my
"dusky demon *and* brother." The Shelleyan ambiguity disappears here.
This marks the end of the parabola that began with "the two feathered
guests from Alabama" (26) and was continued sadly with "the solitary
guest from Alabama" (51) and "the lone singer wonderful" (58). While
the mood of the birds develops from careless rapture to "dusky" melancholy, a contrary change takes place in the sea. "The fierce old mother incessantly moaning" (133), the "savage old mother incessantly crying"
(141) becomes the "old crone rocking the cradle," "hissing melodious,"
"laving me all over." The two opposite developments must be seen in connection. To the degree that the bird is crushed by fate, the sea develops its
soothing qualities; to the degree that beauty fades away, wisdom becomes
manifest. The sea represents the sweet wisdom of death. The forces of

nature are thus ambivalent, Janus-like. Nature wills sorrow and joy, life and death, and it may be that death will become or foster life. "Out of the cradle endlessly rocking," that is (we understand it now), out of the cradle of *death*, the poet will sing life. By presenting, in the beginning, the sea only as a cradle gently rocking, there was suggested the idea of birth and life; but now, the gently rocking cradle is seen as the symbol of recurring death and re-birth. A poet is born by the death of the bird who is a brother and a demon. A brother because he teaches the boy; a demon, because he "projects" the poet, anticipates, and heralds him, stirs up in him those creative faculties which must partake of the frightening and of the daemoniac. But while the bird was destined to teach the boy love ("death" being a reality the bird was not able to reconcile with love), the sea, wiser than the bird and the "aroused child's heart," has another message to bring to the boy: "Death, death, death, death, death" (173). This line is the counterpart of the mocking-bird's "loved loved loved loved loved!", and it is couched in the same exclamational style, as though it were the organic continuation thereof. The word *death* is "the word final, superior to all," "the key," "the clew" which awakes in the boy the thousand responses, songs, echoes, and the myriad of words; and once he has discovered this *meaning* of life, which is death, he is no longer the boy of the beginning ("never again leave me to be the peaceful boy I was before"). He has become the poet, the "uniter of here and hereafter," able to fuse the voices of the *musica mundana* into one symphony, and we the readers can now understand his words in their full depth. In the conclusion we recognize certain lines of the proem textually repeated but now clarified and deepened by the keyword; we understand at last the symphonic value of "that strong and delicious word" alluded to in the proem. The liquid fusion suggested by the sea of death is symbolized by the fluid syntax of the last three stanzas; the relative constructions which we find in l. 165 "Whereto answering the sea . . ." and l. 174 "Which I do not forget" weld the three stanzas together into one stream or chain which comprehends the question of the boy, the answer of the sea and his choice of avocation, into one melody in which inspiration flows uninterruptedly from the watery element to the poet. The bird and the poet have been given their respective solos in the symphony. The bird's solo is the *aria* and the boy's the *trio* of ears, soul, and tears; the endless counterpoint and contrabasso of the sea has accompanied their detached musical pieces. Now all voices blend in an "*unendliche Melodie*," an infinite melody, the unfixed form of nineteenth-century pantheism, with Wagnerian orchestration. "But fuse the song of my dusky demon and brother . . . with the thousand responsive songs, at random, my own songs . . . and with them the key, the word up from the waves." The last word in the poem, however, is the personal pronoun *me*. Though placed inconspicuously in an unstressed position in the short line "the sea whisper'd me," this personal word nevertheless represents a modest climax. It is to Whitman that

has been revealed the musical meaning of the world, the chord formed by
Eros and Thanatos, the infinite cosmos created from infinite chaos, and,
finally, his own micro-cosmic rôle in the creation. It is the knowledge of
death that will make him the poet of life, of this world, *not* of the
Hereafter. The promise in the beginning to sing of the Here and Hereafter
can be said to have been fulfilled only if the Hereafter is understood as
comprised in the Here. We will note that no reference is made in Whitman's poem to the world harmony of the Christian Beyond in the manner
of Milton. The fullness of life of which Whitman sings can come to an end
only in the sealike, endlessly rocking embrace of nothingness, an end that is
sweet and sensuous ("delicious" is Whitman's epithet), and indeed, he appears sensuously to enjoy the sound of the word *death* that he so often
repeats. We may pause at this point to remember that in 1860, one year
after our lyric was written, Whitman gives expression to the same feeling
in the poem "Scented herbage of my breast":

> You [the leaves] make me think of death,
> Death is beautiful from you (what indeed is finally
>   beautiful except death and love?)
> Oh I think it is not for life I am chanting here
>   my chant of lovers,
> I think it must be for death . . .
> Death or life I am then indifferent, my soul
>   declines to prefer
> (I am not sure but the high soul of lovers welcomes
>   death most).

The same feeling for the voluptuousness of death and the death-like quality of love we find not only in Wagner's *Tristan und Isolde* (1857), in
which we hear the same words applied to the love-scene and to the death-
scene, *unbewusst—höchste (Liebes-) Lust.* There is also the same motif in
Baudelaire's *Invitation* of 1857, in which the "invitation" is the lure of
death, described as voluptuous hashish and scented lotus. Perhaps powerful personalities crave death as a liberation from the burden of their own
individuality, and sensuous poets wish to have a sensuous death. Perhaps
also the concurrence in one motif of three poets not in direct contact with
each other means that their subtle sensitivity instinctively anticipated the
death-germs implanted in a luxuriant, sensuous, worldly civilization of
"Enrichissez-vous," of Victorianism, and the Second Empire. This was
long before the *fin de siècle* generation of D'Annunzio, Barrès, Hofmanns-
thal and Thomas Mann, when the theme of love-death, inherited from
Baudelaire and Wagner, finally became the theme *par excellence.* But
Whitman, unlike his two sickly European contemporary confrères will remain for us not the poet of death (although the idea of death may have
perturbed him more than once), but the unique poet of American *optimism* and love of life, who has been able, naturally and naively, to unite

what in other contemporary poets tends to fall apart, the life of man and that of nature.

A last question arises. To what sub-genre does our lyrical poem belong? It is obviously an *ode*, the genre made famous by Pindar, Horace, Milton, and Hölderlin, if the ode may be defined as a solemn, lengthy, lyric-epic poem that celebrates an event significant for the community, such as, with Pindar, the victory of a champion in the Olympic games. Ancient poems belonging to this very aristocratic genre are filled with erudite mythological allusions since the origin of the heroes must be traced back to gods or demigods. These odes are also written in a difficult language that can not easily be sung, for they are replete with whimsical breaks and changes of rhythm and tone that reflect the fragmentary nature of the inspiration of the poet, carried away as he is by his divine enthusiasm or Θεία μανία. Of course, as is true of all ancient poetry, the ode had no rhymes. In the period of the Renaissance this ancient genre was revived, but enjoyed only a precarious existence in modern literatures because the social set-up of Pindar's Greece was missing in our civilization, filled as it is with social resentment, and because the travesty involved in presenting contemporary figures as ancient heroes could only be sadly disappointing. The genre fared relatively better in Germanic than in Romance literatures because the Romance languages are not free enough in word-formation to offer coinages worthy of Pindar and because Romance needs the rhyme as a constitutive element of verse. Ronsard's Pindaric odes were signal failures. Whitman has acclimated the ode on American soil and democratized it. The lyric-epic texture, the solemn basic tone and the stylistic variation, the whimsical word-coinages and the chaotic fragmentariness are preserved. The latter feature has even found a modern justification in the complexity of the modern world. For the rhymeless Greek verse, Whitman by a bold intuition found an equivalent in the Bible verset, but he used this meter in order to express a creed diametrically opposed to that of the Bible. Theoretically, he could have borrowed expressions of his pantheistic beliefs from the mythology of the Greeks, but in reality, he did away with *all* mythology, pagan as well as Christian. He replaces the pagan Pantheon by the deified eternal forces of nature to which any American of today may feel close. The Ocean is the old savage mother, not Neptune with the trident (a mother, a primeval chtonic goddess) and the bird is not Philomela, but the mocking-bird who is a demon of fertility (only in the phrase "feathered guests of Alabama" do we find a faint reminiscence of Homeric expression, the *epitheton constans*). The Neo-Catholic poet Paul Claudel who, as recently as the last decades, gave the French for the first time a true ode and was able to do so only by a detour through America, by imitating Whitman (even the metric form of his free verse), found it necessary to discard Whitman's pantheistic naturalism and to replace it by the *merveilleux chrétien* which a hundred years ago Chateaubriand had introduced into

French prose. But it can not be denied that Whitman's ode can reach a wider range of modern readers than can Claudel's orthodox Catholic *grande ode*. As for the solemn event significant for the community which the ode must by its nature celebrate—this we have in the consecration of Walt Whitman as a poet, the glorification, not of a Greek aristocratic athlete born of Gods, but of a nameless American boy, a solitary listener and singer on a little-known Long Island shore who, having met with nature and with his own heart, becomes the American national poet, the democratic and priestly *vates Americanus*.

Poetry: The Art

Stanley Burnshaw*

In the Form of an Apostrophe to Whitman

I used to read your book and hear your words
Explode in me and blast new passageways
Deep in my brain, until its crowding rooms
Held more light than my head could balance. Now
That the tunnels all are cut, I pace the rooms
Looking for you, though certain I shall find
No more of you than you yourself could gather
Out of the pieces of self. The years have burned
The sharpness from the edges: I can fit
The pieces, but the mortar must be mixed
Out of our blending wills. Others have tried
And failed. I too shall fail if I forget
How thought can range beyond the last frontiers
That common sense has civilized with names.
Others who looked for you have made you say
Words you might have said if they were you:
Have lost you in their passion for a phrase.
The private man's infinitude defies
The singleness they look for when they strive
To sort your various colors to a scheme
Of thought-and-action. Desperate for pattern,
They make the key *Calamus* and they twist
Your other selves around the centerpiece,
Losing you in that love.

              And others forge
A key of social thought that cracks apart
When words and actions contradict: *Walt Whitman,*
You said you love the common man! Where were you
When Parsons' friends were hanged? Were you asleep
Or writing more fine words about mechanics

*Reprinted from *In the Terrified Radiance* (New York: George Braziller, Inc., 1972), pp. 145–49, by permission of the author. Originally published in *Early and Late Testament* (1952).

228

And farmers?—How much cosier for you
To prate about democracy than live it—
You, its self-appointed poet!

Others,
Seeking you in your plangent celebrations
Of science and the holiness of flesh
And earth, end with a fierce *You too, Walt Whitman,*
You flinched, you stumbled, hankering for a "soul" . . .
The substances of sense too harsh too bitter
A truth for you to live by! Underneath
Your protest boils the soft romantic sickness
Of all the Shelleys, Heines—bright lost leaders
We hoped were men. You were afraid of the dark:
You who had thundered "Science is true religion"
Sang the groveler's wooing song to Death
And God and Spirit! . . . *Hide, at least, the image*
Revealed: the gaudy chaos of man
Reviling his own faith!

But who can dare
To arbitrate the depths of you that anger
Against your tranquil self? I am not certain:
I have seen the signposts of contradiction
Planted by men impotent to discern
The harmony beneath the subtle wholeness,
And in their self-defence erect confusion
On quiet entities. A poet's words
Are signatures of self—the many selves
Subsumed in one profounder sense that knows
An all-according truth: a single eye
Uncovering the countless constellations
Of heart and mind. Wherefore the syllables
Reach outward from the self in an embrace
Of multitudes. The poetries of speech
Are acts of thinking love; and I must find
The thought that grows the center of your passion.

And so I say to those who precontemn
The message of *Calamus* as the flowers
Of twisted love what Plato showed of truths
Uttered by poets. And I say to those
Who spit upon your social thought *"Respondez!"*
The human race is restive, on the watch
For some new era—some divine war—
Whose triumph will entrench a brave good-will
Among the common people everywhere—
The trodden multitudes for whom you clamored
A new and tender reverence.

But for those
Who sneer because you looked for lights beyond
The planes of sense, there is no final answer
If they deny the mind its birthright freedom
To range all worlds of thought and sense and vision.
Everything that can be believ'd is an image of truth—
The images refined to great and small
Will cluster into orbits of belief
And hold together as the planets hold
By kinship and denial, in one vaster
All encompassing circle. Let the sneerers
Proclaim your chief intent or keep their silence
Until its name is found.

It is not found,
The answer to your central search—"the problem,
The only one"—*adjust the individual
Into the mass.* For we have just begun
To fit the world to men, men to the world;
And we shall stumble till the single heart
Discovers all its selves and learns therefrom
How singleness and multitude can live
In valiant marriage. With your hungry hope
You pierced the shells of feeling, trumpeted
Into your country's ears, and flooded strength
Into the wavering hearts of men lonely
For courage to fulfill their need: to thrust
Their single faith against the massed-up wills
Of many. "Sing yourself!" you told them. Listening,
They pledged the valors of the inward man.
And others turned from you with dull, deaf ears,
Afraid to listen, waiting to be taught
The trial-and-error way of rats in a maze . . .

A poem "is," some men believe. I say
A poem "is" when it has spread its root
Inside a listener's thought and grows a tree there
Strong enough to burst a room in the brain,
And bring its branch to blossom. Then the host
Forgets the verse and ponders on the mind
That made this seed of growth . . . as I forget
Your poem: as I strive to learn your mind,
Thinking that when I come to understand,
I may begin to touch serenities
You saw beneath the springs of pain that nourished
Your world that was beginning—dim, green world
Trembling with death-and-birth: divinest war.

Walt Whitman: He Had His Nerve

Randall Jarrell*

Whitman, Dickinson, and Melville seem to me the best poets of the 19th Century here in America. Melville's poetry has been grotesquely underestimated, but of course it is only in the last four or five years that it has been much read; in the long run, in spite of the awkwardness and amateurishness of so much of it, it will surely be thought well of. (In the short run it will probably be thought entirely too well of. Melville is a great poet only in the prose of *Moby Dick*.) Dickinson's poetry has been thoroughly read, and well though undifferentiatingly loved—after a few decades or centuries almost everybody will be able to see through Dickinson to her poems. But something odd has happened to the living changing part of Whitman's reputation: nowadays it is people who are not particularly interested in poetry, people who say that they read a poem for what it says, not for how it says it, who admire Whitman most. Whitman is often written about, either approvingly or disapprovingly, as if he were the Thomas Wolfe of 19th Century democracy, the hero of a de Mille movie about Walt Whitman. (People even talk about a war in which Walt Whitman and Henry James chose up sides, to begin with, and in which you and I will go on fighting till the day we die.) All this sort of thing, and all the bad poetry that there of course is in Whitman—for any poet has written enough bad poetry to scare away anybody—has helped to scare away from Whitman most "serious readers of modern poetry." They do not talk of his poems, as a rule, with any real liking or knowledge. Serious readers, people who are ashamed of not knowing all Hopkins by heart, are not at all ashamed to say, "I don't really know Whitman very well." This may harm Whitman in your eyes, they know, but that is a chance that poets have to take. Yet "their" Hopkins, that good critic and great poet, wrote about Whitman, after seeing five or six of his poems in a newspaper review: "I may as well say what I should not otherwise have said, that I always knew in my heart Walt Whitman's mind to be more like my own than any other man's living. As he is a very great scoundrel this is not a very pleasant confession." And Henry James,

*Reprinted from *The Kenyon Review*, 14 (1952), 63–79, by permission of *The Kenyon Review* and Mrs. Randall Jarrell.

the leader of "their" side in that awful imaginary war of which I spoke, once read Whitman to Edith Wharton (much as Mozart used to imitate, on the piano, the organ) with such power and solemnity that both sat shaken and silent; it was after this reading that James expressed his regret at Whitman's "too extensive acquaintance with the foreign languages." Almost all the most "original and advanced" poets and critics and readers of the last part of the 19th Century thought Whitman as original and advanced as themselves, in manner as well as in matter. Can Whitman really be a sort of Thomas Wolfe or Carl Sandburg or Robinson Jeffers or Henry Miller—or a sort of Balzac of poetry, whose every part is crude but whose whole is somehow good? He is not, nor could he be; a poem, like Pope's spider, "lives along the line," and all the dead lines in the world will not make one live poem. As Blake says, "all sublimity is founded on minute discrimination," and it is in these "minute particulars" of Blake's that any poem has its primary existence.

To show Whitman for what he is one does not need to praise or explain or argue, one needs simply to quote. He himself said, "I and mine do not convince by arguments, similes, rhymes,/We convince by our presence." Even a few of his phrases are enough to show us that Whitman was no sweeping rhetorician, but a poet of the greatest and oddest delicacy and originality and sensitivity, so far as words are concerned. This is, after all, the poet who said, "Blind loving wrestling touch, sheath'd hooded sharp-tooth'd touch"; who said, "Smartly attired, countenance smiling, form upright, death under the breast-bones, hell under the skull-bones"; who said, "Agonies are one of my changes of garments"; who saw grass as the "flag of my disposition," saw "the sharp-peak'd farmhouse, with its scallop'd scum and slender shoots from the gutters," heard a plane's "wild ascending lisp," and saw and heard how at the amputation "what is removed drops horribly in a pail." This is the poet for whom the sea was "howler and scooper of storms," reaching out to us with "crooked inviting fingers"; who went "leaping chasms with a pike-pointed staff, clinging to topples of brittle and blue"; who, a runaway slave, saw how "my gore dribs, thinn'd with the ooze of my skin"; who went "lithographing Kronos . . . buying drafts of Osiris"; who stared out at the "little plentiful mannikins skipping around in collars and tail'd coats,/I am aware who they are, (they are positively not worms or fleas)." For he is, at his best, beautifully witty: he says gravely, "I find I incorporate gneiss, coals, long-threaded moss, fruits, grain, esculent roots,/And am stucco'd with quadrupeds and birds all over"; and of these quadrupeds and birds "not one is respectable or unhappy over the whole earth." He calls advice: "Unscrew the locks from the doors! Unscrew the doors from their jambs!" He publishes the results of research: "Having pried through the strata, analyz'd to a hair, counsel'd with doctors and calculated close,/I find no sweeter fat than sticks to my own bones." Everybody remembers how he told the Muse to "cross out please those im-

mensely overpaid accounts,/That matter of Troy and Achilles' wrath, and
Aeneas', Odysseus' wanderings," but his account of the arrival of the "il-
lustrious emigré" here in the New World is even better: "Bluff'd not a bit
by drainpipe, gasometer, artificial fertilizers,/Smiling and pleas'd with
palpable intent to stay,/She's here, install'd amid the kitchenware." Or he
sees, like another Breughel, "the mechanic's wife with the babe at her
nipple interceding for every person born,/ Three scythes at harvest whizzing in a row from three lusty angels with shirts bagg'd out at their waists,/
The snag-toothed hostler with red hair redeeming sins past and to
come"—the passage has enough wit not only (in Johnson's phrase) to keep
it sweet, but enough to make it believable. He says:

> I project my hat, sit shame-faced, and beg.
>
> Enough! Enough! Enough!
> Somehow I have been stunn'd. Stand back!
> Give me a little time beyond my cuff'd head, slumbers,
>   dreams, gaping,
> I discover myself on the verge of a usual mistake.

There is in such changes of tone as these the essence of wit. And Whitman
is even more far-fetched than he is witty; he can say about Doubters, in
the most improbable and explosive of juxtapositions: "I know every one of
you, I know the sea of torment, doubt, despair and unbelief./ How the
flukes splash! How they contort rapid as lightning, with splashes and
spouts of blood!" Who else would have said about God: "As the hugging
and loving bed-fellow sleeps at my side through the night, and withdraws
at the break of day with stealthy tread,/Leaving me baskets cover'd with
white towels, swelling the house with their plenty"?—the Psalmist himself, his cup running over, would have looked at Whitman with dazzled
eyes. (Whitman was persuaded by friends to hide the fact that it was God
he was talking about.) He says, "Flaunt of the sunshine I need not your
bask—lie over!" This unusual employment of verbs is usual enough in
participle-loving Whitman, who also asks you to "look in my face while I
snuff the sidle of evening," or tells you, "I effuse my flesh in eddies, and
drift it in lacy jags." Here are some typical beginnings of poems: "City of
orgies, walks, and joys. . . . Not heaving from my ribb'd breast only. . . .
O take my hand Walt Whitman! Such gliding wonders! Such sights and
sounds! Such join'd unended links. . . ." He says to the objects of the
world, "You have waited, you always wait, you dumb, beautiful
ministers"; sees "the sun and stars that float in the open air,/ The apple-
shaped earth"; says, "O suns—O grass of graves— O perpetual transfers
and promotions,/ If you do not say anything how can I say anything? Not
many poets have written better, in queerer and more convincing and
more individual language, about the world's *gliding wonders*: the phrase
seems particularly right for Whitman. He speaks of those "circling rivers

the breath," of the "savage old mother incessantly crying,/ To the boy's soul's questions sullenly timing, some drown'd secret hissing"—ends a poem, once, "We have voided all but freedom and our own joy." How can one quote enough? If the reader thinks that all this is like Thomas Wolfe he *is* Thomas Wolfe; nothing else could explain it. Poetry like this is as far as possible from the work of any ordinary rhetorician, whose phrases cascade over us like suds of the oldest and most-advertised detergent.

The interesting thing about Whitman's worst language (for, just as few poets have ever written better, few poets have ever written worse) is how unusually absurd, how really ingeniously bad, such language is. I will quote none of the most famous examples; but even a line like *O culpable! I acknowledge. I exposé!* is not anything that you and I could do—only a man with the most extraordinary feel for language, or none whatsoever, could have cooked up Whitman's worst messes. For instance: what other man in all the history of this planet would have said, "I am a habitan of Vienna"? (One has an immediate vision of him as a sort of French-Canadian halfbreed to whom the Viennese are offering, with trepidation, through the bars of a zoological garden, little mounds of whipped cream.) An *enclaircise*—why, it's as bad as *explicate!* We are right to resent his having made up his own horrors, instead of sticking to the ones that we ourselves employ. But when Whitman says, "I dote on myself, there is that lot of me and all so luscious," we should realize that we are not the only ones who are amused. And the queerly bad and merely queer and queerly good will often change into one another without warning: "Hefts of the moving world, at innocent gambols silently rising, freshly exuding,/Scooting obliquely high and low"—not good, but *queer!*—suddenly becomes, "Something I cannot see puts up libidinous prongs,/ Seas of bright juice suffuse heaven," and it is sunrise.

But it is not in individual lines and phrases, but in passages of some length, that Whitman is at his best. In the following quotation Whitman has something difficult to express, something that there are many formulas, all bad, for expressing; he expresses it with complete success, in language of the most dazzling originality:

> The orchestra whirls me wider than Uranus flies,
> It wrenches such ardors from me I did not know I
>   possess'd them,
> It sails me, I dab with bare feet, they are lick'd by the
>   indolent waves,
> I am cut by bitter and angry hail, I lose my breath,
> Sleep'd amid honey'd morphine, my windpipe throttled in
>   fakes of death,
> At length let up again to feel the puzzle of puzzles,
> And that we call Being.

One hardly knows what to point at—everything works. But *wrenches* and *did not know I possess'd them*; the incredible *it sails me, I dab with bare feet; lick'd by the indolent; steep'd amid honey'd morphine; my windpipe throttled in fakes of death*—no wonder Crane admired Whitman! This originality, as absolute in its way as that of Berlioz' orchestration, is often at Whitman's command:

> I am a dance—play up there! the fit is whirling me fast!
> I am the ever-laughing—it is new moon and twilight,
> I see the hiding of douceurs, I see nimble ghosts whichever
>   way I look,
> Cache and cache again deep in the ground and sea, and
>   where it is neither ground nor sea.
> Well do they do their jobs those journeymen divine,
> Only from me can they hide nothing, and would not if they
>   could,
> I reckon I am their boss and they make me a pet besides,
> And surround me and lead me and run ahead when I walk,
> To lift their sunning covers to signify me with stretch'd arms,
>   and resume the way;
> Onward we move, a gay gang of blackguards! with mirth-
>   shouting music and wild-flapping pennants of joy!

If you did not believe Hopkins' remark about Whitman, that *gay gang of blackguards* ought to shake you. Whitman shares Hopkins' passion for "dappled" effects, but he slides in and out of them with ambiguous swiftness. And he has at his command a language of the calmest and most prosaic reality, one that seems to do no more than present:

> The little one sleeps in its cradle.
> I lift the gauze and look a long time, and silently brush away
>   flies with my hand.
> The youngster and the red-faced girl turn aside up the bushy
>   hill,
> I peeringly view them from the top.
>
> The suicide sprawls on the bloody floor of the bedroom.
> I witness the corpse with its dabbled hair, I note where the
>   pistol has fallen.

It is like magic: that is, something has been done to us without our knowing how it was done; but if we look at the lines again we see the *gauze, silently, youngster, red-faced, bushy, peeringly, dabbled*—not that this is all we see. "Present! present!" said James; these are presented, put down side by side to form a little "view of life," from the cradle to the last bloody floor of the bedroom. Very often the things presented form nothing but a list:

> The pure contralto sings in the organ loft,
> The carpenter dresses his plank, the tongue of his foreplane
>   whistles its wild ascending lisp,
> The married and unmarried children ride home to their
>   Thanksgiving dinner,
> The pilot seizes the king-pin, he heaves down with a strong
>   arm,
> The mate stands braced in the whale-boat, lance and harpoon
>   are ready,
> The duck-shooter walks by silent and cautious stretches,
> The deacons are ordain'd with cross'd hands at the altar,
> The spinning-girl retreats and advances to the hum of the big
>   wheel,
> The farmer stops by the bars as he walks on a First-day loafe
>   and looks at the oats and rye,
> The lunatic is carried at last to the asylum a confirm'd case,
> (He will never sleep any more as he did in the cot in his
>   mother's bed-room;)
> The jour printer with gray head and gaunt jaws works at his
>   case,
> He turns his quid of tobacco while his eyes blur with the
>   manuscript,
> The malform'd limbs are tied to the surgeon's table,
> What is removed drops horribly in a pail; . . .

It is only a list—but what a list! And how delicately, in what different ways—likeness and opposition and continuation and climax and anti-climax—the transitions are managed, whenever Whitman wants to manage them. Notice them in the next quotation, another "mere list":

> The bride unrumples her white dress, the minute-hand of the
>   clock moves slowly,
> The opium-eater reclines with rigid head and just-open'd lips,
> The prostitute draggles her shawl, her bonnet bobs on her
>   tipsy and pimpled neck. . . .

The first line is joined to the third by *unrumples* and *draggles, white dress* and *shawl*; the second to the third by *rigid head, bobs, tipsy, neck*; the first to the second by *slowly, just-open'd*, and the slowing-down of time in both states. And occasionally one of these lists is metamorphosed into something we have no name for; the man who would call the next quotation a mere list—anybody will feel this—would boil his babies up for soap:

> Ever the hard unsunk ground,
> Ever the eaters and drinkers, ever the upward and downward
>   sun,
> Ever myself and my neighbors, refreshing, wicked, real,
> Ever the old inexplicable query, ever that thorned thumb, that
>   breath of itches and thirsts,

> Ever the vexer's hoot! hoot! till we find where the sly one hides
>   and bring him forth,
> Ever the sobbing liquid of life,
> Ever the bandage under the chin, ever the trestles of death.

Sometimes Whitman will take what would generally be considered an unpromising subject (in this case, a woman peeping at men in bathing naked) and treat it with such tenderness and subtlety and understanding that we are ashamed of ourselves for having thought it unpromising, and murmur that Chekhov himself couldn't have treated it better:

> Twenty-eight young men bathe by the shore,
> Twenty-eight young men and all so friendly,
> Twenty-eight years of womanly life and all so lonesome.
>
> She owns the fine house by the rise of the bank,
> She hides handsome and richly drest aft the blinds of the
>   window.
>
> Which of the young men does she like the best?
> Ah the homeliest of them is beautiful to her.
>
> Where are you off to, lady? for I see you,
> You splash in the water there, yet stay stock still in your room.
> Dancing and laughing along the beach came the twenty-ninth
>   bather,
> The rest did not see her, but she saw them and loved them.
>
> The beards of the young men glistened with wet, it ran from
>   their long hair,
> Little streams pass'd all over their bodies.
>
> An unseen hand also pass'd over their bodies,
> It descended tremblingly from their temples and ribs.
>
> The young men float on their backs, their white bellies bulge
>   to the sun, they do not ask who seizes fast to them,
> They do not know who puffs and declines with pendant and
>   bending arch,
> They do not know whom they souse with spray.

And in the same poem (that "Song of Myself" in which one finds half his best work) the writer can say of a sea-fight:

> Stretched and still lies the midnight,
> Two great hulls motionless on the breast of the darkness,
> Our vessel riddled and slowly sinking, preparations to pass
>   to the one we have conquer'd,
> The captain on the quarter-deck coldly giving his orders

> through a countenance white as a sheet,
> Near by the corpse of the child that serv'd in the cabin,
> The dead face of an old salt with long white hair and carefully
>   curl'd whiskers,
> The flames spite of all that can be done flickering aloft and
>   below,
> The husky voices of the two or three officers yet fit for duty,
> Formless stacks of bodies and bodies by themselves, dabs of
>   flesh upon the masts and spars,
> Cut of cordage, dangle of rigging, slight shock of the soothe of
>   waves,
> Black and impassive guns, litter of powder-parcels, strong
>   scent,
> A few large stars overhead, silent and mournful shining,
> Delicate snuffs of sea-breeze, smells of sedgy grass and fields by
>   the shore, death-messages given in charge to survivors,
> The hiss of the surgeon's knife, the gnawing teeth of his saw,
> Wheeze, cluck, swash of falling blood, short wild scream, and
>   long, dull, tapering groan,
> These so, these irretrievable.

There are faults in this passage, and they *do not matter*: the serious truth, the complete realization of these last lines make us remember that few poets have shown more of the tears of things, and the joy of things, and of the reality beneath either tears or joy. Even Whitman's most general or political statements sometimes are good: everybody knows his "When liberty goes out of a place it is not the first to go, nor the second or third to go,/ It waits for all the rest to go, it is the last"; these sentences about the United States just before the Civil War may be less familiar:

> Are those really Congressmen? are those the great Judges?
>   is that the President?
> Then I will sleep awhile yet, for I see that these States sleep,
>   for reasons;
> (With gathering murk, with muttering thunder and lambent
>   shoots we all duly awake,
> South, North, East, West, inland and seaboard, we will
>   surely awake.)

How well, with what firmness and dignity and command, Whitman does such passages! And Whitman's doubts that he has done them or anything else well—ah, there is nothing he does better:

> The best I had done seemed to me blank and suspicious,
> My great thoughts as I supposed them, were they not in reality
>   meagre?
> I am he who knew what it was to be evil,
> I too knitted the old knot of contrariety . . .

Saw many I loved in the street or ferry-boat or public assembly,
    yet never told them a word,
Lived the same life with the rest, the same old laughing,
    gnawing, sleeping,
Played the part that still looks back on the actor and actress,
The same old role, the role that is what we make it . . .

Whitman says once that the "look of the bay mare shames silliness
out of me. " This is true—sometimes it is true; but more often the silliness
and affection and cant and exaggeration are there shamelessly, the Old
Adam that was in Whitman from the beginning and the awful new one
that he created to keep it company. But as he says, "I know perfectly well
my own egotism,/ Know my omnivorous lines and must not write any
less." He says over and over that there are in him good and bad, wise and
foolish, anything at all and its antonym, and he is telling the truth; there
is in him almost everything in the world, so that one responds to him,
willingly or unwillingly, almost as one does to the world, that world
which makes the hairs of one's flesh stand up, which seems both evil
beyond any rejection and wonderful beyond any acceptance. We cannot
help seeing that there is something absurd about any judgment we make
of its whole—for there is no "point of view" at which we can stand to
make the judgment, and the moral categories that mean most to us seem
no more to apply to its whole than our spatial or temporal or causal
categories seem to apply to its beginning or its end. (But we need no
arguments to make our judgments seem absurd—we feel their absurdity
without argument.) In some like sense Whitman is a world, a waste with,
here and there, systems blazing at random out of the darkness. Only an
innocent and rigidly methodical mind will reject it for this disorganiza-
tion, particularly since there are in it, here and there, little systems as
beautifully and astonishingly organized as the rings and satellites of
Saturn:

I understand the large hearts of heroes,
The courage of present times and all times,
How the skipper saw the crowded and rudderless wreck of the
    steam-ship, and Death chasing it up and down the storm,
How he knuckled tight and gave not back an inch, and was
    faithful of days and faithful of nights,
And chalked in large letters on a board, Be of good cheer, we
    will not desert you;
How he follow'd with them and tack'd with them three days and
    would not give it up,
How he saved the drifting company at last,
How the lank loose-gown'd women looked when he boated from
    the side of their prepared graves,

> How the silent old-faced infants and the lifted sick, and the
>   sharp-lipp'd unshaved men;
> All this I swallow, it tastes good, I like it well, it becomes mine,
> I am the man, I suffered, I was there.

In the last lines of this quotation Whitman has reached—as great writers always reach—a point at which criticism seems not only unnecessary but absurd: these lines are so good that even admiration feels like insolence, and one is ashamed of anything that one can find to say about them. How anyone can dismiss or accept patronizingly the man who wrote them, I do not understand.

The enormous and apparent advantages of form, of omission and selection, of the highest degree of organization, are accompanied by important disadvantages—and there are far greater works than *Leaves of Grass* to make us realize this. But if we compare Whitman with that very beautiful poet Alfred Tennyson, the most skillful of all Whitman's contemporaries, we are at once aware of how limiting Tennyson's forms have been, of how much Tennyson has had to leave out, even in those discursive poems where he is trying to put everything in. Whitman's poems *represent* his world and himself much more satisfactorily than Tennyson's do his. In the past a few poets have both formed and represented, each in the highest degree; but in modern times what controlling, organizing, selecting poet has created a world with as much in it as Whitman's, a world that so plainly *is* the world? Of all modern poets he has, quantitatively speaking, "the most comprehensive soul"—and, qualitatively, a most comprehensive and comprehending one, with charities and concessions and qualifications that are rare in any time.

"Do I contradict myself? Very well then I contradict myself," wrote Whitman, as everybody remembers, and this is not naive, or something he got from Emerson, or a complacent pose. When you organize one of the contradictory elements out of your work of art, you are getting rid not just of it, but of the contradiction of which it was a part; and it is the contradictions in works of art which make them able to represent to us—as logical and methodical generalizations cannot—our world and our selves, which are also full of contradictions. In Whitman we do not get the controlled, compressed, seemingly concordant contradictions of the great lyric poets, of a poem like, say, Hardy's "During Wind and Rain"; Whitman's contradictions are sometimes announced openly, but are more often scattered at random throughout the poems. For instance: Whitman specializes in ways of saying that there is in some sense (a very Hegelian one, generally) no evil—he says a hundred times that evil is not Real; but he also specializes in making lists of the evil of the world, lists of an unarguable reality. After his minister has recounted "the rounded catalogue divine complete," Whitman comes home and puts down what has been left out: "the countless (nineteen-twentieths) low and evil, crude

and savage . . . the barren soil, the evil men, the slag and hideous rot."
He ends another such catalogue with the plain unexcusing "All these—all
meanness and agony without end I sitting look out upon,/ See, hear, and
am silent." Whitman offered himself to everybody, and said brilliantly
and at length what a good thing he was offering:

> Sure as the most certain sure, plumb in the uprights,
>   well entretied, braced in the beams,
> Stout as a horse, affectionate, haughty, electrical,
> I and this mystery here we stand.

Just for oddness, characteristicalness, differentness, what more could you
ask in a letter of recommendation? (Whitman sounds as if he were recom-
mending a house—haunted, but what foundations!) But after a few pages
he is oddly different:

> Apart from the pulling and hauling stands what I am,
> Stands amused, complacent, compassionating, idle, unitary,
> Looks down, is erect, or bends an arm on an impalpable certain
>   rest
> Looking with side curved head curious what will come next,
> Both in and out of the game and watching and wondering at it.

Tamburlaine is already beginning to sound like Hamlet: the employer
feels uneasily, *Why, I might as well hire myself.* . . . And, a few pages
later, Whitman puts down in ordinary-sized type, in the middle of the
page, this warning to any *new person drawn toward me*:

> Do you think I am trusty and faithful?
> Do you see no further than this facade, this smooth and
>   tolerant manner of me?
> Do you suppose yourself advancing on real ground to-
>   ward a real man?
> Have you no thought O dreamer that it may be all maya,
>   illusion?

Having wonderful dreams, telling wonderful lies, was a temptation Whitman could never resist; but telling the truth was a temptation he could
never resist, either. When you buy him you know what you are buying.
And only an innocent and solemn and systematic mind will condemn him
for his contradictions: Whitman's catalogues of evils represent realities,
and his denials of their reality represent other realities, of feeling and intuition and desire. If he is faithless to logic, to Reality As It Is—whatever
that is—he is faithful to the feel of things, to reality as it seems; this is all
that a poet has to be faithful to, and philosophers even have been known
to leave logic and Reality for it.

Whitman is more coordinate and parallel than anybody, is *the* poet
of parallel present participles, of twenty verbs joined by a single subject:
all this helps to give his work its feeling of raw hypnotic reality, of being

that world which also streams over us joined only by *ands*, until we supply the subordinating conjunctions; and since as children we see the *ands* and not the *becauses*, this method helps to give Whitman some of the freshness of childhood. How inexhaustibly *interesting* the world is in Whitman! Arnold all his life kept wishing that we could see the world "with a plainness as near, as flashing" as that with which Moses and Rebekah and the Argonauts saw it. He asked with elegiac nostaliga, "Who can see the green earth any more/ As she was by the sources of Time?"—and all the time there was somebody alive who saw it so, as plain and near and flashing, and with a kind of calm, pastoral, Biblical dignity and elegance as well, sometimes. The *thereness* and *suchness* of the world are incarnate in Whitman as they are in few other writers.

They might have put on his tombstone WALT WHITMAN: HE HAD HIS NERVE. He is the rashest, the most inexplicable and unlikely—the most impossible, one wants to say—of poets. He somehow *is* in a class by himself, so that one compares him with other poets about as readily as one compares *Alice* with other books. (Even his free verse has a completely different effect from anybody else's.) Who would think of comparing him with Tennyson or Browning or Arnold or Baudelaire?—it is Homer, or the sagas, or something far away and long ago, that comes to one's mind only to be dismissed; for sometimes Whitman *is* epic, just as *Moby-Dick* is, and it surprises us to be able to use truthfully this word that we have misused so many times. Whitman *is* grand, and elevated, and comprehensive, and real with an astonishing reality, and many other things—the critic points at his qualities in despair and wonder, all method failing, and simply calls them by their names. And the range of these qualities is the most extraordinary thing of all. We can surely say about him, "He was a man, take him for all in all. I shall not look upon his like again"—and wish that people had seen this and not tried to be his like: one Whitman is miracle enough, and when he comes again it will be the end of the world.

I have said so little about Whitman's faults because they are so plain: baby critics who have barely learned to complain of the lack of ambiguity in *Peter Rabbit* can tell you all that is wrong with *Leaves of Grass*. But a good many of my readers must have felt that it is ridiculous to write an essay about the obvious fact that Whitman is a great poet. It is ridiculous—just as, in 1851, it would have been ridiculous for anyone to write an essay about the obvious fact that Pope was no "classic of our prose" but a great poet. Critics have to spend half their time reiterating whatever ridiculously obvious things their age or the critics of their age have found it necessary to forget: they say despairingly, at parties, that Wordsworth is a great poet, and *won't* bore you, and tell Mr. Leavis that Milton is a great poet whose deposition *hasn't* been accomplished with astonishing ease by a few words from Eliot and Pound[1]. . . . There is something essentially ridiculous about critics, anyway: what is good is good without our saying so, and beneath all our majesty we know this.

Let me finish by mentioning another quality of Whitman's—a quality, delightful to me, that I have said nothing of. If some day a tourist notices, among the ruins of New York City, a copy of *Leaves of Grass*, and stops and picks it up and reads some lines in it, she will be able to say to herself: "How very American! If he and his country had not existed, it would have been impossible to imagine them."

Note

1. In a subsequent reprinting of this essay Jarrell dropped Pound's name from this sentence.

Walt Whitman and the American Tradition

Floyd Stovall*

In the development of the American tradition during the last two centuries, Whitman occupies a central position. He was the product of the first half of this period, in which liberal thought advanced from the rationalism of Franklin to the romantic idealism of Emerson, and he was in part the shaper of the second half, in which idealism survived the impact of realism, Darwinism, and materialistic determinism. To reveal the extraordinary importance of Whitman in absorbing and transmitting the American tradition it now becomes necessary to survey briefly his characteristic ideas in their relation to that tradition.

The first and perhaps the most notable of these was his idea of independence. He was an individualist who insisted upon the right to go his own way. This was in part a matter of temperament, but it was also the living up to a principle, for he conceded the same privilege to every other person. He was a child of the Revolution, which in turn was an outgrowth of the Enlightenment. Among Whitman's heroes were the radicals Thomas Paine, Frances Wright, and Elias Hicks, and in his own time he was a friend of Robert Ingersoll. He spoke in defense of Paine in 1877 before the Liberal League of Philadelphia, and he wrote in terms of eulogy of Elias Hicks, the radical Quaker, who had been the friend of his grandfather and whom Whitman himself at the age of ten had heard in an unforgettable sermon. When at seventy he recalled the enthusiasms of his youth, it seemed to him that he had fairly knelt at the feet of Fanny Wright, whose paper, the Free Inquirer, his father subscribed to, and whose picture he treasured to the end of his life. He longed to write at length about her, but he never did. Whitman thought that even Voltaire, though he could never be dear to the memory of man, was in some respects a fit precursor of the American era. He owned a copy of the "Philosophical Dictionary" and was familiar with other writings of Voltaire, as well as with the chief works of Rousseau and some of Volney's. There can be little doubt that his persistent anti-clerical feeling owed something to the French writers of the Enlightenment.

*Reprinted from the *Virginia Quarterly Review*, 31 (1955), 546–57, with permission of the journal and the author.

In politics he was, as everybody knows, a follower of the democratic republicanism born of the American Revolution and developed by Jefferson, Jackson, and Lincoln. In his youth he was a Democrat of the radical "Barnburner" faction, became a Free-Soiler about 1848, and voted with the Republican Party from 1864 to 1884, though he did not wholly endorse its principles. With the advent of Cleveland he returned, it seems, to the Democratic Party. In effect, however, he had ceased after about 1850 to give allegiance to any political party, thus setting a precedent which many thoughtful people have since followed. In the late 1880's, under Traubel's prodding, he was induced to express sympathy for the aims of Henry George and the mild socialism of that time; but he would not advocate any definite means by which those aims might be achieved. One feels that he had then but little genuine interest in politics in general, and that towards Marxian socialism he was cold as he had been cold towards the socialism of Fourier in his youth. He remained from youth to age an individualist at heart, suspicious of governmental authority, yet recognizing the necessity of social organization and cautiously conceding such authority as might be required to conserve individual rights. The poem he chose to set first in his final arrangement of *Leaves of Grass* begins with the lines:

> One's-self I sing, a simple separate person
> Yet utter the word Democratic, the word En-Masse.

The individual and the community were for him the two poles of democracy, between which it maintains an effective but perpetually shifting center of balance. A similar balance is to be maintained between the states and the federal government, and between cities and the state, as we learn in another of his "Inscriptions":

> To the States or any one of them, or any city of the
>   States, *Resist much, obey little*.
> Once unquestioning obedience, once fully enslaved,
> Once fully enslaved, no nation, state, city of this
>   earth, ever afterwards resumes its liberty.

Though Whitman was a child of the Enlightenment and the Revolution, he was nurtured by the Romantic Movement. As a youth he read the sentimental literature of his day, graduating in turn to the novels of Cooper, Scott, Dickens, and George Sand. In the theater he was delighted by the feudal pomp of Shakespeare's historical plays. He was equally pleased by the sweet singing of Mrs. Austin in a musical version of *The Tempest*, by the impressive acting of Junius Brutus Booth in *Richard III*, by the stentorian rhetoric of Edwin Forrest in the Old Bowery, and by the polished art of Fanny Kemble and her father at the Park. A little later, at the opera, he was entranced by the liquid music of Rossini, Donizetti, and Bellini on many an unforgettable evening. Reform movements caught him up, and he wrote a temperance novel in 1842, inveighed against capital punishment, and otherwise attacked man's inhumanity to man. He tried, with indifferent success, poems in the manner of Bryant and stories in the manner of Poe and Hawthorne. At some time in his youth, possibly as early as 1845, he discovered Emerson and Carlyle, and during the following ten years, as his intellect matured, he developed a transcendentalism of his own that owed much to them and was a great advance over his juvenile romanticism. Through Carlyle he was introduced to German thought, and through Emerson he was helped to his vision of a national literature as vital as the American people and as broad as the continent they inhabited.

Already, as editor of the *Brooklyn Eagle*, he had deplored American imitativeness and championed nationality in our literature. He did not underestimate the greatness of European literature nor its importance for American readers, but he did asseverate that America requires something different. He said that even the plays of Shakespeare and the novels of Scott, much as he loved them, were contrary to the spirit of American democracy and should not be accepted in lieu of American models. A democratic nation, he insisted, must have a democratic literature. He held to this view throughout his life and expressed it anew in *Democratic Vistas* (1871), in *Collect* (1882), and in *November Boughs* (1888). In music too, though he loved the Italian opera, he advocated as best for America what he called "heart-singing" as distinguished from "art-singing," and he cited by way of illustration the simple yet accomplished singing of the Cheney and Hutchinson families, both popular singing groups in the 1840's. Always he valued the natural and indigenous more than the artificial and the imported work of art. In 1863 he wrote half-seriously in one of his letters to the New York Times that he would be sorry to see removed from the Capitol dome in Washington the huge derrick, so symbolic of the constructive spirit of his age and nation, and raised in its place the odd figure in bronze that was called the Genius of America, which looked to him like a combination of a Greek goddess and a Choctaw girl.

In politics Whitman was equally nationalistic in conformity with the expansive spirit of the nineteenth century. It seemed to him that Mexico should recognize the advantage she would derive from becoming one of our own union of free states, and he expected as a matter of course that Cuba and Canada would eventually, on some terms, by incorporated. This expansiveness, perhaps the most characteristic feature of the American national mind in the two decades before the Civil War, became the controlling mood of Whitman's poetry and prose. The poet-hero of *Leaves of Grass* identifies himself at once with the character and with the geography of the United States and in the later poems moves in the direction of world identity. If he does not become an imperialistic hero waving the banner of "Manifest Destiny" it is because he was imbued, like Whitman himself, with the moral sense and the doctrine of natural rights that were the foundation of American democracy.

Whitman was too much a child of the Enlightenment, as I have shown, to succumb to the enthusiasm of the Evangelical movement that swept the country in the years of his youth—and indeed he condemned it for its spirit of intolerance that destroyed the reputation of Thomas Paine—but he shared the Evangelical faith in the power of the individual to establish an effective relationship with God without the intermediation of the institutional church, and he shared the missionary spirit of Evangelicalism. Even in his newspaper prose of the early 1840's, in which he often wrote with conventional piety, it is clear that his sentiments were grounded in genuine morality and a religion of the heart rather than of the head. His conception of Jesus was that of a good man and a loving comrade, a man of sufferings and charities, not a giver of commandments and prohibitions. Of course he rejected the theology and the ascetic morality of the Evangelical churches. In his talk with Traubel in 1889 he assented to Traubel's suggestion that in a world where Christians were rare, Tolstoy might be called one; yet he disliked Tolstoy's "ascetic side" as a reversion to medievalism. Though Christ was patient and tender, he was not a denier, and in "Song of Myself" the image of Christ as a sufferer and affirmer is unmistakable. Christ dies, but he also rises from the grave, and having done so he becomes the teacher of men. What he teaches, as reported by Whitman, is the immensity and immortality of the soul, forever fed yet never filled, and forever dying yet never dead.

In the identification of himself with Christ through a common experience, the hero-poet of *Leaves of Grass* does not lose his individuality. Some critics, citing Whitman's statement that he sometimes felt himself as two and noting the frequent occurrence of such duality in his poems, have concluded that he had an abnormally divided personality and was at war with himself. I think, on the contrary, that Whitman has merely accentuated in his hero a condition that exists in every individual. The sense of duality is merely a recognition of man's finite and infinite selves and of his consciousness of being both subject and object, the knower and the thing known. In short, it is simply the phenomenon of self-consciousness. When the knower looks into himself he may at rare moments have glimpses of a being more profound than he can compass, and this being, this "deep heart," as Emerson called it, is the infinite self that feeds his spirit from an inexhaustible fountain. Explain such an experience as you will—in terms of mysticism or in terms of imagination—it is equally close to the source of all poetry and all religion.

Of course this is Transcendentalism, but is is also akin to Evangelical religion as it was experienced in America. The mystery of conversion, the trance, the sense of purification and salvation, the consciousness of dying out of sin and being reborn to life and power—all these accompaniments of the revival meeting were implicit in the experience of Whitman's hero-poet. It is true that the repentance of the revival-meeting convert did not always prove enduring; backsliding was all too common. But there is evidence of backsliding in Whitman's hero and his followers, and the devil is just as wily in *Leaves of Grass* as in any wavering human heart. "I know the sea of torment, doubt, despair and unbelief," the hero-poet confesses; "I take my place among you as much as among any." There is no unpardonable sin in these poems, but there is evil enough with its attendant torment. The development of the hero-poet from "Song of Myself" through "Passage to India" is that of a passionate and rebellious yet essentially religious person whose soul is purged by its own fires and stands at last tranquil and free.

This may be also, in general, the development of Whitman himself. Yet the critic must beware of the temptation to interpret *Leaves of Grass* as autobiography. The hero-poet is a mythical person and is no more identifiable with Whitman himself than with the American people, or even the human race. The end of the journey visualized in "Passage to India" is certainly not accomplished in his personal life, though doubtless he has come nearer the goal than most persons; otherwise he could not describe it so well. Even so we must give most of the credit to the poet's imagination. It is the passage of the soul from the dominant sense of physical life to the dominant sense of physical death. When the sense of life is strong, the spirit must content itself with mere moments of vision and freedom, but as the sense of death becomes dominant, the spirit sees more steadily and is less constrained. It is Christian's pilgrimage to the Celestial City seen not as Bunyan saw it but in the light of modern science and evolution. The journey image occurs in many of Whitman's poems, in some where it is not recognized at once. In "When Lilacs Last in the Dooryard Bloom'd" it is suggested in the fact that the poet-hero hears the hermit thrush singing its song of death from the beginning of the poem but he is only gradually drawn to it away from the powerful hold of the symbolic star of life.

In other terms, the journey theme is one from chaos to form, from diversity to unity, from freedom to law, and it is readily discernible in Whitman's increasing attention to poetic form in *Leaves of Grass* from 1855 to 1868. If there is a relapse in the later poems to the formlessness of some of the earlier ones, it proves merely that Whitman's power of execution, particularly after his paralysis, was inferior to his power of conception. It is also evident in the increasing certainty with which he foresees the triumph of man through the moral law. In "Thou Mother with Thy Equal Brood" (1872) he foresees in a successful American democratic nationality the confirmation of man's faith in himself:

> Scattering for good the cloud that hung so long, that
>   weigh'd so long upon the mind of man,
>
> The doubt, suspicion, dread, of gradual, certain
>   decadence of man.

A little later in the same poem he images Ensemble, Evolution, and Free-dom as three stars set in the sky of Law. Here Law may be interpreted as the rule of God, embracing both the moral law and natural law as con-verging tendencies, whereas the three stars are the three terms of the Hegelian formula, Ensemble (or community) being the thesis, Freedom (or individual entity) the antithesis, and Evolution (or compromise) the synthesis. Something like the same scheme had been earlier indicated in the poem of cosmic order, "Chanting the Square Deific." This faith in the eventual triumph of law without denying freedom, expressed often in Whitman's prose as well as in his poetry, is a fundamental condition of the success of American democracy.

These are poetic illustrations of the American conception of progress. The will of God, whether it operates as natural law, as moral law, or by direct intervention, must prevail in the end. Man, as distinguished from nature, is a free moral agent, but his freedom is provided for by the will of God in the fundamental law that governs the universe. In human affairs progress is possible only through the interaction of man's free will and a previously established, though not an unchangeable, order. Many people who cannot accept the reasoning that attempts to justify this theory of progress nevertheless conduct their lives as if they accepted it.

Man is, more than other creatures, attended by the twin sisters, Memory and Hope, and he cannot exist as a human being without them. He is perpetually scanning the backward vista, and when he turns his eyes to the future he sees a similar pattern, only the images are less distinct, and if his mind is healthy they tend to be more agreeable. In proportion as a man's dreams advance beyond his interpretation of history does he believe in progress. What James Truslow Adams has called the "American Dream" is an eloquent testimonial to Western man's belief in progress. Among our literary men the dream is best told by Emerson and Whitman, and of the two, Whitman's version is the more positive and substantial. "Allons!" he cries, "after the great Companions, and to belong to them!" But progress is not an uninterrupted advance. It depends on memory as well as on hope. The end pre-exists in the means. As we are told in "Song of Myself,"

> Every condition promulges not only itself, it promulges
>   what grows after and out of itself.
> And the dark hush promulges as much as any.

In other words, death grows out of life, and life is implicit in death, just as the future grows out of the past and will in turn become the past to some other future. Earth's words, he writes in "A Song of the Rolling Earth," are motion and reflection. The ocean of life ebbs, but the flow will return. Asia that for centuries had been in eclipse was reviving in Whitman's day, and he foresaw that she would have much to teach America in the future.

In "Going Somewhere," a memorial poem to his friend Mrs. Gilchrist, he wrote:

> The world, the race, the soul—in space and time
>   the universes,
> All bound as is befitting each—all surely going
>   somewhere.

And he made it clear that the going is towards something better, that evolution is progressive.

I have said that the American tradition, growing out of European culture and clinging to it even while opposing it, developed from the Enlightenment, through several phases of romanticism, through wars, through bohemianism, materialism, realism, naturalism, and various experimental movements, to the present age of spiritual crisis and hopeful skepticism. I have indicated that Whitman was a product of this development up to about the middle of the nineteenth century, the period of waning romanticism. I should now like to suggest that he was also in the main stream of the tradition in the second half of that century, and that he helped to prepare the way for its development in the twentieth century.

The bohemianism of *Leaves of Grass* in the editions of 1855, 1856, and 1860 is sometimes thought to be a truer expression of Whitman's real personality than the spiritual poems of later years. This is certainly not the case; it is but one of many phases of the character of Whitman's hero. It was, I believe, in some degree the reflection of the influence of Henry Clapp and his bohemian friends who made the Saturday Press, according to Howells, for a while the rival in importance to the *Atlantic Monthly* among the younger literary men. They were in rebellion against conventionality. Howells said that "if respectability was your *bête noire*, then you were a bohemian." Whitman's open letter to Emerson in the 1856 edition of *Leaves of Grass* probably offended Emerson because it seemed to confuse his radicalism with that of the bohemians.

It is not always easy to separate the bohemian from the revolutionary, the anti-clerical, the Jacksonian, the transcendental, and the realistic phases of Whitman's personality, for all were no doubt genuine. The error most to be avoided is that of identifying the poet with any one or two to the exclusion of the rest. Each has won friends for him, and these friends, less ample in their sympathies than he, have occasionally tried to impose their own boundaries on him. Emerson was the first and the greatest of those who, for a while at least, saw Whitman in their own image. He took him to be a Transcendentalist, and when Whitman flaunted his bohemianism Emerson could not conceal his disappointment. Later John Addington Symonds thought he saw in "Leaves of Grass" an expression of homosexuality akin to that of ancient Greece, and others, for one reason or another, have emphasized this aspect of the poems, particularly as it appears in the "Calamus" group, and made it the key not only to the poems but to the personality of Whitman himself. Dr. Bucke, a psychologist, was confident that Whitman possessed what he called "cosmic consciousness." Being also a mystic, Dr. Bucke further believed that *Leaves of Grass* would prove to be the bible of a new religion. William O'Connor, an enthusiast, was most happy when leading a crusade in defense of the "Good Gray Poet." During the 1930's Marxian critics thought they found in his work support for Communistic ideals. Modern experimenters in new verse forms have been encouraged by *Leaves of Grass*, and writers of naturalistic fiction have seemed to find comfort in him, though he was not in sympathy with their pessimistic interpretations of life nor their predilection for characters with criminal or diseased minds. His own realism was akin to that of Howells. He told Garland in 1888 that writers should introduce evil only as a foil for good, as Shakespeare did. "Somewhere in your play or novel," he counseled, "let the sunlight in."

It must be admitted that opponents of democracy and those who deny the existence of an American culture independent of European culture have never claimed Whitman as an authority. Yet there are passages in Whitman's work which, removed from their context, might be cited by them with some effect, for he was in no sense either a political or a cultural isolationist. He believed passionately in the American political union, and he dreamed of the brotherhood of man throughout the world. Probably he would have approved a limited form of union among the nations if it had been proposed in his lifetime, but he would undoubtedly have shied away from the theory of a world state. He believed vigorously in the necessity of creating a distinctive American culture with its own characteristic literature, art, and social institutions, and he sharply reproved any and all who were content to follow European patterns. But he did not reject Europe nor minimize the value for Americans of its culture. He would not have agreed with the line in a poem by Carl Sandburg that calls the past a bucket of ashes, nor with Henry Ford's alleged declaration that history is the bunk. Did Whitman not say in the 1855 Preface that America "does not repel the past," and did he not in "Passage to India" ask, "For what is the present after all but a growth out of the past?" He was not blind to the imperfections of democracy. He knew the seamy side of life, such as a journalist may see in great cities, and he did not like it. He recognized the wolf, the snake, and the hog in human nature; but he also recognized the divinity. It is the fashion in some quarters now to cite the earlier pages of *Democratic Vistas* in support of contemporary pessimism and anti-democratic sentiments, but it is not honest to do so without calling attention to the other and larger part of the essay which supports democracy. In spite of its imperfections, he concludes that "the democratic formula is the only safe and preservative one for coming times." And this is so because "it alone can bind and ever seeks to bind, all nations, all men, of however various and distant lands, into a brotherhood, a family."

This then is Whitman's faith, as it is likewise the democratic faith, the seed and the fruit of the American tradition: that man is born to be free, that the only true freedom is freedom under the law, and that he will attain to it only when he becomes a law unto himself through moral perfection.

An Analysis of "When Lilacs Last in the Dooryard Bloom'd"

Richard Chase*

There remained for Whitman, however, the writing of one more great poem. Apparently stemming from the mood of "Out of the Cradle," "When Lilacs Last in the Dooryard Bloom'd" is also related to "Crossing Brooklyn Ferry," capturing, as it does, the richness of the former and the vital abstractness and serene austerity of the latter. In the unique beauty of the Lincoln elegy one perceives both a farewell to poetry and the dim lineaments of a possible "late manner."

Lincoln had, of course, meant much to Whitman. He had voted for Lincoln in 1860 and had seen the President-elect when he stopped at the Astor House in New York on his way to Washington. Whitman noted how Lincoln "looked with curiosity" at the sullen, silent crowd that had gathered to see him, how he uttered no word but merely stretched his long limbs and stood there, an "uncouth" figure in his black suit and tall hat, gazing at the crowd with "perfect composure and coolness." Whitman thought he saw in Lincoln's posture "a dash of comedy, almost of farce, such as Shakespeare puts in his blackest tragedies," a description so accurate that one might imagine Lincoln unconsciously to describe himself in the same manner.

Matthiessen has pointed out the relevance of the Lincoln lecture Whitman was accustomed to give in later years to one's understanding of the genesis of the elegy. In this lecture Whitman recalled seeing the President on the occasion of the second inaugural address and noting how deeply cut were the marks of fatigue and worry on the "dark brown face" which still showed, however, "all the old goodness, tenderness, sadness, and canny shrewdness." Whitman recalled that just before the President stepped forth to the portico of the Capitol, the violent storm of the morning ceased and the day became so preternaturally clear that in the afternoon the stars shown "long, long before they were due." He recalled, too, the dramatic changes of weather in the weeks preceding the inauguration and how superbly beautiful some of the nights had been in the intervals of

*Reprinted from *Walt Whitman Reconsidered* (New York: William Sloan Associates, 1955), pp. 138–45; copyright 1955 by Richard Chase; reprinted by permission of William Morrow & Co.

fair weather. Especially beautiful was the star he was to use with such effect in the elegy—"The western star, Venus, in the earlier hours of evening, has never been so large, so clear; it seems as if it told something, as if it held rapport indulgent with humanity, with us Americans."

It is of some psychological interest that when Whitman learned of the assassination, he was with his mother in Brooklyn. He described the scene in *Specimen Days*: "The day of the murder we heard the news very early in the morning. Mother prepared breakfast—and other meals afterward—as usual; but not a mouthful was eaten all day by either of us. We each drank half a cup of coffee; that was all. Little was said. We got every newspaper morning and evening, and the frequent extras of that period, and pass'd them silently to each other." The mood of hushed consecration in Whitman's poem, its treatment of death as a providential mother or bride, the large part played in the poem by reminiscences of childhood, such as the singing bird, the lilac that once bloomed in the dooryard of the Whitman farm—all these elements might have entered into the poem in any case but they are doubtless more of the poem's essence because of the circumstances under which Whitman first reflected upon the death of the President. (It is of some interest, too, that in *Specimen Days* Whitman described the star by which he symbolizes Lincoln as "maternal"; he had watched the setting of Venus on the night on March 18, 1879 and had jotted down the following: "Venus nearly down in the west, of a size and lustre as if trying to outshow herself, before departing. Teeming, maternal orb—I take you again to myself. I am reminded of that spring preceding Abraham Lincoln's murder, when I, restlessly haunting the Potomac banks, around Washington city, watch'd you, off there, aloof, moody as myself.")

The feelings expressed in this poem are exceedingly personal and exceedingly abstract. The death of the great person stirs the poet not to a tragic sense of life but to its exquisite pathos. The idea of redemption and eternal life is present, but the mood is aesthetic and moral rather than religious. In these qualities, as in its rather theatrical decor, Whitman's poem is closer in spirit to *The Wings of the Dove* than to the classic elegy.

If we compare "When Lilacs Last in the Dooryard Bloom'd" with "Lycidas," the greatest of English elegies, certainly notable differences emerge. "Lycidas" is, of course, written in the pastoral tradition, the convention of which is that a society of shepherds and more or less mythical personages mourns for the loss of a fellow shepherd. Nature, or its presiding geniuses, is chidden for its cruelty but joins in the universal mourning. And the consolatory thought is expressed that the dead person has actually escaped death and is assured of immortality. Whitman's democratic elegy departs from the practice of Milton exactly as we might expect. There is no society of shepherds in Whitman's poem; there is no image of any society at all, except of the sketchiest kind—on the one hand there are brief concrete images of "separate houses" with their "daily usages" and little groups of somber citizens at the depots watching the coffin, and, on the other hand, a generalized sense of the whole nation in mourning. Lincoln himself is absent from the poem, there being hardly a trace of either his person or his personality until the very end of the poem, where Whitman speaks vaguely of "the sweetest, wisest soul of all my days and lands." By comparison we are told a good deal in "Lycidas" about Edward King, his youthful accomplishments and the promise of his career; and we are made very poignantly to feel the loneliness of the unfortunate youth as his body is tossed by the whelming tide. Whitman had formed sharp impressions of the powerful individuality of Lincoln, as we know from his graphic remarks about him elsewhere. He had even complained, in *Specimen Days*, that none of the portraits he had seen had at all caught the essential qualities of Lincoln's face, "the peculiar color, the lines of it, the eyes, mouth, expression." So that the impersonality of his elegy is all the more strongly brought home to us when Whitman writes:

> Here, coffin that slowly passes,
> I give you my sprig of lilac,

and we realize that not only has the poet not thought directly of the man in the coffin but that he has moved immediately into the absract and universal, for he adds:

> Nor for you, for one alone,
> Blossoms and branches green to coffins all I bring,
> For fresh as the morning, thus would I chant a song
>   for you O sane and sacred death.

Whitman's unacknowledged convention, here as everywhere, makes it impossible for him to conceive either the being or the value of the individual without conceiving him as an example of mankind in general. Were he to read Whitman's poem, Milton would doubtless observe that instead of bestowing flowers upon Lincoln, as he should, the poet bestows them first on all the dead equally and then on death itself.

Elegiac feeling in American literature does not, in fact, characteristically take for its occasion the death of an individual—a Bion, an Edward King, a Keats, a Wellington. Or if it does, as in Whitman's poem, it moves quickly away from the particularity of the occasion, and without proposing the dead person as an example of tragic crisis in the human spirit or in human history. The American elegiac sensibility—in Cooper, Melville, Thoreau, Mark Twain, James, and others—is most strongly engaged by the sense of lost modes of innocence, lost possibilities of brotherhood, magnanimity, and freedom, lost sources of moral spontaneity and spiritual refreshment. The tone is of pathos, nostalgia, and despair. The emotions come to rest, if at all, in the personal virtues of forebearance and resignation—not in metaphysical, religious, or political orders of meaning. There is kinship in Cooper's lament for Lake Glimmerglass, Mark Twain's musings over Huck Finn and Jim on their raft, Isabel Archer's cry, "Oh my Brother," at the death of Ralph Touchett, and Walt Whitman's plea to his dim, evanescent "companions" in the Lincoln poem.

To set off the large abstractions of the Lincoln elegy there is really only one individual in the poem, the poet himself. To be sure, in "Lycidas" the poet makes his personal grief, his personal presence, and his own aspirations strongly felt; yet he finds solace for his grief and an enhanced understanding of his own probable fate by representing a society of actual and mythical persons who also grieve, and by showing the profound involvement of the dead man, and thus of himself and of all men, in the alternately destructive and healing motions of nature in a divinely directed order. In Whitman's poem the poet finds solace for his grief, not by placing himself in a grieving society but by withdrawing from the world and, in effect, curing his grief by feeling the more powerful emotion of loneliness. And the poem then recounts the poet's search for comrades, whom he finds in the symbolic star and singing bird and finally in death itself. There is no doubt that something morally incomplete has taken place when a poet is unable to speak of the death of a man—and he a beloved man—except in terms of his own loneliness. Yet there can be no doubt about the surpassing beauty of the verse:

> Then with the knowledge of death as walking one
>   side of me,
> And the thought of death close-walking the other side
>   of me,
> And I in the middle as with companions, and as holding
>   the hands of companions,
> I fled forth to the hiding receiving night that talks not,
> Down to the shores of the water, the path by the
>   swamp in the dimness,
> To the solemn shadowy cedars and ghostly pines so
>   still.

If the poet of "When Lilacs Last in the Dooryard Bloom'd" does not place himself in any ostensible society, neither does he very profoundly place himself in nature. Had he read *Moby-Dick*, Tocqueville might have found an exception to his prediction that American writers, though they might be profoundly moved by the majestic spectacle of mankind, would not attempt to grasp the deeper implications of man's involvement in nature. But like much of Whitman's poetry, the Lincoln elegy bears out this prediction. Whitman is entirely incapable of conceiving anything like Milton's image of Lycidas, who "visit'st the bottom of the monstrous world." In contrast to Milton's tragic conception of nature, Whitman's grasp upon nature issues, not in a vision of universal order (or disorder), but either in the affective pathos of somewhat theatrical symbols like the lilac and the cedars and pines or in the brooding, lyric but abstract meditations upon death.

It must be noted finally that in contrast to that in "Lycidas" the feeling of immortality is extremely weak in Whitman's poem. There is no liberating promise of personal immortality to the dead man, and at the end we find a beautiful but very sad recessional instead of the buoyant promise of "fresh fields, and pastures new." The symbol of the lilac "blooming, returning with spring" recurs, with its suggestion of resurrection. But this does not at all succeed in releasing the poet from his conviction that he has found the ultimate felicity of comradeship in the equalitarian democracy of death itself.

What we do supremely have in the Lincoln elegy is the expression of Whitman's native elegance and refinement. These are not qualities which we usually assign to this poet. When T. S. Eliot referred to that excessive American refinement which did not belong to civilization but was already beyond it, he was thinking of the refinement of Boston. He might have added the conventional opinion that Whitman well represents the opposite strain of American life. But as we have noted before, Whitman is in some ways an extremely sophisticated, even a decadent poet. There is a premature old age in his poetry, as there was in the man himself. His elegiac utterances sound an unmistakable note of Virgilian weariness. And if the mind whose imprint we read on the Lincoln elegy is harmonious and moving, it is also in danger of an excessive refinement. It is in danger of wishing to substitute antiseptics for the healing processes of nature in which it cannot quite believe any more. How else is one to account for the sterile, the really Egyptian, atmosphere of odors, perfumes, herbage, pine, and cedar, to say nothing of the outright lyric worship of death itself?

Yet despite its artificiality "When Lilacs Last in the Dooryard Bloom'd" stands up well if we compare it with other expressions of the refined American spirit—the "Sunday Morning" of Wallace Stevens, let us say, and James's *The Wings of the Dove* and *The Golden Bowl*, and Eliot's *Four Quartets*. Different as these works are they share a tendency toward the abstract forms of myth and music, allegations of portents and miracles, appeals to the restorative cosmic forces. It is a "late" work, and (within the Whitman canon) it has the sound, as well as the emotional appeal, of a swan song.

An Analysis of "Song of Myself"

Malcolm Cowley*

1

First statement: that the long opening poem, later miscalled "Song of Myself," is Whitman's greatest work, perhaps his one completely realized work, and one of the great poems of modern times. Second, that the other eleven poems of the first edition are not on the same level of realization, but nevertheless are examples of Whitman's freshest and boldest style. At least four of them—their titles in the Deathbed edition are "To Think of Time," "The Sleepers," "I Sing the Body Electric," and "There Was a Child Went Forth"—belong in any selection of his best poems. Third, that the text of the first edition is the purest text for "Song of Myself," since many of the later corrections were also corruptions of the style and concealments of the original meaning. Fourth, that it is likewise the best text for most of the other eleven poems, but especially for "The Sleepers"—that fantasia of the unconscious—and "I Sing the Body Electric." And a final statement: that the first edition is a unified work, unlike any later edition, that it gives us a different picture of Whitman's achievement, and that—considering its very small circulation through the years—it might be called the buried masterpiece of American writing.

All that remains is to document some of these statements, not point by point, but chiefly in relation to "Song of Myself."

2

One reason among others why "Song of Myself" has been widely misprized and misinterpreted, especially by scholars, is that they have paid a disproportionate share of attention to its sources in contemporary culture. Besides noting many parallels with Emerson, they have found that it reflected a number of popular works and spectacles. Among these are Italian opera (notably as sung at the Astor Place Theatre in the great

*Reprinted from Introduction to *Walt Whitman's "Leaves of Grass": The First (1855) Edition* (New York: Viking Press, 1959), pp. x–xxvi; copyright 1959 by The Viking Press, Inc.; reprinted by permission of Viking Penguin, Inc.

season of 1852–1853, when "Alboni's great self" paid her long and only visit to New York); George Sand's novel, *The Countess of Rudolstadt*, which presented the figure of a wandering bard and prophet (as well as another of her novels, *The Journeyman Joiner*, in which the hero was a carpenter and a proletarian saint); Frances Wright's then famous defense of Epicurean philosophy, *A Few Days in Athens*; the Count de Volney's *Ruins*, predicting the final union of all religions; Dr. Abbott's Egyptian Museum, on Broadway; O. M. Mitchel's book, *A Course of Six Lectures on Astronomy*, as well as other writings on the subject; and a number of essays clipped from the English quarterly reviews, of which the poet seems to have been a faithful reader. All these works and shows had a discernible influence on Whitman, but when they are listed with others and discussed at length they lead to one of the misconceptions that are the professional weakness of scholars. They tempt us to conclude that "Song of Myself" was merely a journalist's report, inspired but uneven, of popular culture in the 1850s. It was something more than that, and something vastly different from any of its literary sources.

I might suggest that the real nature of the poem becomes clearer when it is considered in relation to quite another list of works, even though Whitman had probably read none of them in 1855. Most of them he could not have read, because they were not yet written, or not published, or not translated into English. That other list might include the *Bhagavad-Gita*, the *Upanishads*, Christopher Smart's long crazy inspired poem *Jubilate Agno*, Blake's prophetic books (not forgetting *The Marriage of Heaven and Hell*), Rimbaud's *Illuminations, The Chants of Maldoror*, and Nietzsche's *Thus Spake Zarathustra*, as well as *The Gospel of Sri Ramakrishna* and a compendious handbook, *The Philosophies of India*, by Heinrich Zimmer (New York, 1951). I am offering what might seem to be a curious list of titles, but its double purpose is easy to explain. "Song of Myself" should be judged, I think, as one of the great inspired (and sometimes insane) prophetic works that have appeared at intervals in the Western world, like *Jubilate Agno* (which is written in a biblical style sometimes suggesting Whitman's), like the *Illuminations*, like *Thus Spake Zarathustra*. But the system of doctrine suggested by the poem is more Eastern than Western, it includes notions like metempsychosis and karma, and it might almost be one of those *Philosophies of India* that Zimmer expounds at length.

What is extraordinary about this Eastern element is that Whitman, when he was writing the poems of the first edition, seems to have known little or nothing about Indian philosophy. It is more than doubtful that he had even read the *Bhagavad-Gita*, one of the few Indian works then available in translation. He does not refer to it in his notebooks of the early 1850s, where he mentions most of the books he was poring over. A year after the first edition was published, Thoreau went to see him in Brooklyn and told him that *Leaves of Grass* was "Wonderfully like the

Orientals." Had Whitman read them? he asked. The poet answered, "No: tell me about them." He seems to have taken advantage of Thoreau's reading list, since words from the Sanskrit (notably "Maya" and "sudra") are used correctly in some of the poems written after 1858. They do not appear in "Song of Myself," in spite of the recognizably Indian ideas expressed in the poem, and I would hazard the guess that the ideas are not of literary derivation. It is true that they were vaguely in the air of the time and that Whitman may have breathed them in from the Transcendentalists or even from some of the English quarterly reviewers. It also seems possible, however, that he reinvented them for himself, after an experience similar to the one for which the Sanskrit word is samadhi, or absorption.

What it must have been was a mystical experience in the proper sense of the term. Dr. Richard Maurice Bucke, the most acute of Whitman's immediate disciples, believed that it took place on a June morning in 1853 or 1854. He also believed that it was repeated on other occasions, but neither these nor the original experience can be dated from Whitman's papers. On the other hand, his notebooks and manuscripts of the early 1850s are full of sidelong references to such an experience, and they suggest that it was essentially the same as the illuminations or ecstasies of earlier bards and prophets. Such ecstasies consist in a rapt feeling of union or identity with God (or the Soul, or Mankind, or the Cosmos), a sense of ineffable joy leading to the conviction that the seer has been released from the limitations of space and time and has been granted a direct vision of truths impossible to express. As Whitman says in the famous fifth chant of "Song of Myself":

> Swiftly arose and spread around me the peace and joy and
>   knowledge that pass all the art and argument of the earth;
> And I know that the hand of God is the elderhand of my own,
> And I know that the spirit of God is the eldest brother of my own,
> And that all the men ever born are also my brothers . . . and the
>   women my sisters and lovers.

It is to be noted that there is no argument about the real occurrence of such ecstasies. They have been reported, sometimes in sharp detail, by men and women of many different nations, at many historical periods, and each report seems to bear a family resemblance to the others. Part of the resemblance is a feeling universally expressed by mystics that they have acquired a special sort of knowledge not learned from others, but directly revealed to the inner eye. This supposed knowledge has given independent rise to many systems of philosophy or cosmology, once again in many different cultures, and once again there is or should be no argument about one feature of almost all the systems or bodies of teaching: that they too have a family resemblance, like the experiences on which they are based. Indeed, they hold so many principles in common that it is possible for Aldous Huxley and others to group them all together as "the perennial philosophy."

The arguments, which will never end, are first about the nature of the mystical state—is it a form of self-hypnosis, is it a pathological condition to be induced by fasting, vigils, drugs, and other means of abusing the physical organism, or is it, as Whitman believed, the result of superabundant health and energy?—and then about the source and value of the philosophical notions to which it gives rise. Do these merely express the unconscious desires of the individual, and chiefly his sexual desires? Or, as Jungian psychologists like to suggest, are they derived from a racial or universally human unconscious? Are they revelations or hallucinations? Are they supreme doctrines, or are they heretical, false, and even satanic? They belong in the orthodox tradition of Indian philosophy. In Western Christianity, as also in Mohammedanism, the pure and self-consistent forms of mysticism are usually regarded as heresies, with the result that several of the medieval mystics were burned at the stake (though Theresa of Avila and John of the Cross found an orthodox interpretation for their visions and became saints).

Whitman cannot be called a Christian heretic, for the simple reason that he was not a Christian at any stage of his career, early or late. In some of the poems written after the Civil War, and in revisions of older poems made at the same time, he approached the Christian notion of a personal God, whom he invoked as the Elder Brother or the great Camerado. But then he insisted—in another poem of the same period, "Chanting the Square Deific"—that God was not a trinity but a quaternity, and that one of his faces was the "sudra face" of Satan. In "Song of Myself" as originally written, God is neither a person nor, in the strict sense, even a being; God is an abstract principle of energy that is manifested in every living creature, as well as in "the grass that grows wherever the land is and the water is." In some ways this God of the first edition resembles Emerson's Oversoul, but he seems much closer to the Brahman of the *Upanishads*, the absolute, unchanging, all-enfolding Consciousness, the Divine Ground from which all things emanate and to which all living things may hope to return. And this Divine Ground is by no means the only conception that Whitman shared with Indian philosophers, in the days when he was writing "Song of Myself."

3

The poem is hardly at all concerned with American nationalism, political democracy, contemporary progress, or other social themes that are commonly associated with Whitman's work. The "incomparable things" that Emerson found in it are philosophical and religious principles. Its subject is a state of illumination induced by two (or three) separate moments of ecstasy. In more or less narrative sequence it describes those moments, their sequels in life, and the doctrines to which they give rise. The doctrines are not expounded by logical steps or supported by arguments; instead they are presented dramatically, that is, as the new convictions of a hero, and they are revealed by successive unfoldings of his states of mind.

The hero as pictured in the frontispiece—this hero named "I" or "Walt Whitman" in the text—should not be confused with the Whitman of daily life. He is, as I said, a dramatized or idealized figure, and he is put forward as a representative American workingman, but one who prefers to loaf and invite his soul. Thus, he is rough, sunburned, bearded; he cocks his hat as he pleases, indoors, or out; but in the text of the first edition he has no local or family background, and he is deprived of strictly individual characteristics, with the exception of curiosity, boastfulness, and an abnormally developed sense of touch. His really distinguishing feature is that he has been granted a vision, as a result of which he has realized the potentialities latent in every American and indeed, he says, in every living person, even "the brutish koboo, called the ordure of humanity." This dramatization of the hero makes it possible for the living Whitman to exalt him—as he would not have ventured, at the time, to exalt himself—but also to poke mild fun at the hero for his gab and loitering, for his tall talk or "omnivorous words," and for sounding his barbaric yawp over the roofs of the world. The religious feeling in "Song of Myself" is counterpoised by a humor that takes the form of slangy and mischievous impudence or drawling Yankee self-ridicule.

There has been a good deal of discussion about the structure of the poem. In spite of revealing analyses made by a few Whitman scholars, notably Carl F. Strauch and James E. Miller, Jr., a feeling still seems to prevail that it has no structure properly speaking; that it is inspired but uneven, repetitive, and especially weak in its transitions from one theme to another. I suspect that much of this feeling may be due to Whitman's later changes in the text, including his arbitrary scheme, first introduced in the 1867 edition, of dividing the poem into fifty-two numbered paragraphs or chants. One is tempted to read the chants as if they were separate poems, thus overlooking the unity and flow of the work as a whole. It may also be, however, that most of the scholars have been looking for a geometrical pattern, such as can be found and diagramed in some of the later poems. If there is no such pattern in "Song of Myself," that is because the poem was written on a different principle, one much closer to the spirit of the Symbolists or even the Surrealists.

The true structure of the poem is not primarily logical but psychological, and is not a geometrical figure but a musical progression. As music "Song of Myself" is not a symphony with contrasting movements, nor is it an operatic work like "Out of the Cradle Endlessly Rocking," with an overture, arias, recitatives, and a finale. It comes closer to being a rhapsody or tone poem, one that modulates from theme to theme, often changing in key and tempo, falling into reveries and rising toward moments of climax, but always preserving its unity of feeling as it moves onward in a wavelike flow. It is a poem that bears the marks of having been conceived as a whole and written in one prolonged burst of inspiration, but its unity is also the result of conscious art, as can be seen from Whitman's corrections in the early manuscripts. He did not recognize all the bad lines, some of which survive in the printed text, but there is no line in the first edition that seems false to a single prevailing tone. There are passages weaker than others, but none without a place in the general scheme. The repetitions are always musical variations and amplifications. Some of the transitions seem abrupt when the poem is read as if it were an essay, but Whitman was not working in terms of "therefore" and "however." He preferred to let one image suggest another image, which in turn suggests a new statement of mood or doctrine. His themes modulate into one another by pure association, as in a waking dream, with the result that all his transitions seem instinctively right.

In spite of these oneiric elements, the form of the poem is something more than a forward movement in rising and subsiding waves of emotion. There is also a firm narrative structure, one that becomes easier to grasp when we start by dividing the poem into a number of parts or sequences. I think there are nine of these, but the exact number is not important; another critic might say there were seven (as Professor Miller does), or eight or ten. Some of the transitions are gradual, and in such cases it is hard to determine the exact line that ends one sequence and starts another. The essential point is that the parts, however defined, follow one another in irreversible order, like the beginning, middle, and end of any good narrative. My own outline, not necessarily final, would run as follows:

First sequence (chants 1–4): the poet or hero introduced to his audience. Leaning and loafing at his ease, "observing a spear of summer grass," he presents himself as a man who lives outdoors and worships his own naked body, not the least part of which is vile. He is also in love with his deeper self or soul, but explains that it is not to be confused with his mere personality. His joyful contentment can be shared by you, the listener, "For every atom belonging to me as good belongs to you."

Second sequence (chant 5): the ecstasy. This consists in the rapt union of the poet and his soul, and it is described—figuratively, on the present occasion—in terms of sexual union. The poet now has a sense of loving brotherhood with God and with all mankind. His eyes being truly open for the first time, he sees that even the humblest objects contain the infinite universe—

> And limitless are leaves stiff or drooping in the fields,
> And brown ants in little wells beneath them,
> And mossy scabs of the wormfence, and heaped stones, and elder
> and mullen and pokeweed.

Third sequence (chants 6–19): the grass. Chant 6 starts with one of Whitman's brilliant transitions. A child comes with both hands full of those same leaves from the fields. "What is the grass?" the child asks—suddenly we are presented with the central image of the poem, that is, the grass as symbolizing the miracle of common things and the divinity (which implies both the equality and the immortality) of ordinary persons. During the remainder of the sequence, the poet observes men and women—and animals too—at their daily occupations. He is part of this life, he says, and even his thoughts are those of all men in all ages and lands. There are two things to be noted about the sequence, which contains some of Whitman's freshest lyrics. First, the people with a few exceptions (such as the trapper and his bride) are those whom Whitman has known all his life, while the scenes described at length are Manhattan streets and Long Island beaches or countryside. Second, the poet merely roams, watches, and listens, like a sort of Tiresias. The keynote of the sequence—as Professor Strauch was the first to explain—is the two words "I observe."

Fourth sequence (chants 20–25): the poet in person. "Hankering, gross, mystical, nude," he venerates himself as august and immortal, but so, he says, is everyone else. He is the poet of the body and of the soul, of night, earth, and sea, and of vice and feebleness as well as virtue, so that "many long dumb voices" speak through his lips, including those of slaves, prostitutes, even beetles rolling balls of dung. All life to him is such a miracle of beauty that the sunrise would kill him if he could not find expression for it—"If I could not now and always send sunrise out of me." The sequence ends with a dialogue between the poet and his power of speech, during which the poet insists that his deeper self—"the best I am"—is beyond expression.

Fifth sequence (chants 26–29): ecstasy through the senses. Beginning with chant 26, the poem sets out in a new direction. The poet decides to be completely passive: "I think I will do nothing for a long time but listen." What he hears at first are quiet familiar sounds like the gossip of flames on the hearth and the bustle of growing wheat; but the sounds rise quickly to a higher pitch, becoming the matchless voice of a trained soprano, and he is plunged into an ecstasy of hearing, or rather of Being. Then he starts over again, still passively, with the sense of touch, and finds himself rising to the ecstasy of sexual union. This time the union is actual, not figurative, as can be seen from the much longer version of chant 29 preserved in an early notebook.

Sixth sequence (chants 30–38): the power of identification. After his first ecstasy, as presented in chant 5, the poet had acquired a sort of microscopic vision that enabled him to find infinite wonders in the smallest and most familiar things. The second ecstasy (or pair of ecstasies) has an entirely different effect, conferring as it does a sort of vision that is both telescopic and spiritual. The poet sees far into space and time; "afoot with my vision" he ranges over the continent and goes speeding through the heavens among tailed meteors. His secret is the power of identification. Since everything emanates from the universal soul, and since his own soul is of the same essence, he can identify himself with every object and with every person living or dead, heroic or criminal. Thus, he is massacred with the Texans at Goliad, he fights on the *Bonhomme Richard*, he dies on the cross, and he rises again as "one of an average unending procession." Whereas the keynote of the third sequence was "I observe," here it becomes "I am"—"I am a free companion"—"My voice is the wife's voice, the screech by the rail of the stairs"—"I am the man. . . . I suffered. . . . I was there."

Seventh sequence (chants 39–41): the superman. When Indian sages emerge from the state of samadhi or absorption, they often have the feeling of being omnipotent. It is so with the poet, who now feels gifted with superhuman powers. He is the universally beloved Answerer (chant 39), then the Healer, raising men from their deathbeds (40), and then the Prophet (41) of a new religion that outbids "the old cautious hucksters" by announcing that men are divine and will eventually be gods.

Eighth sequence (chants 42–50): the sermon. "A call in the midst of the crowd" is the poet's voice, "orotund sweeping and final." He is about to offer a statement of the doctrines implied by the narrative (but note that his statement comes at the right point psychologically and plays its part in the narrative sequence). As strangers listen, he proclaims that society is full of injustice, but that the reality beneath it is deathless persons (chant 42); that he accepts and practices all religions, but looks beyond them to "what is untried and afterward" (43); that he and his listeners are the fruit of ages, and the seed of untold ages to be (44); that our final goal is appointed: "God will be there and wait till we come" (45); that he tramps a perpetual journey and longs for companions, to whom he will reveal a new world by washing the gum from their eyes—but each must then continue the journey alone (46); that he is the teacher of men who work in the open air (47); that he is not curious about God, but sees God everywhere, at every moment (48); that we shall all be reborn in different forms ("No doubt I have died myself ten thousand times before"); and that the evil in the world is like moonlight, a mere reflection of the sun (49). The end of the sermon (chant 50) is the hardest passage to interpret in the whole poem. I think, though I cannot be certain, that the poet is harking back to the period after one of his ten thousand deaths, when he slept and slept long before his next awakening. He seems to remember vague shapes, and he beseeches these Outlines, as he calls them, to let him reveal the "word unsaid." Then turning back to his audience, "It is not chaos or death," he says. "It is form and union and plan. . . . it is eternal life. . . . it is happiness."

Ninth sequence (chants 51–52): the poet's farewell. Having finished his sermon, the poet gets ready to depart, that is, to die and wait for another incarnation or "fold of the future," while still inviting others to follow. At the beginning of the poem he had been leaning and loafing at ease in the summer grass. Now, having rounded the circle, he bequeaths himself to the dirt "to grow from the grass I love." I do not see how any careful reader, unless blinded with preconceptions, could overlook the unity of the poem in tone and image and direction.

4

It is in the eighth sequence, which is a sermon, that Whitman gives us most of the doctrines suggested by his mystical experience, but they are also implied in the rest of the poem and indeed in the whole text of the first edition. Almost always he expresses them in the figurative and paradoxical language that prophets have used from the beginning. Now I should like to state them explicitly, even at the cost of some repetition.

Whitman believed when he was writing "Song of Myself"—and at later periods too, but with many changes in emphasis—that there is a distinction between one's mere personality and the deeper Self (or between ego and soul). He believed that the Self (or atman, to use a Sanskrit word) is of the same essence as the universal spirit (though he did not quite say it *is* the universal spirit, as Indian philosophers do in the phrase "Atman is Brahman"). He believed that true knowledge is to be acquired not through the senses or the intellect, but through union with the Self. At such moments of union (or "merge," as Whitman called it) the gum is washed from one's eyes (that is his own phrase), and one can read an infinite lesson in common things, discovering that a mouse, for example, "is miracle enough to stagger sextillions of infidels." This true knowledge is available to every man and woman, since each conceals a divine Self. Moreover, the divinity of all implies the perfect equality of all, the immortality of all, and the universal duty of loving one another.

Immortality for Whitman took the form of metempsychosis, and he believed that every individual will be reborn, usually but not always in a higher form. He had also worked out for himself something approaching the Indian notion of karma, which is the doctrine that actions performed during one incarnation determine the nature and fate of the individual during his next incarnation; the doctrine is emphatically if somewhat unclearly stated in a passage of his prose introduction that was later rewritten as a poem, "Song of Prudence." By means of metempsychosis and karma, we are all involved in a process of spiritual evolution that might be compared to natural evolution. Even the latter process, however, was not regarded by Whitman as strictly natural or material. He believed that animals have a rudimentary sort of soul ("They bring me tokens of myself"), and he hinted or surmised, without directly saying, that rocks, trees, and planets possess an identity, or "eidólon," that persists as they rise to higher states of being. The double process of evolution, natural and spiritual, can be traced for ages into the past, and he believed that it will continue for ages beyond ages. Still, it is not an eternal process, since it has an ultimate goal, which appears to be the reabsorption of all things into the Divine Ground.

Most of Whitman's doctrines, though by no means all of them, belong to the mainstream of Indian philosophy. In some respects he went against the stream. Unlike most of the Indian sages, for example, he was not a thoroughgoing idealist. He did not believe that the whole world of the senses, of desires, of birth and death, was only maya, illusion, nor did he hold that it was a sort of purgatory; instead he praised the world as real and joyful. He did not despise the body, but proclaimed that it was as miraculous as the soul. He was too good a citizen of the nineteenth century to surrender his faith in material progress as the necessary counterpart of spiritual progress. Although he yearned for ecstatic union with the soul or Oversoul, he did not try to achieve it by subjugating the senses, as advised by yogis and Buddhists alike; on the contrary, he thought the "merge" could also be achieved (as in chants 26–29) by a total surrender to the senses. These are important differences, but it must be remembered that Indian philosophy or theology is not such a unified structure as it appears to us from a distance. Whitman might have found Indian sages or gurus and even whole sects that agreed with one or another of his heterodoxies (perhaps excepting his belief in material progress). One is tempted to say that instead of being a Christian heretic, he was an Indian rebel and sectarian.

Sometimes he seems to be a Mahayana Buddhist, promising nirvana for all after countless reincarnations, and also sharing the belief of some Mahayana sects that the sexual act can serve as one of the sacraments. At other times he might be an older brother of Sri Ramakrishna (1836–1886), the nineteenth-century apostle of Tantric Brahmanism and of joyous affirmation. Although this priest of Kali, the Mother Goddess, refused to learn English, one finds him delivering some of Whitman's messages in—what is more surprising—the same tone of voice. Read, for example, this fairly typical passage from *The Gospel of Sri Ramakrishna*, while remembering that "Consciousness" is to be taken here as a synonym for Divinity:

> The Divine Mother revealed to me in the Kali temple that it was She who had become everything. She showed me that everything was full of Consciousness. The Image was Consciousness, the altar was Consciousness, the water-vessels were Consciousness, the door-sill was Consciousness, the marble floor was Consciousness—all was Consciousness. . . . I saw a wicked man in front of the Kali temple; but in him I saw the Power of the Divine Mother vibrating. That was why I fed a cat with the food that was to be offered to the Divine Mother.

Whitman expresses the same idea at the end of chant 48, and in the same half-playful fashion:

> Why should I wish to see God better than this day?
> I see something of God each hour of the twenty-four, and each
> moment then,
> In the faces of men and women I see God, and in my own face in
> the glass;
> I find letters from God dropped in the street, and every one is
> signed by God's name,
> And I leave them where they are, for I know that others will
> punctually come forever and ever.

Such parallels—and there are dozens that might be quoted—are more than accidental. They reveal a kinship in thinking and experience that can be of practical value to students of Whitman. Since the Indian mystical philosophies are elaborate structures, based on conceptions that have been shaped and defined by centuries of discussion, they help to explain Whitman's ideas at points in the first edition where he seems at first glance to be vague or self-contradictory. There is, for example, his unusual combination of realism—sometimes brutal realism—and serene optimism. Today he is usually praised for the first, blamed for the second (optimism being out of fashion), and blamed still more for the inconsistency he showed in denying the existence of evil. The usual jibe is that Whitman thought the universe was perfect and was getting better every day.

It is obvious, however, that he never meant to deny the existence of evil in himself or his era or his nation. He knew that it existed in his own family, where one of his brothers was a congenital idiot, another was a drunkard married to a streetwalker, and still another, who had caught "the bad disorder," later died of general paresis in an insane asylum. Whitman's doctrine implied that each of them would have an opportunity to avoid those misfortunes or punishments in another incarnation, where each would be rewarded for his good actions. The universe was an eternal becoming for Whitman, a process not a structure, and it had to be judged from the standpoint of eternity. After his mystical experience, which seemed to offer a vision of eternity, he had become convinced that evil existed only as part of a universally perfect design. That explains his combination of realism and optimism, which seems unusual only in our Western world. In India, Heinrich Zimmer says, "Philosophic theory, religious belief, and intuitive experience support each other . . . in the basic insight that, fundamentally, all is well. A supreme optimism prevails everywhere, in spite of the unromantic recognition that the universe of man's affairs is in the most imperfect state imaginable, one amounting practically to chaos."

Another point explained by Indian conceptions is the sort of democracy Whitman was preaching in "Song of Myself." There is no doubt that he was always a democrat politically—which is to say a Jacksonian Democrat, a Barnburner writing editorials against the Hunkers, a Free Soiler in sympathy, and then a liberal but not a radical Republican. He remained faithful to what he called "the good old cause" of liberty, equality, and fraternity, and he wrote two moving elegies for the European rebels of 1848. In "Song of Myself," however, he is not advocating rebellion or even reform. "To a drudge of the cottonfields," he says, "or emptier of privies I lean. . . . on his right cheek I put the family kiss"; but he offers nothing more than a kiss and an implied promise. What he preaches throughout the poem is not political but religious democracy, such as was practiced by the early Christians. Today it is practiced, at least in theory, by the Tantric sect, and we read in *Philosophies of India*:

> All beings and things are members of a single mystic family (*kula*). There is therefore no thought of caste within the Tantric holy "circles" (*cakra*). . . . Women as well as men are eligible not only to receive the highest initiation but also to confer it in the role of guru. . . . However, it must not be supposed that this indifference to the rules of caste implies any idea of revolution within the social sphere, as distinguished from the sphere of spiritual progress. The initiate returns to his post in society; for there too is the manifestation of Sakti. The world is affirmed, just as it is—neither renounced, as by an ascetic, nor corrected, as by a social reformer.

The promise that Whitman offers to the drudge of the cottonfields, the emptier of privies, and the prostitute draggling her shawl is that they too can set out with him on his perpetual journey—perhaps not in their present incarnations, but at least in some future life. And that leads to another footnote offered by the Indian philosophies: they explain what the poet meant by the Open Road. It starts as an actual road that winds through fields and cities, but Whitman is doing more than inviting us to shoulder our duds and go hiking along it. The real journey is toward spiritual vision, toward reunion with the Divine Ground; and thus the Open Road becomes Whitman's equivalent for all the other roads and paths and ways that appear in mystical teachings. It reminds us of the Noble Eightfold Path of the Buddhists, and the Taoist Way; it suggests both the *bhakti-marga* or "path of devotion" and the *karma-marga* or "path of sacrifice"; while it comes closer to being the "big ferry" of the Mahayana sect, in which there is room for every soul to cross to the farther shore. Whitman's conception, however, was even broader. He said one should know "the universe itself as a road, as many roads, as roads for traveling souls."

I am not pleading for the acceptance of Whitman's ideas or for any other form of mysticism, Eastern or Western. I am only suggesting that his ideas as expressed in "Song of Myself" were bolder and more coherent than is generally supposed, and philosophically a great deal more respectable.

"There was a child"

Edwin Haviland Miller*

"There Was a Child Went Forth" is one of the most sensitive lyrics in the language and one of the most astute diagnoses of the emergent self. Whitman recaptures the awakening consciousness of the child-poet and the lovely but lonely landscape in which the American child matures. The opening line with its biblical cadence evokes the edenic past and presages the future of the boy who "received with wonder or pity or love or dread." At first he perceives only beautiful natural objects—the lilacs, the grass, the morning glories, the clover. Gradually sounds intrude—"the song of the phoebe-bird" and "the noisy brood of the barnyard." With wonder the child observes the miracle of birth in the barnyard—"the sow's pink-faint litter." Quietly he moves to the "pondside," where he sees "the fish suspending themselves so curiously below there . . . and the beautiful curious liquid.

With deceptive understatement Whitman introduces a pivotal symbol in the poem and in his writings. When the boy looks into the water, he is, of course, reenacting the Narcissus myth, like Eve in the Garden of Eden. Unlike Milton, since he is not given to moral judgments or to didactic oversimplifications, Whitman recognizes that love originates in self-love before its evolution into outgoing love, and that only negation stems from self-hatred. In other words, he perceives that narcissism with its creative aspects is a complex phenomenon in the growth process. Whitman's "doting" on the self, which has so frequently and simplistically been labeled egocentricity, is better explained in Marcuse's formulation in *Eros and Civilization*:

> The striking paradox that narcissism, usually understood as egotistic withdrawal from reality, here is connected with oneness with the universe, reveals the new depth of the conception: beyond all immature autoeroticism, narcissism denotes a fundamental relatedness to reality which may generate a comprehensive existential order. In other words, narcissism may contain the germ of a different reality principle: the

*Reprinted from *Walt Whitman's Poetry: A Psychological Journey* (New York: New York Univ. Press, 1968) by permission of the New York Univ. Press. Copyright © 1968 by Edwin Haviland Miller.

libidinal cathexis of the ego (one's own body) may become the source and
reservoir for a new libidinal cathexis of the objective world—transform-
ing this world into a new mode of being.[1]

Somewhat like Proust dipping the madeleine into the teacup, except
that Whitman keeps the incident within the framework of a child's
limited perception, the boy sees in miniature the totality of his and human
life. Unknowingly he journeys to the source, for as he watches the fish in
"the beautiful curious liquid" he is observing the fetus in the amniotic
fluid, the eternally creative womb of life and art. The fish also introduce
the phallic motif, which is invariably present in Whitman's most successful poems: the grass in "Song of Myself," the calamus plant in his love
songs, and even the lilacs in "When Lilacs Last in the Dooryard
Bloom'd." Here the phallicism leads to the "fatherstuff" in the child's account of his own birth.

In this tightly structured poem, psychologically and artistically, the
pond is crucial to the emotional and intellectual development of the child
protagonist and to the progression of the poem itself. Similarly, the boy-
poet in "Out of the Cradle Endlessly Rocking" discovers the "word," the
unifying principle, near the "hissing" sea; and the protagonist in "As I
Ebb'd with the Ocean of Life" will have doubts about his identity along
the shore. In the "Calamus" poem "In Paths Untrodden," the "I" listens to
"tongues aromatic" near the "margins of pond-waters," "away from the
clank of the world." In Whitman's verse, then, the pond serves a complex
function, as, coincidentally, it does in *Walden*; and Melville's Pierre
writes enigmatically: "Not yet had he dropped his angle into the well of
his childhood, to find what a fish might be there; for who dreams to find
fish in the well?" (Book xxi).

The child in Whitman's poem now wanders blithely in a world filled
with animals, "field-sprouts," and "appletrees," when suddenly his idyllic
world is shattered. For the first time another human being, significantly
an adult, appears, and with his appearance comes fear: "And the old
drunkard staggering home from the outhouse of the tavern whence he had
lately risen." The drunken motion of the man clashes with the natural
order, but at the same time may be the human equivalent of the jerky,
darting movements of the fish. Here Whitman's associations are subtle,
since the drunkard is linked both with the father who is to be introduced
shortly and with the boy himself. The disgusting appearance of the
drunkard is to be paralleled in the boy's disgust with his father's crafti-
ness, and both adults evoke fear in the child's heart. The "staggering"
parallels the crude description of the father who "had propelled the
fatherstuff at night." The drunkard, we are told, "had lately risen" "from
the outhouse," and the father from the marital bed. (If Whitman's father
was, as some would have it, a drunkard, these associations take on added
significance.) But the lonely lot of the besotted man is also that of the

child, for as the man makes his uncertain way home alone, so the child sees a group of happy schoolchildren from afar and is not part of the group.

Now the poet turns to the most mysterious and haunting event in his life—his own conception. With fascination and perhaps dread he alludes to "the fatherstuff at night [that] fathered him" and to the mother who "conceived him in her womb and birthed him." Next there is a picture of the mother "with mild words. . . . clean her cap and gown"—one of Whitman's idealized maternal figures. Perhaps the phrase "a wholesome odor falling off her person and clothes as she walks by" is to be contrasted with the somewhat odorous drunkard. From this portrait of the mother we move abruptly to the repellent one of the father, who, as already indicated embodies the intemperateness and dread associated in the child's mind with the drunkard:

> The father, strong, selfsufficient, manly, mean, angered,
> unjust,
> The blow, the quick loud word, the tight bargain, the
> crafty lure. . . .

It means little whether this passage is autobiographical and literally true, since truth in family relationships is usually the emotional response of the participants. What is important is the self-revelation—the emphasis, perhaps overemphasis, upon the mother's purity and perfection and the ambivalence toward the father, whose genital prowess the boy reluctantly admires but whose "crafty" disposition he scorns.

The section on the family, rightly the longest in the poem, for Whitman is almost invariably correct in his psychological values, is followed by a passage reflecting the uncertainty of the child's "yearning and swelling heart":

> The sense of what is real. . . . the thought if after all it
> should prove unreal,
> The doubts of daytime and the doubts of nighttime . . . the
> curious whether and how,
> Whether that which appears so is so. . . . Or is it all flashes
> and specks?
> Men and women crowding fast in the streets . . . if they are
> not flashes and specks what are they?

Here the doubts and deep-seated fears of the boy are understated, unlike the painful confessions later in the "Calamus" sequence. Just as in life Whitman left home at an early age, presumably because the family provided neither emotional nor intellectual security, so in this poem the child seeks his own answers to his "curious whether and how" when he begins what is to become a familiar journey motif in Whitman's poetry, as he wanders along urban streets and observes teams of horses moving along the peopleless streets and ferries crossing the river. In the course of the journey—and the pattern established in "There Was a Child Went Forth" is characteristic of most of his poems—the child-man in some mysterious way overcomes the paralysis of doubt and arrives at certainty.

Ascending images gradually lead to "light falling on roofs and gables of white and brown," and, finally, to

> The strata of colored clouds. . . . the long bar of maroontint
>   away solitary by itse 'ᶜ. . . . the spread of purity it lies
>   motionless in,
> The horizon's edge, the flying seacrow, the fragrance of salt-
>   marsh and shoremud;
> These became part of that child who went forth every day,
>   and who now goes and will always go forth every day. . . .

The reader's eye follows the child-poet in the ascent to cosmic peace and harmony. Here as elsewhere Whitman makes a "leap," as it were, from despair or uncertainty to affirmation. The abrupt transition is perhaps rationally unconvincing, but emotionally there is satisfaction in Whitman's expression of the personal and cultural hunger for an edenic state. Such is the subterranean appeal that we forget that the protagonist finds reality and identity far from the troubling movements of life (the drunkard's "staggering" and coitus), and that, like Melville's Ishmael, the child-man is alone at the beginning and the end of the poem. He, like "the long bar of maroontint" or "the flying seacrow," is "away solitary by itself," a solitary singer in a vast landscape. Thus Whitman creates a lovely rationalization, or sublimation, of human loneliness, which the protagonist (and the poet himself) will endure without a whimper.

To put it another way, the journey comes to its conclusion with a leap that restores the idyllic landscape of the child; the movement, in short, is circular. For the imagery at the conclusion of the poem suggests retreat to the womb. "Purity" and "fragrance" recall the mother's cleanliness and "wholesome odor"; and "the spread of purity it lies motionless in" refers back to the fish in the pond, the fetus in the amniotic fluids. Paradise is regained—through the restoration of the shattered infantile relationship with the mother.

It has been said too loosely and too often that Whitman is the first of the urban poets. Despite the brilliance of lines like "the blab of the pave" and the graphic, but fleeting, pictures of city life in "Song of Myself" and elsewhere, the settings of his greatest poems are almost invariably rural. "The open road" may lead the "I" through city streets, and comrades may be found in "A populous city," but the road invariably leads to rustic sites, and love is consummated, or companionship temporarily found, while "the waters roll slowly continually up the shores" ("When I Heard at the

Close of the Day"). As in "There Was a Child Went Forth," harmony and peace come out of earshot of the city's "dark" or the dynamo's whirring.

Understandably so, since in his evocation of childhood Whitman re-creates not only the child's relationship to the family but also the physical environment the child knew. Whitman lived most of his life in Brooklyn, Washington, and Camden, but in his first years, at Huntington, Long Island, he had never been far from the "hissing" of the Atlantic Ocean, and he had roamed freely in a rural setting. His art, like Proust's, is a remembrance of things past. It is more than coincidence that he did not begin to recover from the debilitating paralysis of 1873 and the death of his mother in May of that year until he found at the Stafford farm in Kirkwood, New Jersey, an approximation of his childhood environment on Long Island, and in the impoverished and barely literate Staffords, mother, father, and children, the equivalent of his own family.

Grace Gilchrist, the daughter of the woman who journeyed to America out of her impassioned desire to marry the poet, records Whitman as saying that "the time of my boyhood was a very restless and unhappy one: I did not know what to do."[2] There is no way of verifying the accuracy of Miss Gilchrist's recollection, but poems like "There Was a Child Went Forth" tend to corroborate her report, for the visual setting in Whitman's poetry is ordinarily not unlike that of the solitary shepherd in the painter's landscape, where lovely colors, like Whitman's beautiful language, keep us from pondering upon the character's isolation. The protagonist in "Song of Myself" withdraws from the intoxicating "distillation" of his artificial or social environment in order to observe "a spear of summer grass." The first line of "Starting from Paumanok," in the 1860 edition, characterizes the poet as "Free, fresh, savage," but the last line in the opening section belies the description and reveals the true state, "Solitary, singing in the west, I strike up for a new world"; Whitman had again "withdrawn to muse and meditate" alone. By a significant addition in 1871, he qualifies his paeans in "A Song of Joys," when he speaks of "Joys of the free and lonesome heart, . . . / Joys of the solitary walk." The original opening line of "As I Walk These Broad Majestic Days" is quite different from its later title: "As I Walk, Solitary, Unattended." In "As I Ebb'd with the Ocean of Life," there is a line as appropriate to the despairing mood as a similar one in The Waste Land, "I, musing, late in the autumn day." Even in the rejuvenation of another season, in "These I Singing in Spring," the poet is "Far, far in the forest, . . . / Solitary."

Repeatedly he refers to "lonesome walks" ("Recorders Ages Hence") during which "I stand and look at the stars" ("Night on the Prairies") or "I sit and look out upon all the sorrows of the world" ("I Sit and Look Out") or "I sit alone, yearning and thoughtful" ("This Moment Yearning and Thoughtful"). Whitman sings of union and companionship and sees himself as the comrade of people unborn, but the song comes from the yearning depths of a solitary observer, of a withdrawn child who, as a man, still reflects the child's estrangement in lines like these from "Not Heaving from My Ribb'd Breast Only":

> Not in many a hungry wish, told to the skies only,
> Not in cries, laughter, defiances, thrown from me when alone,
>   far in the wilds. . . .

Although Whitman sometimes creates a marvelous fantasy of a joyous overman or "savage" speaking with a "barbaric yawp"—an American Pan, as it were, who impregnates the earth with his poetry—the wish gushes forth from a withdrawn soul; like Thoreau's, his Pan is an imaginative fiction. "I am not to speak to you," Whitman writes in "To a Stranger," "I am to think of you when I sit alone, or wake at night alone." Or in "Poets To Come," the celebrator of comrades cannot permit himself the simple gratification of social contact: "I am a man who, sauntering along, without fully stopping, turns a casual look upon you, and then averts his face." But why avert his face? And why must this liberator of the senses write like a latter-day disciple of Puritan duty and asceticism in "All Is Truth": "Meditating among liars, and retreating sternly into myself"? "Sternly" conjures up duty and deep-rooted repressions. "Retreating sternly into myself" is an evasive act out of fear. The fear the drunkard arouses in "There Was a Child Went Forth" anticipates the avoidance of human interaction in Whitman's writings. (Except for the accounts of his experiences in wartime hospitals, *Specimen Days* consists mostly of ramblings about nature; people appear infrequently.) The fear is generally submerged or disguised, since Whitman attempts to deny it in order to play the role of the comrade or lover, but as in dreams we cannot ignore the latent content. This fear is not unlike that which keeps Henry James's most autobiographical characters, Ralph Touchett and Lambert Strether, from acknowledging their affections and entering normal human and sexual relationships. Although critics intent upon neat categories like to make James and Whitman antithetical, this kind of oversimplification will not withstand scrutiny. Just as most of Whitman's protagonists retreat to the forests to meditate upon existence, so the Lambert Strethers retreat to the United States to live out their lonely lives of virtue and self-reliance. For despite James's depiction of class structure and his dramatization of the emergent consciousness in a social context, his heroes and heroines, if death does not snuff them out, have at the conclusion of his fable only the self—no "connections."

In many of Whitman's poems there are crowds of people, particularly in his inventories of occupations and his kaleidoscopic catalogues of urban and rural activities. In "There Was a Child Went Forth," it will be recalled, the child sees the drunkard

> And the schoolmistress that passed on her way to the
>   school . . . and the friendly boys that passed . . . and the
>   quarrelsome boys . . . and the tidy and freshcheeked girls
>   . . . and the barefoot negro boy and girl. . . .

But at no point in the poem does the child speak to these people or interact
with them. The "I" in "Song of Myself," although he speaks forcefully and
amorously to an anonymous audience, does not converse with even one of
the innumerable people who appear in more than 1,300 lines. Sometimes
he talks to himself, as in this passage:

> Speech is the twin of my vision. . . . it is unequal to measure
>   itself.
> It provokes me forever,
> It says sarcastically, Walt, you understand enough. . . . why
>   don't you let it out then?

The rest is monologue with deceptive trappings of dialogue. So, too,
Henry James creates *ficelles* to relieve the monologue of the unraveling
consciousness with a dialogue that is more illusionary than real, since for
the Isabel Archers, Christopher Newmans, Lambert Strethers, and Merton Denshers—and the Huck Finns, for that matter—the territory ahead
is the silence of monologue.

Though Whitman sympathizes with prostitutes, criminals, hunted
slaves, and abject failures, at no time does he do more than express sympathy and suggest in general terms their anguish. More often than not, he
confines himself to descriptions of the life-and-death heroics of firemen or
soldiers, nude male swimmers in danger or in sportive play, mothers nurs-
ing or tending their children, parents honored by their children. But the
brave fireman, unlike the Greek warrior of whom he is the modern
counterpart, is never given the dignity even of a name, and is simply one
of the "divine average," an anonymous and previously unsung hero.

Whitman, then, describes people externally and superficially, as representatives of meaningful activities in a democratic society. These
descriptions are often Michelangelesque in their fascination with the
muscular movements of the beautiful male bodies, as in this well-known
passage in "Song of Myself":

> The butcher-boy puts off his killing clothes, or sharpens his
>   knife at the stall in the market,
> I loiter enjoying his repartee and his shuffle and breakdown.
> Blacksmiths with grimed and hairy chests environ the anvil,
>
> . . . .
>
> The lithe sheer of their waists plays even with their massive
>   arms,
>
> . . . .

> The negro holds firmly the reins of his four horses . . .
>
> . . . .
>
> His blue shirt exposes his ample neck and breast and
>   loosens over his hipband,
>
> . . . .
>
> The sun falls on his crispy hair and moustache. . . . falls on
>   the black of his polish'd and perfect limbs.

The throbbing flesh reduces these men from human status to anatomical functions. They are movements, not humans. Except in "Faces," the people are even faceless, Whitman's eye being drawn to the flesh as though fearful of eye-to-eye contact.

The people in Whitman's poems are like those of Maurice Prendergast, another lonely, isolated American artist. With lovely color and exquisite delicacy Prendergast fills his canvases with people promenading in parks, congregating at beaches, participating in various social functions. Always crowds of people in everyday activities, yet when one looks closely, often there are no faces, only bodies (or colors) in motion. The hedonism evoked by the beautiful pastel colors vanishes as one becomes aware of the artist's shrinking temperament, gregarious in fantasy but painfully timid and withdrawn.

Though Whitman is the greatest singer of love in nineteenth-century American literature, almost always he chants of unrequited love or asserts his love of collective democratic man. The lover portrayed in his poems is for the most part a passive, timid individual who avers his satisfaction with the passing glances of a stranger or a fleeting touch in a crowd. (What little sexual aggression there is resembles autoerotic fantasy.) The beloved, who is neither named nor individualized, is a stranger whose sudden disappearance the lover seems to welcome, for it is easier (and safer) to lament the loss of love than to consummate it. It is also easier to make love to an unknown audience, except that to do so is scarcely to make love at all.

Whitman's fear of personal involvement is part of the hidden or "indirect" meaning of "There Was a Child Went Forth," since the poem records the failure of basic relationships. Whitman, it will be recalled, notes the child's "yearning and swelling heart" and his search for "what is real," but whatever the child discovers he discovers for himself through his own observations of nature, strangers, and parents. There is no interaction between the youth and his parents, only the summarizing statements about the mother's gentleness and the father's harshness. They do not fulfill their parental roles of offering guidance and affection to the boy. In view of their failure, it is scarcely surprising that the child does not interact with other people, that he retreats "sternly" into himself. It is also significant that, although Whitman was the second of seven children and grew up in a large household, the child in the poem has neither brothers nor sisters. In fact, it can be said that Whitman, like Proust and James, acknowledged the reality of sibling rivalry by having his poetic expression of childhood follow two patterns: either the youth enjoys, as in "There Was a Child Went Forth," an exclusive relationship with parents as an only child, which is a kind of paradise, or the boy is more or less an "orphan" who, in his fantasy, enjoys the illusory freedom of a parentless world. The latter situation is more frequent—"Out of the Cradle Endlessly Rocking" and "The Sleepers" are examples—but the only child and the orphan invariably find at the end of their journeys the same haven—the protective maternal figure.

The mature man depicted in "Song of Myself" leaves "Houses and rooms . . . full of perfume," but apparently no family, and in his meditation creates a vision of the free and fulfilled self. However, he establishes no enduring connections:

> I am a free companion . . .
>
> I turn the bridegroom out of bed and stay with the bride
>   myself,
> And tighten her all night to my thighs and lips.

He is, ironically, "free" to roam, to revel in natural and human beauties, and to gather to himself a large group of admirers, but he is not "free" to establish lasting relationships, except imaginary ones. Although it can be argued that Whitman follows the protestant tradition in his insistence that each man is the determiner of his own lot—and this is certainly a partial explanation—it is also true that his fear of personal involvement was such that in his poetry he woos his readers and then holds them off through barriers which he erects between himself and his (imaginary) admirers. When the idolaters in "Song of Myself" become too insistent, he reminds them, "He most honors my style who learns under it to destroy the teacher." No one must approach too close. Only the superficial egocentricity of "Song of Myself" keeps us from recognizing Whitman's sometimes strained attempts to hide feelings of inadequacy and fears of rejection.

For a century detractors have heaped contempt upon Whitman for ignoring or at least minimizing the existence of evil. So-called evil appears everywhere in his writings, although he refuses to stand in judgment or to insist upon the human bond of shared responsibility. His position seems to me to be tenable. Man's great problem is not the world's evils; it is the absence of relationships, or love. Man may think that he is troubled by the world's evils, but his greatest horror is of an emotional lack, of utter loneliness in an indifferent universe. For Whitman heaven or joy is relatedness, real or imaginary; hell or agony is its absence. And so Whit-man dwells at length on the difficulties of becoming human through the establishment of what E. M. Forster calls "connections." Thus Whitman's poetic journeys lead from the self to relatedness to nature and man, at least on the verbal level. The qualification must be introduced, since, as close examination reveals, at the conclusion of a poem the protagonist fre-quently has achieved only sublimation through art or attributes too much to a future union, or relationship, with "unborn admirers." But, although his conclusions are evasive, he wrestles honestly and bravely with *the greater drama going on within myself & every human being.*

The tensions in Whitman's poetry stem from the shifting moods of the narrator as fear and joy vie with each other, the one now dominant, then the other, until resolution, or reconciliation, is achieved. Despite the quiet mood of "There Was a Child Went Forth," these alternations are present: the joy in natural phenomena, the momentary fear of the stag-gering drunkard, the lonely glances at the children, the ambivalence toward "fatherstuff," the reverence for the mother and the fear of the father, and then the peace the child finds at the end of his journey. The phrase "the yearning and swelling heart" succinctly describes the shifts of mood. Perhaps even better is "the curious systole and diastole within." For Whitman's verse does not so much correspond to a symphony or to the waves of the sea, comparisons he and his interpreters are fond of, as to inner tensions, contractions in fear and release into joy and peace. The tensions closely approximate, as the eroticism in his poetry testifies, the sexual rhythm of desire, frustration, and release through consummation or sublimation.

Notes

1. Herbert Marcuse, *Eros and Civilization: A Philosophical Inquiry into Freud* (Boston: Beacon Press, 1955), p. 169.

2. Quoted by Roger Asselineau in *The Evolution of Walt Whitman* (Cambridge, Mass.: Harvard Univ. Press, 1960), I, 276n. Miss Gilchrist's recollections appear in *Temple Bar Magazine*, 113 (1898), 200–12.

The Realm of Whitman's Ideas: Nature

Gay Wilson Allen*

One can only speak of Walt Whitman's "philosophy" in a loose and colloquial sense, for, like Emerson, he was not a systematic thinker, and his conceptions of the world he lived in and man's place in it came from various sources, some of them contradictory. But by the time he had written what was to be the first edition of *Leaves of Grass* he had found a blend of concepts and abstractions which satisfied his own needs both as a person and a poet. Since they were eclectic, they carried over some connotations from their sources, with consequent ambiguity. Moreover, Whitman used these concepts and terms both as expressions of faith in the things he held sacred and as metaphors for his cosmic visions, but they meshed sufficiently to form the semblance of an intelligible *Weltanschauung*. If he was not a philosopher, he was at least concerned with answers to the most profound questions regarding the destiny of man:

> To be in any form, what is that?
>
> . . . .
>
> What is a man anyhow? what am I? what are you?[1]

And in his 1855 Preface he declared: "The poets of the kosmos [he may have meant cosmic poets] advance through all interpositions and coverings and turmoils and stratagems to first principles."[2] What these "first principles" were the poet revealed not in a single preface, an ontological poem like Lucretius's *De rerum natura,* or a prose treatise, but piecemeal through the progressive versions of *Leaves of Grass.*

First of all, Whitman was heir to the Cartesian dualism which separated *mind* and *body*, a dualism which no theory has ever satisfactorily explained. Whitman himself often used the word *soul*, in a variety of contexts (some of which will be examined later), always with the con-

*Reprinted from *The New Walt Whitman Handbook* (New York: New York Univ. Press, 1975), pp. 173–81; reprinted by permission of New York Univ. Press; copyright © 1975 by New York University.

viction that it was "immortal." But exactly what Whitman meant by immortality of the soul is not easy to determine—possibly not survival of
personal identity as most Christians believed. When he used the word
heaven (usually plural) he almost invariably designated the region of the
stars and planets. He never referred to a Day of Judgment, or to the Christian *Atonement*, for he did not believe in "original sin," or that men
needed to atone for anything except acts of greed and selfishness. We have
seen above in his personal social creed striking resemblances to the
"Beatitudes" of Jesus. Yet he did not look to a future life for rewards or
punishments in any orthodox Christian sense—though in an evolutionary
sense he did, as we shall see below. The idea of *resurrection* also occurs
frequently in Whitman's poems, but on the analogy of the life cycles of
plants and animals: that is, the sequence of seed, germination, growth,
organic death, and rebirth from another seed. This favorite theme is
prominent in all Whitman's writings and is one of the best clues to his
philosophy of man and nature.

What most shocked Whitman's contemporaries was his emphasis on
the physicality of life, in which sex was as prominent and necessary as
birth and death. Throughout most of its history the Christian Church had
tolerated sexual intercourse as a necessity for procreation, but regarded it
as shameful, degrading, and sinful if indulged in for pleasure. The
Catholic Church had always held chastity to be one of the highest virtues,
and in nineteenth-century America several Protestant sects, most con-
spicuously the Shakers, had founded celibate communities. In practically
all Christian denominations sex was associated with the forbidden fruit in
the Garden of Eden.

When Christianity assimilated Neo-Platonism, it exalted mind over
body, and gave Nature an inferior position. According to the Platonic
myth the soul domiciled in a human body is a homesick exile, longing
always to return to its spiritual home, which it might be able to do if not
too much defiled by its association with the body and the world of
material things. To return, of course, the body must die, but some Neo-
Platonists such as Plotinus believed that in a state of mystical ecstasy the
soul could catch glimpses of the world of pure spirit. These fleeting experiences were the highest and most desirable possible for the human mind.

Doctrines of the supremacy of the soul over the body had come down
to Whitman by too many channels of religious instruction and literary
tradition not to have strong impacts on his thinking, but they were rivaled
by other, more materialistic, concepts. The most influential of these was
eighteenth-century rationalism and early nineteenth-century science. In
Tom Paine's *Age of Reason*, which Whitman read in his youth,[3] he was
taught that God's true revelation was in Nature, not in the Bible or other
religious documents. From science he learned that the world was not six
thousand years old, as both the Jewish and Christian churches had taught

for centuries, but millions of years old, as the geologists had proven from the strata of rocks and paleontologists from fossils of plants and animals embedded in the ancient rocks. Moreover, the fossils seemed to reveal strong resemblances and gradations of form and structure between the widely distributed specimens of plants and animals of the different geological ages. These resemblances and gradations suggested kinships and systematic variations which led to the idea of "evolution" long before Darwin published his *Origin of Species* in 1859.

In addition to the *Age of Reason*, the discoveries of geologists about the age of the earth, and of prehistoric life by paleontologists, Whitman found in Count Volney's *Ruins* (one of the books he said he had been "raised" on[4]) a complete philosophy of "Natural Religion" and a rationalistic account of the various religions of the world. The title of this book means the "ruins" of great nations,[5] which had fallen because of the greed of their rulers and the ignorance of their peoples. Volney was not a disciple of Rousseau, who believed in the innate goodness of human nature and blamed man's corrupt condition on society. Like Thomas Hobbes, Volney thought that man in a "savage state" was "A brutal, ignorant animal, a wicked and ferocious beast, like bears and Ourang-outangs.[sic]"[6] The strong ruled the weak, and the weak were too ignorant to find means of protecting themselves. Even after the beginning of an organized society, the strong deified themselves and demanded worship and obedience from the ignorant masses. Religion began with men's worship of the stars, and especially of the sun, whose life-giving effects they could see and feel, but tyrannical rulers exploited the natural religious sentiment as a means of gaining power over their subjects.

Aside from the perverse history of religions, Volney pointed out that they all claimed divine origin and presented their doctrines as the only truth. Obviously, with their different gods and theologies, they could not all be right; how then could an honest man choose the *true* religion? Volney said this was easy, that the God who created the universe had revealed his divine truths through his creation. Therefore, to understand God's plan for man, study Nature. The laws of nature were discernible to man's senses, and did not depend upon hearsay traditions or texts which had several times been translated and probably garbled. The laws of nature could be observed and tested. The only authority a man needed was the evidence of his own senses and experiences:

> To establish therefore an uniformity of opinion, it is necessary first to establish the certainty, completely verified, that the portraits which the mind forms are perfectly like the originals: that it reflects the objects correctly as they exist. . . . we must trace a line of distinction between those that are capable of verification, and those that are not, and separate by an inviolable barrier, the world of fantastical beings, from the world of realities . . .[7]

Of course Volney's sensational epistemology had its own naive assumptions, as John Locke's critics of his similar theory of knowledge pointed out, but it appealed to men's "common sense." Volney granted that men could be deceived by their senses, but only when they were swayed by ignorance (superstition) or passion, both of which could be avoided by rational study of the physical world.[8] By "law of nature" Volney meant:

> . . . the constant and regular order of facts, by which God governs the universe; an order which his wisdom presents to the senses and to the reason of men, as an equal and common rule for their actions, to guide them, without distinction of country or of sect, towards perfection and happiness.[9]

Like Bishop Paley and the other "Natural Religion" theologians, Volney argued that no intelligent person could examine "the astonishing spectacle of the universe" without believing in "a supreme agent, an universal and identic mover, designated by the appellation of God. . . ." Men whose ideas of God were formed on the "law of nature" would entertain "stronger and nobler ideas of the Divinity than most other men," for they would "not sully him with the foul ingredients of all the weaknesses and passion entailed on humanity."[10] (One example of Volney probably had in mind was the jealous and vindictive God of Calvinism.) In deriving a whole code of ethics and morality from the impartial, undeviating, and inexorable "Law of Nature," as Volney did in twelve chapters under this heading, he had to make more assumptions than he realized; and the virtues derived from them resembled those of the Judeo-Christian religion—except for holding pleasure, self-love, and egotism to be positively good so long as they did no harm to anyone.

It was not from Volney, however, that Whitman got his idea of "evolution." Volney believed that societies, or nations, had progressed from barbarism to civilization in various places at various times, but they had also just as frequently regressed. A decadent nation became the easy prey of a stronger nation or of revolt by its oppressed masses, resulting either in social chaos or rejuvenation. Although these cycles could be said to resemble the growth and decay of plants and animals, and thus to obey some law of nature, Volney did not make this connection, perhaps because he regarded the death of a nation as unnatural, man-made, and thus avoidable.

Walt Whitman actually got his ideas of evolution not directly from biologists, but indirectly from lectures and books on geology and astronomy—discussed below. To judge from the nature of his ideas on this subject, they came indirectly from Jean Baptiste Lamarck (1744–1829), who was the most influential evolutionist during the half-century preceding Darwin. Lamarck believed that all plants and animals had continuously evolved throughout the periods of geological time, each species making gradual alterations in structure and form to adapt to its environment.

The most controversial part of Lamarck's theory was that acquired characteristics could be transmitted to the offspring. Moreover, the hypothesis implied purpose, that somewhere in the process of change intelligence was at work making choices. Of course this confirmation of cosmic teleology appealed to religious leaders, who saw in it a means of preserving faith in a benevolent Creator. But before the end of the century most scientists had accepted Darwin's theory of fortuitous mutations, accidental changes in structure which happened to give an individual plant or animal an advantage in the struggle for survival, thereby enabling it to live long enough to produce offspring. This was the Darwinian "law" of "natural selection." Meanwhile Gregory Mendel was discovering the mathematical laws of hybridization, but his work did not become generally known until about 1900.

Although we know today that Darwin never ceased wondering whether some intelligent direction of energy might be aiding the mutations—what came to be called "Vitalism"—he never found any proof that this was actually true, though his *Movement and Habits of Climbing Plants* (1876) has been thought to leave room for the operation of psychic energy.[11] At any rate, by the end of the century the vitalists had lost credibility and Darwinian mechanical chance had won the field. However, in recent years something like Vitalism has been creeping back into speculations on the origin and development of living organisms.[12] A few scientists now suspect that even plants have some sort of mind or psychic energy, and that they, as well as animals, may have survived not because they were lucky but clever. Or as Emerson says, "Nature's dice are always loaded."[13]

Walt Whitman himself would have doubtless approved this speculation on the minds of plants, or Pierre Teilhard de Chardin's theory that every cell and molecule has some kind of innate intelligence, which multiplies and gains in strength with each increase in the combining of cells into more complex organisms, and the process is always toward greater complexity—the true evolutionary trend of the cosmos.[14] The great mystery is how the life of each cell in an organized complex obeys the command of some mysterious center of control. Teilhard speculated that mind is that controlling force, and that cosmic evolution is the order of the universe. Eventually the whole "biosphere" will become a "Noosphere" (realm of mind).[15]

Walt Whitman actually seems to have anticipated Teilhard in some ways—and here no specific source for Whitman is known. In his preparatory notes written between 1847 and the printing of his first edition of *Leaves of Grass* he declared:

> The soul or spirit transmits itself into all matter—into rocks, and can live the life of a rock—into the sea, and can feel itself the sea—into the oak, or other tree—into an animal, and feel itself a horse, a fish, or bird—into the earth—into the motions of the suns and stars—[16]

Whitman cautions himself: "Never speak of the soul as any thing but intrinsically great.—The adjective affixed to it must always testify greatness and immortality and purity.—" What he means by "intrinsic" greatness is elaborated in a theory strongly tinged with Neo-Platonism:

> The effusion or corporation of the soul is always under the beautiful laws of physiology—I guess the soul itself can never be anything but great and pure and immortal; but it makes itself visible only through matter—a perfect head, and bowels and bones to match is the easy gate through which it comes from its embowered garden, and pleasantly apears to the sight of the world.—[17]

This is a plain statement of the Platonic idea of the "pre-existence of the soul" (expressed by Wordsworth in his "Ode: Intimations of Immortality"), but Whitman's physiological application has the stamp of his own mind and character: "A twisted skull, and blood watery or rotten by ancestry or gluttony, or rum or bad disorders [in Whitman's editorials bad disorders meant venereal disease],—they are the darkness toward which the plant will not grow, although its seed lie waiting for ages.—"[18] Similar to this thought, he says, "Wickedness is most likely the absence of freedom and health in the soul." But if the soul is "pure" (inviolable?) and "immortal," how can matter have any influence on it? We might conclude that a degraded human body has no soul—or at least is not able to expand in it: "the darkness toward which the plant will not grow. . . ." But then in another note Whitman adds: "The universal and fluid soul impounds within itself not only all good characters, and hero[e]s, but the distorted characters, murderers, thieves[.]"[19]

Perhaps these contradictory statements cannot be logically reconciled, and maybe they were only *trial thoughts* anyway. But they reveal attitudes toward mind and matter, and the miraculous nature of both, which carried over into Whitman's poetry and sustained his childlike wonder at existence, "being in any form . . ."

> My life is a miracle and my body which lives is a miracle; but of what I can nibble at the edges of the limitless and delicious wonder I know that I cannot separate them, and call one superior and the other inferior, any more than I can say my sight is greater than my eyes.—[20]

In short, these are mysteries which the poet himself does not understand, but he *feels* their existence, and simply accepts them as facts in his experience—an attitude resembling the Buddhist's non-intellectual acceptance of the existence of the unseen God. This faith was also accompanied by an over-belief in what Whitman called "dilation," which he conceived to be a cosmic evolutionary process:

> I think the soul will never stop, or attain to any growth beyond which it shall not go.—When I walked at night by the sea shore and looked up at the countless stars, I asked of my soul whether it would be filled and satisfied when it should become god enfolding all these, and open to the life and delight and knowledge of everything in them or of them; and the answer was plain to me at the breaking water on the sands at my feet; and the answer was, No, when I reach there, I shall want to go further still.—[21]

Here are more enormous ambiguities. How will the "soul . . . become god enfolding" the innumerable stars of stellar space? Certainly this is no vision of a Christian heaven or of eternal happiness, for it is the nature of Whitman's "soul" never to be satisfied, or to cease growing. This concept has led many critics and scholars to find parallels to Vedanta and other religious-philosophical concepts of India. While still others are content simply to label Whitman a "mystic." Certainly the far-traveling soul is *migrating* if not transmigrating. But some definite clues both to the source of these huge soul-concepts and to Whitman's future literary use of them are given in some of the poet's trial lines for "Song of Myself":

> I am the poet of reality
> I say the earth is not an echo
> Nor man an apparition;
> But that all things seen are real,
>
> The witness and albic dawn of things equally real.
>
> I have split the earth and the hard coal and rocks and the solid bed of
>   the sea
> And went down to reconnoitre there a long time,
> And bring back a report,
> And I understand that those are positive and dense every one
> And that what they seem to the child they are.

. . . .

> Afar in the sky was a nest,
> And my soul flew thither and squat, and looked out
> And saw the journeywork of suns and systems of suns,
> And that a leaf of grass is not less than they
> And that the pismire is equally perfect, and all grains of sand, and
>   every egg of the wren,
> And the tree-toad is a chef d'oeuvre for the highest,
> And the running blackberry would adorn the parlors of Heaven
> And the cow crunching with depressed neck surpasses every
>   statue, . . .[22]

Notes

1. "Song of Myself," sec. 27 and sec. 20.

2. *Leaves of Grass*, Comprehensive Reader's Edition, ed. Harold W. Blodgett and Sculley Bradley (New York: W. W. Norton and Co., 1968), p. 721.

3. Horace Traubel, *With Walt Whitman in Camden, July 16–October 31, 1888* (New York: D. Appleton and Co., 1908), p. 205. See also David Goodale, "Some of Walt Whitman's Borrowings," *American Literature*, 10 (1938), 202–13.

4. Traubel, p. 445.

5. Full title: *The Ruins; or Meditations on the Revolutions of Empires*, by Count C. F. Volney, Count and Peer of France . . . To Which is Added *The Law of Nature* . . . (New York: Calvin Blanchard, n.d.). The French edition was published in 1791; the American translation after Volney's visit to Philadelphia in 1797—probably around 1800.

6. *Ruins*, p. 184.

7. *Ibid.*, p. 173.

8. *Ibid.*, p. 182.

9. *Ibid.*, p. 175.

10. *Ibid.*, p. 179.

11. See Peter Tompkins and Christopher Bird, *The Secret Life of Plants* (New York: Harper and Row, 1972), pp. 125–26.

12. In addition to Tompkins and Bird (note 11) see also Arthur Koestler's discussion of "Evolution" (Chaps. XI and XII) in *The Ghost in the Machine* (New York: Macmillan, 1967), pp. 151–71.

13. *Nature* (1836), part V. In *The Collected Works of Ralph Waldo Emerson*, ed. Robert E. Spiller and Alfred R. Ferguson (Cambridge, Mass.: Harvard Univ. Press, 1971), I, 25.

14. This is the argument of Pierre Teilhard de Chardin in *Man's Place in Nature: The Human Zoological Group*, translated by René Hague (New York: Harper and Row, 1966); and *The Phenomenon of Man*, translated by Bernard Wall (New York: Harper and Row, 1961).

15. *Man's Place in Nature*, pp. 79–121.

16. *The Uncollected Poetry and Prose of Walt Whitman*, ed. Emory Holloway (New York: Doubleday, Doran, and Co., 1921), II, 64.

17. *Ibid.*, p. 65.

18. *Ibid.*

19. *Ibid.*, pp. 65–66.

20. *Ibid.*, p. 66.

21. *Ibid.*

22. *Ibid.*, pp. 69–70.

The Care and Feeding of Long Poems: The American Epic from Barlow to Berryman

James E. Miller, Jr.*

1

Since the Declaration of Independence in 1776, and even before, American poets have dreamed of providing these States with a—perhaps *the*—Supreme Fiction, a delineated ideal, a set of beliefs, a model for living, a summation of the essence of what it means to be an American. This epic, sometimes anti-epic, ambition runs in the most profound currents from Timothy Dwight and Joel Barlow to John Berryman and Allen Ginsberg, with such important way stations in between as Ezra Pound, T. S. Eliot, Hart Crane, William Carlos Williams, Wallace Stevens, Charles Olson—and many more. There is one pivotal figure whose pronouncements and practice have loomed large enough to dominate—or to be elaborately rejected by—all succeeding poets, and who remains today the somewhat noisy skeleton sounding his barbaric yawp in America's poetic closet: Walt Whitman. As a saint, an embarrassment, or a joke, old Walt haunts the American poetic psyche. Every American poet must come to terms with his presence and is influenced as deeply in rejecting as in accepting him.

The New Criticism once thought that it had written Walt Whitman off, had buried him with the same finality as Fortunato is buried in "The Cask of Amontillado"—bricked up deep in the dank cellars of the mind. The irrelevance of Whitman seemed permanently established when the academies and the little magazines all extolled the consciously structured, elaborately patterned, brilliantly imaged, rigorously impersonal, subtly ironic poem. All poetry was remeasured, and when it smacked of the naively celebratory, the expansively confessional, the intuitively shaped, the shamelessly personal, the improvisationally spoken or chanted, it was dismissed with amusement or contempt; the well-made poem rendered Whitman obsolete.

*Reprinted from *The American Quest for a Supreme Fiction: Whitman's Legacy in the Personal Epic* (Chicago: Univ. of Chicago Press, 1979), pp. 13–29; reprinted by permission of the University of Chicago Press and the author.

289

But like steam built up under a cap too long sealed, Whitman's long dormant live energy blew the lid off modern poetry and released new poetic energies in the land, some of them so vigorous that they swept over the New Criticism and its precious well-made poem, leaving little in their wake except some glistening, fragmentary debris. William Carlos Williams replaced T. S. Eliot as a modern touchstone some four decades after what Williams designated the "catastrophe" of American poetry: the appearance and canonization of *The Waste Land* in 1922.[1] In 1956 Allen Ginsberg "howled" in the measure of Whitman's "yawp." And like many poets of a turbulent time, Robert Lowell began his career with allegiances in one camp, but at a critical moment folded his tent and stole away to the other camp. *Life Studies* (1959) was the turning point, and *Notebook* (1970) revised into *History* (1973) represented his struggle with the new Whitmanian forms. John Berryman cut out of the Eliot path, too, and joined the journey on Whitman's open road; he confessed (in his posthumously published *Paris Review* interview, winter 1972) that he took Eliot's *Waste Land* as his model for *Homage to Mistress Bradstreet* (1956), but turned to Whitman's "Song of Myself" as his model for *The Dream Songs* (finished, more or less, in 1968).[2]

One of the marvels of the deep division that separates the two traditions in modern American poetry is that both trace their origins to identical sources. The New Criticism and its poets, such as John Crowe Ransom, Allen Tate, the early Robert Lowell, took over many of their principles, it is true, from T. S. Eliot, but all realized that these principles derived in some manner from the man who had shaped Eliot, Ezra Pound. On the other hand, such anti-New Critical poets as Charles Olson, Allen Ginsberg, and Robert Creeley came back to Pound by way of William Carlos Williams—especially the Pound of the *Cantos*, the Pound that is most like Whitman. How Pound ended up a prophet in both of two opposed poetic camps makes for one of those ambiguities sufficiently baffling to puzzle a legion of literary historians.

An even greater irony, perhaps, is Whitman's lurking presence in each of these shapers of modern American poetry. If Ezra Pound is sometimes conceived of as the father of the modern movement, and Eliot and Williams as his odd offspring often at odds, then Whitman must clearly be cast in the role of grandfather; his poetic genes flowed through Pound into both Eliot and Williams—and on beyond into those who declare their allegiance to one or the other, or even declare their independence of all, self-generated poets without ancestry (Whitman's own role, more or less).

From Whitman to Pound and from Pound to Eliot and Williams, and thus to the latest moderns of whatever school: this lineage, the focus of this book, appears to be a natural development for American literature, but the idea may come as something of a shock to those accustomed to discovering the sources of American modernism abroad, especially in France. That Pound derived from the French Symbolists (among them

Stéphane Mallarmé), and Eliot also (for example, Jules Laforgue), has long been common critical knowledge if not critical commonplace. That the French Symbolists derived from an American source, Edgar Allan Poe, is a fact on which sophisticated criticism has gagged in disbelief for some time (Eliot expressed his wonder and revulsion at the notion in "From Poe to Valéry," 1948).

No one would want to deny that Pound and Eliot drew from multiple sources and were nourished by many traditions. And it is doubtful that any single context or source could illuminate all the cryptic and enigmatic lines of such a complex poem as *The Cantos*; but I believe that the American and specifically Whitmanian context will shed light on the poem's growth, method, and form—as, indeed, the American context will help us to understand what Eliot was about in *The Waste Land*, William Carlos Williams in *Paterson*, Hart Crane in *The Bridge*, and many other American poets in a multitude of long American poems. There *is* something especially American in the American poet's recurring ambition to write a long poem, sometimes a poem that takes a lifetime in the composition. The American roots of this ambition do much to explain the poem's meaning and shape. And every American poet who has written a long poem has, consciously or unconsciously, measured the length of his reach, tested the depth of his thrust, by the American poem that stands as the pivotal work for all American poetry: *Leaves of Grass*.

This theme was touched on, in part, by Roy Harvey Pearce in *The Continuity of American Poetry* (1961), in a section called "The Long View: An American Epic." Here Professor Pearce took exception to my view, expressed in the conclusion of *A Critical Guide to Leaves of Grass* (1957), that Whitman's entire work constituted (in Whitman's view as well as mine) an American epic. He defined Whitman's epic as "Song of Myself," and placed it in relation to *The Columbiad* before it and *The Cantos*, *The Bridge*, and *Paterson* after it.[3] Taking many hints from this seminal discussion, as well as offering some demurrers, I have endeavoured in these pages to trace some of the important implications of this almost obsessive impulse in the American poet to write a long poem: not just another long poem, but a long poem for America, that will serve as its epic, and if not its epic, then as the embodiment of its "Supreme Fiction" (in Wallace Stevens's sense), as a particularly American way of conceiving or perceiving or receiving the world.

That the impulse is obsessive seems clear enough from the beginning, especially for anyone who has tried to read either of the two versions of Joel Barlow's epic, *The Vision of Columbus* (1787) or *The Columbiad* (1807). Barlow's ambition was epic, but he found that he had to modify the form to suit his American materials (he gave up narrative in favor of sweeping vision), and the form has gone through radical transformation ever since. Whitman, at the beginning of his career as a poet, outlined in his 1855 Preface to *Leaves of Grass* a recipe for the "great psalm of the republic," whose theme "is creative and has vista."[4] In John Berryman's *Dream Songs*, published in 1969, we find in Song 354:

> "The Care & Feeding of Long Poems" was Henry's title
> for his next essay, which will come out when
> he wants it to.
> A Kennedy-sponsored bill for the protection
> of poets from long poems   will benefit the culture
> and do no harm to that kind lady, Mrs. Johnson.[5]

And in *Sphere: The Form of a Motion* (1974), A. R. Ammons wrote:

>   I don't know about you,
> but I'm sick of good poems, all those little rondures
> splendidly brought off, painted gourds on a shelf: give me
> the dumb, debilitated, nasty, and massive, if that's the
> alternative: touch the universe anywhere you touch it
> everywhere.[6]

Irony sounds through Berryman's many voices, and the greatest irony is perhaps that his lines come in the middle of his most ambitious, most obsessive long poem. And Ammons writes his words in the middle of *his* poem, tossing off what appears to be one of the assumptions basic to the American long poem: its ego-centrifugality (as well as ego-centripetality), the notion that anyone can be everyman, that the poet can represent his time, his place, his world, "touch the universe anywhere you touch it/everywhere." Ah yes, but to *touch the universe*: how is that done? The answer to this question is in some sense the answer sought through two centuries of America's quest for a Supreme Fiction.

2

Had John Berryman's Huffy Henry, who throughout the *Dream Songs* shields himself as best he can from the suffering of his "irreversible loss," and who, to the reader's delight, repeatedly discovers that he has a "sing to shay"[7]—had Henry lived to finish his essay on "The Care & Feeding of Long Poems," he could have dealt with some strange works in American literature. He might well have gone back to the beginnings to stare in amazement at that poem of cataclysmic conclusions, the Puritan epic and best-seller, Michael Wigglesworth's *Day of Doom*, published in 1662; surely he would have sympathized with the sinners who "put away the evil day, / and drown'd their care and fears, / Till drown'd were they, and swept away / by vengeance unawares."[8] And he would certainly have paused over Edward Taylor's poetic sequences, *God's Determinations* and the two series of *Preparatory Meditations*, written in the seventeenth century but not published until the twentieth; he would have wondered at the American poet's penchant from the first for the scatological image, as in Meditation 8 (First Series): "In this sad state, Gods Tender Bowells run

/ Out streams of Grace: And he to end all strife / The Purest Wheate in Heaven, his deare-dear Son / Grinds, and kneads up into this Bread of Life."⁹ He probably would have agreed with Albert Gelpi's recent judgment (in *The Tenth Muse*, 1975) that Taylor's work "is the first instance of what may be a distinctly American genre: the open-ended poem written over years, perhaps even over a lifetime, in separate but interacting segments."¹⁰

Moving from the seventeenth century to the eighteenth, Henry could not avoid encountering what its author claimed to be the first epic written in America—Timothy Dwight's *The Conquest of Canaan*, begun in the early 1770s but not published until 1785 (John Trumbull's *M'Fingal*, 1782, as a *mock-epic* did not qualify for the honor). Its eleven books, written in a seemingly endless sequence of heroic couplets, was an attempt by the grandson of Jonathan Edwards to wed religion and politics by making the biblical story of Joshua's leading the Israelites into the land of Canaan suggest or symbolize George Washington's triumph over the British in the American Revolutionary War. It is not a matter of record that this epic's allegorized hero, and the man to whom the poem is, with a rhetorical flourish, dedicated—George Washington—ever got around to reading its some three hundred pages.¹¹ For that matter, it is not clear that anyone except the dedicated scholar has read the work in its entirety, a fate not uncommon to America's long poems.

Had Henry survived his encounter with Dwight's epic, he would next stumble up against another blockbuster, Joel Barlow's *Columbiad* (1787, 1807). Here he could test his own reaction against that of William Cullen Bryant, who said: "The plan of the work is utterly destitute of interest and that which was at first [in its 1787 form as *The Vision of Columbus*] sufficiently wearisome has become doubly so by being drawn out to its present length."¹² That length, with notes, extended over four hundred pages, or ten books of relentless heroic couplets. Barlow's epic device was to invent a guardian Genius who rescued Columbus from his old-age prison and took him to the top of the "mount of vision," whence he could witness the whole bloody history of the conquest of the American continents, the formation of the American nation, and on into the glorious future and utopian fulfillment. Clearly Columbus was enthralled by the vision of America's special destiny in the world presented by his guardian Genius, as shown in these lines closing Book the Ninth:

> As thus he spoke, returning tears of joy
> Suffused the Hero's cheek and pearl'd his eye:
> Unveil, said he, my friend [that is, Hesper, his guardian
>   Genius], and stretch once more
>
> Beneath my view that heaven-illumined shore;
> Let me behold her silver beams expand
> To lead all nations, lighten every land,

> Instruct the total race and teach at last
> Their toils to lessen and their chains to cast,
> Trace and attain the purpose of their birth
> And hold in peace this heritage of earth.
> The Seraph smiled consent; the Hero's eye
> Watcht for the daybeam round the changing sky.[13]

If Henry found himself turned off, or put to sleep, by such passages drawn out at such tedious length, in works diligently attempting to transfigure Christopher Columbus or George Washington into an epic hero, and slavishly courting the Old World muse of past epics, he might have dug out such native-seeming works as Daniel Bryan's *Adventures of Daniel Boone* (1813), with its attempt to develop a different kind of epic hero—the frontier, native-born American. But though he started with an original New World hero, the poet evoked, in startlingly elevated language, the Old World muse: "And thou my Muse! with wildly melting grace, / Strike softly from the angel-woven wires, / Of poesy's bright Harp, sweet flowing strains."[14] From lines like these, Henry might have turned quickly to Thomas Ward's *Passaic* (1842), with its attempt to embody an epic landscape, elevating to hero status an American river—later to figure importantly in a twentieth-century American epic, William Carlos Williams's *Paterson* (the Ward poem has been conveniently excerpted for the epic hunter in Mike Weaver's *William Carlos Williams: The American Background*, 1971).[15]

But if the rustic and the local might have bored Henry after a time, he could have become enthusiastic about a work that is overwhelmingly elegant and universal, Edgar Allan Poe's *Eureka: A Prose Poem* (1848). By writing his poetry in prose, Poe violated most of the tenets he had developed for the writing of poetry (such as the nonexistence of a *long poem*) and at the same time set the pattern for the prosy or prose-filled poems of the twentieth century (as in Williams, Charles Olson, Karl Shapiro, and others). Moreover, *Eureka* is suffused with the epic impulse, the impulse to "get it all together," to elevate science into metaphysics, and to erect thereon a system of belief, a myth for the mythless American. And the epic hero? It could be no other than the poem's speaker himself, Edgar Allan Poe, perceiving for his readers the unity of seemingly disparate things, reconciling the conflicts of science and religion.

What might Henry make of Henry Wadsworth Longfellow's *Song of Hiawatha?*

> Swift of foot was Hiawatha;
> He could shoot an arrow from him,
> And run forward with such fleetness,
> That the arrow fell behind him!
> Strong of arm was Hiawatha;
> He could shoot ten arrows upward,
> Shoot them with such strength and swiftness

That the tenth had left the bow-string
Ere the first to earth had fallen![16]

This American epic took over the hypnotic trochaic tetrameter of the Finnish epic, *Kalevala*, and appeared in that signal year of 1855 (signal because it was the year of the first edition of Whitman's *Leaves of Grass*). The one poem, Longfellow's, was hailed as a masterpiece; the other, Whitman's, almost still-born, was hailed only, or primarily, by the author's own stealthily placed reviews. Henry might raise a glass to this inconspicuous crossing of the old and new, the one epic rushing into the past and near-oblivion (at least critically), the other wobbling uncertainly toward the future and many strange reincarnations.

Henry might have paused and puzzled over the case of Emily Dickinson, like Poe the seeming genius of the short poem. He might examine those packets in which she placed and fixed her poems, apparently out of some obscure notion that there was an arrangement that would turn short poems into a long poem which would penetrate to a truth perhaps greater than the sum of the individual insights, which by the juxtaposition of disparate subjects would make a transcendent leap to the unity behind all subjects.[17] But Henry's pause with Emily would surely have turned into a prolonged stay with Herman Melville if he had attempted to comprehend Melville's incredibly long poem, *Clarel: A Poem and Pilgrimage in the Holy Land* (1876). Henry might have agreed with those who said that Melville's greatest poetry was written in prose, that *Moby Dick* was his, and America's, epic. But such statements do not make *Clarel* disappear, and Henry's keen interest in the "care & feeding of long poems" would surely impel him into a close investigation of its agonizing search, through six hundred pages of rhyming iambic tetrameter, for a way of belief for an American in the modern world, or, perhaps, for an American way of belief (or an American way of living with unbelief).

When Henry turned his attention to the early twentieth century, he would find, in poetry as in prose, attention focused on the American village, the small town (to turn up later in dramatic form in Thornton Wilder's *Our Town*, 1938). Edward Arlington Robinson produced a body of such poetry in which there lurked the long poem that was extracted and published as *Tilbury Town* (1953).[18] But another long poem of similar nature that Henry could add to his list is Edgar Lee Masters's *Spoon River Anthology* (1915), which includes "The Spooniad"[19] at the end—perhaps a tipoff to the epic (even if comic) ambition of the book. Henry might come to speculate that *Spoon River Anthology* was in a sense a climax in the evolution of the American long poem—poles apart from those early attempts to find a hero in George Washington or Christopher Columbus, stumbling instead on a "democratic" hero in the glory of his anonymity living his anonymous life in an anonymous village—Everyman in Everytown, USA.

Beginning with Ezra Pound, Henry would find that the "care & feeding of long poems" became something else. Something else, but also something the same—the same, that is, as the "care & feeding" by that pivotal poet who unobtrusively changed literary history beginning quietly—unnoticed—in 1855. Like *Leaves of Grass*, Pound's *Cantos* grew over a lifetime, assuming the shape of a life. No other long poem of the twentieth century seems to have taken so long in the writing. Though conceived earlier, the first Canto was published in 1917 (Pound was thirty-two), the last in 1969, a period of fifty-two years. Whitman, thirty-six in 1855, was to work thirty-seven years on *Leaves of Grass*—until his death and the Deathbed Edition in 1892. By comparison with such spectacular devotion to the "care & feeding of long poems," other twentieth-century poets appear to be pikers. But as Henry would surely know, a poem's excellence or impact cannot be measured by the years of its production. T. S. Eliot's *The Waste Land* was seemingly produced in a great surge of emotion and inspiration, revised by Pound, and issued at a stroke in 1922. Less sudden in execution and appearance, *The Four Quartets* appeared in 1943. If Henry examined their feeding closely, he might find both poems shaped to the poet's life more closely than anyone imagined possible on their appearance and for long after.

After Pound and Eliot, Henry's reading list would be long and arduous. One line of inquiry would carry him through long poems that grew over more or less long periods and that relate themselves more or less directly to the Whitman-Pound-Eliot patterns (or anti-patterns): Hart Crane's *The Bridge* (1930), William Carlos Williams's *Paterson* (1946–63), Charles Olson's Maximus Poems (1960–75), Henry's own John Berryman and his *Dream Songs* (1964–68), Allen Ginsberg's *Fall of America* (1972). This is the line I shall be tracking, using in addition Wallace Stevens's "Notes toward a Supreme Fiction" (1942) as a focal point for discussion of the theory of an American long poem. Wallace Stevens's long poem is divided into three sections, each of which bears a title that appears to be a rule: "It Must Be Abstract," "It Must Change," "It Must Give Pleasure."[20] And Stevens's letters reveal that he once contemplated adding a fourth section to be entitled, "It Must Be Human."[21] The antecedents of all the "Its" of these rules, although left ambiguous by Stevens, must be a work that attempts to embody a "Supreme Fiction" (a viable truth or reality, a usable myth)—that is, an epic, or a specifically American epic, in short, a Significant Long Poem (like "Notes toward a Supreme Fiction" itself).

But in tracking the American long poem, Henry might find, aside from Crane, Williams, Berryman, and Ginsberg, other possible paths to investigate, side trips to make. He (and we) might follow another line that leads through materials bearing the clear stamp of America: Stephen Vincent Benét's *John Brown's Body* (1928), Archibald MacLeish's *Conquistador* (1932), Robert Penn Warren's *Brother to Dragons* (1953). In a way most such works struggle to connect with a narrative epic tradition that Whitman rendered obsolete with *Leaves of Grass*. Henry would, however, surely find ample Whitmanian echoes in a modern master of the long narrative (and yet also intricately lyric) poet, Robinson Jeffers, but he would just as surely note the basic Whitmanian brightness transfigured into gloom in Jeffers's masterpiece, *The Women at Point Sur* (1927), or in his later work, *The Double Axe* (1948).[22] And if Henry found Jeffers fascinating, he might seek out the work of Brother Antoninus—William Everson (who has styled himself Jeffers's "only disciple"),[23] as for example his *Man-Fate: The Swan Song of Brother Antoninus* (1974), an account of the poet's feelings on giving up monkhood for marriage. Or if Henry tired of the Jeffers gloom he might prefer to immerse himself for a time in Carl Sandburg's *The People, Yes!* (1936), a long poem that seems to out-Whitman Whitman in its embrace of Americans "En-Masse." And if Sandburg's expansiveness began to pall, Henry could turn to H. D.'s more restrained *Trilogy* ("The Walls Do Not Fall," 1944; "Tribute to the Angels," 1945; "The Flowering of the Rod," 1946), and its lyric account of an intensely personal reaction to an overwhelming public event, World War II. A passage from "The Walls Do Not Fall" may be read as a kind of general motto of the American long poem:

> we know no rule
> of procedure,
>
> we are voyagers, discoverers
> of the not-known,
>
> the unrecorded;
> we have no map;
>
> possibly we will reach haven,
> heaven.[24]

Henry's ardor for "the care & feeding of long poems" might have cooled had he become lost in the labyrinths of Louis Zukofsky's *A*, begun in 1928, elaborated and extended for almost fifty years, and brought ostensibly to a conclusion in 1976.[25] Or Henry might have become bemused by the contemporary proliferation of the long poem in a seemingly infinite variety of forms, as he spun in circles trying desperately to keep up with its hydra-headed manifestations. Robert Duncan, *The Structure of Rime*, launched in his volume *The Opening of the Field* in 1960; and also *Passages*, which began to appear in his volume *Bending the Bow* in 1968; Louis Simpson, *At the End of the Open Road* (1963), and *Searching for the Ox* (1976); Melvin B. Tolson, *Harlem Gallery* (1965); A. R. Ammons, *Tape for the Turn of the Year* (1965), and *Sphere: The Form of a Motion* (1974); John Ashberry, *The Skaters* (1966), and *Three Poems* (in prose)

(1972); James Schuyler, *Hymn to Life* (1976); Edward Dorn, *Slinger* (1975); James Dickey, *The Zodiac* (1976).

Henry might have concluded, after attempting to read as many of America's recent long poems as he could find, that for a poet to choose the form of the long poem as it has evolved is to opt for many freedoms, but it also is to venture many risks. In a way, the form denudes the poet, displaying, it is true, all his genius, but mercilessly exposing, too, all his frailties. Whatever else its nature, the form offers no place to hide mediocrity, banality, conformity. In a short, well-made poem, these traits might be cleverly concealed, hidden behind the meter or metaphor or conceit; but in the American long poem, they will out, willy-nilly—and the poem can quickly become, instead of a daring adventure and journey, a colossal and predictable bore.

The risks involved and the hazards incurred Henry might find symbolized by A. R. Ammons's *Tape for the Turn of the Year* (1965), which was composed entirely on an adding-machine tape, started through the typewriter in early December and continued daily until the tape ran out in mid-January. The poem opens on 6 December.

> today I
> decided to write
> a long
>   thin
>   poem
>   employing certain
> classical considerations:
>   this
> part is called the pro-
> logue: it has to do with
>   the business of
>   getting started.
>
>   first the
>   Muse
>   must be acknowledged,
> saluted, and implored:
> I cannot
> write
>   without her help
>   but when
> her help comes it's
> water from spring heights,
>   stream
>   inexhaustible:
> I salute her, lady

of a hundred names—
        Inspiration
        Unconscious
        Apollo (on her man side)[26]

Here, in a witty, seemingly disposable, epic, one hundred years and more
after the appearance of Whitman's *Leaves of Grass*, is a limit reached, an
extreme explored—improvisational, a free-flowing comically organic
form, a poem about the writing of a poem, an anti-epic about the writing
of an epic. Henry may well look quizzical, scratch his head, and now
wander back to his own familiar habitat, *The Dream Songs* of John Berryman, to meditate at length over the gargantuan dimensions of the
materials accumulated on "the care & feeding of long poems."

3

Where are the beginnings of this epic impulse, this impassioned quest
for a Supreme Fiction? The origins lie deep in the national psyche, and
those poets who fled America in search of a more congenial tradition
(Eliot, Pound) succeeded only in demonstrating their deepest American
nature. There is one side of the American character that shouts: throw
over all tradition, cut off the past, start and build anew; but there is the
counterpart that whispers: take all traditions as yours, connect firmly
with the past, build the new only on the old. Walt Whitman's 1855
Preface to *Leaves of Grass*, with its call for the new, made T. S. Eliot's
1917 "Tradition and the Individual Talent," with its praise for the past,
inevitable. Both are solidly American documents, treating of peculiarly
American issues. Only a country without much past, without long traditions, can be so self-conscious about them, either in rejecting or in seeking
them.

America needed a new literature to match the new land and the new
society, the land largely empty, the society hardly established. This was
the recurring note sounded by almost every literary and cultural critic to
comment on American literature from the time of America's political independence on. For example, Solyman Brown, a sometime poet,
clergyman, and dentist of Connecticut, opened his 1818 "Essay on American Poetry" thus: "The proudest freedom to which a nation can aspire,
not excepting even political independence, is found in complete emancipation from literary thraldom. Few nations, however, have arrived at
this commanding eminence." After a sweeping survey of all civilization,
Brown comes to America, and instead of finding the causes for her continuing literary dependence within, he finds the causes abroad—in a British
conspiracy. "It has ever been the policy and practice of England to decry
Scotch and Irish intellect and affect a sovereign contempt for all that are
born on the Forth or the Liffey. As these countries have now coalesced

under the crown of England, it has become less her interest to urge hostilities in those directions. America is therefore the principal object of her literary persecution." Persecution? That, indeed, is what Solyman Brown means, and he goes on to point out that this persecution is accomplished through the British reviews, through the "importation of books into the United States, often at reduced prices," and through the refusal of British men of letters to give "the smallest credit to American productions, how meritorious soever."[27] Although the specifics might and did change, the literary or intellectual hostility toward England and British literary dominance would continue for many decades, even into our own time.

William Cullen Bryant, in a review of Solyman Brown's book laying out his conspiracy theory, surveyed American poetry in 1818. Although Bryant ridiculed Brown's theories, his concern for an American poetry runs through all his comments: "Abroad, our literature has fallen under unmerited contumely from those who were but slenderly acquainted with the subject on which they professed to decide: and at home, it must be confessed that the swaggering and pompous pretensions of many have done not a little to provoke and excuse the ridicule of foreigners. Either of these extremes exerts an injurious influence on the cause of letters in our country." Bryant found Brown's boasting merely embarrassing: "We make but a contemptible figure in the eyes of the world and set ourselves up as objects of pity to our posterity when we affect to rank the poets of our own country with those mighty masters of song who have flourished in Greece, Italy, and Britian."[28]

Mighty masters of song? Would America ever have them? Henry Wadsworth Longfellow may well have had himself in mind when he posed essentially this question, at eighteen years of age, in 1825:

> Is then our land to be indeed the land of song? Will it one day be rich in romantic associations? Will poetry, that hallows every scene, that renders every spot classical, and pours out on all things the soul of its enthusiasm, breathe over it that enchantment which lives in the isles of Greece, and is more than life amid the "woods, that wave o'er Delphi's steep." Yes!—and palms are to be won by our native writers!—by those that have been nursed and brought up with us in the civil and religious freedom of our country. Already has a voice been lifted up in this land, already a spirit and a love of literature are springing up in the shadow of our free political institutions.

In answering the British charge that America had no "finished scholars," Longfellow set forth in embryo the lines of a literary argument that would flourish in the twentieth century:

> But there is reason for believing that men of mere learning, men of sober research and studied correctness, do not give to a nation its great name. Our very poverty in this respect will have a tendency to give a national

character to our literature. Our writers will not be constantly boiling and panting after classical allusions to the vale of Tempe and the Etrurian river. . . . We are thus thrown upon ourselves: and thus shall our native hills become renowned in song, like those of Greece and Italy.[29]

It was left to Ralph Waldo Emerson to offer the classic statement that all these critics (and many more) were stammering to make. And although Emerson's 1837 "American Scholar," with its cry—"We have listened too long to the courtly muses of Europe"[30]—has come to be considered the American intellectual declaration of independence, it was not until "The Poet" (1844) that Emerson made his most eloquent plea and prophecy for American poetry:

I look in vain for the poet whom I describe. We do not with sufficient plainness or sufficient profoundness address ourselves to life, nor dare we chaunt our own times and social circumstance. If we filled the day with bravery, we should not shrink from celebrating it. Time and nature yield us many gifts, but not yet the timely man, the new religion, the reconciler, whom all things await. Dante's praise is that he dared to write his autobiography in colossal cipher, or into universality. We have yet had no genius in America, with tyrannous eye, which knew the value of our incomparable materials, and saw, in the barbarism and materialism of the times, another carnival of the same gods whose picture he so much admires in Homer; then in the Middle Age; then in Calvinism. . . . Yet America is a poem in our eyes; its ample geography dazzles the imagination, and it will not wait long for meters.[31]

From 1844 to 1855. The wait was not long for *Leaves of Grass*. In response to the copy Whitman sent him, Emerson replied in the most famous letter in American literature: "It meets the demand I am always making of what seemed the sterile and stingy nature, as if too much handiwork, or too much lymph in the temperament, were making our Western wits fat and mean. I give you joy of your free and brave thought."[32]

Emerson's role in shaping the concept of an American bard and an American epic is vital, and there is justification in recognizing him as one of the Whitmanian "Beginners": "How they are provided for upon the earth (appearing at intervals)."[33] The relationship between Emerson and Whitman has been the subject of repeated exploration, two of the most recent commentaries, by Hyatt Waggoner and Harold Bloom, providing some of the most interesting—and debatable—conjecture.[34] It is as gross a mistake to claim that Emerson's and Whitman's ideas are identical in all respects (as Yvor Winters astonishingly claimed in attacking Hart Crane's *The Bridge*; see chapter 8, section 2, below) as it is to claim that Whitman owes nothing to Emerson. Whitman himself once said that he was "simmering, simmering" and Emerson brought him "to a boil"[35]—an image that perhaps most fairly delineates the complex relationship without diminishing the genuine originality or denying the remarkable innovation of either writer. Never would Whitman's poetry (or prose) be mistaken for Emerson's. Both were "Beginners" and both spoke with strongly individual voices. But only Whitman can lay claim to the title of America's epic poet—as Emerson himself seems to suggest in his glowing letter thanking Whitman for the gift of *Leaves of Grass*.

4

But before turning to the "free and brave thought" of Whitman's poem, we must note still one more cultural commentator—from another land—who seemed more acutely aware than most that the nature of the American democratic experiment would shape the nature and theme of American poetry in special ways: Alexis de Tocqueville, whose *Democracy in America* appeared in 1835, with an American edition in 1838 (when Whitman was nineteen years of age). Whatever Whitman took from Ralph Waldo Emerson, and it was surely a great deal, he may well have been first inspired in his ambition as a native American poet by Alexis de Tocqueville's vision. Consider, for example, the following Tocqueville comments:

On style:

> Taken as a whole, literature in democratic ages can never present, as it does in the periods of aristocracy, an aspect of order, regularity, science, and art; its form will, on the contrary, ordinarily be slighted, sometimes despised. Style will frequently be fantastic, incorrect, over-burdened, and loose,—almost always vehement and bold. Authors will aim at rapidity of execution, more than at perfection of detail. Small productions will be more common than bulky books: there will be more wit than erudition, more imagination than profundity; and literary performances will bear marks of an untutored and rude vigor of thought,—frequently of great variety and singular fecundity. The object of authors will be to astonish rather than to please, and to stir the passions more than to charm the taste.

On the past:

> Democratic nations care but little for what has been, but they are haunted by visions of what will be; in this direction, their unbounded imagination grows and dilates beyond all measure. . . . Democracy, which shuts the past against the poet, opens the future before him.

On the subject and theme of poetry:

> Amongst a democratic people, poetry will not be fed with legends or the memorials of old traditions. The poet will not attempt to people the universe with supernatural beings, in whom his readers and his own fancy have ceased to believe; nor will he coldly personify virtues and vices, which are better received under their own features. All these resources fail

him; but Man remains, and the poet needs no more. The destinies of mankind—man himself, taken aloof from his country and his age, and standing the presence of Nature and of God, with his passions, his doubts, his rare prosperities and inconceivable wretchedness—will become the chief, if not the sole, theme of poetry amongst these nations.[36]

Alexis de Tocqueville's predictions for a democratic or American poetry, in spite of their occasional quaintness of concern, of language, of focus, are remarkably accurate when measured against the poetry that America has produced and critically acclaimed. And Tocqueville is instructive too in that he brought together in his commentary many of the literary notions hanging in the air at the time and linked them to their political and cultural contexts, pointing out connections and causes where others could only express their feelings of involvement. Whether Emerson or Whitman read him is not so important as the simple fact he saw in his book of the 1830s what they were to express in the decades following, Emerson in "The Poet" in 1844, and Whitman in his Preface and volume of poems, *Leaves of Grass*, in 1855. In his Preface Whitman announced: "The expression of the American poet is to be transcendent and new. It is to be indirect and not direct or descriptive or epic. Its quality goes through these to much more. Let the age and wars of other nations be chanted and their eras and characters be illustrated and that finish the verse. Not so the great psalm of the republic. Here the theme is creative and has vista."[37]

A final word:
"American Poetry"

Louis Simpson

Whatever it is, it must have
A stomach that can digest
Rubber, coal, uranium, moon, poems.

Like the shark, it contains a shoe.
It must swim for miles through the desert
Uttering cries that are almost human.[38]

Notes

1. See the radical reassessment of Williams in *William Carlos Williams*, ed. J. Hillis Miller (Englewood Cliffs, N.J.: Prentice Hall, 1966). For an account of Williams's views on *The Waste Land*, see chap. 7 of the book from which this chapter is reprinted.

2. See chaps. 1 and 10.

3. Roy Harvey Pearce, *The Continuity of American Poetry* (Princeton: Princeton Univ. Press, 1961), pp. 59–136.

4. Walt Whitman, "1855 Preface," *Complete Poetry and Selected Prose*, ed. James E. Miller, Jr. (Boston: Houghton Mifflin Co., 1959), p. 413.

5. John Berryman, *The Dream Songs* (New York: Farrar, Straus and Giroux, 1969), p. 376.

6. A. R. Ammons, *Sphere: The Form of a Motion* (New York: W. W. Norton and Co., 1974), p. 72.

7. Berryman, *Dream Songs*, p. 39.

8. Michael Wigglesworth, "They Day of Doom," *Seventeenth Century American Poetry* (New York: New York Univ. Press, 1968), p. 56.

9. Edward Taylor, "Preparatory Meditations," *The Poems of Edward Taylor* (New Haven: Yale Univ. Press, 1960), p. 18.

10. Albert Gelpi, *The Tenth Muse* (Cambridge, Mass.: Harvard Univ. Press, 1975), p. 32.

11. See the facsimile reprint of the 1785 edition of Timothy Dwight's *The Conquest of Canaan* in *The Major Poems of Timothy Dwight (1752–1817)*, ed. William J. McTaggart and William K. Bottorf (Gainesville, Fla.: Scholars' Facsimiles and Reprints, 1969).

12. William Cullen Bryant, "Essay on American Poetry," *The American Literary Revolution, 1783–1837*, ed. Robert E. Spiller (New York: New York Univ. Press, 1967), p. 201.

13. See the facsimile reprint of the 1825 edition of Joel Barlow's *The Columbiad* in *The Works of Joel Barlow*, ed. William K. Bottorf and Arthur L. Ford (Gainesville, Fla.: Scholars' Facsimiles and Reprints, 1970), Vol. II. The quoted passage appears on p. 747 of the volume or p. 329 of the facsimile.

14. Daniel Bryan, "The Adventures of Daniel Boone," *The Mountain Muse* (Harrisonburg, Va.: Davidson and Bourne, 1813), p. 111.

15. Mike Weaver, *William Carlos Williams: The American Background* (Cambridge, Eng.: Cambridge Univ. Press, 1971), p. 165–200.

16. Henry Wadsworth Longfellow, *Song of Hiawatha* (Boston: Ticknor and Fields, 1855), pp. 49–50.

17. See chap. 10 ("The Fascicles") and Appendix I ("The Fascicle Numbering") of Ruth Miller's *The Poetry of Emily Dickinson* (Middletown, Conn.: Wesleyan Univ. Press, 1968).

18. Edward Arlington Robinson, *Tilbury Town: Selected Poems of Edward Arlington Robinson*, ed. Lawrance Thompson (New York: Macmillan Co., 1953).

19. Edgar Lee Masters, "The Spooniad," *Spoon River Anthology* (New York: Collier Books, 1962), pp. 281–91.

20. Wallace Stevens, *The Collected Poems* (New York: Alfred A. Knopf, 1965), pp. 380–408.

21. ———, *Letters* (New York: Alfred A. Knopf, 1966), pp. 863–64.

22. See Tim Hunt, Afterword to *The Women at Point Sur*, by Robinson Jeffers (New York: Liveright, 1977), for a comparison of *The Women at Point Sur* with Whitman's "Song of Myself" (pp. 198–200).

23. See Brother Antoninus, *Robinson Jeffers: Fragments of an Older Fury* (Berkeley: Oyez, 1968), p. 3.

24. H. D., *Trilogy* (New York: New Directions, 1973), p. 43.

25. In a review of "A" 22 & 23 (presumably the last of Zukofsky's poem; "A" 24 was published previously), Hugh Kenner called "A" the "most hermetic poem in English" and predicted that "they" will "still be elucidating [it] in the 22nd century" (*New York Times Book Review*, 14 Mar. 1976, p. 7).

26. A. R. Ammons, *Tape for the Turn of the Year* (Ithaca: Cornell Univ. Press, 1965; rpt. W. W. Norton and Co., 1972), p. 1.

27. Solyman Brown, "Essay on American Poetry," *American Literary Revolution, 1783-1837*, pp. 187-92.

28. William Cullen Bryant, "Essay on American Poetry," *ibid.*, pp. 195-96.

29. Henry Wadsworth Longfellow, "Our Native Writers," *ibid.*, pp. 387-88, 389.

30. Ralph Waldo Emerson, "The American Scholar," *ibid.*, p. 362.

31. ——, "The Poet," *Selections from Ralph Waldo Emerson*, ed. Stephen E. Whicher (Boston: Houghton Mifflin Co., 1957), p. 238.

32. ——, "To Walt Whitman," *ibid.*, p. 362.

33. Walt Whitman, "Beginners," *Complete Poetry and Selected Prose*, p. 10.

34. Hyatt H. Waggoner, *American Poets from the Puritans to the Present* (Boston: Houghton Mifflin Co., 1968), chaps. 5 and 6; Harold Bloom, *A Map of Misreading* (New York: Oxford Univ. Press, 1975), chaps. 9 and 10.

35. Quoted in Gay Wilson Allen, *The New Walt Whitman Handbook* (New York: New York Univ. Press, 1975), p. 19.

36. Alexis de Tocqueville, *Democracy in America*, ed. Richard D. Heffner (New York: New American Library, 1956), pp. 177, 181, 183.

37. Whitman, "1855 Preface," *Complete Poetry and Selected Prose*, p. 413.

38. Louis Simpson, *At the End of the Open Road* (Middletown: Wesleyan Univ. Press, 1963), p. 55.

Emerson, Whitman, and the Paradox of Self-Reliance

Jerome Loving*

> "Doubt not, O Poet but persist. . . . Stand there, balked and dumb, stuttering and stammering, hissed and hooted, stand and strive, until at last rage draw out of thee that *dream*-power which every night shows thee is thine own."

My epigraph is taken from "The Poet," an essay that Walt Whitman denied reading until 1856.[1] Yet studies of the Emerson-Whitman relationship invariably point to it as the Emersonian fountainhead of Whitman's poetry. Emerson's "By God it is in me and must go forth," for example, is apparently echoed in Whitman's "There is that in me—I do not know what it is—but I know it is in me" ("Song of Myself," Section 50). Ralph Waldo Emerson also anticipated Whitman in "The Poet" when he wrote that "the vocabulary of an omniscient man would embrace words and images excluded from polite society" and that "bare lists of words are found suggestive to an imaginative and excited mind." There are simply too many parallels between "The Poet" and *Leaves of Grass* in 1855 to make Whitman's disclaimer even remotely credible. Certainly, one thinks of Whitman as the Emersonian poet who "is inflamed and carried away by his thought, to that degree that he forgets the authors and the public and heeds only this one dream. . . ." "I was simmering, simmering, simmering," Whitman allegedly admitted in 1860, "Emerson brought me to a boil."[2] Whitman was, it would appear from the consensus of studies that have looked into his "foreground,"[3] the poet without the "e" that bubbled forth between 1855 and 1860, his most creative years.

And yet to argue that "The Poet" was above all the essay that emboldened Whitman to issue *Leaves of Grass* is to misunderstand Emerson's essay. For then we misread it as an unqualified celebration of the powers of the poet. Such an interpretation overlooks the fact that Emerson first drafted "The Poet" as a lecture (as he did almost all of his essays) shortly before his son's death in 1842 and finished it as an essay in the wake of his profound melancholy. And unlike the earlier lecture (which Whitman

*This essay, which has not previously been published, was adapted from parts of *Emerson, Whitman, and the American Muse*, scheduled for publication by Univ. of N. Car. Press in December, 1982. It is printed with the permission of the author.

306

heard in 1842 in New York City), the 1844 essay catches Emerson between two world-views, so to speak—in transition between what Stephen Whicher has called freedom and fate.[4] I call them the worlds of Vision and Wisdom.

There is, for example, a significant difference between the Emerson of 1836–1841 who is "the endless seeker with no Past at [his] back" and the Emerson of 1842–1860 who sees our inevitable awakening from the poetic sublime as the discovery that "we exist"—in a biological trap or a life of limitations. "That discovery," he confesses in "Experience," "is called the Fall of Man. Ever afterwards we suspect our instruments. We have learned that we do not see directly, but mediately. . . ." But back in 1836, in *Nature*, poetry could make "all mean egotism" vanish. In the "American Scholar Address" of 1837 and the "Divinity School Address" of 1838, the possibility of seeing *directly* is undeniable. The theme of man coming into (his own) nature also pervades the three lecture series that followed, culminating with the lecture-draft of "The Poet" (called "Nature and the Powers of the Poet"). Throughout this period Emerson is what Harold Bloom calls a "strong" poet—the poet of Vision who invents himself in "colossal cipher." There is no fear of flying here. Rather, like Orpheus whose songs tamed the beasts of the wilderness, Emerson's poet of 1836–1841 is undaunted. "When he lifts his great voice," Emerson proclaimed in the lecture-draft, "men gather to him and forget all that is past, and then his words are to the hearers, pictures of all history." Here we find no sour notes of pessimism regarding the poet and his "*dream-power.*" "To doubt that the poet will yet appear is to doubt of day and night."[5]

It is, of course, nothing new to point out the realism that creeps into Emerson's prose with the composition of "Experience." One has only to scan the worldly titles in *Essays; Second Series* (1844) and *The Conduct of Life* (1860): "Manners," "Gifts," "Politics," "Power," "Wealth," "Culture." One quickly finds in Emerson's prose the growth of Wisdom, or *good advice under the circumstances*. In "Culture," for example, Emerson defines his subject as that which "kills [man's] exaggeration [of himself]; his conceit of his village or his city." Culture is the antidote to self-love, to the kind of egotism the earlier advocate of Vision sought in himself and encouraged in others between 1836 and 1841. We should remember, however, that the opening essay of Emerson's 1844 volume is "The Poet," not "Experience." And appropriately so, for it does not belong with the essays of 1836–1841, before Emerson had begun to doubt that the American poet would appear. By this time many of his "discoveries" had faded: Amos Bronson Alcott was "an intellectual *torso*, without hands or feet"; Jones Very was "hopelessly mad"; the thoughts of Henry David Thoreau disclosed no "new matter"—simply Emerson's "own originally drest"; the poems of William Ellery Channing II lacked polish; and so on.[6] Emerson told Carlyle in 1842 that these poets were "all religious but hate the churches: they reject all the ways of living of other men, but have nothing to offer in their stead. Perhaps, one of these days, a great Yankee shall come, who will easily do the unknown deed."[7]

By 1842 Emerson must have believed that if the American poet was possible, he would have to be a "great Yankee" indeed. For earlier that year he had suffered the loss of his first son—and with it much of the Vision that he thought possible in himself and his American poets. "Must every experience—those that promised to be dearest & most penetrating," he asked a friend within a week of young Waldo's death, "—only kiss my cheek like the wind & pass away?" With this letter he in effect began the composition of "Experience." "Alas! I chiefly grieve that I cannot grieve," he exclaimed in the same letter—and used almost the same language in the essay.[8] He could not grieve now because he was convinced of the brevity of Vision, of the inevitable return of the Orphic flight to a world whose very existence required change, often ruthless and brutal change. In such a world balance, or culture, was necessary—that reminder of who we are (or who we are *not*); hence, the Wisdom or *good advice* in "Experience" and the works that followed it.

It is in the revision of "The Poet," though, that we find Emerson acting out the catharsis that carried him from Vision to Wisdom. Unlike the lecture-draft of 1841, the final version is ultimately ambivalent. And indeed without this ambivalence, it would vary little from the positive statements on egotism in *Nature*, the "American Scholar" and "Divinity School" addresses, and the first *Essays*, including especially "Self-Reliance." To say, as Emerson does in "The Poet," that this individual "re-attaches things to nature and the Whole," for example, is to say nothing that is not found in the Transcendentalist doctrine of the earlier essays and lectures evolving directly from *Nature*. On the other hand, this celebration of self-reliance in "The Poet" is strangely mixed. Certainly there is more than a murmur of pessimism in the admission: "I look in vain for the poet whom I describe." The possibility of such an individual is perhaps too lofty in the face of life's relentless change. Emerson, to be sure, persists in his description of the poet; yet he betrays his anxiety in his exhortation to this "great Yankee" to "Doubt not . . . but persist. Say 'It is in me and shall out.' Stand there, balked and dumb, stuttering and stammering, hissed and hooted, stand and strive, until at last rage draw out of thee that *dream*-power which every night shows thee is thine own." In *Nature* Emerson had suggested that we would not overlook the miracle of nature if, for example, the stars "should appear one night in a thousand years." In "The Poet," however, it appears that Emerson may believe that our conversation with nature is inaudible. It is as if Emerson himself is now "balked and dumb, stuttering and stammering, hissed and hooted"—a poet fully exposed to what he describes earlier in the essay as "the accidents of the weary kingdom of time."

If my reading is correct, if "The Poet" signals the end of Emerson's boundless faith in the possibilities of poetry, it has to be one of the great ironies of American literary history that this essay inspired Whitman to celebrate himself with such abandon and originality in "Song of Myself." If such was the case, he misread the essay as badly as we have misread it ever since, misread Emerson as seriously as Melville, who was fascinated by the "blackness" in Hawthorne's fiction as he wrote *his* masterpiece, *Moby-Dick* (1851). And doubtless Whitman did. But like Melville (as I have argued elsewhere),[9] Whitman was well on his way to writing his *magnum opus* long before he read "The Poet." And yet also like Hawthorne's influence, Emerson's upon Whitman was not without its effect because it helped to bring the poet's vision of himself into focus. After hearing the lecture-draft of "The Poet" in 1842, the young reporter for the New York *Aurora* called it "one of the richest and most beautiful compositions, both for its matter and style, we have ever heard anywhere, at any time."[10] This was perhaps the real beginning of that "long foreground" that Emerson spoke of in his now-famous letter of July 21, 1855. Whitman did not need to read the 1844 version (and if he had, he would have found only the optimistic statements he sought) to "simmer" toward the creation of *Leaves of Grass* in 1855. It would, of course, take thirteen long years for the editorial "we" of the *Aurora* piece to metamorphose into the self-reliant "I" of "Song of Myself," but Emerson's words had found and stirred the "great Yankee" he had described with a mixture of hope and despair in his letter to Carlyle and in the 1844 essay on "The Poet."

The metamorphosis from Walter Whitman the journalist to Walt Whitman the poet was largely, however, a process of self-discovery—the result of a successful quest for self-reliance. It was only after he had studied his group as a journalist that he was able to define himself as a "single, separate person." His journalistic peregrination (that covered everything from boarding house life to abandoned children, from married life to prostitution) was ultimately a journey into the self, a search for that quality, or Character, that was at once representative of the divinity of all men and uniquely his own. The search for Whitman's foreground will of course continue—as it has since the study of American literature became inseparable from the study of *Leaves of Grass*. And no study that counts Emerson out of that foreground can ever be termed judicious. By the same token, it is a mistake to give Emerson all the credit for Whitman's "original energy" (his term for self-reliance) in "Song of Myself." As Stephen Whicher notes, to credit Emerson "is often to give conceptual definition to attitudes and insights which are too close to Whitman for definition, which he does not state because he lives them."[11]

Emerson himself would refute those who presume to crown him master of Whitman. In 1859—four years after he had sent his letter of greeting to Whitman and three years after he had opened the 1856 edition of *Leaves of Grass* to find himself addressed as "Master"—he confided to his journal: "I have been writing & speaking what were once called novelties for twenty five or thirty years, & have not now one disciple. Why? Not that what I said was not true . . . but because it did not go from any wish in me to bring men to me, but to themselves."[12] That Whitman's "Master" letter in the second edition of his book (which also carried on its spine in gold letters, "I greet you at the beginning of a great career . . .) was little more than a promotional trick (anticipating the dustjacket blurbs of today) Emerson surely realized. He wanted no disciples and would not have encouraged an imitator; he would not have been so keenly interested in the third edition.[13] But perhaps Whitman more lucidly summed up what Emerson would have agreed was his actual role in the making of *Leaves of Grass*: "The best part of Emersonianism is, it breeds the giant that destroys itself. Who wants to be any man's mere follower? lurks behind every page. No teacher ever taught, that has so provided for his pupil's setting up independently—no truer evolutionist."[14] Emerson had emboldened Whitman to set up independently. And to do so, he had to learn—or to believe—that death was harmless in the face of self-love; and so he "doted" on himself in "Song of Myself." The Understanding saw death, while the Reason saw immortality, Emerson had taught in his "strong" poetry. But no one could *teach* the Poet. Not even Emerson could show Whitman how to charm the Understanding out of its fear of death—how to use the fable of poetry to invent himself in "colossal cipher." Such an achievement required "original energy"—not simply the chant of self-reliance coming from one who was the product of Harvard College and a proud New England heritage. As I have said, Emerson helped to adjust Whitman's self-view, but only Whitman could make Whitman believe the fable.

That fable eventually came to be called "Song of Myself" (in 1881). And yet it was a misnomer. There is a defensiveness in the title that suggests that Whitman's Orphic flight into himself had ended years before. In 1855 the poem had no title—surely evidence of self-reliance. No explanation was necessary. He had only to proceed with the celebration without apologies: "I CELEBRATE myself, / And what I assume you shall assume." We sense almost a military precision in this confident announcement—a "direct order" to the soul and those of humanity. After 1855 the poem needs a name tag: "Poem of Walt Whitman, an American" in 1856; "Walt Whitman" in 1860. The changes follow a change in the poet's self-view as his Orphic flight moves, as it were, toward its crash landing, which is manifested in the poems of 1860. Roy Harvey Pearce considers this third edition of *Leaves of Grass* Whitman's most important. The poet of this edition, Pearce writes, "is, par excellence, Emerson's 'secretary,' reporting 'the doings of the miraculous spirit of life that everywhere throbs and works.' "[15] He argues that the edition justifies Whitman as a poet because it is the culmination of the first three editions, which he views as a "complete sequence." While not wishing to quibble over which edition (really, the first or the third) is superior, I do think that the 1860 edition is distinguished in the sense that Whitman here bids farewell to the power of poetry to lull the Understanding into the illusion that the self-lover is invulnerable to the anxieties produced by death-in-life.

It is also distinguished in the sense that it is Whitman's most Emersonian edition. In other words, by including "Song of Myself" and the "farewell" poems ("Out of the Cradle Endlessly Rocking" and "As I Ebb'd with the Ocean of Life"), Whitman travels the same cycle Emerson had travelled between *Nature* and "Experience." It was a cycle that began and concluded with the self. In the middle—in such 1856 poems whose final titles are "Salute au Monde!," "Crossing Brooklyn Ferry," "Song of the Open Road," and "Song of the Rolling Earth"—Whitman tries to embrace the world, as Emerson had as unsuccessfully in such essays as "Love" and "Friendship." "The only joy I have in [a friend's] being mine," Emerson wrote in the latter, "is that the *not mine* is *mine*." In "Song of the Rolling Earth," Whitman too suspects that self-love is the only permanent love in the face of death: "Not one can acquire for another—not one! / Not one can grow for another—not one!" Both poets are thrown back here in their quest for love of another by the truth that the Open Road of life is inevitably a lonely road. At this stage, however, the truth that we are spiritual deafmutes who travel together but cannot speak to each other is but a fear—a suspicion at best. It is fully realized for each in "Experience" and Whitman's "farewell" poems.

Probably because these two poems of Whitman's strip away the facade of self-reliance, their harsh view of the human condition was later softened through changes (both in title and content) and hidden away in the "Deathbed" edition of *Leaves of Grass*—their positioning explained away by a fiction that Whitman's "language experiment" had derived from some sort of master plan. Hidden away is Emerson's poet of "Experience"—who painfully reports, as Emerson's "secretary," his confrontation with the truth that the self is the only permanent lover or "comrade" in life. Death-in-life is the experience he reports, and this truth is both celebrated and lamented.

If 1842 was Emerson's watershed year, 1859 was Whitman's—or at least the year in which he weighed the impact of the preceding two years when he may have come down from the spiritual heights of "Song of Myself" in search of personal love. He describes the search as "paths untrodden" in "Calamus," where he is "resolved to sing no songs . . . but those of manly love." In his recent biography of Whitman, Justin Kaplan calls 1859 the year of the poet's "slough," when he found himself a lonely and unrequited lover. One of the objects of Whitman's intimacy, Kaplan speculates, may have been his younger brother Thomas Jefferson Whitman. The poet's favorite sibling and clearly the only family member who "understood" *Leaves of Grass*, Jeff had accompanied Walt to New Orleans in 1848 and grown up to share his brother's fondness for the opera and (to a lesser extent) his interest in literature. "When Jeff was born I was in my 15th year," Whitman wrote after his brother's death in 1890, "and [I] had much care of him for many years afterward, and he did not separate from me. He was a very handsome, healthy, affectionate, smart child, and would sit on my lap or hang on my neck half an hour at a time. . . ." It may be significant, therefore, that Walt's "slough" and Jeff's marriage in 1859 coincided, thus removing Jeff to separate Brooklyn quarters and Walt from the object of his affection. As Kaplan puts it, "after the marriage Jeff was Walt's ward and companion no longer."[16]

Further evidence of Whitman's longing for intimacy with another and not simply himself is found in notebooks he penned during the 1857–1859 period. "Why be there men I meet, and others I know. . . ," he asked himself, "that when I walk with an arm of theirs around my neck, my soul scoots and courses like an unleashed dog—that when they leave me the pennants of my joy sink flat and lank in the deadest calm? . . . What is the meaning, any how, of my adhesiveness toward others?—What is the cause of theirs toward me? Am I loved by them boundlessly because my love for them is more boundless?"[17] Whitman's exasperation at his failure to satisfy himself in the quest for personal love is described in "Calamus." He records in these poems, he tells us, "the secret of [the] nights and days" in which he attempted to climb out of his "slough." "I will escape from the sham that was proposed to me," he says in No. 2 of "Calamus." "I will sound myself and comrades only—I will never again utter a call, only their call." But as he discovers, the call of self "and comrades only" reflects his attempt to retreat in the face of on-coming death. The "sham" is the truth that Love and Death are fused together—"folded together above all." And therefore the only love worth seeking is that which makes "death exhilarating." He is speaking of the realization that personal love makes death ominous. It fears death because it can exist only in the realm of the Understanding, which sees life in particulars ("atom after atom," Emerson said). Personal love or "Adhesiveness" clings to the moment; self-love to the procession of moments toward death and beyond.

By the end of "Calamus" the poet *fears* that "I effuse unreturned love." And if the belief in personal love is not utterly defeated at this juncture in the composition of the new poems in the 1860 edition,[18] it is certainly shaken—leaving the poet temporarily confused. He is left, it appears, with little more than his shadow. And even this external object may not be fused with the self: "How often I find myself standing and looking at it where it flits, / How often I question and doubt whether that is really me." In fact, the only thing—and the very thing—he has gained from the "Calamus" quest is the memory of the particular infatuations and its expression in the "Calamus" poems. But this is enough: ". . . in these, and among my lovers, and carrolling my songs, / O I never doubt whether that is really me." The Memory and the Song are the sole possessions that the poet can carry down the Open Road of life toward death. "Calamus," it might be said, was merely a preparation for the greatest poem of the 1860 edition, later entitled "Out of the Cradle Endlessly Rocking." For it is here that the Memory and the Song—Love and Death—are fused.

By the time Whitman composed "A Word Out of the Sea" ("Out of the Cradle"), he was coming out of his "slough." Armed now with the Memory on record in the Song, he was thus prepared to act out the ultimate vocation of the poet: to celebrate and lament at once the fusion of Love and Death. The poem, which first appeared in the *Saturday Press* for Christmas 1859 as "A Child's Reminiscence," is not concerned so much with a child's reminiscence as it is with that point in Whitman's life when the recollection of a childhood experience served as a catalyst in his transformation from a belief in "Adhesiveness" to a mild form of nihilism. The "reminiscence" (whether of an actual or imaginary event) concerns "two guests from Alabama—two together":

> And every day the he-bird, to and fro, near at hand,
> And every day the she-bird, crouched on her nest,
>   silent, with bright eyes,
> And every day I, curious boy, never too close, never
>   disturbing them,
> Cautiously peering, absorbing, translating.

The he-bird becomes the "solitary guest from Alabama" when his mate vanishes among the "white arms out in the breakers tirelessly tossing." As the "lone singer" stands before the sea and pours forth his lament, the "peaceful child" listens. The cry is one of loneliness, and though the boy listened but passively, the poet that the boy has finally become "of all men" knows what it feels like to be halted at the land's edge in pursuit of love. The speaker is a "man—yet by these tears a little boy again, / Throwing myself on the sand, confronting the waves."

At the time of the childhood experience recalled, the boy basked emotionally in the warmth of the sun as did the two lovers before their separation. *"Shine! Shine!"* they exclaim. *"Pour down your warmth, great Sun! / While we two bask together."* And yet the crucial moment in the event remembered—hearing the solitary mate's *"Loved—but no more with me, / We two together no more"*—takes place at midnight under the "yellow half-moon, late-risen, and swollen as if with tears." The *late-risen* moon reflects, I believe, Whitman's dark night of the soul, his "Calamus" experience. It is a period of spiritual blackness that separates the full-risen moon from the warm sun under which the two from Alabama—and all personal lovers—bask, *"singing all the time, minding no time."* When the truth comes due, however, it is never in the light of common day. "O give me some clew!" the poet begs. "O if I am to have so much, let me have more!" he demands *in the very act of the poet* who is the "uniter of the here and the hereafter." He presides now over the union of Love and Death. In perhaps an unconscious echo of Hawthorne's

"Moonlight, in a familiar room," Whitman uses this "neutral territory" of the mind to fuse Love and Death. As the poet stands before the sea and begs for "some clew" ("a word out of the sea") for the thousand singers or unrequited lovers, he hears the word—"Death" repeated five times. This is *the* clue to man's destiny, and the poet now knows and realizes his vocation: "Now in a moment I know what I am for—I awake, / And already a thousand singers—a thousand songs, clearer, louder, more sorrowful than yours, / A thousand warbling echoes have started to life within me, / Never to die." He is to use the Memory and the Song to fuse Love and Death. He has duly loved—or suffered—and is now fully prepared to sing of that universal experience. His theme is that the Self—Emerson's real "Me"—is the only lover available to man, and that it lies on the other side of Death: "The word of the sweetest song, *and all songs*." (My italics.)

"A Word Out of the Sea," then, articulates the lesson learned in "Calamus." It both celebrates and laments the inevitable return of Love to the sea from which all life emanates. Death is the answer the poet hears from the sea, and with this epiphany he exchanged one world view for another, the boy's for the man's. In a real sense, the poem is Whitman's version of Emerson's "Experience." Both the poem and the essay re-enact the discovery that *true* love is fused with death.

In Emerson's case as in Whitman's, it marks the end of his Orphic vision which gives death no quarter in the face of self-love. Waldo's death in 1842, we will recall, was not the first to traumatize Emerson so. His favorite brother Charles died in 1836, and his first wife Ellen Tucker died in 1831 before the age of twenty. With Ellen's passing, he could no longer believe in Christianity which, he clearly implies in *Nature*, gropes "among the dry bones of the past"; in other words, it focuses upon the particular example of Christ rather than on the principle of universal divinity Christ's life exemplified. A year earlier he could tell his Aunt Mary with regard to Ellen's death, the "severest truth would forbid me to say that ever I had made a sacrifice. . . . I loved Ellen, & love her with an affection that would ask nothing but its indulgence to make me blessed. Yet when she was taken from me, the air was still sweet, the sun was not taken down from my firmament, & however sore was that particular loss, I still felt that it was particular, that the Universe remained to us both. . . ."[19] He could then accept life as change and see the hope for permanence in the particular as life's greatest folly.

And so he could not grieve, finding how shallow grief was. He said the same thing after Waldo's death—but with a significant difference. "In the death of my son, now more than two years ago, I seem to have lost a beautiful estate—no more," he writes in "Experience." Now he says—in a shockingly bathetic comparison—that he can get no nearer the loss than he could a financial reverse. All the particulars are now "caducous": "The dearest events are summer-rain, and we the Para coats that shed every drop." The trouble with grief, or the longing for that summer rain, is that it takes us from realism to idealism—to the kind of idealism which at its neoplatonic pinnacle allowed Emerson to experience "the currents of the Universal Being." This is what grief had taught him in the wake of Ellen's death: that death could not remove her from Emerson's life, that the Universe remained to them both. In "Experience," on the other hand, Waldo's death forced that universe behind the same cloud cover that preceded Whitman's "late-risen" moon. "Nothing is left us now," Emerson concedes (as Whitman would in "A Word Out of the Sea") "but death. We look to that with grim satisfaction, saying There at least is a reality that will not dodge us." There at last *is* reality. And under its long shadow, "the mid-world is best"—Wisdom, or *good advice under the circumstances*.

"Experience" is Emerson's "farewell" poem. Like Whitman in "A Word Out of the Sea," he is now forever "out of the rocked cradle," out of the youthful illusions about personal love. Waking from that *"dream-power"* of poetry on the "stair" of experience, Emerson nevertheless protests in "Experience" that "Our life is not so much threatened as our perception." But for the poet, of course, such perception or *"dream-power"* is the key to life, for it is the only means to the poetry of self-reliance. Without it the poet's life may be compared to the cat in pursuit of her tail, described in "Experience":

> Do you see that kitten chasing so prettily her own tail? If you could look with her eyes you might see her surrounded with hundreds of figures performing complex dramas, with tragic and comic issues, long conversations, many characters, many ups and downs of fate,—and meantime it is only puss and her tail.

Perception is everything to the artist. Without this fable of what Whitman envisioned as the "single, separate person," Emerson is left with only culture—essentially his theme after "Experience." No longer can he honestly seek spiritual analogies in nature. Or "types" as Whitman confesses in his other "farewell" poem, "As I Ebb'd with the Ocean of Life."

I should like to conclude my essay with a brief examination of this poem. For it is Whitman's most dramatic farewell to the poetry of self-reliance; more exactly, it is his farewell to self-reliance itself, the very conceit upon which all great poems are constructed. Although the poem precedes "A Word Out of the Sea" in the third edition (as No. 1 of the "Leaves of Grass" poems), it was probably written as a sequel to Whitman's "Reminiscence." As the 1892 arrangement of the "Deathbed" edition suggests, Whitman was at the very least myopic when it came to general structure. Furthermore, the poem was first published as "Bardic Symbols" in the *Atlantic Monthly* for April 1860—three months after "A Child's Reminiscence" had appeared in the *Saturday Press*.

"As I Ebb'd" explores the paradox of self-reliance. Like Emerson's "Experience," it neither celebrates nor condemns the conceit; it merely laments it. To put the matter another way, Whitman laments the tension that self-reliance produces between the mortal self and its lover on the other side of Death. Self-reliance, he has discovered, effectively blurs the mortal vision, dissolves the impact of Death. It sees beyond or through Death to the other half. As Emerson had told Whitman in 1842, "The man is only half himself; the other half is his Expression."[20] The Understanding told Whitman who he was *not*; the Reason taught him who he *was*. But paradoxically to attempt to cross that line—to walk the shores of Paumanok, as Whitman does in the poem, "with that eternal self of me, seeking types"—is at the same time to deny the mortal self. Such abnegation, of course, calls for the denial of personal love as well. We find in this poem, it appears, Whitman's version of Emerson's "The Poet." Both are ambivalent. Poetry not only allows one to overcome the limitations of his mortality but by its very success demonstrates those limitations or the inadequacy of the mortal self.

This paradox is dramatically rendered in "As I Ebb'd." For the poem records the collapse of "bardic symbols." The poet walks the shores of Paumanok, "the shores I know," in search of "the shores I know not." And yet he walks in fear: "Alone, held by the eternal self of me *that threatens to get the better of me, and stifle me.*" (My italics.) The "eternal self"—the offspring of self-reliance—is the villain that threatens to expose life for what it is—shallow. As Emerson realized in "Experience," life turns out to be "scene-painting and counterfeit"—Ahab's "paste-board mask." And hence to yearn for life is to "pay the costly price of sons and lovers." The price is grief, which had taught Emerson only "how shallow it is." *Shallow* because it longs for what was never really there. It is a longing at best for halfness—the fragments of life ("little corpses" in Whitman's poem) which relentlessly drive man into the hands of Death.

Probably no American poet was more sensitive to the fragmentary nature of life than Emily Dickinson, who after the death of yet another "lover" exclaimed rhetorically, "Is God Love's Adversary?"[21] But this was an attitude that Whitman would ultimately reject. He would not allow its nihilism to stifle his ability to write poetry—as it did Dickinson's. To resist, however, he had to make the ultimate compromise: he was forced to turn from self-reliance to God-reliance. We find it in such post-Vision poems as "Proud Music of the Storm" and "Passage to India," where the poet goes on about a "new rhythmus" and an "elder brother." These poems and others simply fly in the face of the tragic vision of his "farewell" poems. Too well aware now of the arrogance implicit in their Orphic flight, he would write poems of "religious purpose" instead. Now the poetry of self-reliance is viewed as that fable which dangerously inflates the ego, the product of a "*dream*-power" which lulls man into the arrogant belief that he can experience the elusive identity of his source. But with "As I Ebb'd" Whitman realizes that his poems are "insolent poems—that the real Me still stands untouched, untold, altogether unreached." It is not only unreached but withdrawn "with peals of distant ironical laughter at every word I have written or shall write,/ Striking me with insults till I fall helpless upon the sand." Like the grown child of "A Word Out of the Sea," the persona of this poem lies helpless and ridiculed on the eternal shore. Joining him this time is the humanity he would speak for—lying like "drowned corpses" at the feet of God: "We, capricious, brought hither, we know not whence, spread out before You, up there, walking or sitting,/ Whoever *you* are—we too lie in drifts at your feet."

I have supplied the emphasis on "you" because the statement acknowledges Whitman's rejection now of the arrogance of self-reliance in favor of the humility of God-reliance. In "Song of Myself" Whitman could boldly ask:

Listener up there! Here you. . . . what have you to confide to me?
Look in my face while I snuff the sidle of evening,
Talk honestly, for no one else hears you, and I stay only a minute longer.

There he was on personal terms with the Creator. This poet was indeed privileged—the only one who could hear God. But in "As I Ebb'd" the poet no longer dares to believe—as Emerson could no longer believe—that he is "part or parcel of God." In a real sense, "Song of Myself" acts out this whole cycle, the paradox of self-reliance; for the poem opens with the celebration of the "I" and concludes waiting for the "you." If not the entire cycle, it sets the stage for the "you" (or personal lover) poems found in the 1856 edition—which, in turn, take him back to self-love and its collapse in the "farewell" poems. Like Emerson, he comes full circle. And nothing is left him but Wisdom: faith in the benevolence of God instead of the powers of the poet. For self-reliance, on the one hand, denies the possibility of personal love in its insistance on transcendence; and on the other, it denies self-love in its failure to experience ultimately the "real Me." It was the hoax, therefore, that led Whitman up Emerson's spiral staircase to nowhere.

Notes

1. John Burroughs, *Notes on Walt Whitman As Poet and Person* (New York: American Book Company, 1867), pp. 16–17. Whitman is known to have written part of this volume; see Frederick P. Hier, Jr., "The End of a Literary Mystery," *American Mercury*, 1 (1924), 471–78.

2. John Townsend Trowbridge, "Reminiscences of Walt Whitman," *Atlantic Monthly*, 89 (1902), 166; the essay in which the quote is given is reprinted in his *My Own Story, With Recollections of Noted Persons* (Boston: Houghton Mifflin, 1903).

3. Studies of the relationship in which Emerson is generally credited with Whitman's success as a poet include Emerson Grant Sutcliffe, "Whitman, Emerson and the New Poetry," *New Republic*, 19 (1919), 114–16; Norman Foerster, "Whitman and the Cult of Confusion," *North American Review*, 213 (1921), 799–812; John B. Moore, "The Master of Whitman," *Studies in Philology*, 23 (1926), 77–89; Killis Campbell, "The Evolution of Whitman as an

Artist," *American Literature*, 6 (1934), 254–63; Hyatt H. Waggoner, *American Poets from the Puritans to the Present* (Boston: Houghton Mifflin Co., 1968); and Harold Bloom, *A Map of Misreading* (New York: Oxford Univ. Press, 1975) and *Poetry and Repression; Revisionism from Blake to Stevens* (New Haven: Yale Univ. Press, 1976). Few studies (which confront the Emerson-Whitman connection directly) argue convincingly for Whitman's originality: Leon Howard, "For a Critique of Whitman's Transcendentalism" *Modern Language Notes*, 47 (1932), 79–85; F. O. Matthiessen, *American Renaissance: Art and Expression in the Age of Emerson and Whitman* (New York: Oxford Univ. Press, 1941); Roy Harvey Pearce, *The Continuity of American Poetry* (Princeton: Princeton Univ. Press, 1961); and Lawrence Buell, "Transcendentalist Catalogue Rhetoric: Vision Versus Form," *American Literature*, 40 (1968), 235–39, and *Literary Transcendentalism: Style and Vision in the American Renaissance* (Ithaca: Cornell Univ. Press, 1973).

4. *Freedom and Fate; An Inner Life of Ralph Waldo Emerson* (Philadelphia: Univ. of Pennsylvania Press, 1953).

5. *Early Lectures of Ralph Waldo Emerson*, ed. Robert E. Spiller and Wallace E. Williams (Cambridge: Harvard Univ. Press, 1972), III, 363.

6. James Elliot Cabot, *A Memoir of Ralph Waldo Emerson* (Boston: Houghton, Mifflin and Company, 1887), I, 281; *Letters of Ralph Waldo Emerson*, ed. Ralph L. Rusk (New York: Columbia Univ. Press, 1939), II, 191; *Journals and Miscellaneous Notebooks of Ralph Waldo Emerson*, ed. William H. Gilman and J. E. Parsons (Cambridge: Harvard Univ. Press, 1970), VIII, 96. See also William M. Moss, " 'So Many Promising Youths': Emerson's Disappointing Discoveries of New England Poet-Seers," *New England Quarterly*, 49 (1976), 46–64.

7. *Correspondence of Emerson and Carlyle*, ed. Joseph Slater (New York: Columbia Univ. Press, 1964), p. 332.

8. *Letters*, III, 9; and *Complete Works of Ralph Waldo Emerson*, ed. Edward W. Emerson (Boston: Houghton Mifflin, 1903–1904), III, 52.

9. "Melville's Pardonable Sin," *New England Quarterly*, 47 (1974), 262–78.

10. *Walt Whitman of the New York Aurora*, ed. Joseph Jay Rubin and Charles H. Brown (State College, Pa.: Bald Eagle Press, 1950), p. 105.

11. "Whitman's Awakening to Death: Toward a Biographical Reading of 'Out of the Cradle Endlessly Rocking,' " in *The Presence of Walt Whitman*, ed. R. W. B. Lewis (New York: Columbia Univ. Press, 1962), p. 3.

12. *Journals and Miscellaneous Notebooks of Ralph Waldo Emerson*, ed. Susan Sutton Smith and Harrison Hayford (Cambridge: Harvard Univ. Press, 1978), XIV, 258.

13. Emerson made it his business to discover what Whitman had added in the 1860 edition as it went through the press that winter at the firm of Thayer & Eldridge. Afterward he tried unsuccessfully to persuade Whitman to omit the "Enfans d'Adam" poems from the volume—for reasons, Whitman later recalled, that were practical and not aesthetic. For the details of their confrontation on the Boston Common in 1860, see *Walt Whitman: Prose Works 1892*, ed. Floyd Stovall (New York: New York Univ. Press, 1963–1964), I, 281–82; and *With Walt Whitman in Camden*, ed. Horace Traubel (Boston: Small, Maynard Co., 1906), I, 50; and (New York: Mitchell Kennerley, 1914), III, 321, 439, 453.

14. *Prose Works 1892*, II, 517–18.

15. "Whitman Justified: The Poet in 1860," in *The Presence of Walt Whitman*, p. 81.

16. *Walt Whitman; A Life* (New York: Simon and Schuster, 1980), p. 236.

17. *Walt Whitman: Daybooks and Notebooks*, ed. William White (New York: New York Univ. Press, 1978), III, 764–65.

18. In other words, I am arguing that "Calamus" precedes "Out of the Cradle Endlessly Rocking" in order of composition. I base this conjecture upon the evidence gathered in *Whit-*

man's Manuscripts: "Leaves of Grass" (1860), A Parallel Text, ed. Fredson Bowers (Chicago: Univ. of Chicago Press, 1955), pp. lxiii–lxxiv.

19. *Journals and Miscellaneous Notebooks of Ralph Waldo Emerson*, ed. Merton M. Sealts, Jr. (Cambridge: Harvard Univ. Press, 1975), V, 19–20.

20. *Early Lectures*, III, 349.

21. *Letters of Emily Dickinson*, ed. Thomas H. Johnson (Cambridge: Harvard Univ. Press, 1958), III, 755.

Nationalism vs. Internationalism in *Leaves of Grass*

Roger Asselineau*

As Whitman himself fully realized, *Leaves of Grass* is full of contradictions. These contradictions in general do not result from the mere static juxtaposition of opposite elements, but rather from the dynamic clash of divergent tendencies and conflicting ideas. They correspond to perplexities which he could not eliminate or resolve. Thus, just as he sang "One's-Self . . . a simple separate person" as well as its antagonist "the word Democratic, the word En-Masse,"[1] he celebrated with equal fervor his native country, his "nation," as well as "all nations, colors, barbarisms, civilizations, languages."[2] In other words, he was both the whole world and a 20th century American: "Walt Whitman, a Kosmos, of Manhattan the son"[3]—both an ardent patriot and a convinced internationalist before the word came into current use.[4]

One of the most obvious characteristics of *Leaves of Grass* is indeed that it is firmly and deeply rooted in American soil. The words "America" and "American" recur again and again; the United States and "these States" are constantly referred to. Foreign readers are warned from the start that the poet's purpose is "to prove this puzzle, the New World,/ And to define America, her athletic Democracy . . ."[5] and he keeps apostrophizing America: "Listen, America . . . America! I do not vaunt my love for you . . . To thee, America . . . And thou America . . . And you America . . ."[6] He even proclaims: "I chant America the mistress"[7] and in his self-portrait, in "Song of Myself," he insists on his rootedness. He was, he tells us, "Born here of parents born here from parents the same, and their parents the same,"[8] and in *Specimen Days* he boasts—with a pride worthy of a "Son of the American Revolution": "The later years of the last century found the Van Velsor family, my mother's side, living on their own farm at Cold Spring, Long Island, New York State . . . My father's side—probably the fifth generation from the first English arrivals in New England . . . were at the same time farmers on their own land . . . John Whitman . . . came over in The True Love in

*This essay, which has not previously been printed, was read before the International Federation for Modern Languages and Literatures in September, 1981, at Phoenix, Arizona. It is printed here with the permission of the author.

1640 to America.["]9 Thus, his first paternal ancestor landed in Massachusetts only twenty years after the Pilgrim fathers.

So America is one of the main themes of *Leaves of Grass*. In Whitman's as in Emerson's eyes, the United States was a poem. "The United States themselves are essentially the greatest poem," Whitman posited as early as 1855 in his preface.[10] In his own words, he heard America singing:[11]

> Chants of the prairies,
> Chants of the long-running Mississippi, and down to the
>   Mexican sea,
> Chants of Ohio, Indiana, Illinois, Iowa, Wisconsin, and
>   Minnesota.[12]

When the Civil War broke out, he exultantly inventoried all the resources of the Union in "Song of the Banner at Daybreak": "the populous cities with wealth incalculable," the "numberless farms," the "buildings everywhere founded, going up or finish'd," and the Southern plantations, the "ships sailing in and out," "thirty-eight spacious and haughty States" constituting one identity.[13] In "Apostrophe," words almost failed him, he could only accumulate exclamations:

> O mater! O fils!
> O brood continental!
> O flowers of the prairies! . . .

and the ecstatic enumeration goes on for over two pages.[14] The reader grows tired of it long before Whitman does. At a time when no one thought yet of writing "the great American novel," he was in a way attempting to write the great American poem containing the whole of the United States. "Starting from fish-shaped Paumanok where [he] was born,"[15] after dwelling in Mannahatta of the "ship-fringed shore,"[16] he travelled (in imagination most of the time rather than in person) through the South and the West, over the Rockies, as far as California's shores where he dreamt of "the flowery peninsulas and the spice islands" of Asia beyond "[his] Western sea."[17] He thus constantly bore in mind the myriad-faceted image of "Our Old Feuillage,"

> The eighteen thousand miles of sea-coast and bay-coast
>   on the main, the thirty thousand miles of river navi-
>   gation,
> The seven millions of distinct families and the same
>   number of dwellings . . .
> . . . the prairies, pastures, forests, vast cities . . .

from "Florida's green peninsula" to "California's golden hills and hollows."[18] Like all good Americans, he was in raptures over statistics; high figures made him grow lyrical.

Such visions of beauty, immensity and limitless possibilities inspired him with infinite love for his native land, a love which he expressed in particular in "Thou Mother With Thy Equal Brood," which he called a "recitative." It was almost a religious hymn in praise of America and democracy.[19] He placed what he called "Nationality" (what we would rather call patriotism or nationalism) very high in the scale of poetical values: "In estimating first-class song," he wrote in "A Backward Glance O'er Travel'd Roads," "a sufficient Nationality . . . is often, if not always, the first element."[20] And here he had the support of no less an authority than Taine whose *History of English Literature* he read with passion as soon as it was translated into English.[21] For, according to Taine, a work of art is wholly determined by three factors: race, time and place.

Whitman included race too (the English race in particular) in his worship of America:

> Great is the English brood—what brood has so
>   vast a destiny as the English?
> It is the mother of the brood that must rule the earth
>   with the new rule . . ."[22]

This he wrote in 1855. He was moved by an intense pride in the new American race:

> A breed whose proof is in time and deeds,
> What we are we are, nativity is answer enough to
>   objections,
> We wield ourselves as a weapon is wielded,
> We are powerful and tremendous in ourselves. . . .[23]

He sang at the top of his voice "the youthful sinewy races," the "resistless restless race" of the pioneers who cleared and conquered the West.[24] As he explained in the "Prayer of Columbus," "the brutish measureless human undergrowth" of the Old World once "transplanted" in America rose to a "stature [and] knowledge worthy" of God.[25] As a result, the dying redwood tree could but resign himself to making room for "a superior race," for "the new culminating man" destined to grow "hardy, sweet, gigantic" and "tower proportionate to Nature," fully "unfold[ing] himself" at last.[26]

There were thus times when Whitman completely forgot that he came himself from a melting-pot in which impure Welsh and Dutch elements had been mixed with the English blood of his remote paternal forefathers. During the Civil War, for instance, he wrote to one of his young soldier friends who came from a good Massachusetts family: ". . . seven-eighths of the army are Americans, our own stock—the foreign element in our army is much overrated and is of not much account anyhow."[27] Though twenty years before, as editor of the *Brooklyn Eagle*, he broke lances with the "Nativists" of the "American Party," in such contexts, he almost gives a derogatory sense to the word "foreign" and sounds nearly like a "wasp" in whose eyes the English stock is by nature superior to all others.[28]

However, despite such quasi-visceral reactions directed mostly against the Irish in the privacy of his correspondence, Whitman, as a rule, was:

> Pleas'd with the native and pleas'd with the foreign,
>   pleas'd with the new and old.[29]

Again and again in *Leaves of Grass* he enthusiastically welcomes the immigrants landing in New York from Europe:

Immigrants arriving, fifteen or twenty thousand in a week,[30] all easily assimilated thanks to "the simple elastic scheme" for which he praised the United States in "By Blue Ontario's Shore,[31] and elsewhere:

> See, in my poems immigrants continually coming and landing,[32]
> The groups of newly-come immigrants cover the wharf or
>   levee. . . .[33]

For the United States is "the modern composite Nation, formed from all, with room for all, welcoming all immigrants," he affirmed in the preface to the 1872 edition of *Leaves of Grass*,[34] and he called up "the copious humanity streaming from every direction toward America,"[35] the most hospitable of nations. In his most idealistic moments, his admiration for the English race was completely eclipsed by his fervid internationalism. He attached so much importance to this fraternity of all people and all races that he originally wound up *Specimen Days* with a paragraph specially devoted to it and clumsily entitled "The Last Collective Compaction"—for lack of a better word:

"I like well our polyglot construction-stamp, and the retention thereof, in the broad, the tolerating, the many-sided, the collective. All nations here—a home for every race on earth. British, German, Scandinavian, Spanish, French, Italian—papers published, plays acted, speeches made, in all languages—on our shores the crowning resultant of those distillations, decantations, compactions of humanity. . . ."[36]

Incidentally, we can see here why he sprinkled his poems with foreign words like "camerado" or "ma femme." They were the linguistic projection of his internationalistic faith—a faith which was not limited to the various European nationalities which he lists in this passage; he truly meant "every race on earth." He was quite explicit on this point in his open letter to Emerson in 1856 when he specified: "Of course, we shall have a national character, an identity . . . with cheerfully welcomed immigrants from Europe, Asia, Africa. . . ."[37]

As the word "internationalism" did not exist yet, he used the word "solidarity" instead, and, in his old age, talking with Traubel, said for instance—for his faith in it had not abated: "I like much to see that word—solidarity, intercalation, fusion, no one left out." "Solidarity is the future," he added.[38] As Traubel pointed out, he was here joining hands with Victor Hugo and Tolstoy. Whitman was quite aware of it. "Yes," he answered, "Comte makes much of it [the word solidarity]; it is peculiarly a French word: comes naturally from the French [language]. That is a fact I always remember in the connection with Hugo. . . ."[39] He was right. Though his belief in human solidarity did not come from Victor Hugo himself, it did come through his and George Sand's humanitarian romanticism from the enlightened philosophies of French 18th century "philosophs" (as he spelt the word). Far from being a narrowly national poet with a parochial culture, he was well-read in them (he was particularly fond of Volney's *Ruins*) and he knew and admired George Sand's socialistic romances.[40] He had even read Béranger's poem on "La Sainte Alliance des Peuples" and he extolled its message of international brotherhood in the *New York Times* in 1858.[41]

In his old age his faith in solidarity was as ardent as ever and he declared to Traubel: "I know in my own heart that every line I ever wrote—every line—not an exception—was animated by that feeling," and he loved to quote "the little line or two in the preface to the English edition of *Specimen Days* wherein [he] expressed this feeling"[42] and proclaimed the "eligibility to Enlightenment, Democracy and Fair-Show for the bulk, the common people of all civilized nations."[43] So his internationalism was a disinterested form of political idealism. The United States and democracy were synonymous terms in his eyes: "I shall use the words America and Democracy as convertible terms," he warns us in *Democratic Vistas*,[44] and in 1860 he entitled a group of poems "Chants Democratic and Native American." He believed from the beginning of his career in "constructing a nation of nations,"[45] a "New, indeed new Spiritual World."[46] He dreamt in 1876, the year of the Centennial, of a kind of International "of all the Workmen of all the Nations of the World," so "welcome and inspiring a theme,"[47] he said, and even of an International of poets: "a vaster, saner, more splendid COMRADESHIP, typifying the People everywhere, uniting closer not only the American States, but all Nations, and all Humanity. (That, O Poets! is not *that* a theme, a Union worth chanting for? Why not fix our verses henceforth to the gauge of the round globe? the whole race?)."[48] "My dearest dream is for an internationality of poems and poets, binding the lands of the earth closer than all treaties and diplomacy," he added in *Specimen Days*.[49]

From the dizzy height of this idealistic internationalism he sometimes looked down rather severely on the failings of his native land and he thus lamented in "Respondez":

> (Stifled! O days! O lands! . . .
> Let there be money, business, imports, exports, custom,
>   authority, precedents, pallor, dyspepsia, smut, igno-
>   rance, unbelief![50]

It seemed to him that American democracy was a complete failure and he debunked it *avant la lettre*: "I myself see clearly enough the crude, defective streaks in all the strata of the common people, the specimens and the vast collections of the ignorant, the credulous, the unfit and un-couth, the incapable and the very low and poor."[51] "Never was there more hollowness of heart than at present and here in the United States . . . The underlying principles of the States are not honestly believed in (for all this hectic glow and these melodramatic screamings), nor is humanity itself believed in."[52]

Despite such moments of doubt and even despair, Whitman's patriotism subsisted at the core of his internationalism and to some extent tainted it. In his enthusiasm and zeal he was, for instance, ready to annex Cuba and Canada in order to liberate them from the feudal tyranny of Europe. This attitude went back to his youth. At the time of the Mexican War he had already declared himself in favor of the annexation of new territories in his editorials for the *Brooklyn Eagle*.[53] In his eyes the cause of humanity was identical with that of his native country. So if the United States expanded, it would necessarily be a gain for human happiness and liberty. Mexico, with her weak and corrupt government, could offer only a parody of democracy and was unworthy of the great mission, devolving upon the new world, to populate America with a noble race. Only the United States, he thought, could fulfil it. He therefore expected the U.S. government one day to annex not only Mexico, but also Alaska and Canada: "Yankeedoodledom is going ahead with the resistless energy of a sixty-five-hundred-thousand-horse-power steam engine! It is carrying everything before it South and West, and may one day put the Canadas and Russian America [i.e. Alaska] in its fob pocket!"[54]

Carried away by his democratic proselytism, he saw liberty diffused all over the world thanks to the United States:

> Shapes of a hundred Free States, begetting another hundred
> north and south. . . .[55]

In 1856 he quite naturally included Montreal and Havana in a list of American cities in his open letter to Emerson[56] and his poems of 1860 similarly reflect his expansionist zeal. He dreams of the time when the same current of life will circulate from Mexico and Cuba to New York, when the Canadian will readily sacrifice himself for the Kansan and vice versa.[57] (He spells Kanada with a K to preserve the Indian flavor of the word.) He even sings of the supremacy of the United States over the Pacific Islands, of "the new empire grander than any before" of which America will be the "mistress."[58] In 1857, consistently with his principles, he had advocated an American intervention in Cuba in an article in the *Brooklyn Times*.[59]

His convictions in this respect never changed. In 1871, he affirmed with the greatest confidence in *Democratic Vistas*: "Long ere the second centennial arrives [in 1976], there will be from forty to fifty great States, among them Canada and Cuba."[60] In 1873, in a letter to Peter Doyle, he once more declared himself in favor of military intervention in Cuba,[61] and in 1880, while visiting Canada and the Great Lakes region, he noted: "It seems to me a certainty of time, sooner or later, that Canada shall form two or three grand States, equal and independent, with the rest of the American Union."[62]

This pan-Americanism, definitely tainted with nationalism and even chauvinism at the beginning, was gradually purified and rose from a rather narrow Americanism to a very broad internationalism based on the universal brotherhood of men. At the end of the Civil War, in "Years of the Modern," Whitman evoked the universal democracy of the future for which "not America only, not only Liberty's nation, but other nations" were preparing,[63] and in 1889 he thus sent the fraternal salute of the United States to the young republic of Brazil.[64] He had "One Thought Ever At the Fore," he said:

> All peoples of the globe together sail, sail the same
> voyage, are bound to the same destination.[65]

The "Salut au Monde" which he extended to all the nations of the world as early as 1856 was returned to him in later years by many idealistic writers and poets. Identifying himself to Columbus, he already heard them in imagination in his lifetime:

> . . . anthems in new tongues I hear saluting me.[66]

Spanish American poets were among the most enthusiastic and eloquent of his admirers. They forgave him his nationalism. José Martí, Rubén Darío, Pablo Neruda saluted him with equal fervor. Pablo Neruda in particular very perspicaciously pointed out: "His patent nationalism forms part of a total and organic universal vision."[67]

But there have been dissenting voices. A few Spanish American writers have been unable to forgive and forget the superficial pan-Americanism of Whitman's political essays. There thus appeared in Guatemala in 1952 a violent *Contracanto a Walt Whitman* by one Pedro Mir, who accused him of hiding under his "sublime beard" the Banks, the Trusts and the Monopolies, which, he claimed, have enslaved Central and South America.[68] The most systematic attack was made by a Mexican critic, Mauricio González de la Garza, who accused Whitman of being a racist, an imperialist in general and an anti-Mexican in particular.[69] For him, Whitman was fundamentally a madman who mistook himself not only for Whitman, but also for God, democracy and the United States. The caricature he draws in his book is so much exaggerated that it loses all contact with reality and soon ceases to be believable. De la Garza has failed to see that in Whitman as in everyone of us there were two men: a Sancho Panza and a Don Quixote. Whitman-Sancho Panza was a "wasp" journalist, a chauvinistic conservative and even occasionally a racist, whereas Whitman-Don Quixote dreamt of a universal democracy in which all men were brothers without any distinction of nation or race. These two characters were not quite the same man, however. The former wrote in prose about the real and the latter was a poet and sang the ideal. They could thus co-exist peacefully without suffering from their contradictions. One lived in the present (sometimes even in the past) and the other in the future.

Notes

1. "One's Self I Sing," *Leaves of Grass*, Comprehensive Reader's Edition, ed. Harold W. Blodgett and Sculley Bradley (New York: W. W. Norton, 1968), p. 1, 11. 1-2. All subsequent references to *Leaves of Grass* will be to this edition designated as *L of G*.

2. "On the Beach at Night Alone," *L of G*, p. 261, 1. 10.

3. "Song of Myself," *L of G*, p. 52, 1. 497.

4. According to the *Oxford English Dictionary*, the word "international "did not appear in print before 1801 (in a non-technical publication), and the word "internationalism" before 1877. In France the word "international," which was coined first, was accepted by the French Academy only in 1878.

5. "To Foreign Lands," *L of G*, p. 3.

6. See Edwin Harold Eby, *A Concordance of Walt Whitman's "Leaves of Grass" and Selected Prose Writings* (Seattle: Univ. of Washington Press, 1955), pp. 17, 700-701.

7. "A Broadway Pageant," *L of G*, p. 245, 1. 59.

8. "Song of Myself," *L of G*, p. 29, 1. 7.

9. *Prose Works 1892*, vol. I, *Specimen Days*, ed. Floyd Stoval (New York Univ. Press, 1963), pp. 4-5.

10. *L of G*, p. 711, 11. 11-12.

11. "I Hear America Singing," *L of G*, p. 12.

12. "Starting from Paumanok," *L of G*, p. 17, 11. 40-42.

13. "Song of the Banner at Daybreak," *L of G*, pp. 287-288, 11. 67-76.

14. *L of G*, pp. 600-602.

15. "Starting from Paumanok," *L of G*, p. 15, 1. 1.

16. "As the Greek's Signal Flame," *L of G*, p 533, 1. 5.

17. "Facing West from California's Shores," *L of G*, p. 111, 1. 7.

18. "Our Old Feuillage," *L of G*, pp. 171-176, especially 11. 6-9. See also "Starting from Paumanok," p. 17, section 3.

19. "Thou Mother with Thy Equal Brood," *L of G*, pp. 455-461.

20. *L of G*, p. 566.

21. See Roger Asselineau, "A Poet's Dilemma: Walt Whitman's Attitude to Literary History and Literary Criticism," in Leon Edel, ed., *Literary History and Literary Criticism* (New York University Press, 1964), pp. 50-61.

22. "Great Are the Myths," *L of G*, p. 587, 11. 45-46.

23. "By Blue Ontario's Shore," *L of G*, p. 341, 11. 12-15.

24. "Pioneers! O Pioneers!", *L of G*, p. 229, 1. 7, p. 230, 1. 37.

25. "Prayer of Columbus," *L of G*, p. 422, 11. 36-37.

26. "Song of the Redwood Tree," *L of G*, pp. 209-211, 11. 39, 53, 67, 70.

27. Letter to William S. Davis, dated 1 Oct 1863, in *Correspondence of Walt Whitman*, ed. Edwin H. Miller (New York Univ. Press, 1961), I, 153.

28. See *The Gathering of the Forces*, ed. Cleveland Rodgers and John Black (New York: Putnam's Sons, 1920), I, 14–22.

29. "Song of Myself," *L of G*, p. 64, 1. 774.

30. "Mannahatta," *L of G*, p. 475, 1. 12.

31. "By Blue Ontario's Shore," *L of G*, p. 344 1. 89.

32. "Starting from Paumanok," *L of G*, p. 27, 1. 254.

33. "Song of Myself," *L of G*, p. 42, 1. 285.

34. *L of G*, p. 743, 11. 50–51.

35. "Poem of Remembrances for a Girl or a Boy of These States," *L of G*, pp. 588–589, 1.6.

36. *Prose Works 1892*, vol. II. *Collect and Other Prose*, p. 540.

37. "Whitman to Emerson," *L of G*, p. 739, 11. 287–291.

38. Horace Traubel, *With Walt Whitman in Camden*, vol. III (New York: Mitchell Kennerley, 1914), p. 360.

39. *Ibid.*

40. See Esther Shephard, *Walt Whitman's Pose* (New York: Harcourt Brace, 1936), on George Sand's influence and especially Betsy Erkkila, *Walt Whitman Among the French* (Princeton, N.J.: Princeton Univ. Press, 1980).

41. See "The Moral Effect of the Cable," in Emory Holloway and Vernolian Schwarz, eds. *I Sit and Look Out* (New York: Columbia Univ. Press, 1932), pp. 159–160. However, Whitman's article contained the following sentence which Béranger would certainly not have subscribed to: "It is the union of the great Anglo-Saxon race, henceforth forever to be a unit, that makes the States throb with tumultuous emotion and thrills every breast with admiration and triumph."

42. *With Walt Whitman in Camden*, vol. III, *op. cit.*, p. 367.

43. "Preface to 'Democratic Vistas'—English Edition," *Prose Works 1892, Collect and Other Prose*, vol. II, *op. cit.*, p. 600, 11. 75–76.

44. *Ibid.*, p. 363, 1. 50.

45. "MS Notebook dated 1847," in *The Uncollected Poetry and Prose of Walt Whitman*, ed. Emory Holloway (New York: Doubleday, Doran and Co., 1921), p. 76.

46. "Thou Mother With Thy Equal Brood," *L of G*, p. 461, 1. 128.

47. "Preface to 1876 Edition," *L of G*, p. 751, 11. 94–96.

48. Clifton J. Furness, *Walt Whitman's Workshop* (Harvard Univ. Press, 1928), p. 163. This text was also written in 1876.

49. *Prose Works 1892, vol. II, Collect and Other Prose, op. cit.*, p. 512, 11. 23–24.

50. "Respondez," *L of G*, p. 591, 1. 19, p. 593, 1. 43.

51. "Democratic Vistas," *Prose Works 1892*, vol. II, *op. cit.*, p. 379 11. 532–535. See also the next two or three pages.

52. *Ibid.*, p. 369, 11. 240–244.

53. See *The Gathering of the Forces, op. cit.*, I, 242–266.

54. *Ibid.*, pp. 32–33.

55. "Song of the Broad-Axe," *Leaves of Grass—A Textual Variorum of the Printed Poems*, ed. Sculley Bradley, Harold W. Blodgett, Arthur Golden, William White (New York Univ. Press, 1980), p. 189, variant reading of 1. 251.

56. *L of G*, p. 738, 11. 195, 198.

57. "States," *L of G*, p. 609, 11. 19–24.

58. "A Broadway Pageant," *L of G*, pp. 244–245, 11. 58–59.

59. *I Sit and Look Out, op. cit.*, p. 52.

60. *Prose Works 1892*, vol. II, *Collect and Other Prose*, p. 413, 11. 1626–27.

61. *Calamus*, ed. Richard M. Bucke (London, Ontario, 1899), p. 127.

62. "A Zollverein between the U.S. and Canada," *Prose Works 1892*, Vol. I, p. 241.

63. "Years of the Modern," *L of G*, p. 489, 1. 3.

64. "A Christmas Greeting," *L of G*, p. 548.

65. "One Thought Ever at the Fore," *L of G*, p. 577, 1. 3.

66. "Prayer of Columbus," *L of G*, p. 423, 1. 66.

67. "We live in a Whitmanesque age," in *Walt Whitman in Europe Today*, ed. Roger Asselineau and William White (Detroit: Wayne State Univ. Press, 1972), p. 42.

68. Pedro Mir, *Contracanto a Walt Whitman—Canto a Nosotros Mismos* (Guatemala: Ediociones Saker-Ti, 1952).

69. Mauricio González de la Garza, *Walt Whitman—Racista, Imperialista, Antimexicano* (Mexico: Collección Málaga, 1971).

INDEX